D0993498

BANKING AND CAPITAL MARKETS

BANKING AND CAPITAL MARKETS

David Adams LLB, Solicitor

Published by

College of Law Publishing,
Braboeuf Manor, Portsmouth Road, St Catherines, Guildford GU3 1HA

© The University of Law 2014

David Adams has asserted his moral rights under ss 77– 80 of the Copyright, Designs and Patents Act 1988

All rights reserved. No part of this publication may be reproduced, stored in a retrieval system, or transmitted in any way or by any means, including photocopying or recording, without the written permission of the copyright holder, application for which should be addressed to the publisher.

British Library Cataloguing-in-Publication Data

A catalogue record for this book is available from the British Library.

ISBN 978 1 909176 98 0

Typeset by Style Photosetting Ltd, Mayfield, East Sussex

Printed in Great Britain by Polestar Wheatons, Exeter

Preface

The hardest part in writing this book was deciding what should be left out; a work entitled 'Banking and Capital Markets' could justifiably run to a dozen volumes. However, from a solicitor's perspective, banking practice is essentially 'document driven', and so Part I of this book is devoted to the fundamentals behind drafting loan facility documentation. Probably the most legally complex area of a banking solicitor's practice is that of security: Part II therefore explains the fundamental issues of secured lending. Lastly, Part III of the book introduces capital markets financing and, in particular, the process of issuing a eurobond. The reader should be aware that this book is primarily designed as an integral part of the Legal Practice Course elective, 'Banking and Debt Finance'.

In true preface tradition, I must record my thanks to the people who saved me from making countless mistakes. In particular, I must thank ex-client Ian Brown, colleagues Patrick O'Connor, David Dunnigan and Julia Machin, and ex-colleague Frances George. Following preface tradition still further, I take all responsibility for the mistakes that remain. This book is dedicated to Jayne, who supported me through the pregnancy pains of its creation whilst suffering her own, and to little Tabitha and Francesca for giving me the best incentive to finish writing.

In the interest of brevity, the masculine pronoun is used throughout to include the feminine.

The law is stated as at 1 October 2013 (unless indicated otherwise).

Lastly, the *Financial Times* articles reproduced throughout the book are from various years and are intended to provide contextual illustrations of topics rather than current market positions.

DAVID ADAMS
London

Contents

PREFACE   v

TABLE OF CASES   xiii

TABLE OF STATUTES   xv

TABLE OF SECONDARY LEGISLATION, ACCOUNTING STANDARDS AND RULES   xvii

TABLE OF ABBREVIATIONS   xix

Chapter 1   RAISING FINANCE: AN OVERVIEW OF PLAYERS AND PRODUCTS   1
             1.1   Introduction   1
             1.2   Borrowers   1
             1.3   Lenders   4
             1.4   A bank is a bank is a bank   4
             1.5   The finance solicitor's role   6
             1.6   Perspectives   7

Part I   FACILITY AGREEMENTS   9

Chapter 2   DUE DILIGENCE, COMMITMENT LETTERS AND THE TERM SHEET   11
             2.1   Introduction: understanding the context   11
             2.2   Due diligence   12
             2.3   The term sheet and commitment letter   14
             2.4   What should the commitment letter cover?   15
             2.5   What should a basic term sheet cover?   15
             2.6   Legal effect of the term sheet   16
             2.7   Private equity term sheets   16
             2.8   From commitment documents to loan: duty to negotiate in good faith?   16
             2.9   Sample term sheet   17
             2.10   Confidentiality letter   18

Chapter 3   PLAIN VANILLA OR BELLS AND WHISTLES?   19
             3.1   Introduction   19
             3.2   Common types of facility   19
             3.3   Syndicated facilities   23
             3.4   Leveraged acquisition facilities   26
             3.5   Other forms of short-term lending   27
             3.6   Which facility is appropriate?   27
             3.7   Anatomy of a facility agreement   27
             3.8   Matched funding   29
             3.9   Further reading   29

Chapter 4   WHEN, WHO, WHERE, WHAT AND WHY?   33
             4.1   Introduction   33
             4.2   Date   34
             4.3   Parties   34
             4.4   Interpretation/definitions   34
             4.5   The facility   35
             4.6   Purpose clause   36
             4.7   Conditions precedent   39
             4.8   Availability   41
             4.9   Floating rate interest   42
             4.10   Fixed rate interest   45
             4.11   Interest periods   45

	4.12	Apportionment: the 'day count fraction'	46
	4.13	Ratchets	46
	4.14	Hedging	47
	4.15	Default interest	47
	4.16	Basis points	47
		Summary	48
Chapter 5		REPRESENTATIONS AND WARRANTIES	49
	5.1	Introduction	49
	5.2	Representations and warranties in a facility agreement	49
	5.3	Representations – the bank's perspective	55
	5.4	Representations – the borrower's perspective	55
	5.5	Representations in contract law	56
		Summary	58
Chapter 6		A REVIEW OF COMPANY ACCOUNTS	59
	6.1	Introduction	59
	6.2	Financial statements	59
	6.3	The balance sheet	60
	6.4	Profit and loss account	65
	6.5	Directors' report, auditor's report, and notes to the accounts	68
	6.6	Cash flow statements	69
	6.7	Consolidated accounts	69
	6.8	Management accounts	70
	6.9	Accounting regulations	70
		Summary	73
Chapter 7		UNDERTAKINGS	75
	7.1	Introduction	75
	7.2	What is an undertaking?	75
	7.3	Financial covenants	76
	7.4	Information undertakings	82
	7.5	General undertakings	83
	7.6	Undertakings – the bank's perspective	86
	7.7	Undertakings – the borrower's perspective	87
Chapter 8		EVENTS OF DEFAULT	89
	8.1	Introduction	89
	8.2	Why have events of default?	89
	8.3	Common events of default	90
	8.4	Events of default and other clauses	95
	8.5	Action on default	95
	8.6	Potential events of default	96
	8.7	LMA definition	97
	8.8	Events of default – the bank's perspective	97
	8.9	Events of default – the borrower's perspective	97
Chapter 9		BOILER PLATE, MECHANICS AND MISCELLANEOUS CLAUSES	99
	9.1	Introduction	99
	9.2	Repayment, prepayment and cancellation	99
	9.3	Margin protection	102
	9.4	Costs and expenses	108
	9.5	Fees	109
	9.6	Remedies, waivers, partial invalidity and amendments	110
	9.7	Force majeure	112
	9.8	Governing law and jurisdiction	112
	9.9	Miscellaneous	114
	9.10	Schedules	116
	9.11	Execution	116
	9.12	US and English law loan facilities	118

Chapter 10	NOVATION, ASSIGNMENT AND SUB-PARTICIPATION	121
	10.1 Introduction	121
	10.2 Why sell a loan?	121
	10.3 Moving rights and obligations	122
	10.4 Selling assets	123
	10.5 Global Transfer Agreement	130
	10.6 Type of assets sold	130
	10.7 Tax implications	130
	10.8 Financial Services and Markets Act implications	131
	10.9 Borrower transfers	131
	10.10 Other jurisdictions	131
	10.11 Securitisation	131
	10.12 Asset sales – the bank's perspective	131
	10.13 Asset sales – the borrower's perspective	131
	10.14 Further reading	132
Chapter 11	DRAFTING TIPS	135
	11.1 Introduction	135
	11.2 Creating the document	135
	11.3 The aims of drafting	136
	11.4 Templates and precedents	136
	11.5 Drafting techniques	137
	11.6 Key words	140
	11.7 Time computations	142
Part II	SECURED LENDING	143
Chapter 12	COMMON FORMS OF SECURITY	145
	12.1 Introduction	145
	12.2 Categorising security	145
	12.3 Giving rights over assets	146
	12.4 Transfer of ownership	149
	12.5 Giving physical possession	150
	12.6 Assignment	152
	12.7 Some terminology	152
	12.8 Further reading	153
Chapter 13	QUASI-SECURITY	155
	13.1 Introduction	155
	13.2 Third party support – guarantees and comfort letters	155
	13.3 Negative pledge	159
	13.4 Retention of title	159
	13.5 Set-off	159
	13.6 Why take security?	160
	13.7 Security – the bank's perspective	162
	13.8 Security – the borrower's perspective	163
	13.9 Further reading	163
Chapter 14	FURTHER ISSUES ON TAKING SECURITY	165
	14.1 Introduction	165
	14.2 Perfection through registration	165
	14.3 Priority of security	173
	14.4 Contractual subordination	174
	14.5 Tacking	175
	14.6 Ruling off accounts	176
	14.7 Fixed or floating charge?	177
	14.8 Hardening periods	178
	14.9 Capacity	179
	14.10 Corporate benefit	179

	14.11	Financial assistance	180
	14.12	Applicable law	180
	14.13	UNCITRAL Model Law	181
	14.14	Other considerations on taking security	181
	14.15	Further reading	182
Chapter 15		SECURITY DOCUMENTATION – DEBENTURES	183
	15.1	Introduction	183
	15.2	Structure of a typical debenture	183
	15.3	Execution	189
Chapter 16		LEGAL OPINIONS	191
	16.1	Introduction	191
	16.2	What are legal opinions?	191
	16.3	Preamble	192
	16.4	Assumptions	193
	16.5	Opinion	193
	16.6	Qualifications	194
	16.7	Foreign counsel legal opinions	195
	16.8	Conclusion	196
Part III		**CAPITAL MARKETS**	**197**
Chapter 17		INTRODUCTION TO INTERNATIONAL CAPITAL MARKETS	199
	17.1	Introduction	199
	17.2	What is a capital market?	199
	17.3	Domestic and euromarkets	200
	17.4	Debt and equity securities	203
	17.5	Bonds and notes	203
	17.6	Other debt securities	207
	17.7	Primary and secondary markets	210
	17.8	Clearing systems	210
	17.9	International Capital Markets Association	211
	17.10	The issuers	212
	17.11	Credit rating	212
	17.12	Further reading	214
Chapter 18		THE FORMS AND LEGAL CHARACTERISTICS OF A BOND	215
	18.1	Introduction	215
	18.2	The form of a bond	215
	18.3	Legal nature of a bond	218
	18.4	Comparing registered and bearer bonds	219
	18.5	The legal effect on bearer bonds held in clearing systems	221
	18.6	Further reading	222
Chapter 19		ISSUING A BOND – THE PARTIES AND DOCUMENTATION	223
	19.1	Introduction	223
	19.2	Parties to a bond issue	223
	19.3	Documentation of a bond issue	227
	19.4	Terms and conditions of a bond	232
Chapter 20		BOND PROSPECTUS AND LISTING PARTICULARS	239
	20.1	Introduction	239
	20.2	Obtaining a London listing	239
	20.3	When is an approved prospectus required?	240
	20.4	Contents of a prospectus	241
	20.5	General duty of disclosure	244
	20.6	Omission of information	244
	20.7	Liability for prospectus and listing particulars	245
	20.8	Other jurisdictions	247

Chapter 21   ISSUING A BOND – THE PROCESS   249
              21.1   Introduction   249
              21.2   The stages of a bond issue   249
              21.3   Mandate   251
              21.4   Due diligence   251
              21.5   Documentation   252
              21.6   Marketing   252
              21.7   Launch and syndication   252
              21.8   Listing   253
              21.9   Signing   255
              21.10 Closing   255

GLOSSARY   259

BIBLIOGRAPHY   271

INDEX   273

Table of Cases

A

Agnew and Another v Commissioner of Inland Revenue ('Brumark') [2001] UKPC 28, [2001] 3 WLR 454 — 186
Al Nakib Investments (Jersey) v Longcroft [1990] 3 All ER 321 — 246
Argo Fund Ltd v Essar Steel Ltd [2005] EWHC 600 (Comm) — 131
Atlantic Computers plc (in administration), Re; National Australia Bank Ltd v Soden [1995] BCC 696 — 158

B

Barbudev v Eurocom Cable Management Bulgaria [2012] EWCA Civ 548 — 17
Barclays Bank Ltd v Quistclose Investments Ltd [1970] AC 567 — 39
BNP Paribas v Yukos Oil Company [2005] EWHC 1321 (Ch) — 95
BNY Corporate Trustee Services Ltd v Eurosail-UK-2007-3BL Plc & Others [2011] EWCA Civ 227 — 93
Bradman v Trinity Estates plc [1989] BCLC 757 — 115
Brightlife, Re [1987] Ch 200 — 185

C

Caparo Industries v Dickman [1990] 1 All ER 568 — 246
Chalk v Kahn and Another [2000] 2 BCLC 361 — 178, 186
Company (No 005009 of 1987), Re A [1989] BCLC 324 — 86
Concord Trust v The Law Debenture Trust Corporation plc [2005] UKHL 27 — 97, 225
Corinthian Securities v Cato [1970] 1 QB 377 — 106
Credit Suisse International v Ramot Plana OOD [2010] EWHC 2759 (Comm) — 115
Credit Suisse v Allerdale Borough Council [1997] QB 306 — 39
Cryne v Barclays Bank plc [1987] BCLC 548 — 184

D

Dearle v Hall (1828) 3 Russ 1 — 174
Devaynes v Noble (1816) 1 Mer 572 — 176
Dodds v Walker [1981] 2 All ER 609 — 142
Dunlop Pneumatic Tyre Co Ltd v New Garage & Motor Co Ltd [1915] AC 79 — 47

E

Enviroco Ltd v Farstad Supply A/S [2009] EWCA Civ 1399 — 140, 186

G

Gate Gourmet Australia (in liquidation) v Gate Gourmet Holding AG [2004] NSWSC 149 — 158
Goldsoll v Goldman [1915] 1 Ch 292 — 111
Goodridge v Macquarie Bank Limited [2010] FCA 67 — 125
Griffiths v Yorkshire Bank plc [1994] 1 WLR 1427 — 173
Grosvenor Place Estates v Roberts (1960) 39 TC 433 — 107

H

Habibsons Bank Ltd v Standard Chartered Bank (Hong Kong) Limited [2010] EWCA Civ 1335 — 125
Hedley Byrne & Co Ltd v Heller & Partners Ltd [1964] AC 465 — 57, 246
Hooper v Western Counties and South Wales Telephone Co Ltd (1892) 68 LT 78 — 100

I

IFE Fund SA v Goldman Sachs International [2007] EWCA Civ 811 — 26
Introductions Ltd v National Provincial Bank [1970] Ch 199 — 37

J

Jet2.com Ltd v Blackpool Airport Ltd [2011] EWHC 1529 (Comm) — 138

K

Keenan Bros, Re [1986] BCLC 242 — 185
Kleinwort Benson Ltd v Malaysia Mining Corpn [1989] 1 All ER 785 — 158

L

Lee-Parker v Izett (No 2) [1972] 2 All ER 800   40
Lester v Garland (1808) 15 Ves 248   142
Lordsvale Finance plc v Bank of Zambia [1996] QB 752   47

M

Manurewa Transport Ltd, Re [1971] NZLR 909   148
McGuinness v Norwich and Peterborough Building Society [2010] EWHC 2989 (Ch)   156
Morris v Agrichemicals Ltd [1997] 3 WLR 909   185

N

National Westminster Bank plc v Spectrum Plus Limited [2005] UKHL 41   186
New Bullas Trading, Re [1994] 1 BCLC 485   186

P

Petromec Inc v Petroleo Brasileiro SA Petrobras and Others [2006] 1 Lloyd's Rep 121   16
PFTZM Ltd, Re [1995] BCC 280   86

Q

Quest Cae Limited, Re [1985] BCLC 266   184

R

R (on the application of Mercury Tax Group and Another) v HM Revenue and Customs Commissioners
    and Others [2008] EWHC 2721   117
Raiffeisen Zentralbank Osterreich AG v The Royal Bank of Scotland plc [2010] EWHC 1392 (Comm)   26
Rhodia International Holdings v Huntsman International LLC [2007] All ER (D) 264   138
Rolled Steel Products (Holdings) Ltd v British Steel Corporation [1986] Ch 246   36, 38

S

Shaker v Vistajet Group Holding SA [2012] EWHC 1329 (Comm)   17
Slavenburg's Bank NV v Intercontinental National Resources Ltd [1980] 1 All ER 955   172
Smith New Court Securities Ltd v Scrimgeour Vickers (Asset Management) Ltd [1997] AC 254, HL   57
Smith v Henniker-Major & Co [2002] BCC 544   38
SSSL Realisations Limited [2004] EWHC (Ch) 1760   175
Sumitomo Bank Ltd v Banque Bruxelles Lambert SA, QBD (Commercial Court), 1 October 1996   26

T

Tele2 International Card Company SA v Post Office Limited [2009] EWCA Civ 9   111
Three Rivers DC v Bank of England [1995] 4 All ER 312   127
Tolhurst v Associated Portland Cement Manufacturers (1900) Ltd [1902] 2 KB 660   127
Tournier v National Provincial and Union Bank of England [1924] 1 KB 461   92, 129
Trade Indemnity Co Ltd v Workington Harbour and Dock Board [1937] AC 1   156
Trafalgar House Construction (Regions) Ltd v General Surety & Guarantee Co Ltd [1995] 3 WLR 204   136
Triodos Bank v Ashley Charles Dobbs [2005] EWCA Civ 630   156

V

Vita Food Products Inc v Unus Shipping Co Ltd (in Liquidation) [1939] AC 277   112

W

Walford and Others v Miles and Another [1992] 2 AC 128   16
Walter and Sullivan Ltd v Murphy (J) and Sons Ltd [1955] 2 QB 584   125
Westmaze Ltd, Re (1998) The Times, 15 July   186

Y

Yorkshire Woolcombers Association Ltd, Re [1903] 2 Ch 284   178

Table of Statutes

Bank of England Act 1946 6
Bills of Exchange Act 1882 126, 219
Bills of Sale Act 1878 173
Bills of Sale Act 1882 173

Companies Act 1985
    s 35 36
    s 35(1) 37
    s 35A 38
    s 35B 38
Companies Act 1989 36, 37
    ss 111 112 36
Companies Act 2006 36, 37, 53, 66, 70, 71, 72, 80, 81, 86,
    126, 140, 141, 148, 152, 165, 172, 175
    s 17 37
    s 39 37, 39
    s 40 38, 39
    s 40(1)–(3) 38
    s 44 189
    s 44(6) 116
    s 79 186
    s 170 86
    s 172 86, 157, 179
    ss 173–177 86
    s 251 86
    s 382 71
    ss 394–396 59, 71
    s 400 52
    s 415 68, 71
    s 423 35, 71
    ss 424–425 35
    s 426 35, 73
    ss 427–429 35
    s 430 35, 71
    ss 431–432 35
    s 442 60
    s 466 71
    s 477 71
    s 482 72
    s 495 71
    s 550 206
    ss 561–573 206
    ss 641–653 64
    s 678 157, 180
    ss 679–680 157
    s 738 35
    s 741 35
    ss 859A–859Q 166
    s 859A(2) 166
    s 859A(4) 167
    s 859A(6) 166
    s 859A(7) 166
    s 859C 172
    s 859D 166
    s 859F 167
    s 859G 167
    s 859H 167

Companies Act 2006 – *continued*
    s 859P 172
    s 859Q(2) 172
    s 860 150, 166, 173
    ss 861–894 150
    s 885(3) 159
    s 1105 172
    s 1159 140, 141
    s 1162 69, 140
    Sch 7 140
Company Directors Disqualification Act 1986 86, 178
    s 22 86
Contracts (Rights of Third Parties) Act 1999 34

Enterprise Act 2002 93, 148, 160, 161, 162, 177, 194
    s 250 161, 162
    s 251 148
Environment Act 1995 53
Environmental Protection Act 1990 53

Finance Act 1986
    s 79(4) 130
    s 99(5)(a) 130
Financial Services Act 2013
    s 89 247
    s 90 247
Financial Services and Markets Act 2000 35, 86, 106, 127,
    131, 226, 245, 246, 259, 264
    s 19 131
    ss 21–25 252
    Part VI (ss 72–103) 239
    s 79 241
    s 80 244, 245
    s 84(1)(d) 242
    s 86 240
    s 87A 241, 244, 245
    s 87A(6) 241
    s 90 245
    s 102 240
    s 397 247
    s 397(3) 247
    s 417 86, 87
    Sch 10 245
    Sch 11A 240
Fraud Act 2006 247

Income and Corporation Taxes Act 1988 107
Income Tax Act 2007 105, 106, 107
    s 874 106
    s 878 106, 107
    s 879 106, 130
    s 930 106
    s 991 106
Insolvency Act 1986 86, 149, 157, 160, 178
    s 9 160
    s 29(2) 160, 161, 183
    s 40 148

Insolvency Act 1986 – *continued*
  s 72A 162
  ss 72B–72G 161
  s 123 93
  s 123(1)–(2) 93
  s 176A 149
  s 214(7) 86
  s 238 125, 157, 160, 178, 194
  s 239 100, 125, 157, 160, 178, 194
  ss 240–241 125
  s 245 125, 149, 179
  s 248(b) 152
  s 249 149, 178
  s 251 86
  s 344 172, 173
  s 386 148
  s 423 194
  Sch 6 148
  Sch B1
    para 14 177
Interpretation Act 1978 141

Land Registration Act 2002 149, 173, 184
Law of Property Act 1925 126, 149, 152
  s 52 189
  s 61 141, 142
  s 87 146, 150
  s 94 175, 176
  s 101 150, 189
  s 136 125, 127, 152
Law of Property (Miscellaneous Provisions) Act 1989 117, 189
  s 2(1) 117
  s 2(3) 117
Limitation Act 1939 183

Merchant Shipping Act 1894 173
Misrepresentation Act 1967 56, 57, 76, 247
  s 2(1) 56, 57
  s 2(2) 57

Pensions Act 2004 186
Powers of Attorney Act 1971
  s 1 189
  s 4 188
  s 7(1) 117

Stamp Act 1891 109
  s 14(1) 109
Statute of Frauds 1677
  s 4 157

Theft Act 1968 247
Trustee Act 1925
  s 16 179

Unfair Contract Terms Act 1977 26

International legislation
Basel I 103
Basel II 103, 104, 105
Basel III 103, 104, 105
Lugano Convention on Jurisdiction and Enforcement of Judgments in Civil and Commercial Matters 1988 114
Lugano Convention on Jurisdiction and Enforcement of Judgments in Civil and Commercial Matters 2007 113
UNCITRAL Model Law 181

US legislation
Glass-Steagall Act (Banking Act 1933) 5

Table of Secondary Legislation, Accounting Standards and Rules

Civil Procedure Rules 1998 (SI 1998/3132)
  r 6.11 114
Cross Border Insolvency Regulations 2006 (SI 2006/1030) 181

Environmental Damage (Prevention and Remediation) Regulations 2009 (SI 2009/153) 53

Insolvency Rules 1986 (SI 1986/1925)
  r 4.90 160
Insolvency (Amendment) Rules 2005 (SI 2005/527) 160
Insolvency (Amendment) Rules 2008 (SI 2008/737) 148

Land Registration Rules 2003(SI 2003/1417) 173

Mortgaging of Aircraft Order 1972 (SI 1972/1268) 173

Overseas Companies (Execution of Documents and Registration of Charges) Amendment Regulations 2011 (SI 2011/2194) 172

Prospectus Regulations 2005 (SI 2005/525) 239

Accounting Standards
FRS 71, 72, 80
  FRS 1 (Revised 1996) 69
  FRS 3 68
  FRS 10 79
  FRS 12 65
  FRS 15 65
General Accepted Accounting Practice (GAAP) 52, 59, 60, 65, 68, 69, 71, 79, 81
International Accounting Standards (IAS) 59, 72
  IAS 16 65
  IAS 39 65
International Financial Reporting Standards (IFRS) 59, 61, 64, 65, 68, 70, 72, 73, 79, 243
  IFRS 3 79
SSAPs 71, 72, 80
  SSAP 6 68
  SSAP 13 79
  SSAP 21 80

Rules
Disclosure and Transparency Rules 72, 239, 255, 268
  r 4.1 72
  r 4.1.3 60
  r 4.2 72

ICMA Rules 212, 218, 228, 230, 249, 252, 253
  r 251 234
Land Registry
  Rule 139 184
Listing Rules 72, 224, 239, 240, 241, 244, 245, 255, 268
  r 2 253
  r 3 254
  r 3.2.2 255
  r 3.4.4 254
  r 4 242
  r 9.6 236
  r 9.8.2R 72
  r 9.8.4 72
  r 12.5 234
  r 17 254
  Appendix 3 269
Prospectus Rules 239, 240, 242, 244, 245, 268
  r 1.2.1 240
  r 2.1 241
  r 2.2 241
  r 2.2.7 241
  r 2.4 244
  r 2.4.4 244
  r 2.5 245
  r 3 254
  r 3.1.3 252, 254
  r 5.5 242
  r 5.5.4 242
  Appendix 3
    Annex IV 242
    Annex V 242
    Annex IX 242
    Annex XIII 242
    Annex V 243

EU secondary legislation
Directive 2003/71/EC Prospectus Directive 239, 242, 244
Directive 2004/35/EC EU Environmental Directive 53
Directive 2010/73/EU Amendment Directive 239, 240
Regulation 1346/2000 EU Insolvency Regulation (EUIR)
  Preamble 13 180
  Art 3(1) 180
Regulation 44/2001 (Brussels I) 113, 114
Regulation 1606/2002 59
Regulation 864/2007 (Rome II Regulation) 113
Regulation 593/2008 (Rome I Regulation) 113
Regulation 1289/2008 243
Regulation 311/2012 243
Rome I Regulation *see* Regulation 593/2008

Table of Abbreviations

ACT	Association of Corporate Treasurers
CA 1985	Companies Act 1985
CA 1989	Companies Act 1989
CA 2006	Companies Act 2006
CD	certificate of deposit
CDDA	Company Directors Disqualification Act 1986
COMI	Centre of Main Interest
CP	conditions precedent
EA 2002	Enterprise Act 2002
EEA	European Economic Area
EPA 1990	Environmental Protection Act 1990
FCA	Financial Conduct Authority
FPC	Financial Policy Committee
FRN	floating rate note
FRSs	Financial Reporting Standards
FSA	Financial Services Authority
FSMA 2000	Financial Services and Markets Act 2000
GAAP	Generaly Accepted Accounting Practice
IA 1986	Insolvency Act 1986
IAS	International Accounting Standard
ICMA	International Capital Markets Association
ICTA 1988	Income and Corporation Taxes Act 1988
IFRS	International Financial Reporting Standards
IPMA	International Primary Markets Association (now part of ICMA)
IRB	internal ratings-based
ISIN	International Securities Identification Number
ISMA	International Security Markets Association (now part of ICMA)
Libor	London Interbank Offered Rate
LMA	Loan Market Association
LPA 1925	Law of Property Act 1925
LRA 2002	Land Registration Act 2002
LSE	London Stock Exchange
MAC	material adverse change
MTN	medium term note
PRA	Prudential Regulation Authority
PSM	Professional Securities Market
RCF	revolving credit facility
RIS	Regulatory Information Service (Listing Rules, Rule 12.5)
SA 1891	Stamp Act 1891
SDRT	stamp duty reserve tax
SPV	special purpose vehicle
SSAPs	Statements of Standard Accounting Practice

TLC	transferable loan certificate
TLI	transferable loan instrument
UKLA	UK Listing Authority

CHAPTER 1

RAISING FINANCE: AN OVERVIEW OF PLAYERS AND PRODUCTS

1.1	Introduction	1
1.2	Borrowers	1
1.3	Lenders	4
1.4	A bank is a bank is a bank	4
1.5	The finance solicitor's role	6
1.6	Perspectives	7

> 'We're in the risk business. We take positions. We lend money. We get most of it back.'
>
> Martin Taylor, Chief Executive, Barclays Bank, reporting losses of £325m
>
> (Source: *Financial Times*, September 1998)

1.1 INTRODUCTION

Most people will never be party to litigation. Many of us, including a good few lawyers, will die without making a will. Some people will never own property, and so avoid the nuances of conveyancing, and very few people will run their own business. Almost all of us, however, will borrow money.

Whether it is to buy a car, a house, to fund education, or to bridge from one payday to the next, borrowing is almost a 'requirement' of our society. Banking services available to individuals have grown in number and sophistication over recent years, with innovations such as telephone and internet banking making borrowing increasingly more accessible.

However, borrowing is not the sole preserve of the individual. Businesses must also borrow money, and they usually require more versatile, more complex, and far larger loans than individuals. Banks and business borrowers will therefore frequently rely on the skills of specialised solicitors to help establish their required financing.

This book is not about banking for individuals. It is about financing a business; and in particular it is about the solicitor's role in the two dominant forms of corporate financing: commercial loan facilities and capital markets finance. Beyond this chapter the book is divided into three parts: the first part concentrates on raising money by way of a commercial loan facility, the second deals with taking security for a commercial loan, and the third part considers raising money on international capital markets.

1.2 BORROWERS

1.2.1 Types of borrower

The most common borrowers of capital on a commercial basis can conveniently be placed into the following three broad categories.

1.2.1.1 Governments

All governments borrow; this is usually referred to as 'sovereign debt'. The borrowing may be short term, to bridge a shortfall between their income (primarily from taxation) and the money they require to fulfil their policies and meet their general obligations, or it may be long term (eg, to fund specific projects). The global financial crisis, which began in 2007 and is still affecting financial markets, brutally exposed governments' borrowing needs, with Greece, Spain, Portugal and others struggling to meet their requirements (Spain alone is estimated to require over €121 billion of borrowing in the capital markets through 2013).

Local authorities and municipalities

Part of a government's borrowing may be used to fund local authorities; however, those authorities will also have the capacity to borrow for some purposes, typically to invest in infrastructure. For example, the Greater London Authority hoped to raise £600 million through a bond issue to help fund the Crossrail project (see the article at the end of this chapter) although the plan was later shelved.

1.2.1.2 Companies

By far the most prevalent borrowers are companies. These range from public companies with diverse interests and a vast network of subsidiaries to small local businesses. Furthermore, banks and other financial institutions are voracious corporate borrowers. Companies, particularly public companies, enjoy a broader range of techniques for raising money (and providing security for borrowing) than any other type of borrower. Since they are so numerous, corporates usually account for the majority of a solicitor's borrower clients. The following chapters will therefore concentrate on borrowing by a limited company, and references to 'borrower' should be read accordingly.

1.2.1.3 Others

Whilst the three categories above cover most of the entities raising substantial finance, it should not be thought that they account for every type of borrower: partnerships, sole traders and supranational organisations (eg, the World Bank or the European Investment Bank) will all borrow capital.

1.2.2 The need for finance

It is not difficult to think of reasons why a *new* business might require considerable 'start up' capital. Assets such as premises, office equipment, and plant and machinery must be purchased or leased. Manufacturing businesses will need to buy raw materials, and almost all businesses must pay employees' wages. They will need to pay electricity bills, advertise to attract customers, and initially they may even have to run at a loss to win business from competitors.

Most existing businesses will also need to borrow capital in order to trade successfully. Consider Tesco plc, one of the world's leading retailers. According to its latest (2013) audited accounts, the Tesco group had a net worth of around £16.7 billion, with profit before tax in 2013 of nearly £2 billion. It might be thought that a well-established company generating such immense profit would have little need for borrowing. However, the group had outstanding commercial borrowing of around £10.8 billion (with a further £2.8 billion of available borrowings which were undrawn). Tesco plc almost certainly has continuing working capital requirements not dissimilar to those listed above for a newly-formed business (albeit on a larger scale!). But the Tesco group will also have required capital to expand its businesses through acquisitions and opening new stores.

1.2.3   Financing a company

There are, broadly, four methods by which a large company might raise the money it requires to run its business:

(a)   share capital;

(b)   retained profits;

(c)   loan facilities; and

(d)   capital markets instruments.

1.2.3.1   Share capital

All companies have 'ordinary' shareholders who invest money in the company in return for a 'share' in the business. This money is effectively 'non-returnable' so far as the company is concerned (other than on a winding-up), and so it can be used to invest in the company's assets on a long-term basis. Furthermore, while most shareholders expect to share in some of the profits their company makes (by way of a dividend), there is no absolute obligation on the company to provide a return on its shares.

Most companies will issue shares both on incorporation (to provide initial capital) and at a future date (to raise additional capital). However, each time a company issues more shares it will generally entail any profit which is distributed to the shareholders being spread more thinly. The existing shareholders may therefore prefer their company to borrow capital on which it pays a 'fixed' return, rather than a return linked to profits. In other words, the company can borrow money at a (relatively) fixed cost, and use it to make greater profits for its shareholders. This is known as 'gearing', or 'leverage'. (A fuller explanation of share finance is given in **Business Law and Practice**.)

1.2.3.2   Retained profit

Once a company starts trading successfully, it will make a profit. The directors will decide how to use any profit, and a substantial amount will usually be distributed to the shareholders as a return on their investment in shares. However, part (and occasionally all) of a company's profits will be retained in the company to provide working capital and to finance other funding requirements. These retained profits are shown in a company's balance sheet as 'retained profits' or 'retained earnings' (see **6.3.5**).

1.2.3.3   Loan facilities

Whilst share capital and retained profits can provide substantial levels of funding, they are unlikely to be entirely sufficient for all a company's needs. For example, share capital cannot generally be raised in small amounts on a regular basis, and only public limited companies may offer their shares to the general public. Meanwhile, the timing and amount of a company's profits are often unpredictable.

Borrowing by way of a loan (usually known as a 'loan facility') can provide a company with a flexible and 'reliable' source of funds, and allow very diverse methods of borrowing capital. An overdraft facility, for example, provides an instant source of variable borrowing, helping a company with its cash flow. Alternatively (or additionally), a company might borrow a lump sum for a period of time (known as a 'term loan') to fund a specific project. Loan facilities can cater for borrowing in a choice of currencies. Interest may be payable at a fixed or variable rate, whilst the capital may be repayable in stages through the life of the loan, or in one repayment when the loan 'matures'. The most common forms of loan facility are dealt with more fully in **Chapter 3**.

1.2.3.4   Capital markets instruments

Large companies may obtain financing from another source of funds known as the 'capital markets'. In simplistic terms, this will involve a company issuing a series of instruments (ie, a form of certificate) to investors in acknowledgement of an amount of capital it has borrowed from them (these instruments are known generically as 'debt securities'). The most common forms of capital markets debt security involve the issuer agreeing to repay the borrowed capital on a specified date (on 'maturity') and to pay interest on the borrowed capital in the meantime. The debt security may be sold by the original investor to subsequent investors at any time, allowing it to recover some or all of its capital investment before the maturity date. The subsequent investor will then be entitled to claim any remaining interest payments, and to receive the borrowed capital on maturity. The debt security can be re-sold any number of times; the issuer simply pays interest to the current owner, and repays capital to the owner at maturity.

Debt securities issued on the capital markets include bonds, notes, commercial paper, certificates of deposit, and loan stock. Raising finance through issuing debt securities is dealt with in **Part III**.

1.3 LENDERS

For most people the word 'lender' is probably synonymous with 'bank'. There are, however, two main types of commercial lender: banks and so-called 'institutional' lenders (also known as 'non-bank lenders' or, rather loosely, 'funds'). Both are intermediaries, that is they generally lend money raised from others rather than their own capital. Banks raise money primarily from depositors (eg, you and I opening savings accounts), from issuing debt securities and by borrowing from each other (see **4.9.1.2**). Individuals also 'lend' indirectly through their contributions to pension funds and insurance policies, because the institutions which receive the contributions invest them in order to raise the money they need to meet their obligations under the funds and policies. Institutional lenders usually raise money from investors by creating a series of 'funds' which then reinvest the money in various ways. These 'non-bank lenders' have become prominent participants in term loans in recent years, commonly making up at least half the syndicate (by value) once a loan is in secondary syndication (see **3.3.2**).

In basic terms, therefore, individuals and companies fund all the forms of lending outlined above by putting 'spare' cash with banks or into investment funds, and by buying debt securities. However, it is usually a bank, of one type or another, with which a borrower must initially deal in order to arrange most types of borrowing. For the sake of brevity, the generic term 'bank' is used throughout this book to refer to the financial institution which acts as lender. The main types of bank are examined below.

1.4 A BANK IS A BANK IS A BANK

It is inconceivable that any of us will go through life without some form of interaction with a bank. To some extent, the banks which provide us with current accounts, credit cards, savings products and loans are also the bankers to businesses. However, the financial markets are awash with different labels such as 'accepting houses', 'merchant banks', 'commercial banks', 'high street banks', 'universal banks', 'retail banking' and 'wholesale banking'. The key to understanding these terms is to distinguish commercial banks and investment banks.

1.4.1 Commercial banks

Commercial banks essentially raise money by attracting deposits and then lend that money to individuals ('retail' banking), companies ('corporate' or 'wholesale' banking), governments and others who need it. We are all familiar with the retail divisions of commercial banks such as Barclays, Lloyds, HSBC and Nat West because they have branches on most high streets (they are known as 'high street banks'). They clear cheques, provide current accounts, savings accounts, overdrafts and mortgages for individuals and many businesses. We take these services for granted, but they are so woven into our lives that even a short interruption can be traumatic, as demonstrated by the computer failure suffered by the RBS Group in June 2012 (see article below). If we lose trust in a high street bank, the consequence can be catastrophic, as demonstrated by the collapse of Northern Rock and its subsequent nationalisation in 2008. In essence then, commercial banks do what you might expect of a bank: they are intermediaries, 'moving money' to where it is required and providing basic banking services. So long as they lend prudently, it is a relatively low risk and lucrative business.

1.4.2 Investment banks

You and I are unlikely to have direct dealings with investment banks. They do not take deposits or lend in the traditional sense. The term 'investment bank' was originally used for US institutions such as Goldman Sachs, JP Morgan and Merrill Lynch; the equivalent banks in the UK, such as Barings, NM Rothschilds, Samuel Montagu and Hambros, were known as 'merchant banks'. Their origins were in financing trade in the 18th and 19th centuries (they were sometimes known as 'accepting houses' from their traditional role of accepting bills of exchange – see **17.6.4**). Over time, the role of these banks expanded and the term merchant bank was largely dropped. Modern day investment banks sell advice (for example, advising on bond or share issues, or corporate acquisitions) and underwrite securities issues. They also trade and speculate on bonds, shares and complex financial instruments, and it is these activities that can bring huge reward but also the risk of large losses. It has attracted the tabloidesque label of 'casino banking'.

1.4.3 Glass-Steagall, universal banks and 'ring-fencing'

In 1929 the US suffered the Wall Street Crash, the most devastating stock market collapse in its history. It was followed by years of economic depression. Many US banks collapsed over this period, due in part to their exposure to the stock market through their own trading and their loans to others to buy shares. This led to the Banking Act 1933 (commonly known as the 'Glass-Steagall Act' after its sponsor) which regulated the investments of many commercial banks and effectively prohibited commercial banks and investment banks from combining their businesses. The aim of the regulation was to protect depositors' money held by commercial banks from the investment risks taken by investment banks.

The European banking market had no equivalent to Glass-Steagall and, stimulated by the deregulation in the UK financial markets in the 1980s (the 'Big Bang'), European banks grew in size and complexity. Banks such as Barclays, Royal Bank of Scotland and HSBC combined retail, wholesale and investment bank services in one institution. These 'universal banks' were intended to benefit from economies of scale and reap synergies, with the capital and customer base of the commercial business feeding the investment and advisory activities of the investment banking arm. The investment business also benefited from being married to a retail business that markets knew governments would not allow to fail. In 1999, following heavy lobbying from the banks, Glass-Steagall was repealed and US banks largely followed suit through institutions such as Citigroup and JP Morgan Chase.

It would not be fair to lay the blame for the financial crisis of 2007–08 entirely at the feet of universal banks: proponents would argue that the largest institutions provide a 'full service' to customers and are better able to weather financial storms. However, many governments and regulators now see stricter bank regulation as critical and the separation of investment and commercial bank business is high on the agenda. The UK Independent Commission on Banking (the 'Vickers Report'), set up to consider reforms of the UK banking sector to promote financial stability, recommended forcing bank groups to separate their retail and investment bank businesses. This 'ring-fencing' of the retail banking business was adopted by the subsequent HM Treasury White Paper. Meanwhile, the US Government is also looking to restrict the trading of certain banks under proposals known as the Volcker Rule. Universal banks will almost certainly have to make changes to their structure as a result.

1.4.4   Central banks

All countries with developed economies have a central bank, although the functions performed by that institution will vary between jurisdictions. The central bank of the United Kingdom is the Bank of England, which was founded in 1694 as a private bank and nationalised under the Bank of England Act 1946. The main functions of the Bank of England are to act as the Government's banker (holding its main account and borrowing on its behalf) and adviser on monetary policy, to issue bank notes, to regulate the money markets by lending or borrowing and to set interest rates. The Bank of England will also help other banks with short-term liquidity problems as a lender of last resort (eg, in September 2007 the Bank provided a short-term 'emergency' facility to the Northern Rock bank which feared it could not borrow sufficient short-term funds in the markets because of a general liquidity crisis). Longer-term problems are more likely to be met with advice than money (when Northern Rock's depositors decided an 'emergency facility' signalled time to withdraw their savings, the Government had to nationalise the bank).

The Bank's historic function as regulator of other banks was almost entirely transferred to the Financial Services Authority (FSA) in June 1998. However, on 16 June 2010, the UK's Chancellor of the Exchequer, George Osborne, announced plans to replace the FSA with three new entities (the Financial Policy Committee (FPC), the Prudential Regulation Authority (PRA) and the Financial Conduct Authority (FCA)). On 1 April 2013, the three new regulators were formally established. The FPC (part of the Bank of England) is primarily charged with monitoring, and removing or reducing, systemic risks to protect the UK financial system; the PRA (an operationally independent subsidiary of the Bank of England) is responsible for prudential regulation and supervision of banks, building societies, insurers, credit unions and major investment firms; and the FCA supervises and regulates around 26,000 firms in the UK financial services industry, primarily with a view to consumer protection and market integrity.

RBS: systems down

Houston, we have a problem. Banks often plan for disasters, such as a rival bank failure, currency collapse or terrorist attacks. But Royal Bank of Scotland has been caught out by an internal IT problem after a routine software upgrade last week. This laid low the retail banking operation's payment processing system. RBS has fixed the problem, but still has to clear a backlog of client payments. Many banks have service interruptions when installing patches or upgrades. But big upsets are rare for a UK banking system that handled more than 6.5bn interbank payments (£70tn worth) in 2010, according to British Bankers' Association data.

The mess will further dent RBS's reputation, but the final cost should be manageable.

Clients will surely claim back late payment charges and other indirect costs. RBS and its Nat-West and Ulster Bank units, with almost 17m customers in total, have said clients will not be left out of pocket. The administrative cost of proving and settling claims could be burdensome for a business that generated £6bn of operating profit last year. But it is likely to be a small fraction of the £1.2bn it has provided against payment protection insurance mis-selling claims.

The Financial Services Authority does not stress test bank IT systems. But it expects banks "to take reasonable care to establish and maintain such systems and controls as are appropriate to its business", and to ensure business continuity.

The key, however, as Research In Motion, Perrier and Toyota learnt, is to communicate clearly and often with stakeholders. RBS has struggled to get ahead of the problem. It may be that a line of programming code was wrong, or the bank lost vital IT staff in its cost-cutting zeal. Either way, RBS must once again take the financial and reputational rap for its actions. "The computer says no" is no longer a satisfactory response.

Source: *Financial Times*, 25 June 2012

1.5   THE FINANCE SOLICITOR'S ROLE

This chapter has provided a very brief overview as to why a business might need to borrow money, how that money might be raised, and the role of various banks in the financing process. What part does a finance solicitor play? Newly-formed companies will usually require relatively straightforward financing: typically a simple term loan to supplement their initial shareholders' capital, together with an overdraft facility to aid cash flow and provide flexibility. Many banks provide their own specialist small business advisers, and will usually insist that basic loans are transacted on their standard form documents, with minimal negotiation. There is little requirement at this stage for a specialist finance solicitor.

Larger companies, however, will tend to have more complex financial requirements, and so both the company and the bank will frequently instruct their own specialist finance solicitors. The depth of a solicitor's involvement depends upon the stage at which he is instructed by his client. In very complicated facilities, or for specialised transactions such as an acquisition finance, project finance or securitisation, the finance solicitors will be involved at a very early stage assisting with the structure of the deal. For more straightforward facilities, the structure and basic terms of the facility will usually be agreed between the director with executive responsibility for supervising the company's finances (the 'finance director') and the company's bankers. The finance solicitors will then be instructed to draft and negotiate the loan documentation. Together with good drafting and negotiation skills, a finance solicitor must also be aware of current market practice, since this will dictate the terms that most banks are likely to accept.

Most City firms will split a large finance department into a number of areas with specific responsibilities. The common divisions are:

(a)   general banking (ie, loan facilities – acting for bank or borrower);

(b)   capital markets and securitisation (see **10.10** for a brief explanation);

(c)   project finance (ie, the financing of specific projects in which the return on investment is linked to the project itself) and asset finance (ie, the financing of the purchase or lease of specific assets such as aircraft or ships); and maybe

(d)   separate derivatives and regulatory practices.

1.6   PERSPECTIVES

Banking practice is usually a particularly constructive form of legal work; both parties will be anxious for the loan transaction to go ahead, and this invariably results in a fair degree of co-operation between them. It is important to remember, however, that each party will see certain matters from a slightly different perspective, with various matters up for negotiation. As a finance solicitor, your perspective on certain matters will therefore depend on your client. Where appropriate, this book will try to give a brief summary of both the borrower's and the bank's perspectives.

Bond issue to raise Crossrail funds

By Bob Sherwood, London and South-East Correspondent

London will become the first local authority to tap into the capital markets for 17 years with a £600m bond issue to raise funds for the £14.8bn Crossrail project.

At a time of tight financial constraints on local authorities, Boris Johnson, London mayor, intends to use the public debt market model for further funding of the Greater London Authority's capital programme in the belief that it is cheaper than more conventional arrangements. The GLA has finalised the £600m bond issue through a new vehicle developed with Lloyds Bank Corporate Markets.

Leicester and Salford councils turned to the bond market in 1994 to raise money for housing and infrastructure and Transport for London (TfL) issued a £200m bond in 2006 to finance Tube upgrades.

However, the Lloyds Bank advisers who worked on the deal said they fully expected other local authorities to follow London's lead and seek similar bond deals to finance capital projects.

Mr Johnson said: "This is a great example of the public and private sectors coming together and delivering an innovative solution to bear down on borrowing costs. I hope this is a model local government can develop for other important improvements we make to the capital and beyond."

Given equivalent savings on future borrowings scheduled to fund the cross-London rail link, the GLA believes the bond option could shave £65m off the costs of long-term borrowing for the scheme. The GLA is required to borrow a total of £3.5bn for Crossrail, just under 25 per cent of the total construction bill, which is to be funded by a supplement to the business rates (BRS) paid by larger companies in the capital. The government and TfL are financing the balance.

The GLA had previously raised £800m, the first tranche of its borrowing, through the government's Public Works Loan Board. But ministers made borrowing through the board about 1 per cent more expensive in October.

The mayor's advisers say the bond will prove around 0.17 per cent cheaper than the loan board. If used for future borrowings, the strategy could give the GLA the option to repay its loans earlier, potentially shortening the period that the business rate supplement, due to run until 2035, remains in operation. The GLA said it could save the equivalent of a year's levy of the BRS on outer-London businesses, or £4,000 per business property.

Andrew Géczy, chief executive of wholesale markets and co-head of Lloyds Bank Corporate Markets, said: "It is more than 17 years since a mainstream local authority has secured finance via the public markets, so this transaction is significant as well as innovative."

He said the framework created for the GLA could benefit the local authority sector as a whole. He added: "Local authorities wanting to raise financing, even relatively small sums in comparison to that raised by the GLA, will be able to access the capital markets to help them deliver their local projects and to do so in a more cost-effective manner."

An article illustrating a local authority bond finance.
Source: *Financial Times*, 3 July 2011

PART I

FACILITY AGREEMENTS

DUE DILIGENCE, COMMITMENT LETTERS AND THE TERM SHEET

2.1	Introduction: understanding the context	11
2.2	Due diligence	12
2.3	The term sheet and commitment letter	14
2.4	What should the commitment letter cover?	15
2.5	What should a basic term sheet cover?	15
2.6	Legal effect of the term sheet	16
2.7	Private equity term sheets	16
2.8	From commitment documents to loan: duty to negotiate in good faith?	16
2.9	Sample term sheet	17
2.10	Confidentiality letter	18

'Every journey begins with a single step.'

Mao Tse-Tung

2.1 INTRODUCTION: UNDERSTANDING THE CONTEXT

Before considering loan documentation, it is important to understand that the context in which a loan facility is to be used will influence its final terms and the process of its creation. The three main contexts are:

(a) *investment grade loans (or 'corporate credit')* – where the borrower is typically a large established company requiring cash to run and expand its business, and possibly make small acquisitions;

(b) *leveraged loans* – where the borrower's debt is a multiple of its share capital (equity). Because this involves greater risk for a bank, the controls in the facility agreement are usually tighter. Leveraged loans are usually used for 'acquisition finance' in which companies, or private equity funds, buy other companies or groups.

(c) *cross-over credit* – where a borrower is borderline investment grade and so subject to controls in the facility agreement stricter than usual investment grade loans but not usually as strict as leveraged loans.

Almost as important as the context is the liquidity of the market: the more money available to borrow, the more borrowers can dictate the terms of the loan facility, whatever the context. For example, investment grade borrowers, having a lower risk of payment default, traditionally demand more relaxed terms than a leveraged loan. However, the early years of this century saw leveraged markets flooded with cash from institutional lenders ('funds'), resulting in certain terms being more relaxed than investment grade loans. Then, since August 2007, the so-called 'credit crunch' has made negotiating borrowing difficult for almost all borrowers.

This book generally explains the process and terms relevant to an investment grade loan made to a company, but with an indication of certain leveraged terms, and relaxations that a strong corporate borrower might request.

If a borrower is refinancing an existing loan it will probably approach its current syndicate. Not only will there be an existing relationship, but the current facility agreement will usually form the basis of the new loan document. If it has no existing facilities, is dissatisfied with its current bank, or even requires a loan facility of a type that the current bank cannot or will not provide, then the borrower will have to approach a new institution. It should not be assumed, however, that the borrower is always the 'suitor'. When the lending market is flush with money, banks are generally more pro-active and may approach businesses with the offer of a loan.

Once initial contact has been made, a bank cannot proceed further without obtaining approval for the transaction in accordance with its internal credit procedures. Approval must always be obtained before a loan is offered. If the loan is approved, the next stage involves the drafting of an initial summary of terms (the 'term sheet') from which the loan facility will grow. This chapter explains the first steps in the lending process with a review of a typical credit procedure and term sheet.

2.2   DUE DILIGENCE

Before lending several hundred million pounds, it is necessary to know a little bit about the borrower! When a bank considers lending to a would-be borrower, its initial job is to assess the credit risk: put simply, what is the risk that the borrower will be unable to pay interest ('service' the loan), or be unable to repay the capital? If the credit risk is small, many banks will be prepared to lend to that borrower, and so the fees and margin (ie, profit) that can be charged will be driven down. Conversely, the higher the chance of default, the larger the fees and margin a bank will demand to compensate for the greater risk, and at some point the risk will become too great for the bank to offer a loan. The more information about a borrower that a bank can get, the better it can assess the risk. A bank will therefore conduct a fact-finding exercise known as 'due diligence'.

The breadth and depth of any due diligence process will depend on a number of factors (see **2.2.1**), but in broad terms it will be in two parts.

2.2.1   Initial investigation

The format and scope of the investigation will vary with the identity of the bank and the borrower as well as a number of factors, including:

(a)   the size of the loan;

(b)   the type of loan and its purpose;

(c)   whether the loan is to be secured;

(d)   whether the borrower is already known to the bank;

(e)   market liquidity (ie, whether there are numerous or few lenders willing to lend); and

(f)   whether the loan is an integral part of a larger transaction, such as a flotation or an acquisition (where the due diligence process will have to take account of the larger transaction).

There is no 'standard' due diligence procedure applied by all banks. However, a typical initial investigation for an existing borrower requiring a loan for general corporate purposes might be as follows.

2.2.1.1   Account officer

Each borrower is assigned a particular individual (usually known as an 'account officer') within the bank who provides a consistent point of contact and someone with whom the borrower's officers (in particular its Finance Director) can build a relationship. The account officer will put together a very basic package of terms for the proposed loan. This will usually cover matters such as the amount and term of the loan, repayment dates and principal financial covenants, and will be based largely on the account officer's knowledge of the borrower.

2.2.1.2 Credit analysis

The account officer's proposal will then undergo a credit analysis. Some banks will have a separate committee which meets regularly to analyse lending proposals. Many banks will rely on the account officer to create his own assessment, often with the help of a credit assessment manual which provides checklists of the points to be covered. This will also include any policy guidelines peculiar to the bank, for example, the mandatory inclusion of a material adverse change, or cross-default clause (see **Chapter 8**). The source of information for the credit analysis depends on the borrower and the proposed deal. The borrower's most recently published accounts will always be reviewed. Since a private company has nine months after its year end in which to publish accounts (a public company has six months and a (London) listed company has four months), a bank might require more current information. Smaller borrowers will, therefore, probably be asked to produce interim accounts or management accounts. Larger borrowers (eg, those in the FTSE 250) would treat such a request with derision if the loan was for general purposes. Generally, the better credit rating the borrower has, the less information it is likely to provide. If a borrower provides sensitive unpublished information, it will ask the bank to give an undertaking not to disclose it to third parties (a 'confidentiality letter').

As mentioned above, the scope of the analysis will also depend on the size of the loan. It is also important for any analysis to take into account the 'global' exposure the bank will have with respect to the borrower, its affiliated entities and that business sector, since these factors may affect the risk assessment.

2.2.1.3 Credit clearance

Once the credit analysis has been completed it will be sent to a credit department for sanctioning by a more senior officer of the bank. The credit department (or a 'credit committee') will see all credit requests and therefore have an overview of overall lending. They will also check that internal limits and policies, as well as any external restraints (eg, for exposure), will not be breached. Occasionally, they may defer the analysis to an industry department (which has expertise in a particular industry) or Area Credit Officer (with geographical expertise) to obtain a more specialised view of the borrower in the context of contemporary businesses.

The credit department might reject the proposal. Alternatively, they may either approve a loan on the basis of the analysis, or make approval subject to revised terms being agreed (eg, a smaller loan, stricter undertakings, or a shorter term). Once clearance has been given, the account officer can finalise a draft term sheet. If the deal is particularly complex, the account officer might involve a solicitor at this stage, to help construct the term sheet.

2.2.2 Subsequent investigation

The borrower may immediately accept the bank's draft of the term sheet, or there may be a small amount of negotiation (any major changes would require reapproval by the credit department). Once the bank and borrower have agreed the term sheet, a second phase of the due diligence process will begin. It is at this point that the bank is most likely to involve advisers (although smaller loans and 'repeats' may be dealt with largely 'in house'). The bank will instruct solicitors to put together an initial draft facility agreement on the basis of the term sheet. The bank may also instruct accountants to compile a report on the borrower.

During this stage, a solicitor might obtain copies of the memorandum and articles, the charges register and company records relating to the borrower. Obtaining a copy of a corporate borrower's registered documents (typically from the Companies Registry online service) is a quick and cost-effective way of getting information. However, the register does have its limitations. For example, the borrower may not have filed its returns properly. Whilst this may result in a fine for a company and its officers, there is no provision for compensating a third party who suffers any loss. Primarily, therefore, the bank and its advisers will turn to the borrower to supply information as 'conditions precedent' to the loan facility becoming available.

2.2.3   Ongoing information

It is important to realise that a bank's information gathering does not end with the signing of the loan document. A bank must monitor the borrower to ensure it has a reasonable chance of getting its loan repaid. This is the practical reason behind the repeated representations and undertakings in a facility agreement (see **Chapters 5** to **7**).

2.2.4   Acquisition finance

The position is different here. Traditionally, acquisition financings involve greater due diligence since they are leveraged financings with increased risk. However, in very liquid markets, with multiple bidders for each target company, due diligence may be very limited. In particular, if the target is already owned by a private equity house, due diligence may consist of just a few documents and reports about the target company made available to view for a limited time in a 'data room' (either a 'virtual' data room – ie, online – or a designated room at the vendor's solicitor). In a hostile acquisition of a public company, information will also be limited.

2.3   THE TERM SHEET AND COMMITMENT LETTER

2.3.1   What are they?

A term sheet is a document which records, in writing, the principal terms of a transaction. It is signed by the parties to the transaction, but it is not usually intended to be contractually binding (see **2.5**). Term sheets are often attached as an Appendix to a short letter (the 'commitment letter' or 'mandate letter'), which contains any legally binding terms required at the outset of the lending process (see **2.4**).

After initial meetings with the borrower to discuss the fundamentals of the proposed loan, the bank will produce a commitment letter and term sheet reflecting the terms on which it is prepared to lend. The borrower will then be given a date by which it must accept those terms by signing and returning the commitment letter (known as granting the bank a 'mandate'). Occasionally, the bank will instruct solicitors to assist in drafting the commitment letter and term sheet, but more frequently it will be produced by the bank's in-house legal department. Typically, the term sheet aims to provide an overview and will not include substantial detail (but see **2.7**).

2.3.2   Why have a term sheet?

The key reason for producing a term sheet is to focus the minds of bank and borrower on the fundamental issues of the deal. If the pricing and structure of the loan cannot be agreed in outline then there is little point instructing solicitors or performing substantial due diligence. When markets are flush with cash (as was the case for acquisition finance before the economic downturn started in late 2007) borrowers tend to have the whip hand in negotiating terms. This may result in borrowers drafting their own term sheets in an attempt to dictate terms to prospective lenders (see **2.7**).

If the proposed facility is to be syndicated (ie involve more than one lender), it will be helpful for the bank which is arranging the loan to have an accurate summary of the main terms when trying to sell the deal to early syndicate members before an information memorandum has been produced (see **Chapter 3** for further explanation).

Finally, the term sheet acts as an outline from which the bank's solicitor can extract the key information necessary to prepare the first draft of the facility agreement. Whilst not usually intended to be legally binding, neither party will expect any derogation from the broad outline of the term sheet, and so the solicitor has some certainty on which to begin his drafting.

2.4 WHAT SHOULD THE COMMITMENT LETTER COVER?

The commitment letter (also known as a 'mandate letter') is a letter sent from the bank which is arranging the facility to the borrower. It contains any terms which need to be legally binding before the loan itself is executed, and usually has the term sheet attached as an appendix. The key points covered in the letter are:

(a)   whether the bank's obligation to arrange the facility (see **3.3.2.1**) is 'best efforts' or 'underwritten';

(b)   any general conditionality to the offer to arrange, eg time limit for executing the facility document, obtaining credit committee approvals, completion of satisfactory due diligence, etc;

(c)   a material adverse change provision allowing the bank to withdraw from the offer if there is a material adverse change to the market generally (known as the 'market mac') or to the borrower's situation specifically (known as the 'business mac');

(d)   a 'clear market' clause in which the borrower agrees not to raise other finance whilst this facility is being arranged;

(e)   a 'market flex' clause which allows the bank to change aspects of the negotiated facility agreement if it is necessary to attract other banks to participate; and

(f)   provisions for the bank to recover fees, costs and expenses if the deal does not go ahead, as well as an indemnity for any losses the bank might suffer.

The intention is that the commitment letter is signed and returned by the borrower within a few days, although it must be said this is not always enforced in practice.

2.5 WHAT SHOULD A BASIC TERM SHEET COVER?

A 'sample' of a straightforward bilateral, investment grade type term sheet appears at **2.10**, although many are more complex (see **2.7**). As explained earlier, a signed term sheet is usually the first thing a solicitor will know about the transaction. If called upon to help draft the term sheet, however, there are a number of general points a solicitor should keep in mind.

2.5.1 What the term sheet should not cover

A term sheet is not a facility agreement, neither is it a first attempt at drafting. Too much detail will neutralise its purpose. For example, the term sheet may specify the *type* of undertakings (see **Chapter 7**) that are to appear in the final agreement, but it will not include a draft clause.

The aim is towards brevity; the details will need careful negotiation at a later stage. For example, the term sheet might state:

> Guarantees will be given by all material subsidiaries of the borrower.

It is not usually necessary to define what is meant by 'material subsidiary' at this stage: the term sheet simply makes it clear that guarantees will be required between companies within the borrower's group; which companies actually give the guarantees will be a focus of subsequent negotiation.

2.5.2 'Inclusive' lists

There is a danger, when listing specific points to be included in the agreement, that one party might claim during later negotiation that they believed the list to be exhaustive. Where appropriate, therefore, language such as '… including, but not limited to …' should be used to preface a list of requirements.

2.5.3 Only specify 'unusual' provisions

It is quite common to see the following in a term sheet:

> Conditions Precedent:
>
> The facility agreement will contain the usual conditions precedent applicable to this type of facility.

This wide language can also be used with other generic terms such as undertakings, events of default or representations and warranties. Any provisions peculiar to the deal, for example a condition precedent that a borrower must win a particular contract before the loan facility can be utilised, should be referred to specifically in the term sheet.

2.6 LEGAL EFFECT OF THE TERM SHEET

The term sheet is not usually intended to be legally binding. This is because it is drafted in broad terms, and based on limited information. More detailed investigation by the bank and its advisers will follow the signing of the term sheet (see **5.2**). These investigations will guide the bank as to the terms required in the facility agreement, and occasionally may cause it to withdraw from the deal altogether although this would be unusual: term sheets have considerable 'moral' authority.

Term sheets are usually not binding as a matter of English common law. An 'agreement to agree' will not be legally enforceable if there is a material term of the future contract which has not been expressly or impliedly agreed (this is not the same as an ambiguous or meaningless term, which might be disregarded whilst the remaining terms stand). A binding contract would also require consideration. To avoid any doubt, however, it is usual practice to head a term sheet with language making clear that the parties do not intend it to be legally binding, for example:

> Please note that the terms set out in this term sheet are indicative only and do not constitute an offer to arrange or finance the Facility. The provision of the Facility is subject to due diligence, credit committee approval, the terms and conditions of the Mandate Letter and satisfactory documentation.

If any sections of a term sheet are required to be legally binding, they should be moved to the commitment letter (see **2.4**) or a separate side letter which can be made legally binding.

2.7 PRIVATE EQUITY TERM SHEETS

In acquisition finance deals, the private equity house borrowing to finance the acquisition commonly produces its own term sheet from which to negotiate the loan. In contrast to the traditional term sheet described above, these private equity (or 'sponsor') term sheets are long (90–100 pages), detailed (containing complete definitions and clauses) and favour the borrower. This strong borrower position was the result of high market liquidity in recent years, which brought stiff competition to lend but also easy syndication, allowing banks to sell almost any loans.

2.8 FROM COMMITMENT DOCUMENTS TO LOAN: DUTY TO NEGOTIATE IN GOOD FAITH?

The commitment letter and term sheet are usually intended to set parameters for negotiating the facility agreement. There is no implied duty to negotiate in good faith under English law (although many other European jurisdictions do imply some sort of duty): in other words, either party may withdraw at any time without reason. There is also long-established authority that even an express contractual obligation to negotiate in good faith would be unenforceable for lack of certainty (see *Walford and Others v Miles and Another* [1992] 2 AC 128). A surprising departure from that doctrine was delivered in *Petromec Inc v Petroleo Brasileiro SA Petrobras and Others* [2006] 1 Lloyd's Rep 121, where the Court of Appeal stated that an express obligation to negotiate in good faith may be enforceable in some cases. However, the comment was obiter (the point was *not* a point of appeal before the Court) and so the statement is not binding precedent. Furthermore, the Court of Appeal recently chose not to follow the *Petromec* statement and reiterated the established view that an agreement to negotiate in good faith without more is always unenforceable in English Law (see *Barbudev v Eurocom Cable Management Bulgaria* [2012] EWCA Civ 548). A similar line was taken by the High Court in *Shaker v Vistajet Group Holding SA* [2012] EWHC 1329 (Comm).

2.9 SAMPLE TERM SHEET

The format of a term sheet will depend on the type of loan facility being proposed. Set out below is an imaginary term sheet for a simple bilateral term loan to illustrate typical content and structure.

DATE 1 March 2014   SUBJECT TO CONTRACT

Borrower:	Bashum Car Rental Co Ltd (the 'Company').
Lender:	Loadido Bank plc.
Facility:	£10,000,000 term facility to be drawn in advances of sterling.
Fees:	Commitment fee at 3 per cent per annum on daily unused and uncancelled amount (payable monthly in arrear).
Purpose:	To finance part of cost of acquisition by the Company of entire issued share capital of Wrecker Rent Ltd ('Target'), together with costs and expenses in connection therewith.
Availability:	The facility will be available for utilisation for 2 months after execution of documentation.
Interest:	Floating rate interest at Loadido Bank plc's (prime bank) LIBOR + 5.5 per cent per annum + Mandatory Cost (payable quarterly in arrear).
Maturity:	5 years from execution of loan documentation.
Repayment:	The facility will amortise as follows:

Repayment date:	Amount:
years 1–3	zero
42 months	2,000,000
48 months	2,000,000
54 months	2,000,000
60 months	4,000,000

Prepayment:	Prepayment permitted with 5 business days' notice to coincide with any interest payment. Prepayment amounts to be no less than £50,000 or a multiple thereof, and may not be redrawn.
Security:	The facility will be secured by:

    a. First ranking security over all shares in Target being acquired by the Company.

    b. First ranking fixed and floating security over all current and future assets (including revenues) of the Company.

    c. Guarantee from Target supported by first ranking fixed and floating security.

Conditions Precedent:	All conditions precedent which are customary for such financings including, without limitation:

    a. Payment of Arrangement fee.

    b. Satisfaction with the terms of the acquisition documentation in connection with Target.

    c. Satisfaction with the terms of financing for the balance of Target's acquisition cost, in particular as regards the equity contribution.

    d. All documentation required to comply with the Financial Assistance Relaxation Procedures.

Representations:	The usual reps and warranties in connection with this type of facility shall be included in the loan documentation, including but not limited to:
	a. No withholding taxes on payments.
	b. Pari passu ranking.
	c. No material adverse change.
Undertakings:	The loan documentation will include standard undertakings for this type of facility, including, without limitation, restrictions on:
	a. Liens and encumbrances.
	b. Guarantees.
	c. Sale of assets.
	d. Loans and advances.
Financial Covenants:	The loan documentation will contain financial covenants to be negotiated, including, without limitation:
	a. Minimum net worth to be £10 million at all times.
	b. Borrowings not more than 1.5 times net worth.
Events of Default:	Customary events of default for a facility of this type, including, but not limited to:
	a. Default in payment or other obligation.
	b. Cross-default.
	c. Material adverse change.
Taxes:	All payments to be free of withholding and other taxes.
Costs:	Notwithstanding that this term sheet is 'subject to contract', the following provision shall be binding on the Company from the date hereof. All expenses in the preparation, negotiation, execution and delivery of the facility, including, but not limited to, legal fees, to be paid by the Company whether or not the facility is put in place. All expenses associated with administering the facility to be paid by the Company.
Assignment:	Loadido may transfer or assign all or part of the facility at any time.
Other:	All other standard terms for documents of this nature shall be included.
Available:	These terms will be available until 11 March 2014. In the event that documentation is not executed within 30 days of acceptance of this offer, Loadido reserves the right to renegotiate the term sheet, or withdraw the offer.
Law:	English law and jurisdiction shall apply.

Accepted by:

....

on behalf of Bashum Car Rental Co Ltd   Date ....

2.10   CONFIDENTIALITY LETTER

A bank may, at some stage in the loan negotiation, be given information about the borrower which is highly confidential. This may be information about the purpose for which the borrower requires the loan, such as a project finance, management buy out, or funding for a flotation. Alternatively, it may be information specifically concerning the borrower which the bank requires to enable it to make a decision on whether it can lend, or to enable it to form a syndicate to provide the loan (see **3.3**).

Whilst a bank is subject to common law confidentiality obligations (based on agency principles) due to the banker/customer relationship (see **8.3.4**), most borrowers will require the bank to sign a confidentiality letter. The short letter contains an undertaking by the bank not to disclose confidential information other than in limited circumstances to aid syndication. Any bank which is considering participating in the facility will have to sign the confidentiality letter before receiving any information.

CHAPTER 3

PLAIN VANILLA OR BELLS AND WHISTLES?

3.1	Introduction	19
3.2	Common types of facility	19
3.3	Syndicated facilities	23
3.4	Leveraged acquisition facilities	26
3.5	Other forms of short-term lending	27
3.6	Which facility is appropriate?	27
3.7	Anatomy of a facility agreement	27
3.8	Matched funding	29
3.9	Further reading	29

'The Golden Rule is that there are no golden rules.'

George Bernard Shaw

3.1 INTRODUCTION

A facility agreement is a contract. In order to be valid under English law, it will require offer and acceptance, consideration, an intention to create legal relations and agreement on all material terms. In common with most commercial contracts, the detailed provisions of a facility agreement will be tailored to the specific requirements of the parties. From a wider perspective, however, there is a handful of categories within which most loan facilities can be placed. This chapter explains the most common types of facility, before providing a broad anatomy of a facility agreement as a preliminary to more detailed review in the ensuing chapters.

3.2 COMMON TYPES OF FACILITY

The three most common types of general purpose loan facility are:

(a)   overdraft;

(b)   term loan;

(c)   revolving credit facility.

The feature which distinguishes one type of loan from another is the way in which it allows the borrower to utilise credit. Facilities with relatively straightforward mechanics were traditionally referred to as 'plain vanilla' loans, whilst any additional features were known as 'bells and whistles'. Which particular loan is appropriate for a borrower will depend largely on the purpose for which the money is required.

Before looking more closely at the features of different loan facilities, it is important to understand a further categorisation: a loan facility may be either 'committed' or 'uncommitted'. A facility is committed if the facility agreement, once executed, obliges the bank to advance monies at the borrower's request (subject to the borrower complying with certain pre-agreed conditions – see **4.7**). If the facility agreement allows the bank some discretion before advancing any loan monies, the facility will be an 'uncommitted' facility.

3.2.1 Overdraft facility

This is the one type of facility of which most of us have first-hand experience! The corporate overdraft is little different from the personal one, apart from its size (see also **3.2.5** below).

3.2.1.1 Purpose

In the long term, a business will survive only if its income is greater than its expenditure. From day to day, however, it is very difficult for a business to ensure that it has sufficient receipts to cover all outgoings: the week in which the employees are paid will not necessarily coincide with the business selling products, or customers paying their bills. An overdraft is, essentially, a tool to aid cash flow by providing a reserve of easily accessible money to meet any shortfall in working capital (it is sometimes known as a 'working capital facility').

3.2.1.2 Basic features

An overdraft is an 'uncommitted' facility (see **3.2**). Furthermore, it will be 'on demand', which means that it must be repaid (reduced to zero) whenever the bank demands, even if the borrower has not defaulted (ie, failed to comply with a term of the loan). This position is not quite as precarious for the borrower as it first seems; there is generally an understanding that the bank will not 'pull the plug' and demand repayment without good reason. Even so, since it is technically on demand, an overdraft must appear as a current liability on a borrower's balance sheet (see **6.3.2**).

As a result of being on demand and uncommitted, an overdraft facility does not usually require substantial documentation. It is often provided on the bank's 'standard terms', with little room for negotiation by the borrower.

An overdraft will always be subject to a maximum aggregate amount which may be borrowed at any one time and may be subject to a 'clean-down' provision (see **3.2.3.3**). If a business is being run efficiently, each utilisation of its overdraft should be temporary, and once cash flow recovers, it should be used to reduce borrowing under the overdraft.

An overdraft is a relatively expensive way of borrowing capital. Interest is calculated on the amount outstanding each day, and usually charged at a fixed percentage above the bank's base rate (see **4.9** for interest rate calculations). The bank will also charge a relatively high fee for providing an overdraft, since it requires more administration than other loan facilities.

3.2.2 Term loan

A term loan (or 'term facility': both labels are used for this type of credit) essentially provides a specified capital sum over a set period (the 'term'), with an agreed schedule for repayment (see **Table 3.1** below).

3.2.2.1 Purpose

Term loans provide a borrower with a lump sum of capital usually for a specified purpose, for example setting up a business, renewing assets ('capital expenditure'), or acquiring another business.

TABLE 3.1   £10m one-year term loan: repayment examples

| | | | Type of repayment | |
Date	Total Drawn	Amortised	Balloon	Bullet
1/1	10m	[Repayment	—	—
28/2		Holiday]	—	—
31/3		1m	—	—
30/4		1m	—	—
31/5		1m	—	—
30/6		1m	—	—
31/7		1m	—	—
31/8		1m	½m	—
30/9		1m	1m	—
31/10		1m	1½m	—
30/11		1m	3m	—
31/12	Nil	1m	4m	10m

3.2.2.2   Basic features

Term loans are usually committed facilities (see **3.2**). Typically, a borrower is allowed a short period (the 'availability period' or 'commitment period') after executing the facility agreement during which (provided it has complied with certain pre-conditions – see **4.7**) it can draw down or 'utilise' a lump sum up to a specified amount. Sometimes, a term loan will provide for an extended availability period during which the money can be drawn in a number of portions (known as 'tranches', 'advances' or 'loans') as and when required by the borrower. This allows a borrower to borrow only what it needs, minimising interest payments, and also to spread the incidence of interest payments into manageable amounts at different times.

Term loans will be repayable in accordance with an agreed timetable. The schedule of repayment may be structured in a number of different ways (see also **9.2**), most commonly:

(a)   'amortisation' – repayment in equal amounts at regular intervals over the term of the loan. There will usually be a repayment 'holiday' at the beginning of the loan;

(b)   'balloon repayment' – repayment over several instalments where the instalment amount increases in size towards maturity;

(c)   'bullet repayment' – repayment in a single instalment at the end of the term of the loan (at 'maturity').

Once the capital has been repaid it cannot then be re-borrowed (compare revolving facilities at **3.2.3**). If the loan has a bullet repayment, the borrower might negotiate a renewal of the loan at maturity, or arrange a 'refinancing' to repay the loan by taking out other borrowings. It is unusual to see a general purpose term loan with a life of more than five years, although acquisition finance term loans are usually seven to 10 years (but invariably refinanced long before maturity) and project finance loans may be for 20 years or more.

Term loans are not usually 'on demand': the bank cannot withdraw the facility unless the borrower defaults (see **Chapter 8**). This allows the borrower to plan with certainty when it needs to fund capital repayments, and to commit borrowed money in a way that would not be possible with a loan which was on demand, such as an overdraft.

A multicurrency term loan allows the borrower to draw different tranches in different (pre-agreed) currencies. In addition, drawn amounts may be 'redenominated' (ie, converted into a different currency) at the end of an interest period. For example, a sterling tranche could be redenominated into dollars: the borrower does not receive more capital, but its interest payments and repayment would now be due in dollars.

Interest on a term loan may be at a fixed rate, but more usually floats at a fixed percentage (the bank's 'margin') above the bank's base rate or LIBOR (see **4.9**).

3.2.3 Revolving credit facility

Like a term loan, a revolving credit facility (RCF) provides a maximum aggregate amount of capital, available over a specified period. Unlike a term loan, the RCF allows a borrower to draw down and repay tranches of the available capital, almost as and when it chooses throughout the term of the loan (see **Table 3.2** below).

TABLE 3.2   **£10m one-year RCF: utilisation and repayment example**

Date	Total Drawn	Repayment	Available
1/1	4m	—	6m
7/2	7m	—	3m
1/4	3m	4m	7m
21/6	8½m	—	1½m
7/8	5½m	3m	4½m
31/12	Nil	5½m	Nil

3.2.3.1 Purpose

The RCF combines some of the flexibility of an overdraft, allowing the borrower to draw money when it is required, with the certainty of a term loan (the RCF is usually a committed facility: see **3.2**). Not only can the borrower save money by not drawing the whole loan at once, it can also elect to repay outstanding tranches that it no longer requires. Interest payments can therefore be kept to a minimum. Like an overdraft, the RCF is a 'working capital' facility intended to meet the short-term, fluctuating capital needs of the borrower.

3.2.3.2 Basic features

Each tranche is usually borrowed for a relatively short period (eg, one, three, or six months) after which it is technically repayable. However, if the borrower has not defaulted under the loan, the tranche to be repaid can be immediately re-drawn. This is known as a 'rollover'. The RCF might appear very similar to an overdraft facility, but there are fundamental differences. The first of these is size: an overdraft will rarely exceed a few hundred thousand pounds, whereas many large companies have revolving credit facilities of several hundred million pounds. A second difference is flexibility: utilisation and repayment will usually be subject to more restrictions than an overdraft. For example:

(a)   minimum notice periods before each utilisation;

(b)   maximum and minimum amounts which may be drawn down in one tranche;

(c)   a minimum period for which an amount must be borrowed before it is repaid;

(d)   a maximum number of tranches which may be drawn at any time;

(e)   control over frequency and timing of repayment (final repayment is usually required in a bullet repayment, although an RCF can also be structured with a reducing availability through its life, mimicking term loan amortisation).

Whilst a borrower can avoid unnecessary interest costs by borrowing only as much as it requires, the bank will charge a 'commitment fee' calculated as a percentage of the undrawn facility from time to time. The commitment fee is levied to cover capital adequacy costs suffered by a bank in making a committed facility available. (Capital adequacy requirements are dealt with in more detail at **9.3.3**.)

3.2.3.3 Clean down

A clean down provision may be included to ensure the money borrowed under an RCF (and any overdraft) is used for working capital rather than for 'long term' capital expenditure. The clean down provision typically requires the borrower to reduce the amount drawn under the RCF (overdraft) to a specified sum, during a specified period and for a specified number of (consecutive) days. For example, the borrower might have to reduce these facilities to zero, for at least five consecutive business days, once a year. At first sight this provision appears rather odd. It is, however, intended to ensure that the borrower is utilising its RCF and overdraft properly: they are structured for use in cash flow management, and not intended to be permanently drawn at maximum amount (contrast term loans at **3.2.2**).

3.2.4 '364 day facilities' and 'term-out options'

As the name suggests, '364 day facilities' are loans with an original maturity of up to one year. They are usually revolving credit facilities. Historically, the advantage of these loans was that, to the extent they were unutilised, they did not require regulatory capital to support them (see **9.3.3**). This made them a cost-effective way to provide a 'standby' facility in circumstances where a borrower was unsure whether it would need funds or not.

Furthermore, the borrower could be given the right to convert any outstanding amount on the last day of maturity into a term loan without losing the benefits explained above (during the first 364 days). This was known as a 'term-out option'.

From January 2008, this favourable regulatory capital treatment was largely lost as 'Basel II' came fully into force. As a result, 364 day facilities are less common, though not yet extinct.

3.2.5 Ancillary facilities

Syndicated facility agreement (see **3.3**) may include both a term loan and an RCF in one document. Furthermore, the borrower is typically permitted to take part of the RCF commitment as a bilateral loan with one of the syndicate banks, for example an overdraft or derivatives facility. These are known as 'ancillary facilities'.

3.3 SYNDICATED FACILITIES

3.3.1 Bilateral or syndicated facility

Most small loans and overdraft facilities are provided by a single bank. Because they are between two parties, they are known as 'bilateral' facilities. However, banks try to avoid the risk of making large commitments to single borrowers, and so large or sophisticated facilities (eg, for a project or acquisition funding) are commonly provided by a group of banks known as a 'syndicate'. It is not unusual to find syndicates of more than 30 banks, and sometimes even larger (large facilities with multiple institutional investors, for example, may have several hundred lending entities).

3.3.2 Structuring a syndicate

The majority of syndications involve one bank, the 'arranger', organising a group of banks to participate directly in the facility agreement. This is known as 'primary syndication'. The syndicate members will participate in the syndicate on common terms, and so agree common documentation, although they may contribute different amounts. Most importantly, each syndicate member will assume liability only for its own lending obligations: it will not undertake any responsibility for other syndicate members' commitments.

An alternative form of 'syndication' occurs when a single bank is party to the loan documentation and initially provides the facility, with the intention of immediately transferring part, or all, of its commitment to other banks. These 'post-closing syndications' are dealt with in **Chapter 10**.

As with most banking terminology, the nomenclature is not set in stone, but the main roles of various syndicate members are explained below.

3.3.2.1 Arranger

The arranger (sometimes known as the 'mandated lead arranger' or 'MLA') is the bank originally responsible for advising the borrower as to the type of facility it requires, finding other banks to form the syndicate, and negotiating the broad terms of the loan. It will either be a bank with which the borrower already has a relationship or one which has won the mandate to arrange the loan after pitching for the role.

In a large facility, syndication may be done in stages. The first stage will involve finding a further group of banks to provide a share of the facility with the arranger. These are usually known as 'lead managers' or 'co-arrangers'. The lead managers will then each attempt to find more banks to participate in the syndicate (known as 'participants') by taking a share of the lead managers' commitment (variations on these titles will appear to show banks' relative importance in the syndicate – see pp 30–31). Co-arrangers/managers commonly underwrite the loan, that is, they will have to provide the whole of the loan between them if further syndicate members cannot be found.

Once the facility is made available, the particpating banks might sell part or all of their commitment to other banks (or institutional lenders), known as 'secondary syndication'. However, a borrower will usually require the arranger to retain a substantial part of the facility (known as a 'minimum hold'), since negotiation with the arranger can become more difficult if it does not have any direct interest. The facility agreement should specifically state that the arranger does not owe the other syndicate members any common law fiduciary duties, in order to prevent any argument to the contrary.

3.3.2.2 Administrative agent

Once a syndicated facility is operational, it is not difficult to imagine how the mechanics could become very unwieldy; some of the largest facilities have several hundred named lenders. To avoid a logistical headache, it is common for one bank to act as agent for the others in the day-to-day running of the loan. This bank is known as the 'administrative agent' (or simply the 'agent') and, broadly, it must act as interpreter (maintaining regular contact with the borrower and representing the views of the syndicate), counsellor (dealing with any practical problems concerning the provisions of the agreement), policeman (monitoring the borrower's compliance with its obligations), postman and record keeper (it is the administrative agent to which the borrower must usually give notices (eg, of utilisation), pay interest and make repayments, and through which it will receive loan monies).

The administrative agent is simply empowered to administer the mechanics of the facility. Any material decisions, such as a waiver of facility agreement provisions, must usually be taken by the whole syndicate, or at least by a majority (see **3.3.2.4**). The administrative agent will carry the duties and responsibilities imposed on any agent under English law, but the facility agreement will contain provisions to limit the relationship (known as 'exculpatory provisions'), in particular:

(a)   the agent will not want any obligation to act unless instructed by the syndicate;

(b)   the agent will want the ability to delegate its functions and to take professional advice if necessary;

(c)   the agent will want syndicate members to take responsibility for their own credit assessment of the borrower. It will not want responsibility for any information it passes to the syndicate members with respect to the borrower, for the efficacy of the facility agreement, or for any security or other ancillary documents (see **3.3.4** below);

(d)   syndicate members will also be required to complete their own 'Know Your Customer' (or 'KYC') checks to comply with money laundering regulations;

(e)   an agent must be able to take agency fees and other payments from the borrower without them being classed as secret profit (and therefore prohibited);

(f)   the agent will want a right to resign, and the other syndicate members will want the right to replace it. A borrower will usually be allowed a right of consultation before any change is made, since its relationship with the agent is very important;

(g)   as a result of Lehman's insolvency in 2008, loan facilities now also allow for a requisite majority of lenders (after consulting the borrower) to require the agent to resign. An insolvent agent causes severe problems since it is the conduit for all payments between the lenders and the borrower; and

(h)   the agent will want an indemnity from syndicate members with respect to all costs incurred in its role as agent (unless they are recovered from the borrower).

3.3.2.3   Security trustee

If a syndicated loan is secured, one entity (usually one of the syndicate banks) will usually hold the security on trust for the whole syndicate. This entity is known as the 'security trustee'. In civil law jurisdictions, which may not recognise the trust, a 'security agent' and 'parallel debt' structure may be used instead (see **14.14.4**). The fiduciary duties imposed upon a security agent/trustee will be more extensive than those of a simple agent.

3.3.2.4   Advantages of taking a role

There are several advantages for a bank in taking lead roles within a syndicated facility. The first is prestige: the most prestigious role is lead arranger. The other banks in the syndicate will then be allotted titles to reflect their standing within the syndicate (based on their contributions to the facility, financial and otherwise). The second advantage to taking a leading role in the syndicate is the ability to charge fees (see **9.5**). Lastly, the 'relationship' banks within the syndicate will hope that the borrower comes to them for other financial products.

3.3.3   Tombstones

Historically, once a large deal closed, it would be announced by way of an 'advert' in the financial press with details of the borrower, deal size and main parties. This was known as a 'tombstone' (or sometimes the 'football team'), and some examples are shown at pp 30–31. The tombstone would often be cast in a perspex block and given to parties and advisers as a 'memento' of the deal. Nowadays, both the adverts and mementos are uncommon, due to their cost and the availability of alternative 'online' advertising.

3.3.4   Liability of arrangers

In order to persuade banks to join the syndicate, an arranger will have to provide a considerable amount of information about the borrower and its group companies. This information is usually written as an 'information memorandum', referred to colloquially as the 'info memo'. The info memo is written by the arranger (or sometimes its lawyers) and, importantly, based on documents and other information provided by the borrower. It usually contains:

(a)   financial information relating to the borrower and its group companies (financial statements for previous years, financial projections over the life of the loan including capital expenditure, revenue, details of anticipated expansion, etc);

(b)   general information about the borrower's group companies; and

(c)   information about the group's business and the markets in which it operates.

Since the arranger compiles the info memo, it is potentially liable for any wrong information the info memo contains which is relied on by lenders deciding to join the syndicate. Claims might be brought for misrepresentation (see **5.5**) or negligence. In addition, the courts have confirmed that the relationship between an arranger and syndicate banks is a 'classic example' of a situation where a tortious duty of care will arise (see *Sumitomo Bank Ltd v Banque Bruxelles Lambert SA*, QBD (Commercial Court), 1 October 1996). It is therefore market practice for the arranger to disclaim responsibility for any information given to the syndicate, by including a clause in the info memo which states:

- the borrower has supplied the information and confirms it is true, complete and accurate; has been prepared with reasonable care; is not misleading; and does not omit anything material;
- the borrower confirms that any assumptions or projections it makes are reasonable and in good faith;
- the arranger has not independently verified the information; does not make any representations or undertakings with respect to it; does not take responsibility for it; and accepts no liability for loss caused by reliance on it; and
- participants in the facility acknowledge the info memo is not a valuation of the borrower's credit; that it is not a recommendation to participate; and that they should make their own independent assessment of the documentation and the borrower.

A broad disclaimer of responsibility will also appear in the loan agreement.

The effectiveness of such disclaimers has been questioned. First, as a general proposition, courts are reluctant to uphold exclusion clauses. More specifically, the Unfair Contract Terms Act 1977 will allow a disclaimer of liability for negligence or misrepresentation only if it satisfies a reasonableness test under the Act. Secondly, the disclaimer and warranty clauses are often drafted too narrowly. They should cover:

(a)   excluded, as well as included, information;

(b)   oral, as well as written, information.

Thirdly, the arranger is almost certainly under a duty not to withhold relevant information, and also under a duty to answer fully any specific questions.

However, in *IFE Fund SA v Goldman Sachs International* [2007] EWCA Civ 811, the Court of Appeal ruled that the disclaimer language commonly used in information memoranda is effective to deny an arranger's liability for the accuracy of information and to deny responsibility for updating it. More recently, the judge in *Raiffeisen Zentralbank Osterreich AG v The Royal Bank of Scotland plc* [2010] EWHC 1392 (Comm) considered (*obiter*) that the standard disclaimer language in RBS's info memo (and other transaction documents) was effective to avoid RBS making representations and taking responsibility for information. The judge decided that if commercial parties wished to conduct business on that basis, they were entitled to do so.

3.4 LEVERAGED ACQUISITION FACILITIES

Leveraged acquisition financing usually involves more than one source of lending in order to raise the maximum amount of debt. Until recently this would typically consist of a 'senior' facility providing a term loan and a revolving credit facility ('revolver'), and a 'mezzanine' facility providing a second term loan. If the borrower defaults, the senior lenders enjoy first right to repayment and control of enforcement processes. The mezzanine lenders (so called because they sit between the senior lenders and the shareholders in terms of priority) only get repaid if the senior lenders are fully reimbursed. The shareholders (the 'equity') only recover money if the seniors *and* the mezzanine get fully repaid. The greater risk taken by the mezzanine lenders (often known as the 'mezz') is compensated by a higher interest rate. Mezzanine facilities have become rare in recent years, and leveraged deals have instead seen a combination of a senior facility (term and revolver, or just a revolver) and a 'high yield bond' issued by the borrower which is sold into the US market. The rights of enforcement and priority between the senior lenders and the high yield bondholders vary widely depending on the deal structure.

3.5 OTHER FORMS OF SHORT-TERM LENDING

3.5.1 Standby facility

A standby facility is a generic name for a facility which a borrower does not intend using under normal circumstances but may need to utilise if other uncommitted funding is unexpectedly unavailable (see also swing-line facility at **3.5.3**). It may include a 'utilisation fee', payable (in addition to interest) if the facility is actually drawn.

3.5.2 Bankers' acceptance

A bankers' acceptance is a bill of exchange (essentially a written acknowledgement by one party that it owes a second party money at a future date) which a bank has agreed to be responsible for paying when it falls due. The borrower which asked the bank to accept its bill must eventually reimburse the bank, but in the meantime it is effectively borrowing short term from the bank.

3.5.3 Swing-line facility

A swing-line facility is a facility which is usually made available to a company which has a commercial paper programme ('commercial paper' is a short-term – between one day and one year – uncommitted debt security ('IOU') issued by a company to investors). The swing-line facility can be utilised on very short notice (eg, by a telephone request) to allow the borrower to pay back any maturing commercial paper which it is unable to re-issue ('rollover').

Chapter 17 provides a short explanation of MTNs, bills of exchange and commercial paper.

3.6 WHICH FACILITY IS APPROPRIATE?

This chapter has outlined the common forms of loan facility. It should be appreciated that, rather like primary colours, these can be mixed and matched to suit an individual client's requirements. Furthermore, within a particular type of facility, the mechanics of utilisation, interest payment and the repayment schedule can fundamentally alter its complexion. A banking solicitor must therefore understand his client's needs and business in order to establish the most appropriate facility and properly negotiate its terms.

3.7 ANATOMY OF A FACILITY AGREEMENT

Banks must lend to make money; businesses must borrow to thrive. The ultimate aim of borrower and bank is therefore the same: both want the loan in place as soon as possible. The loan contract could of course be made orally. It is generally accepted, however, that the certainty of a written facility agreement is preferable, especially from an evidential point of view. But how can a facility agreement which might be summarised in a 10-page term sheet grow to a 150-page document? To answer that question, it is important to realise that the provisions in a loan document are almost all designed to protect the bank's position, since it is the bank which is most likely to suffer in the event of any uncertainty or ambiguity.

3.7.1 A bank's concerns

In broad terms, a bank will want to ensure three things:

(a)   its fees are paid;
(b)   it receives interest on the loan;
(c)   it eventually gets its loan capital back.

These aims may be best served by ensuring that:

(a)   the loan monies are used only for a specific purpose(s);
(b)   the borrower does not do anything which might put its ability to service and/or repay the loan at risk;

(c)   the borrower is monitored to give early warning of any possibility that it might be unable to service or repay the loan; and, in some cases,

(d)   all monies due to the bank are secured over the borrower's assets.

These areas of concern provide the pattern for most facility agreements (the first draft of which is usually produced by the bank's solicitor). First, the agreement will need clauses to cover the use and flow of the borrowed money, for example:

(a)   amount and purpose;

(b)   fees;

(c)   interest payment;

(d)   repayment;

(e)   maturity;

(f)   early termination by the bank.

Secondly, there will be a number of clauses designed to protect the bank's profit margin in the event that certain costs or other circumstances change, for example:

(a)   withholding tax is imposed (the 'gross-up clause');

(b)   regulatory capital costs increase (the 'increased costs clause');

(c)   the bank's borrowing cost is not covered (the 'market disruption clause');

(d)   it becomes illegal for the bank to lend to the borrower (the 'illegality clause');

(e)   other unexpected costs are incurred (indemnities).

Thirdly, the facility agreement will usually contain provisions allowing the bank to keep a check on the borrower's 'financial health', and to deal with the possibility of things going wrong, for example:

(a)   conditions to be met before utilisation ('conditions precedent');

(b)   information from the borrower about its status and business ('representations and warranties');

(c)   promises by the borrower about things it will do, or will not do ('undertakings');

(d)   events allowing the bank to cancel the loan ('events of default'); and, in some cases,

(e)   security over the borrower's assets.

Lastly, there will be a number of provisions which the bank's solicitor insists are necessary for smooth operation of the agreement, for example:

(a)   a governing law clause;

(b)   provisions for transferring the loan to another lender; and

(c)   provisions for serving notices.

The clauses in a facility agreement can therefore be classified into four main groups.

(a)   'Mechanics' clauses (ie, clauses dealing with the mechanics of making the money flow).

(b)   Margin protection clauses (ie, clauses protecting the bank's profit).

(c)   General protection clauses (ie, clauses connected with the bank's willingness initially to make the loan, and then to allow it to continue).

(d)   Boiler plate clauses (ie, provisions governing the relationship between the parties, and enforcement of the agreement).

3.7.2 A borrower's concerns

The borrower's primary concern is flexibility. It wants the money to achieve its aims, and the fewer strings that are attached the better. In particular, the borrower wants the bank (and so the facility agreement) to recognise that there are bound to be highs and lows on the road to corporate success, and so if the bank sticks with it, everything will be fine in the end ... probably.

The main areas to be negotiated, therefore, will relate to the monitoring of, and restrictions on, the borrower. The solicitors must try to negotiate a document which both bank and borrower feel is an acceptable and workable compromise. The mechanics will, to a large extent, be a function of the terms agreed initially between bank and borrower, and recorded in the term sheet (see **Chapter 2**). The boiler plate will contain provisions affording protection for the bank, or (occasionally) the borrower, and provisions 'oiling' the mechanics. These will usually be included as a matter of accepted market practice. **Chapters 4** to **9** will focus on the detail of loan documentation.

3.8 MATCHED FUNDING

Before exploring loan facilities further, it is important to understand a concept that permeates many of the mechanics clauses. Most facility agreements assume that when the borrower requests a utilisation, say for £10 million, the facility banks will fund their commitment by borrowing £10 million from other banks in the London interbank market. This is known as 'matched funding'.

Loans in the interbank market are typically short term (eg one, three or six months) and never longer than a year. Thus, if a borrower requests £10 million under a three-year term loan, the banks might take an interbank loan of £10 million for, say, six months. After six months, the interbank loan must be repaid and so the bank will take a second interbank loan for £10 million to repay the first. The interest payable on the first interbank loan ('Libor') is recovered from the borrower and the process is repeated through a succession of these 'interest periods' (see **4.9.2**) until the borrower repays the £10 million at the end of three years.

The matched funding assumption drives numerous provisions in the facility including interest periods (**4.9.2**), repetition of representations (**5.2.4**), repayment, prepayment and break costs (all at **9.2**). It should be noted, however, that loan facilities will not actually *require* the banks to fund this way, and in fact interbank market lending has reduced dramatically since 2007.

3.9 FURTHER READING

Stephen Valdez, *An Introduction to Global Financial Markets* (6th edn, Macmillan, 2010).

Geoffrey Fuller, *Corporate Borrowing: Law and Practice* (4th edn, Jordans, 2009).

Examples of old 'tombstones' from the *Financial Times*; now seldom seen.

This announcement appears as a matter of record only

INVESTCORP S.A.

U.S. $200,000,000
Eurodollar Loan Facility

— Arrangers —

Al Fransi
The Arab Investment Company S.A.A. (TAIC)
rnational PLC
The Bank of Tokyo, Ltd.
Chase Investment Bank, Limited
Deutsche Bank Group
larkets Limited
Lloyds Bank Plc
Société Générale

— Lead Managers —

oration (B.S.C.)
Credit Industriel et Commercial
ebank Luxembourg S.A.
The Royal Bank of Scotland plc

— Managers —

This announcement appears as a matter of record only

S$6,000,000,000
g Credit Facility

Canada

Agent and Arranger:
Citicorp

Senior Managing Agents:
of Tokyo, Ltd. • **Bayerische Landesbank Girozentrale**
Bank AG • Dresdner Bank AG • The Fuji Bank, Limited
mited • The Long-Term Credit Bank of Japan, Limited
ew York • Societe Generale • Swiss Bank Corporation

Managing Agents:
ank • Credit Lyonnais • Dai-Ichi Kangyo Bank, Limited
ubishi Bank, Limited • National Westminster Bank Plc
The Sanwa Bank, Ltd. • The Sumitomo Bank, Limited

Lead Managers:
f America NT&SA • Banca Nazionale del Lavoro S.p.A.

Managers:
ink, Limited • Westdeutsche Landesbank Girozentrale

Co-Managers:
sahi Bank, Ltd. • Bank of Yokohama • Banque Paribas
redit Bank, Ltd. • Republic National Bank of New Yor

Participa
ealand Banking Group, Ltd. • The Shizuoka Bank

May 1.

CITICORP◆®

This announcement appears as a matter of record only.

Montell
POLYOLEFINS

Montell N.V.
U.S.$2,300,000,000
Term Loan and Working Capital Facilities

Arranged by:
Citibank International plc

Underwriters and Senior Lead Managers:
Citibank, N.A. • ABN AMRO Bank N.V.
Banca Commerciale Italiana S.p.A • Banca di Roma SpA
The Bank of Nova Scotia • The Chase Manhattan Bank, N.A
Chemical Bank • Commerzbank (Nederland) N.V. • Deutsche Bank Luxembourg S.A.
The Dai-Ichi Kangyo Bank, Ltd • Crédit Lyonnais
ING Bank • Istituto Bancario San Paolo di Torino S.p.A • Midland Bank plc
NatWest Markets • NationsBank • Société Générale
Banque Paribas Nederland N.V. • Credito Italiano, SpA

Senior Lead Managers:
Banca Nazionale del Lavoro • Bayerische Landesbank International SA
Cariplo-Cassa di Risparmio delle Provincie Lombarde SpA • Commonwealth Bank of Australia
I.M.I.– Is
Mobiliare Italiano SpA • Kredietbank Nederland N.V. • Lloyds Bank plc
The Long-
National Australia
Ltd. • Monte dei Paschi di Siena, New York Branch
The Royal Bank of Scotland plc
WestLB Group

luxembourg
gesellschaft
pe Bank plc
nk, Limited

ntenbar
don Bran

Banca
Credit Nat

Securi
Citib

This announcement appears as a matter of record only

Compagnie Financière Michelin
US $330,000,000
Revolving Credit Standby Facility

Arranger/Underwriter
NatWest Markets

Senior Lead Managers

Bayerische Landesbank Girozentrale
Succursale de Paris
National Westminster Bank Plc

Lead Managers

Caisse Centrale des Banques Populaires
The Long-Term Credit Bank of Japan, Limited
Banco Exterior de España Paris Branch
Argentaria

The Industrial Bank of Japan, Ltd.
Paris Branch
The Sanwa Bank, Limited

Managers

Banque et Caisse d'Epargne de L'Etat, Luxembourg
Bank in Liechtenstein AG
The Fuji Bank, Limited
The Mitsubishi Trust and Banking Corporation
The Sakura Bank, Ltd., Paris Branch

The Dai-Ichi Kangyo Bank, Ltd.

Caixa de Catalunya
NationsBank
Via Banque

Banque Cantonale Vaudoise
Landeskreditbank Baden-Württemberg
National Bank of Abu Dhabi
Scotiabank (Ireland) Limited

Agent
National Westminster Bank Plc

NatWest
NatWest MARKETS

Issued by National Westminster Bank Plc, regulated by IMRO

ILL/S.95/01

CHAPTER 4

WHEN, WHO, WHERE, WHAT AND WHY?

4.1	Introduction	33
4.2	Date	34
4.3	Parties	34
4.4	Interpretation/definitions	34
4.5	The facility	35
4.6	Purpose clause	36
4.7	Conditions precedent	39
4.8	Availability	41
4.9	Floating rate interest	42
4.10	Fixed rate interest	45
4.11	Interest periods	45
4.12	Apportionment: the 'day count fraction'	46
4.13	Ratchets	46
4.14	Hedging	47
4.15	Default interest	47
4.16	Basis points	47
	Summary	48

4.1 INTRODUCTION

Broadly speaking, a facility agreement follows the same pattern as the majority of commercial agreements, namely:

(a)   date, title and parties;

(b)   interpretation/definitions;

(c)   operative provisions;

(d)   schedules;

(e)   execution.

Even if they both provide the same type of facility, no two facility agreements will have identical provisions. Agreements must be tailored to suit borrowers, banks, purpose, market practice and the prevailing economic circumstances. However, **Chapters 4** to **9** endeavour to explain the main provisions that might be found in a typical bilateral or syndicated facility agreement made to an investment grade company for general corporate purposes. Contrast is made between strong and weak borrowers where appropriate. The terms are reviewed in the order in which they are likely to occur within a document, with this chapter covering the following clauses:

(a)   date;

(b)   parties;

(c)   interpretation;

(d)   the facility;

(e)   purpose;

(f)   conditions precedent;

(g)   availability;

(h)   interest.

4.2 DATE

Usually the date clause will appear on the first page of the document, and should be completed, in manuscript, simultaneously with signing. If there are several parties signing on different days, the date should be that on which the last party signs. If there are conditions precedent outstanding, the document will usually become effective when signed and dated, but utilisation will not be possible (see **4.7**) until the conditions are either met or waived.

4.3 PARTIES

Borrower(s)

Any borrower (there may be more than one) must be a party to the facility agreement. There may be a mechanism for new borrowers, usually termed 'Acceding Borrowers', to join at a later stage.

Guarantors

Some deals require a borrower's parent, sister and/or subsidiary companies to provide guarantees ('cross guarantees') for amounts outstanding under the facility. Those companies may be required to execute the facility agreement which will contain a guarantee (and indemnity). Alternatively, a separate guarantee document may be used, particularly for overseas companies (see **13.2**).

The borrowers and guarantors together are typically referred to as 'Obligors' under the facility document.

Banks

In large syndicated facilities, the borrower, parent, arranging bank(s), facility agent plus any issuing bank (providing letters of credit) and security agent will be named on the front page and in the opening clause. Other parties such as subsidiary borrowers, guarantors and the syndicate banks are typically listed in a schedule at the back of the facility. Execution issues are explored at **9.11**.

Note that the Contract (Rights of Third Parties) Act 1999 gives third parties (ie those not party to a contract) rights to enforce a contractual term if the contract expressly so provides, or if the term confers a benefit on the party. Most facility agreements exclude the effect of the 1999 Act other than allowing a bank's employees to benefit from the indemnity and other 'protective' provisions.

Bear in mind that the names of the bank and its representatives are one of the things a bank will always check (along with fees and commitment amounts) and mistakes are embarrassing, particularly at signing!

4.4 INTERPRETATION/DEFINITIONS

This clause marks the beginning of the operative part of the document. The use of a definitions clause is particularly prevalent in facility agreements because there is a great deal of repetition of terms. However, if they are used excessively, definitions can make the document front-heavy and difficult to follow. If a term appears several times in one clause but not in any others, it should be defined in the clause where it appears rather than in the definitions section (this is often the case for financial covenants).

Defined terms should always appear in the document with their initial letters in upper case. Beware, however – most documents have an 'interpretation' section (defining common words, eg, month, year, etc) immediately after the 'definitions' section, and this may include 'lower-case' definitions (watch out in particular for a definition of 'continuing' defaults). Complex definitions are almost mini-clauses and they should be drafted with great care, particularly since any mistake is likely to occur more than once. Finally, you should not negotiate a definition before checking where it is used and thus the full effect of any changes.

4.5 THE FACILITY

The facility clause outlines the type of facility (or facilities) the bank will provide under the agreement, as well as the amount to be made available. From a borrower's perspective it is important to include this clause to create an obligation on the bank to lend (albeit conditional – see **4.7**). It may require just one sentence, for example:

> THE FACILITY
>
> Subject to the terms of this Agreement, the Bank agrees to make available to the Borrower a term loan up to an amount of £5,000,000.

Many facility agreements contain both a term loan and an RCF. The leveraged acquisition market has at times seen several term facilities in one document, traditionally labelled 'Facility A' (an amortising term loan), 'Facility B' and 'Facility C' (bullet term loans with different duration, margin and maybe prepayment rights and other terms), as well as an RCF. Each bank in a syndicated loan will agree to provide a proportion of the total facility, and this is known as the bank's 'commitment'. The agreement will specify that their obligations are 'several' (and not 'joint and several') to ensure that each bank is liable to provide only its own commitment.

4.5.1 Why 'facility'?

In common usage, the terms 'loan facility' and 'loan agreement' tend to be interchangeable. There are, however, two technical reasons why the use of 'loan facility' might be more appropriate in the document:

(a)   The term 'agreement' suggests that the borrower has agreed to borrow money, and is obliged to draw down. The term 'facility' reflects the fact that the loan is available if the borrower wants to use it, but without an obligation to borrow.

(b)   Any written acknowledgement of a company's indebtedness is in danger of being classified as a 'debenture' under s 738 of the CA 2006. If a facility agreement was held to be a 'debenture', it would fall within a number of registration and information requirements under the CA 2006 (eg, ss 423–432, s 741) and, potentially, within provisions relating to regulated activities and financial promotion in the Financial Services and Markets Act 2000 (FSMA 2000). Use of the term 'facility' is less likely to suggest a debenture than 'loan'.

How, then, can a bank prove that a borrower owes it any money? The account records kept by a bank showing the total amount outstanding (the bank's 'book') and certified by an appropriate officer of the bank are, under English law at least, prima facie evidence of the borrower's obligations (the facility agreement will usually require the borrower to accept the account records as conclusive evidence). In some jurisdictions (eg, the United States) the bank's account records would be insufficient evidence of debt. In that case, a certificate is issued acknowledging each utilisation (known as a 'promissory note').

4.5.2 Facility office

The facility office (or 'lending office') is the particular branch of a bank through which a loan is made ('booked'). The facility office will be specified in the facility agreement, and is the place where the borrower must make interest payments and capital repayments. The location of the facility office is of particular concern to a borrower for tax reasons (see **9.3.4**).

4.6 PURPOSE CLAUSE

4.6.1 Control

The bank will want the facility agreement to state explicitly how the loan monies can be used. It is the first point of control which a bank can use to protect its money and maximise the probability of being repaid. The wording may be relatively wide, for example:

> The Facility is to be used for general corporate purposes.

or

> The proceeds of the Facility will be used to support the general corporate requirements of the Borrower.

This would at least make it clear that the borrower must not place the first utilisation on the '2.30' race at Epsom.

Sometimes, however, a purpose clause will be more specific. For example, restricting the use to 'working capital' purposes will probably exclude making a substantial acquisition. If the bank has assessed its credit risk (see **2.2**) on a particular project which the borrower is to finance with the loan monies (known as 'project finance'), or it has taken security over particular assets on which it will want the loan monies spent, the purpose clause should be drafted accordingly.

Some purpose clauses state that money should not be used for certain purposes (eg, an investment in particular companies). The purpose clause might also contain restrictions which are driven by the bank's constitution or policy.

Two matters closely connected with the purpose clause are those of capacity and authority. The questions of whether a borrower has the capacity to enter into a transaction, and who is authorised to bind the borrower, are invariably determined in accordance with the law of the borrower's domicile (for companies, this is the country of incorporation). The position for companies incorporated under English law is considered briefly below.

4.6.2 Capacity

The CA 1989 attempted to clarify the position with respect to a company's capacity to enter into a transaction, by introducing a new s 35 to the CA 1985 (which is, in turn, substantially adopted by the CA 2006). The law on ultra vires acts prior to the new s 35 was complicated, and is now largely obsolete (although it still applies to transactions completed before 4 February 1991, and to certain acts of charitable companies (see CA 1989, ss 111, 112)). However, a brief summary of the pre-s 35 law with respect to borrowing is given below, since it formed the basis of the new law.

4.6.2.1 The position pre-CA 1989

Prima facie, a company could pursue only the objects for which its memorandum stated it was incorporated. Pre-CA 1989, therefore, a company could avoid performing its obligations under a contract which was outside the company's objects (an 'ultra vires' act). However, in *Rolled Steel Products (Holdings) Ltd v British Steel Corporation* [1986] Ch 246, it was confirmed that an ultra vires transaction was not void unless the contracting party had actual or constructive notice of the company's agents (ie, the directors) breaching their fiduciary duties (in which case the contracting party would be a constructive trustee for the company, and be liable to return any property it had received). The directors' breach of duty in allowing an ultra vires act could be ratified by the shareholders.

In the context of a facility agreement, a purpose clause stating that the loan was to be used 'for general corporate purposes' would allow a bank to assume that the purpose of exercising the borrowing power was intra vires. However, if a purpose clause were more specific, the bank might have been unable to assume the loan was within the borrower's objects, and there was a danger of the loan being void. (Note that, whilst all trading and commercial companies have an implied power to borrow (*Introductions Ltd v National Provincial Bank* [1970] Ch 199), this is an implied power not an implied object, and so generally it can be used only in pursuance of a purpose authorised by a company's objects.)

4.6.2.2 The position post-CA 1989

The CA 1989 attempted to consolidate the position at common law by substituting a new s 35(1) into the CA 1985, stating:

> The validity of an act done by a company shall not be called into question on the ground of lack of capacity by reason of anything in the company's memorandum.

Practitioners have, however, been cautious about relying on these provisions, and for a finance transaction they would typically require specific objects allowing borrowing, giving of guarantees, giving of security and entering into derivatives.

4.6.2.3 The position post-CA 2006

As from 1 October 2009, s 39 of the CA 2006 replaces s 35(1) by repeating the same language but replacing 'memorandum' with 'constitution'. This is because the 2006 Act makes the memorandum merely part of the registration process, and any objects clauses are part of the articles: 'constitution' includes the articles together with certain resolutions and agreements (CA 2006, s 17). The CA 2006 also stipulates that unless a company's articles specifically restrict its objects, its objects will be unrestricted.

The intention of the CA 2006 is to remove the concept of ultra vires acts from the perspective of a third party dealing with a company in good faith (the directors remain liable for any losses to the company due to the ultra vires act, unless ratified by two special resolutions – one ratifying the breach of duty, the other ratifying the loss). The section does not, however, provide protection for a transaction which is invalid for other reasons (eg, illegality).

4.6.2.4 Conclusion

The CA 2006 language gives considerable comfort for creditors dealing with a company in good faith. However, practitioners should still check the articles for *specific restrictions* to the objects (eg relating to borrowing, guarantees, security and derivatives) since these could still make a transaction ultra vires. Furthermore, liability of the directors to the company remains.

4.6.3 Authority

The second issue from a bank's perspective is to ensure that a person who acts to bind a corporate borrower has authority to do so, since agency law dictates that a principal will not be bound if an agent acts outside his authority. That authority may be actual or ostensible.

4.6.3.1 Actual authority

The articles of association of most companies provide for the powers of the company to be exercised at a meeting of the board of directors. It is also usual for the board to delegate their powers to a committee, or appoint an attorney to sign on their behalf. Prima facie, there may be several restrictions on this authority:

(a)   The articles of association will often contain specific limitations on borrowing (although see **4.6.3.2**). These might restrict the amount of money which the company may borrow (often by reference to the net asset value of the company), or they may require a specific internal procedure to be followed before borrowing is sanctioned. Furthermore, some borrowers will be restricted under statute (eg, insurance companies).

(b)   It is not uncommon for directors to want to appoint an attorney to execute a document and to agree any 'eleventh hour' changes. However, most articles do not allow directors to delegate their powers to non-directors. Therefore, although a non-director can probably be empowered to execute a settled document, delegation of powers to agree substantial amendments may be ineffective (although see **4.6.3.2**).

(c) An agent cannot have actual authority to bind a company to a transaction which is not for the purpose of, or reasonably incidental to, attaining or pursuing the company's objects (*Rolled Steel Products (Holdings) Ltd v British Steel Corporation* [1986] Ch 246, CA). See **Chapter 14**.

4.6.3.2 Ostensible (apparent) authority

The common law doctrine of ostensible authority implies (subject to certain limitations) authority on an agent which the agent appears to have because of his principal's representations, or because of his 'status'. However, any actual or constructive notice of limitations on the authority will restrict the ability to rely upon it. Furthermore, the scope of ostensible authority is by no means certain.

Nevertheless, s 40 of the CA 2006 (largely repeating CA 1985, ss 35A and 35B) gives some reassurance to a creditor as to an agent's actual or ostensible authority.

The CA 2006, s 40 provides:

(1) In favour of a person dealing with a company in good faith, the power of the directors to bind the company, or authorise others to do so, is deemed to be free of any limitation under the company's constitution.

(2) For this purpose—

    (a) a person 'deals with' a company if he is a party to any transaction or other act to which the company is a party,

    (b) a person dealing with a company—

        (i) is not bound to enquire as to any limitation on the powers of the directors to bind the company or authorise others to do so,

        (ii) is presumed to have acted in good faith unless the contrary is proved, and

        (iii) is not to be regarded as acting in bad faith by reason only of his knowing that an act is beyond the powers of the directors under the company's constitution.

(3) The references above to limitations on the directors' powers under the company's constitution include limitations deriving—

    (a) from a resolution of the company or of any class of shareholders, or

    (b) from any agreement between the members of the company or of any class of shareholders.

4.6.3.3 Conclusion

While s 40 of the CA 2006 is helpful to lenders, it does have limitations: uncertainty over the 'good faith' requirement; the need for non-directors to be given authority by directors; and the possibility that an inquorate board meeting might fall outside the provisions (see *Smith v Henniker-Major & Co* [2002] BCC 544).

The only sure way to avoid problems is to make certain that a company's agents are properly authorised to execute the facility agreement. The bank's solicitor should ensure that the borrower holds a board meeting which explicitly addresses the implications for the borrower of executing the facility agreement and any ancillary documentation, and authorising the borrower to execute all the documentation through specified agents (eg, the directors). The meeting must satisfy any conditions as to quorum, and certified copies of the minutes should be required as a condition precedent to utilisation (see **4.7**). It is also good practice to ensure there are no relevant restrictions in the company's articles of association.

In addition, there are a number of institutions other than limited companies which may seek to borrow, such as partnerships, building societies or local authorities, all with different common law or statutory powers. Companies that are charities are also subject to certain exceptions to ss 39 and 40 of the CA 2006. A solicitor must therefore consider the legal status and nature of a borrower, and then assess its legal capacity and what action is required to provide proper authority (local authorities have been particularly problematic, eg, *Credit Suisse v Allerdale Borough Council* [1997] QB 306, where the local authority's guarantee was held void for being ultra vires).

4.6.4 Resulting trust

Another reason for including a purpose clause is an attempt to create a resulting trust if the purpose fails. For example, imagine a loan made specifically to fund a new factory for borrower B. After two months, B's orders suddenly dry up and it stops work on the factory. If the purpose of the loan was specified then, since that purpose has failed, any money which has been drawn down but remains unspent (and identifiable) will be held by B on resulting trust for the bank (*Barclays Bank Ltd v Quistclose Investments Ltd* [1970] AC 567). While B is solvent, the question of whether unspent monies are held on trust or in contract is largely irrelevant. On its insolvency, however, any money held on trust by B must be paid to the bank, irrespective of any claims by other creditors. If held under contract, the money would become an asset of B to be shared between its creditors in accordance with the liquidation process.

4.6.5 The bank's and borrower's perspectives

The purpose clause is designed to oblige the borrower to use the loan for the purpose stated, but it should also expressly absolve the bank from any liability to ensure that the funds are used in accordance with that purpose. This will avoid any claim by the borrower (or a guarantor of the loan) that the bank has consented to, or waived, any misuse of funds, or has a duty to ensure the money is properly applied.

The borrower's main concern is usually to ensure that the purpose clause is drafted widely enough to allow versatility in using the borrowed money and avoid any possibility that it might breach the clause. For example, the borrower will be responsible for paying all costs incurred in negotiating the loan. A borrower will usually want to ensure that the purpose clause is wide enough to allow him to pay these costs out of the money drawn under the loan.

4.7 CONDITIONS PRECEDENT

4.7.1 Purpose

Conditions precedent (CPs) are, as their name suggests, specific conditions which a bank requires a borrower to fulfil before part or all of a facility agreement takes effect. The CPs provide tangible evidence that the representations and warranties (see **Chapter 5**) are met. The clause is usually found near the beginning of the loan facility, but if there are numerous CPs to satisfy, they may be listed in a schedule at the back of the agreement.

4.7.2 Condition precedent to … ?

Usually, the substantial parts of a loan document will come into effect as soon as it is executed by all the parties, but the borrower will not be able to utilise unless and until the CPs are satisfied. This has a number of advantages for the bank. First, the borrower is locked in to the main provisions of the agreement. This means the bank's fees are payable and remedies for default apply.

Secondly, the representations, warranties, undertakings, events of default and boiler plate (see **Chapters 5** to **9**) will all become operative as soon as the document is executed. This means the bank can begin monitoring the borrower, even whilst the borrower is trying to satisfy the CPs.

4.7.3   Watch out for ...

4.7.3.1   Time limits

In many cases, the CPs will be satisfied by 'closing' (ie, the time the loan documentation is executed and goes 'live'). If a borrower believes it cannot satisfy one or more CPs it will have to ask the banks for a temporary or permanent waiver. Most of the CPs, aside from the legal opinions, are within the borrower's control and so it, through its solicitors, must collect the necessary paperwork and deliver it to the bank's solicitor before execution. In practice, however, the bank's solicitor also takes responsibility for ensuring that the CPs are either satisfied (or waived) and he may have to write a 'CP confirmation letter' to the agent confirming the position. If the loan is for a specific purpose, for example an acquisition, then timing of the CPs and first utilisation will almost certainly be tied in to the acquisition timetable.

4.7.3.2   Uncertainty

It is possible that a CP could be so vague as to make the agreement void for uncertainty. For example, a condition in a contract which stipulated that the sale was 'subject to the purchaser obtaining a satisfactory mortgage' was held to make the entire contract void in *Lee-Parker v Izett (No 2)* [1972] 2 All ER 800. It is, however, common to see wording requiring a CP document to be 'in form and substance satisfactory to the banks'. This is probably certain enough in legal terms, although it may trouble the borrower (see **4.7.6**).

4.7.4   Typical conditions precedent

Obviously the form of the CPs will depend entirely on the particular transaction, but a general purpose term loan is likely to require fewer CPs than a multi-currency term and RCF funding an acquisition. Many CPs to a facility agreement are fairly standard, however, and those most commonly seen are mentioned at **4.7.4.1**.

4.7.4.1   Documentary

Common CPs might include:

(a)   current constitutional documents (eg articles of association) of the borrower and any companies giving guarantees or security;

(b)   a board resolution approving the terms and conditions of the facility agreement and authorising signatories (usually the directors);

(c)   a list of names of authorised signatories, together with a specimen of their signatures;

(d)   a shareholders' resolution from any guarantor, approving the guarantee (if there are any possible corporate benefit issues associated with it);

(e)   legal opinions from the bank's lawyers confirming the validity of the agreement and effectiveness of any security (see **Chapter 16**);

(f)   a comfort letter from the borrower's parent (see **13.2.2**);

(g)   insurance policies (including any 'Keyman' insurance (see **7.6**));

(h)   certificates of title for any properties;

(i)   executed security documents, together with any documents of title (eg, share certificates) which those documents require;

(j)   copies of any other related documents (eg, fee letters, hedging agreements, intercreditor, and of course the loan facility executed by all parties);

(k)   in an acquisition finance, 'Reliance Letters' allowing the bank to rely on expert due diligence reports on the target, commissioned by the purchaser;

(l)   management accounts;

(m)   payment instructions notifying the bank where loan monies should be paid;

(n)   any consents or licences which are necessary in connection with the purpose of the loan;

(o)   an agreement for an agent for service of process to be appointed by a borrower which is domiciled abroad (see also **9.8**).

If a borrower does not want to provide an original document then a 'certified copy' might be sufficient. This is a copy which has been signed, usually by a director or secretary of the borrower, as a true copy of the original as at a given date. Clearly, certified copies of board minutes are acceptable; certified copies of share certificates are usually not. If the borrower is based overseas and original documents are likely to be in a language other than English, the facility agreement should require the borrower to provide translations.

4.7.4.2   Other

Most CPs entail providing documentary evidence. However, it will also be a condition of utilisation that no event of default is continuing (see **Chapter 8**) and CPs might include less tangible things such as obtaining a listing, being granted a licence, or obtaining competition clearance.

4.7.5   Conditions subsequent

In some transactions, notably acquisition finance bids which are required to happen quickly, some of the usual CPs are made 'conditions subsequent'. For example, the borrower may be required to give share security over its subsidiaries as a condition precedent, but the remaining security as a condition subsequent within, say, 90 days of utilisation.

4.7.6   CPs – the bank's perspective

A bank looks to the CPs, alongside the representations (see **Chapter 5**), to satisfy it of the borrower's position before any money is utilised. The bank simply lists what it requires.

4.7.7   CPs – the borrower's perspective

The borrower must approach a list of CPs with some caution: can they be achieved within the required time? The potentially problematic CPs for the borrower are those where a third party is involved. The form and availability of accountants' reports, licences and opinions should all be agreed early in the countdown to signing. There are solutions to most problems, provided they are addressed in good time: a bank may be less flexible if a problem is sprung on it at the last minute in what looks like tactical timing.

Another potential minefield for a borrower is wording, such as 'in form and substance satisfactory to the bank'. This gives a bank plenty of discretion to decide that something is not satisfactory and utilisation cannot be made. Wherever possible, an agreed form should be settled in advance, for example with respect to board minutes and legal opinions. These are sometimes appended in draft form in a schedule to the agreement, so that all parties know what is required. If a form cannot be agreed in advance, qualifying the bank's discretion with the word 'reasonable' gives a borrower some comfort.

Lastly, this is one area where the borrower in a syndicated loan might press for acceptance of documents to be in the discretion of the agent or, if not, a simple majority of the syndicate. The agent is likely to be the entity with which the borrower has the best relationship, and so may be more flexible. Majority decisions entail persuading a number of banks, but at least avoid dissenting minorities causing trouble.

4.8   AVAILABILITY

4.8.1   Single utilisation loan

The availability or 'utilisation' clause deals with the mechanics of when and how the borrower can actually borrow money under the loan. A simple term loan might allow the money to be utilised in one amount on a specified day. The utilisation clause will essentially say: satisfy the CPs, repeat the representations, and so long as you are not in default we will comply with your utilisation request.

4.8.2 Multiple utilisation loan

More sophisticated facilities might allow the borrower to utilise in a number of tranches (or 'loans') as and when required, up to the available amount. Tranches must be utilised within a 'commitment period' (see **3.2.2**). Revolving credit facilities offer even more flexibility, allowing repeated utilisation and repayment throughout the term of the facility. A bank will invariably charge a 'commitment fee' during any commitment period (see **9.5**). In either case, the availability clause must cater for multiple utilisation.

4.8.2.1 Notice of utilisation

A fundamental premise of syndicated facility mechanics is that banks will use the interbank market to fund large advances (sometimes known as 'matched funding') (see **3.8**). They will therefore usually require the borrower to give several business days' notice of utilisation. The number of days depends largely on the currency: in the London market, eurocurrencies (currencies held outside their country of origin – see **Chapter 17**) would technically require a minimum of two clear business days for the bank to fund, whereas domestic sterling, if available, could probably be funded on the day of request. In a syndicated loan, however, the banks will usually require notice no later than the third business day before the day of utilisation for eurocurrencies, or the first business day before for sterling (the extra time allows syndicate members to sub-participate the loan if required – see **Chapter 10**). Often the facility document will specify the latest time in a day when a request can be received (eg, 11 am). Money can always be made available more quickly, but at a cost. If the facility is a revolving one, where fees are usually higher to buy flexibility, the bank is more likely to accept a shorter notice period.

Some utilisation provisions require the borrower's request to be not more than a specified period (eg, two weeks) before the money is required. This is a purely practical point to avoid the situation, not unknown among sovereign borrowers, where a borrower puts in a request several years in advance!

Once a utilisation notice is given, a borrower is usually committed to taking the money requested. Once again, this is based on the assumption that banks will have matched funded a facility, and that 'funding loan' cannot be cancelled without penalty.

4.8.2.2 Representations and defaults

In its utilisation request, a borrower must confirm there is no current default (and that utilisation will not result in a default) (see **Chapter 8**). In a facility allowing multiple utilisations, those requirements must be complied with each time a utilisation is requested.

4.9 FLOATING RATE INTEREST

Banks are intermediaries and so the interest they charge on their loans must cover their cost of raising money as well as an element of profit to keep their shareholders happy. The majority of commercial loans will bear interest at a floating rate: the interest rate will vary through the life of the loan to reflect the fluctuating cost to the bank of raising money in the market. Floating rate loans may be based on 'base rate' or 'Libor', and these concepts are explored below.

4.9.1 Base rates

Commercial banks raise loan capital in a variety of ways, but primarily through attracting depositors and through issuing debt securities (see **Chapter 17**). Along the way they will also incur regulatory costs (see below and **9.3.2**). A bank's base rate amalgamates all those costs to provide a general cost of raising funds. Base rate is then typically used to charge interest (often with a margin) on bilateral loans to individuals and small to medium businesses. Each commercial bank will have its own base rate, though they may be very similar or identical.

The Bank of England also publishes a base rate (the 'official rate') which is decided by its Monetary Policy Committee each month and is designed to influence economic activity and control inflation. The official rate influences the economy because it is the rate at which the Bank lends to financial institutions (primarily through the short term sale and repurchase of gilts) and so it will eventually affect a bank's cost of funding. Thus, while commercial banks' base rates will not usually be as low as the official rate, they will broadly speaking follow its movements. The last four years have seen the official rate unchanged at a historic low of 0.5%.

4.9.2 Libor

Large commercial facilities, which are typically syndicated, will not usually use base rates to calculate interest. Instead, a floating rate is usually the sum of two or maybe three elements:

(a)   Libor (or equivalent): representing the main cost of funding (see **3.8** and below);

(b)   margin: generating the bank's profit and covering regulatory capital costs (see **9.3.3**); and maybe

(c)   mandatory cost: the cost to the bank of its regulatory fees and deposits (although this element is now typically not included, see **9.3.2**).

Libor stands for 'London Interbank Offered Rate' and is the interest rate charged for loans between banks in the London interbank market. The interbank market is intended to provide banks with liquidity: quickly accessible, short-term loans allowing banks to meet their lending commitments or put excess funds to work. As mentioned at **3.8**, large commercial loan facilities typically *assume* that banks will fund their commitments by borrowing on the interbank market (although it is never an *obligation*, and the recent financial crisis and its repercussions have resulted in a much reduced volume of interbank lending). Libor rates will vary depending primarily on:

(a)   the currency of the interbank loan;

(b)   the duration of the interbank loan;

(c)   the credit standing of the borrowing bank; and

(d)   the liquidity of the interbank market.

A Libor-based interest rate definition must therefore specify the first three variables. In addition, since Libor rates fluctuate throughout each day (in contrast, base rates might only change every few months), the definition should specify the date (eg the first day of each interest period) and time (typically 11am when the market is most active) at which the rate is to be set. Lastly, each bank effectively has its own Libor rate. To simplify calculating the interest rate for syndicated loans, most facilities use an average rate calculated and published on market screens (see below).

4.9.3 Screen rate (Libor and Euribor)

In 1986, the British Bankers Association (BBA) started publishing an averaged Libor rate known as 'bbalibor' (or the 'screen rate', or simply 'Libor'). It was intended to provide an easily accessible, impartial benchmark rate for borrowing costs in the London interbank market. The bbalibor rates became widely used across financial products and markets internationally (some estimates suggest it is used in over $300 trillion worth of transactions), and it appears in almost all syndicated facility agreements. The rate is calculated by asking a panel of banks to submit estimated rates at which they could borrow funds if they were to do so by 'asking for and then accepting interbank offers in a reasonable market size just prior to 11am'. The highest and lowest quartile (25%) of submitted rates are discarded and the remaining quotes are averaged. The resulting rates are currently published by Thompson

Reuters for five currencies over seven maturities, ranging from overnight to 12 months. However, the BBA will soon be stripped of the right to administer the rate (see below).

Other interbank rates

Financial markets outside of London have their own interbank rates, for example Mibor in Mumbai, Tibor in Tokyo, and Hibor in Hong Kong. In the eurozone, there is a euro equivalent of bbalibor, known as Euribor. Euribor is compiled by the Euribor-EBF and published by Thomson Reuters. It is calculated by asking a panel of 32 banks throughout the European Union each to submit the rate at which, to the best of their knowledge, euro interbank term deposits are being offered within the EMU zone by one prime bank to another at a specified time. The highest and lowest 15% of rates are discarded and the remainder averaged to give the Euribor rate.

Problems with bbalibor

Concerns about the manipulation of bbalibor surfaced as early as 2005, but in 2012 they came to a head. Several banks were found to have manipulated their rate submissions, in part to create a healthier picture of their credit quality during the financial crisis, in part as a result of individuals collaborating to influence financial trades. Three contributor banks to date have been found guilty of fixing their submissions and fined over £1.6 billion by British and American regulators; other parties are under investigation. Following recommendations of a Government-commissioned review of bbalibor (the Wheatley Review), the BBA is being replaced as administrator of the rate. The new administrator will be NYSE Euronext Rate Administration Ltd, a subsidiary of NYSE Euronext (a global operator of financial markets), and it will take over in early 2014 after a period of transition.

The Wheatley Review also resulted in certain currencies being dropped from Libor quotation on the basis that 'they are both difficult to support using trade data, and are not heavily used by market participants' (for similar reasons, the number of tenors of the currencies still quoted have been reduced from 15 to 7). Australian, Canadian and New Zealand dollars as well as Danish Krone and Swedish Krona are no longer quoted: facilities providing these currencies must look for alternatives such as local market rates in the relevant country (for example 'CDOR' for Canadian Dollars). The absence of screen rates for certain currencies and tenors has also put strain on the typical fallback provisions in facility agreements, as explained below.

4.9.4   Reference banks and market disruption clause

If loan facilities use screen rates, they need to legislate for those rates not being available or being insufficient to cover the banks' actual funding costs. The fallback is to rely on a small group of 'reference banks' (typically three) from within the syndicate to supply their own Libor rates, which are averaged to provide a rate in place of the screen rate (ie margin and mandatory cost are still added to it). The identity of the reference banks is important to the borrower: banks with a high credit rating are likely to have a lower Libor.

If none (or only one) of the reference banks are able to provide a Libor quote, or if a percentage of the syndicate (typically 30%) notify the agent that their actual cost of funding the facility exceeds the screen rates, the banks can invoke the 'market disruption clause'. The market disruption clause allows each bank to notify the agent of its own actual cost of funding, and this is used to calculate the interest owed to that bank in place of the screen rate or reference bank rates (ie margin and mandatory cost are still added to it).

Issues with reference banks and market disruption

The fallback to reference banks rates and the market disruption clause was originally intended to be used in rare circumstances, for example due to technical problems with the screen rate or an irregular interest period (which can happen on first utilisation or in a restructuring).

However, the reduction in currencies covered by the screen rate, and the reduced number of tenors for those currencies still published, means the reference banks are increasingly likely to be asked to quote a Libor rate. This causes two issues. First, there is a vastly increased administrative burden for the reference banks for which they are generally not reimbursed. Secondly, and more importantly, reference banks may be unable to give accurate Libor rates for the same reason as the screen rate is problematic, namely a reduced or non-existent interbank market in some currencies and tenors. At the time of publication, the market is still looking for practical solutions.

4.10 FIXED RATE INTEREST

Fixed rate interest is unusual in commercial loan facilities. The fixed rate must cover the banks' costs of funding, and provide a profit, through the life of the loan, and since their fund raising may be at a floating rate, they will not want to be caught out by unexpected upward interest rate movements. Fixed rates therefore tend to be unattractively high. However, borrowers looking for fixed rate liability under their loans may be able to use hedging (see **4.14**) or possibly look to the capital markets (see **Part III**).

Q&A: What next for Libor?

NYSE Euronext, the transatlantic exchanges operator, has been awarded the contract by the UK government to run the London interbank offered rate contract after the benchmark interbank lending rate was discredited by a rate-rigging scandal that saw banks fined for fixing the rate and individual traders put on trial. The Financial Times looks at the planned reforms.

What happens to the regulation of Libor?

The UK Financial Conduct Authority will supervise the Libor administrator and the rate-setting process. The UK amended its laws amid the scandal to bring rate-setting under the regulatory umbrella as of April 1. The European Commission has proposed transferring responsibility to the pan-EU European Securities and Markets Authority, but no legislation is expected to pass for several years.

The Financial Stability Board, a global group that coordinates regulatory reform efforts, has also set up a committee, headed by top US and UK regulators, to oversee reform of the benchmark-setting process.

What does this mean for the rate-setting process?

Libor will continue to be set by surveying a panel of banks about the rates at which they think they can borrow, at least for the short term. Martin Wheatley, the FCA chief, has said he wants the new administrator to lead the process of finding ways to tie the rates more closely to actual transactions without wreaking havoc with the $300tn in existing contracts tied to the Libor rate. A likely solution may be to run two parallel rates, one based on surveys to support the existing book, and a transaction-based rate for new contracts. NYSE Euronext's Liffe arm has many clients who use the existing rate and their bid emphasised continuity.

Is the scandal over?

Barclays, UBS and Royal Bank of Scotland have already been fined nearly $2.6bn collectively for manipulating Libor rates to make money on derivatives, and Japanese and Singaporean regulators have also taken action against a total of 20 banks for misbehaviour involving other interbank lending rates.

But UK and US enforcers are still investigating other banks and interdealer brokers including Rabobank, Citigroup, Lloyds, Deutsche Bank and ICAP, among others. Further corporate fines are expected and Tom Hayes, a former UBS and Citigroup trader, has been charged with criminal fraud in both the US and UK in connection with the scandal. He has not indicated how he intends to plead in either country.

Will it be a lucrative contract for NYSE Euronext?

Mr Wheatley's report specified that the new administrator should be a private company whose primary responsibility was to compile, distribute and police the daily publication of Libor. Nevertheless the report acknowledged that the winner was permitted to explore the commercial viability of the rate. For the present, however, NYSE Euronext's successful bid is more important for the prestige it will bring the exchange group than any revenues.

Source: *Financial Times*, 9 July 2013

4.11 INTEREST PERIODS

A simple loan might require a borrower to pay interest at regular intervals throughout the term of the loan. More sophisticated agreements will divide the life of each tranche into successive 'interest periods' of varying duration. Interest periods are primarily used to support matched funding (see **3.8**) so that:

(a) the chosen interest period will (theoretically at least) be mirrored by the bank's interbank loan (the borrower's choice is often limited to one, three or six months, since these are the most common interbank funding periods);

(b) the Libor rate is recalculated at the start of each interest period and applies for the duration of that interest period (hence the 'floating rate' loan is really a succession of different fixed rates);

(c) interest is payable at the end of each interest period;

(d) the borrower can usually select the duration of each interest period, giving him some control over the rate he pays and timing of payment to match income;

(e) repayments (and prepayments) are required to coincide with the end of an interest period, when the bank will (theoretically) be repaying its interbank loan. If the borrower prepays mid interest period, it will be charged 'break costs'. These are typically the difference between total interest the bank would have received to the end of the broken interest period, less the interest it can raise by lending the prepaid amount in the interbank market. Strong borrowers will argue they should not pay margin or mandatory cost for the remaining period but just the difference between the Libor on the loan and the current Libor (if less); and

(f) some of the representations will be repeated on the first day of each interest period.

4.12 APPORTIONMENT: THE 'DAY COUNT FRACTION'

Interest rates are almost invariably quoted at an annual rate. However, interest payments are usually due several times a year (ie at the end of each interest period). The bank and borrower must therefore agree the basis on which the annual interest will be apportioned between each interest period (known as the 'day count fraction'). For domestic sterling facility agreements in the London market, the traditional basis for calculating interest is known as '365/365': the annual interest rate is applied to the principal outstanding, and the result is multiplied by the actual number of days in the interest period and then divided by 365.

> **EXAMPLE**
>
> If the annual rate of interest is 6%, and the principal outstanding is £200, then:
>
> Total interest due each year = £12
>
> In February (non-leap year) the interest due will be:
>
> $\dfrac{(12 \times 28)}{365}$ = approx. 92

Interest paid under this method will therefore reflect the exact number of days in the interest period (other currencies and other markets may use methods which 'approximate' periods, for example treating each month as exactly one-twelfth of a year – see **19.4.3**).

4.13 RATCHETS

Some facility agreements provide for their margin to vary in accordance with the health of a borrower, which is measured through monitoring its financial ratios (for cross-over or leveraged facilities) or credit rating (for investment grade facilities) (see **17.11**). These 'margin ratchets' are intended to reflect the variation in risk borne by the bank, and provide an incentive for the borrower to perform well. If the ratios (or rating) worsen, the margin increases; if they improve, the margin falls and the loan is 'cheaper'.

4.14 HEDGING

While most commercial loans will carry floating rate interest, this does leave borrowers vulnerable to upward swings in the floating rate on which they are based (eg Libor). This is particularly acute for leveraged borrowers, which typically have large loans with relatively high margins. Many leveraged borrowers therefore manage ('hedge') their exposure to interest rate fluctuation by entering into an interest rate swap (a type of derivative). Essentially, the borrower contracts to periodically pay a fixed amount to another party (the 'counterparty') in return for an amount which varies in line with the floating rate of interest under the loan facility. The borrower therefore knows (and can budget for) its fixed obligations under the swap whilst also knowing it will receive income from the counterparty to meet its floating rate obligations under the loan.

Not all borrowers will hedge their interest obligations (the swaps can be expensive), and if they do, they may not hedge their entire exposure: in leveraged loans, lenders will typically require them to hedge around two-thirds of their exposure. The counterparty is typically the facility agent under the loan (it is lucrative business for the banks).

4.15 DEFAULT INTEREST

If a borrower fails to pay any sum due under a facility agreement, there will invariably be a provision for default interest. This will charge a rate of interest on any overdue amount (eg, interest, capital or fees) which is a fixed rate above the usual interest rate payable, ie:

(a)   LIBOR (at the rate applicable to each day the amount is overdue); plus

(b)   Mandatory Cost Rate; plus

(c)   the margin; plus

(d)   default interest of around 1%.

As long as the default interest rate can be justified as reasonable compensation for the bank having to deal with a loan in default, the clause should stand. If, however, the rate appears to be more by way of a threat to encourage non-default by the borrower, then it is in danger of offending the rules laid down for trading contracts in *Dunlop Pneumatic Tyre Co Ltd v New Garage & Motor Co Ltd* [1915] AC 79, and being declared void as a 'penalty'. (In *Lordsvale Finance plc v Bank of Zambia* [1996] QB 752, a 1% default interest rate was considered too 'modest' to be construed as a penalty.)

A bank will usually justify the additional rate as compensation for increased risk of lending to a defaulting borrower.

It should be noted that some jurisdictions do not permit interest to be charged on interest (eg, Islamic law prohibits interest per se) and that most solicitors will not opine on the validity of default interest (see **Chapter 16**).

4.16 BASIS POINTS

Traditionally, banks were able to charge a relatively large margin, which would usually be measured in minimum amounts of 0.5%. In the 1980s, however, borrowing became a 'buyer's market', as the number of products increased and world markets shrunk. Banks were forced to trim their margins and, as a result, a smaller measure was required. Margins are now measured in 'basis points'. One basis point (or 'bp') is 0.01%. Thus, 1% is 100 basis points. If LIBOR is running at 2%, then loan interest of 85 basis points above LIBOR is a rate of 2.85%. Sometimes (particularly in capital markets), 1% is referred to as one 'point', and a basis point is referred to as a 'tick'. Most loan documents will simply refer to percentages.

SUMMARY

This chapter has dealt with the following aspects of a facility agreement:

(1)   Who? ... the parties to the agreement.

(2)   When? ... the date, and the conditions precedent to be satisfied.

(3)   What? ... the type of facility and the definitions clause.

(4)   Why? ... the purpose of the facility, and the interest payable.

(5)   Where? ... the availability of the facility.

Most of these provisions deal with the mechanics of lending. The conditions precedent and purpose clause give only a crude control over the borrower. The following four chapters, however, deal with the most important control aspects of a facility agreement (and thus often the most heavily negotiated), namely the representations, undertakings and events of default.

CHAPTER 5

REPRESENTATIONS AND WARRANTIES

5.1	Introduction	49
5.2	Representations and warranties in a facility agreement	49
5.3	Representations – the bank's perspective	55
5.4	Representations – the borrower's perspective	55
5.5	Representations in contract law	56
	Summary	58

'Put all your eggs in one basket, and watch that basket!'

Mark Twain

5.1 INTRODUCTION

A bank will want to lend only if it is happy with the 'status quo' of a borrower. A facility agreement will therefore contain statements which the bank requires the borrower to make about various matters. These representations (occasionally referred to as 'representations' (or just 'reps') and warranties) are made on signing the facility agreement and usually repeated periodically thereafter. The first part of this chapter deals with these representations in the facility agreement. Representations and warranties under general contract law are discussed at **5.5**.

5.2 REPRESENTATIONS AND WARRANTIES IN A FACILITY AGREEMENT

5.2.1 Contractual remedies

Throughout the due diligence process (see **2.2**), the borrower will provide facts, records, forecasts, business plan, documents of title and other unpublished material (eg, management accounts). The most important pieces of information are effectively recorded in the facility agreement as representations: statements of fact made by the borrower and, sometimes, by the guarantor(s) confirming their position.

The three reasons for including borrower representations in the facility agreement are:

(a) to elicit information (part of the due diligence process);

(b) to provide a 'drawstop' (money may not be borrowed) if they are untrue; and

(c) to allow the bank to call a default (see **Chapter 8**) if they are untrue.

The borrower should therefore consider the representations carefully before agreeing to them. A bank will also be entitled to various legal remedies in the event of a misrepresentation, and these are examined further below. Those remedies, however, are of secondary importance.

5.2.2 Examples of common representations

The representations should provide disclosure of any circumstances which might affect the bank's decision to lend, and as such they will be tailored specifically to a particular borrower and particular loan; however, some of the areas commonly covered are outlined below.

5.2.2.1 'Legal' representations

The first group of representations (known as the 'legal' representations) relate to the validity of the borrower, any guarantor and the loan documentation.

Status

A borrower will be required to state that it is duly incorporated under the laws of its jurisdiction, and that it has power to own its assets and carry on its business. In some jurisdictions (eg, the United States) the relevant authorities will produce 'certificates of good standing' to confirm that a borrower is up to date in filing information and paying taxes: reference should be made to these, if appropriate.

Binding obligations

The borrower must confirm that the obligations it undertakes in the facility agreement and associated documents are legal, valid, binding and enforceable. It has become commonplace to qualify this representation by any general principles of law which limit the borrower's obligations and which are referred to in the legal opinion addressed to the bank (see **Chapter 16**), for example insolvency procedures, equitable principles or public policy issues. Banks should resist this qualification applying to other representations since it puts risk back on to the banks.

Non-conflict

Borrowers must usually state that entering into the facility agreement will not conflict with any laws or regulations, their constitutional documents, or any other agreement or instrument to which they are a party. Clearly this is important from a practical point of view: the bank does not want a borrower immediately to be in default under another contract, or in breach of a law, as a result of signing the loan. However, there is also an important legal issue which the third element of this representation is designed to tackle. If entering the loan causes the borrower to breach an existing contract, the other party to that contract might sue the bank in tort for 'procuring a breach of contractual relations' (or 'interference with contractual relations'). The representation that there is no conflict with other agreements should protect the bank, since the tort requires the bank to act with knowledge or indifference to any conflict. Banks should therefore beware of borrowers limiting the representation to 'material' breaches of other contracts, since that would not protect them from the tortious claim (though the claim itself may not be material).

Power and authority

It might be thought that the question of whether a borrower has the power to enter into the loan facility is one for a solicitor to answer rather than the borrower. Indeed, it will usually be addressed in the bank's legal opinion (see **Chapter 16**). If, however, the borrower had no authority to take the loan, suing its solicitor is of only limited comfort to the bank. A borrower must therefore represent that it has the power and authority to enter into the loan, and to perform its obligations. Breach of the representation (as with other representations) will lead to a default and allow the bank to refuse advances or demand repayment ('acceleration'). This is particularly important for this type of representation which cannot usually be remedied.

Validity and admissibility in evidence

The borrower must represent that it has done everything required to ensure that the facility agreement is admissible in evidence in its jurisdiction of incorporation. This will be particularly important if the borrower is incorporated in a different jurisdiction from the governing law. It might include the need for government or regulatory authorisations: if these are extensive, they may be included in a schedule to the facility. Sometimes the facility itself must be signed before obtaining the authorisation, in which case it should be made a condition to utilising the loan ('a condition precedent', see **4.7**) or an undertaking to obtain authorisation within a specific time-frame.

Governing law and enforcement

The last of the common 'legal' representations is that the law governing the facility agreement, and any judgment obtained in relation to it, will be recognised and enforced in the borrower's jurisdiction of incorporation. For obvious reasons this is not a negotiated clause.

All six of these 'legal' representations are usually repeated (see **5.2.4**).

5.2.2.2 'Commercial' representations

The second group of representations (known as the 'commercial' representations) relate to the commercial position of the borrower.

Deduction of tax

The borrower will be required to represent that it is not required to deduct tax from payments made to banks which are defined as 'Qualifying Lenders' (defined as those banks usually exempt from withholding tax or which benefit from a double tax treaty). This is primarily aimed at ensuring there is no withholding tax imposed on interest payments which would mean the banks getting less interest than expected, or the borrower having to increase its interest payment under the gross-up provisions. This representation is not repeated because ongoing tax issues are dealt with in a separate section of the facility agreement (see **9.3.4**).

No filing or stamp duties

Stamp duties are a form of document tax imposed on the execution of certain instruments (ie written documents). In the United Kingdom, stamp duty is imposed on the transfer of 'stock', 'marketable securities' and 'interests in partnership', with rates ranging from 0.5% to 1.5% of the consideration or market value of the property being transferred (known as *ad valorem* stamp duty). Failure to pay stamp duty within 30 days of execution will usually mean that the document is not admissible in evidence or accepted for registration purposes. It may also entail penalties and interest on late payment. Whilst UK stamp duty may apply to transfers of bonds (see **Part III**), loan agreements would not usually be caught. The representation is required, however, to protect against changes to the UK regime, or against possible foreign duties of which the bank was unaware. This representation is not usually repeated unless new borrowers accede to the facility agreement.

There is a separate UK regime imposing stamp duty on the transfer of land.

No event of default

The borrower must represent that there is no event of default (see **Chapter 8**) continuing, or which might reasonably be expected to occur as a result of utilising the facility. In addition it must represent there is no event of default under any other of its agreements which would have a material adverse effect (this is usually a defined term) on the facility agreement. It is hard for a borrower to argue against giving this representation: any negotiation will focus on narrowing the definition of 'material adverse effect'. The bank will insist that this representation is repeated. It is therefore important that the representation refers to 'event of default' and not the LMA definition of 'default' or 'potential event of default' (see **8.6**).

No misleading information

This representation – that the borrower has not supplied information to the bank which is misleading – will usually have three points of focus. First, it will state that the information provided for the information memorandum (see **3.3.4**) was true and accurate. Secondly, it will state that the financial projections prepared by the company's directors (and which usually appear in the information memorandum) are based on recent information and contain reasonable assumptions. Thirdly, it will state that all other information provided to the banks was true, complete and accurate at the time it was given.

The borrower will want to negotiate this clause in at least two ways. It will want the representation to apply only to written information it has provided; oral discussions will be considered too numerous to remember in detail and represent as accurate. This is usually acceptable to banks, unless key oral representations were made; after all, proving what was said would be problematic unless it was recorded. The borrower will also want the representation qualified to say the information was 'true and accurate in all material respects'. Again, this is usually acceptable to the banks. It is not usually necessary to repeat this representation.

Accounting principles

The bank will have closely reviewed the borrower's accounts as part of its due diligence procedures, and it will base lending decisions on the information they provide. Under UK GAAP (Generally Accepted Accounting Practice) it is quite legitimate for a company to use a variety of policies in compiling its accounts (see **6.9.2**), as long as they give a 'true and fair view' (CA 2006, s 400).

The borrower will therefore be required to represent that the original financial statements it provided to the bank were prepared in accordance with the relevant GAAP, consistently applied policies, and give a 'true and fair view' (or equivalent). The borrower will also give an undertaking to deliver future accounts on the same basis, but with a proviso to deal with any change in policies or practice (see **7.4.4.3**).

A third limb of this representation usually states that there has been no material adverse change in the business or financial condition of the borrower since a particular set of financial statements. This is because the financial statements may date from some time earlier, for example audited accounts are produced only annually. The representation effectively brings them up to date, in a material sense at least.

If this representation is to be repeated (it usually will be), there is a point for negotiation on the third limb: should it refer to material adverse change from the original financial statements produced when the facility agreement was executed, or should it refer to the latest financial statements? If the borrower performs well financially in the first few years, referring to the original financial statements is a less severe test, since the good performance will build a cushion for later bad performance. If it refers to the most recent financial statements, the 'no material adverse change' test ratchets up with each improved set of financial statements. Conversely, if a borrower performs poorly from the start, measuring against the latest financial statements allows it to keep failing incrementally so long as no one year is 'material'. If the failure was measured against the original financial statements, the cumulative failings would eventually become a material adverse change and the borrower could not make the representation.

Ranking

The borrower is invariably asked to represent that any claims the bank may have under the loan documentation will rank at least *pari passu* (equally) with any other unsecured creditors, other than as a result of any preference through insolvency regulations (eg, for unpaid employees' wages). In fact this simply states the position under current English law, but if the representation is repeated it protects the bank (by becoming an event of default) if the law should change. In addition, some jurisdictions (eg, Spain) allow a borrower to favour some unsecured creditors over others (eg, by notarisation), and so it may be a provision that overseas syndicate members want to see in the facility (see also **7.6**).

Litigation

It would clearly be disastrous for a bank if, shortly after execution of the facility agreement, the borrower had a crippling judgment given against it. A bank needs to know about any litigation (or similar proceedings), existing or threatened, in order to assess the risk and effect of an unfavourable judgment. The consequences may not just be a heavy fine; they might include loss of licences, bad publicity affecting trade, or cross defaults into other agreements.

The borrower might have a problem with an unqualified statement that it faces no current or threatened litigation, particularly if the statement is to be periodically repeated (see **5.2.4**). Most large companies (particularly those with a US presence) have a number of law suits in which they are involved at any one time. They may involve minimal amounts, they may be a 'try on' by a rival or creditor, or they may be started by the company itself to protect its intellectual property. The solution might be to use a disclosure letter (see **5.2.3**), though these are now uncommon, to include an element of de minimis or materiality (see **11.5.3** and **11.5.5**), to draft the representations to exclude frivolous and vexatious claims, to refer to the 'reasonably likely outcome' or perhaps to use a combination of all the above.

Since 1 October 2007, the CA 2006 has made 'derivative actions' (ie, shareholders bringing claims against directors in the company's name) easier to bring, and so litigation representations are now likely to include claims against the borrower group's directors.

Winding-up proceedings

A bank will want to know that no insolvency proceedings in any form have been started or are threatened against the borrower. At first sight this might seem eminently reasonable. However, non-payment may be due to a genuine mistake or disagreement, and it is not uncommon for creditors to threaten a company over relatively small unpaid amounts. The borrower should press for a de minimis provision and wording to exclude debts which it disputes in good faith. This representation is usually repeated (unless covered by an undertaking or event of default).

Encumbrances

If a loan is to be secured over the borrower's assets, the priority and effectiveness of the bank's security will depend on any existing charges (see **Chapter 12**). It will therefore be of paramount importance that the bank knows exact details of any existing security. In practice, the bank's solicitor will have obtained a company search on the borrower and examined its register of mortgages and charges. In addition, the bank will usually require a representation by the borrower that there are no encumbrances other than those disclosed before execution (see **5.2.3**). A bank might also require a representation from the borrower that it has valid title, in its own name, to all property over which security is to be given. This representation does not usually require repetition.

Environmental

Environmental issues are of increasing concern to banks: quite apart from any civil liability (eg, adopting a nuisance), banks should be aware of increasingly tough legislation in this area. In particular, the Environmental Protection Act 1990 (EPA 1990), as amended by the Environment Act 1995, introduced a licensing system for specified 'polluting' processes, as well as powers to various bodies to enforce clean-up (or 'remediation') of polluted sites. On 1 April 2000, a regime for the clean-up of existing seriously contaminated sites became operational. Primary responsibility for remediation rests with the polluter, however 'innocent'. Owners or occupiers may be held liable if the person with primary responsibility cannot be found. This type of strict liability may mean expense and disruption for which a borrower has not budgeted, and which severely devalues the bank's main security. The Environmental Damage (Prevention and Remediation) Regulations 2009 (SI 2009/153) (as amended) implemented the 2004 EU Environmental Directive (2004/35/EC). In particular, the Regulations impose liability to remedy (or bear the cost of remedying) environmental damage to habitats, species, land and water. The focus is on 'operators' carrying out polluting activities. In the United States (where environmental legislation is more comprehensive than in the UK), lender liability is well established and a bank may find itself liable for clean-up costs.

It is increasingly common for a bank to require an expert's report on environmental issues before lending. The use of an 'environmental audit' will depend on the business of the borrower and the purpose of the loan. However, even if the borrower does not carry on a 'high risk' business, a bank will usually require it to represent that it is in compliance with all environmental laws and has obtained, and complies with, all environmental licences necessary for its business. This representation is usually subject to materiality and, typically, will not be repated because there will be an 'environmental undertaking' in the facility agreement.

Catch all

From time to time, banks have asked for a representation that there is 'nothing the borrower has omitted to tell the banks that if it had told them they would not want to lend'! Most borrowers resist this on the basis that it is almost impossible for them to know if they have complied.

5.2.3 Disclosure letter

When a bank's solicitor is preparing the first draft of the representations, he will try to make them as wide as possible. For example, the borrower may be required to state that it has no litigation against it. However, most businesses will be sued, from time to time, albeit that it may be of no real significance to the bank. A would-be borrower is therefore forced to say that it cannot give the representation, the bank will ask why, and any litigation is revealed. The first objective of the representation has been achieved.

Assuming the bank is not unduly worried by the disclosed litigation, it could simply include it in the representation as a specific exception. An alternative solution, however, is to keep the representation 'clean' and use a separate document to deal with anything which would otherwise amount to a breach. This document is known as a 'disclosure letter'. The disclosure letter is essentially an agreed list of specific items which would ordinarily prevent a borrower from making a representation but which the bank has agreed to waive. The representations in the loan document are then made subject to anything in the disclosure letter.

If a disclosure letter is used (they are now uncommon), the borrower should be wary of pegging a disclosure to one particular representation, because it may breach more than one. The disclosure should therefore be worded to modify all the reps and warranties. At the same time, the bank should be sure that the disclosure is a full and accurate one so that it can properly judge whether it may be waived. Using a disclosure letter to soften the representations is very effective when they are first given, but can lead to problems for the borrower if they are to be repeated (see **5.4**).

5.2.4 Repetition of representations

Representations and warranties are used in many other commercial agreements: the purchaser of a house, or a business, will want numerous representations from the vendor. Unlike many commercial agreements, however, a loan document provides for a continuing relationship, and a bank may therefore want the representations repeated from time to time. Since a representation can be made only as at a given date, the question arises as to when it should be repeated. Some agreements require the representations to be deemed repeated every day throughout the life of the loan (known as 'evergreening'). However, most facility agreements require the reps and warranties to be given on execution and then repeated immediately prior to each utilisation, and on the first day of each interest period (see **4.9**).

If the representations are deemed repeated, the loan document will often specifically state that they are to 'survive' the execution and first utilisation. Some agreements will require a certificate to be provided periodically, by an officer of the borrower, confirming that the representations are still correct (or that there has been no default). Both measures prevent a borrower from arguing that the representations were merely initial pre-conditions of lending. Furthermore, any claim for misrepresentation will depend on the innocent party showing reliance on the representation (see **5.5.1**). Reliance may be harder to prove on a deemed repetition, and so the additional emphasis provided by requiring a certificate or specifying repetition may be helpful.

Some practitioners believe that it is better not to deem someone to have made an incorrect statement and will instead use undertakings (**Chapter 6**) and events of default (**Chapter 8**) to allow the bank to respond to changes during the term of the loan.

5.3 REPRESENTATIONS – THE BANK'S PERSPECTIVE

There is an element of *caveat emptor* which applies when a bank makes a loan: essentially, there is no common law obligation on a borrower to disclose information which might be pertinent to the bank's decision to lend. The representations will need careful drafting to achieve the required disclosure. Some reps and warranties are best cast in very wide terms, for example a representation that a borrower has 'no litigation, arbitration, or similar proceedings pending or threatened'. However, a representation that a borrower has insurance could benefit from being more specific.

Sometimes a borrower will ask to qualify its 'legal' representations by any qualifications used in the bank's legal opinions. This may be accepted for the 'binding obligation' and possibly 'governing law' representations, but a 'blanket' application is not appropriate or necessary. Remember, from the bank's perspective, the representations are about 'risk allocation', allowing them to take action if a situation is not what they had been led to believe.

5.4 REPRESENTATIONS – THE BORROWER'S PERSPECTIVE

If a representation is untrue when made or repeated it will trigger an event of default, and therefore borrowers will want to negotiate wide margins for error. A repeated representation should avoid the need for an undertaking or an event of default on the same issue, but, at the very least, any concessions negotiated in drafting any equivalent or related events of default or undertakings (such as de minimis provisions) should be reflected in any representations which are to be repeated (see **5.2.4**). A borrower should never repeat a representation that there is no 'potential event of default' or equivalent, since that would turn a 'potential' into a 'full' default.

There is a particular danger for the borrower if the representations are to be deemed repeated. The bank will argue that when representations are first made, they should be tightly worded in order to flush out any problems (by way of a disclosure letter: see **5.2.3**). However, on repetition, the disclosure letter is ineffective against new breaches.

EXAMPLE

A borrower is asked to sign a facility agreement which includes a representation that it is not involved in litigation or a dispute of any kind. However, the borrower has a small dispute currently running with a distributor in the United States. The bank suggests the representation remains, but that the borrower lists exact details of the dispute in a disclosure letter. The bank considers the letter and decides that the dispute is in fact trivial, and the loan may go ahead. The representation has therefore served its purpose by exposing the dispute, and allowing the bank to dismiss it as inconsequential to lending. If, however, the agreement provides that the representations are deemed repeated then any new dispute, even although it may be as inconsequential as the first, will cause a default. The disclosure letter is effective only in the first instance.

A borrower will sometimes ask for the representations to be qualified with, 'to the best of our knowledge and belief'. Whilst this might at first sight seem quite reasonable, it confounds the true purpose of the representations, which is to lay the risk of unknown problems on the borrower rather than the bank. The qualification is therefore acceptable to banks only in very limited circumstances (eg, with respect to knowledge of threatened legal proceedings or market information) and may carry the caveat 'after due and careful enquiry'.

Borrowers may want to negotiate a materiality qualification to many of the representations. This is largely a question of risk allocation between the banks and the borrower. The borrower should ensure any materiality qualification will not make a representation too uncertain to be given (using a minimum monetary amount, where appropriate, can help). A borrower should also check whether representations are given in relation to just itself, or whether they also include a defined 'group' or even all its subsidiaries. Is it able to give what is required, or should the representation be limited, for example, to 'Material Subsidiaries'?

Lastly, a borrower should be careful about any information it provides during negotiations. If the information is false, it may be liable for misrepresentation under general law in addition to any sanctions in the facility agreement (see **5.5**).

5.5 REPRESENTATIONS IN CONTRACT LAW

5.5.1 Representations

A representation is a statement of fact, made to induce the party to whom it is addressed to enter into a contract. The statement may be oral or written, and if it is drafted into the contract it also becomes a term of that contract. If the statement is untrue, it constitutes misrepresentation. The due diligence process (see **2.2**) will inevitably involve the borrower in making numerous representations. If a borrower makes a false statement during negotiations, when might it be actionable by the bank under the general law?

5.5.1.1 Misrepresentation Act 1967

The right to claim for contractual misrepresentation is governed by the Misrepresentation Act 1967 (as amended). A claim will be recognised only if the misrepresentation was of a material fact, was intended to induce a party to contract, and did induce the party to contract. The Act effectively places misrepresentations into two categories, one of which is sub-divided.

Fraudulent misrepresentation

A misrepresentation is fraudulent where it is made knowingly, or without any belief in its truth, or recklessly. The test is subjective, ie what did the maker truly believe?

Non-fraudulent misrepresentation

If the maker honestly believed the statement he made was true, the misrepresentation is not fraudulent. Non-fraudulent misrepresentation may be one of two types:

(a) *Negligent misrepresentation.* Negligent misrepresentation presumes that a representation was made negligently. The test here is objective, ie the 'reasonable man' type test.

(b) *Innocent misrepresentation.* If the maker can show that he had reasonable grounds to believe his statement was true, then s 2(1) says the misrepresentation will be innocent.

If the borrower makes a true statement but then learns before the loan document is executed that it has ceased to be true, it must notify the bank or it may be liable for misrepresentation.

5.5.1.2 Remedies for misrepresentation

The reason for categorising misrepresentation is that each category allows a slightly different remedy.

Rescission

Whatever form the misrepresentation takes, the innocent party has a prima facie right to rescind the contract he was induced to enter. Rescission aims to put the parties back into their pre-contractual position. The right to rescind may be lost in two particular circumstances.

First, s 2(2) of the Misrepresentation Act 1967 (as amended) gives a court the discretion to award damages instead of rescission in non-fraudulent cases. The court may exercise this discretion if it feels that the remedy of rescission is too drastic in the circumstances, particularly since the misrepresentation was not fraudulent. The court will lose this discretion if the right to rescind has been lost (see below).

Secondly, rescission is an equitable remedy and will not be available if, for example:

(a)   it is impossible to restore the pre-contractual position;

(b)   bona fide third party rights have been acquired;

(c)   the innocent party, knowing of the misrepresentation, takes action affirming the agreement; or

(d)   there is undue delay in seeking relief.

Damages

If the misrepresentation is innocent but not negligent, there is no right to damages. Damages may, however, be awarded in lieu of rescission as long as the right to rescind is not lost to an equitable bar (see above).

Negligent misrepresentation and fraudulent misrepresentation both entitle the innocent party to damages, under the Misrepresentation Act 1967, s 2(1) and the tort of deceit respectively. In both cases, however, any damages will be on a tortious basis and, therefore, a bank would get no compensation for loss of bargain or profit (see *Smith New Court Securities Ltd v Scrimgeour Vickers (Asset Management) Ltd* [1997] AC 254, HL, for a comprehensive guide to determining damages for fraudulent representation inducing a plaintiff to buy property).

5.5.1.3   *Hedley Byrne & Co Ltd v Heller & Partners Ltd* [1964] AC 465

There is a claim for negligent misstatement in the law of tort, based on the judgment in *Hedley Byrne v Heller*. This depends on there being a relationship between two parties that gives rise to a duty of care. This might occur, for example, if the borrower's in-house accountant provided information to a bank. The rule in *Hedley Byrne v Heller* is, however, eclipsed by the Misrepresentation Act 1967 in a situation of inducement to contract, because the onus of proof in the latter is more favourable to a claimant. The tortious claim is therefore of little relevance in the context of bank lending (other than in a claim for losses where a contract had never actually been signed).

5.5.2   Application to a facility agreement

Whilst the most important remedies for misleading and inaccurate information are built into the facility agreement, the general law of representations does have an application.

It should be clear by now that a borrower would be hard pressed not to make oral and written representations in the negotiations leading to executing a facility agreement. If any of those statements is untrue, the bank may have a claim for misrepresentation, which has the advantage over a simple event of default of applying even if the facility agreement is void.

SUMMARY

The end product of a bank's due diligence process is the inclusion of representations, to be made by the borrower, in the loan document. The purpose of the representations is threefold. First, while the loan is being negotiated, they will force the borrower to disclose information and discuss problems. Secondly, after execution of the loan, the bank will not be obliged to lend unless the representations are (materially) correct. Lastly, once money has been lent, a breach of representation will allow the bank to pursue the remedies provided by the facility agreement, which ultimately includes demanding repayment (see **Chapter 8**).

CHAPTER 6

A REVIEW OF COMPANY ACCOUNTS

6.1	Introduction	59
6.2	Financial statements	59
6.3	The balance sheet	60
6.4	Profit and loss account	65
6.5	Directors' report, auditor's report, and notes to the accounts	68
6.6	Cash flow statements	69
6.7	Consolidated accounts	69
6.8	Management accounts	70
6.9	Accounting regulations	70
	Summary	73

'Fear is that little darkroom where negatives are developed.'

Michael Pritchard

6.1 INTRODUCTION

Chapter 4 considered some of the more important operative provisions at the beginning of a loan document. **Chapter 5** concentrated on how a bank gleans information concerning a borrower. This chapter 'steps back' from the loan document to provide a basic review of company accounts.

Most readers will now protest earnestly that they want to be lawyers, not accountants, which is why they are reading these pages in the first place. However, the most hotly negotiated area of a facility agreement, apart from the events of default, is the financial covenants. Whilst this is an area in which the commercial judgement of clients and expertise of accountants tend to outweigh any legal considerations, no banking solicitor can feel entirely comfortable producing a document where a whole section is beyond his comprehension. Furthermore, to fully understand a business you must understand its accounts. A basic grasp of company accounts is therefore essential. The following summary is not intended to be highly technical, specialised, or comprehensive, but a broad introduction.

The observations in this chapter are based on UK GAAP, a compilation of legislation, accounting standards and accepted practice. However, comparison is made with the International Financial Reporting Standards (IFRS) on key issues and terminology; and in any event, the UK regime is increasingly converging with IFRS principles. European listed companies must now publish *consolidated* accounts under the IFRS (sometimes referred to as International Accounting Standards or 'IAS') pursuant to EU Regulation No 1606/2002.

6.2 FINANCIAL STATEMENTS

Why is a company required to produce accounts? The requirement was originally driven by the principle that members should know how the directors are running their company. Under ss 394–396 of the CA 2006, a company's directors must provide the following financial statements for its shareholders:

(a)   a balance sheet (as at the last day of the company's accounting period); and

(b)   a profit and loss account,

and, under UK GAAP, a cash flow statement (see **6.6**).

These statements must be delivered to members (and registered at the Companies Registry) once a year, and so are often known as 'annual accounts'. Under s 442 of the CA 2006, they must be produced no later than nine months (or six months for public companies – four months if listed on the London Stock Exchange – see the Disclosure and Transparency Rules, DTR 4.1.3) after the end of the company's financial year, accompanied by a directors' report and an auditor's report (see **6.5**). Parent companies must produce group accounts: a consolidated balance sheet and consolidated profit and loss account (see **6.6**).

Although originally intended to keep members informed, the annual accounts are also an essential reference for potential lenders to, and would-be investors in, a company. What information do these financial statements provide?

6.3   THE BALANCE SHEET

6.3.1   What does it show?

In broad terms, a company will raise money to fund its business from two sources:

(a)   lenders (including, for these purposes, anyone allowing the company credit, ie time to pay a debt); and

(b)   shareholders:

(i)   from money they paid for shares, and/or

(ii)   from profits made by the company, which directors retain to invest in the company instead of distributing to the shareholders.

It follows that, once a company has paid back all its debts, anything which remains belongs to the shareholders. To calculate what their share in the company is worth, therefore, the shareholders need to know exactly what assets their company owns, and how much money it owes. This is what a balance sheet shows. A balance sheet is written as a vertical list, and so the equation becomes:

ASSETS

less

LIABILITIES

=

SHAREHOLDERS' FUNDS

This is why a balance sheet will always balance. If a company's assets decrease in value there will be less money left for shareholders once the liabilities are paid off; thus the shareholders' funds will reduce, balancing the equation. The top half of a balance sheet will always equal the bottom half.

If a small company were to list its assets and liabilities, it might look something like this:

EXAMPLE 1

Balance sheet as at 31 December 2013

	£	£	£
ASSETS			
Word processors	1,000		
Money at bank	600		
Delivery van	3,500		
Warehouse	8,000		
Money owed by customers	350		
Unsold stock	3,000		
Petty cash	175		
Licence	1,500		
TOTAL		18,125	
	£	£	£
LIABILITIES			
Long-term loan	6,000		
Overdraft	460		
Money owed to creditors	1,150		
TOTAL		7,610	
TOTAL OF ASSETS LESS LIABILITIES			10,515
CAPITAL AND RESERVES			
Called-up capital			5,500
Share premium account			1,500
Profit and loss account (reserves)			3,515
TOTAL			10,515

6.3.2 Grouping of assets and liabilities

The example at **6.3.1** is essentially correct, but in practice the published accounts will show assets and liabilities in groups, and list a total value for that group, rather than list them individually. The groups will usually be as follows.

6.3.2.1 Fixed assets

Fixed assets (known as 'non-current assets' under IFRS) are assets a company intends to retain on a fairly permanent basis. In the example at **6.3.1** this will include the word processors, the van, and the warehouse. Essentially, these are assets which the company needs to run its business. They may not be easily or quickly realisable. Fixed assets are sub-divided into 'tangible' (such as those listed above), 'intangible' (such as licences, patents, copyrights or acquired goodwill) and 'investments' (such as long-term shareholdings in other companies).

6.3.2.2 Current assets

Current assets are cash and other assets which a company expects to turn into cash in the ordinary course of its business (usually within 12 months). It is these liquid assets that the company intends to use to pay its short-term liabilities. The current assets therefore form part of the company's 'working capital', essential for maintaining its liquidity (see **3.2.1**). Current assets will include any stock which the company holds, money owed by customers (debtors) and any cash. Current assets are usually listed in order of permanence.

6.3.2.3   Current liabilities

Current liabilities are liabilities which the company must pay within 12 months of the balance sheet date. They are usually labelled in a balance sheet as 'Creditors: amounts falling due within one year'. They will include most trade creditors and any short-term loans, including any overdraft facility and any repayments of long-term loans falling due (see **3.2.1**). Current liabilities would also include any dividend declared but unpaid (eg, because it is awaiting shareholder approval).

6.3.2.4   Long-term liabilities

Long-term liabilities are liabilities which the company need not settle until more than 12 months after the balance sheet date, for example long-term loans. They are usually labelled as 'Creditors: amounts falling due after more than one year'.

6.3.3   Bank's balance sheet

The majority of assets on the balance sheet of a commercial bank will be loans it has made to customers and other banks. Conversely, its key liabilities will be deposits by customers and other banks. A typical commercial bank balance sheet is set out below by way of illustration.

As at 31st December	Notes	2010 £m	2009 £m
Assets			
Cash and balances at central banks		**97,630**	81,483
Items in the course of collection from other banks		**1,384**	1,593
Trading portfolio assets	12	**168,867**	151,344
Financial assets designated at fair value	13	**41,485**	42,568
Derivative financial instruments	14	**420,319**	416,815
Loans and advances to banks	15	**37,799**	41,135
Loans and advances to customers	15	**427,942**	420,224
Reverse repurchase agreements and other similar secured lending	17	**205,772**	143,431
Available for sale financial investments	16	**65,110**	56,483
Current tax assets	9	**196**	349
Prepayments, accrued income and other assets		**5,269**	6,358
Investments in associates and joint ventures	18	**518**	422
Goodwill and intangible assets	19	**8,697**	8,795
Property, plant and equipment	20	**6,140**	5,626
Deferred tax assets	9	**2,517**	2,303
Total assets		**1,489,645**	1,378,929
Liabilities			
Deposits from banks		**77,975**	76,446
Items in the course of collection due to other banks		**1,321**	1,466
Customer accounts		**345,788**	322,429
Repurchase agreements and other similar secured borrowing	17	**225,534**	198,781
Trading portfolio liabilities	12	**72,693**	51,252
Financial liabilities designated at fair value	21	**97,729**	87,881
Derivative financial instruments	14	**405,516**	403,416
Debt securities in issue		**156,623**	135,902
Accruals, deferred income and other liabilities	22	**13,233**	14,241
Current tax liabilities	9	**646**	992
Subordinated liabilities	23	**28,499**	25,816
Deferred tax liabilities	9	**514**	470
Provisions	24	**947**	590
Retirement benefit liabilities	28	**365**	769
Total liabilities		**1,427,383**	1,320,451
Shareholders' equity			
Shareholders' equity excluding non-controlling interests		**50,858**	47,277
Non-controlling interests	31	**11,404**	11,201
Total shareholders' equity		**62,262**	58,478
Total liabilities and shareholders' equity		**1,489,645**	1,378,929

6.3.4   Ordering of assets and liabilities

Rather than simply listing the groups of assets and then subtracting all the liabilities (as in Example 1 at **6.3.1**), a balance sheet re-orders these items slightly. First, it will list the groups of fixed assets. It will then show the current assets and the current liabilities, then deduct the latter from the former to show 'net current assets' (or 'liabilities'). This provides an indication of whether the company can cover short-term liabilities with its current assets.

Finally, the long-term liabilities are listed and then subtracted from the above figure to give a total value for the company once all its liabilities have been paid. This is the amount which belongs to the shareholders, and would be returned to them if the company was wound up at that point. Thus the re-written balance sheet from Example 1 would look like this:

EXAMPLE 2

Balance sheet as at 31 December 2013

	£	£	£
FIXED ASSETS			
Tangible assets	12,500		
Intangible assets	1,500		
CURRENT ASSETS			14,000
Stock	3,000		
Debtors	350		
Cash at bank and in hand	775		
		4,125	
LESS CREDITORS: amounts falling due within one year			
Trade creditors	1,150		
Bank overdraft	460		
		1,610	
NET CURRENT ASSETS			2,515
TOTAL ASSETS LESS CURRENT LIABILITIES			16,515
LESS CREDITORS: amounts falling due after more than one year			
Borrowings			6,000
NET ASSETS			10,515
CAPITAL AND RESERVES			
Called-up capital			5,500
Share premium			1,500
Retained profit			3,515
			10,515

Some balance sheets will present the equation in a different order:

Assets = Shareholders' funds (ie capital and reserves) plus liabilities

This is the format required under IFRS.

6.3.5 Capital and reserves

As explained at **6.3.4**, the top part of the balance sheet calculates a figure representing all the company's assets less all the debts it owes (in Example 2, that figure is £10,515). These are the 'shareholders' funds' referred to at **6.3.1** – the amount which would be paid back to shareholders if the company were wound up. The bottom part of the balance sheet, headed 'Capital and reserves', takes the figure representing shareholders' funds and shows how it is comprised.

6.3.5.1 Share capital

This is the total amount of money which shareholders have invested in the company through buying shares. It is divided into:

(a)   called-up share capital, ie the nominal value of the shares which has either been paid by the shareholders, or called to be paid ('nominal' or 'par' value is the value attributed to shares when they are first issued, usually £1); and

(b)   share premium, ie any amount paid for the issued shares over and above their nominal value.

6.3.5.2   Retained profit

This is profit which directors have, over time, retained in the company instead of distributing it to shareholders. The retained profit entry (known as 'retained earnings' under IFRS) is part of a company's 'reserves' (see also revaluation reserve at **6.3.7**). These amounts are not represented by money held in an account or by specific assets; they are simply retained value in the company.

6.3.6   Restrictions on disposal of assets

One of the reasons for splitting the shareholders' funds into categories showing their origins is that there is statutory control over the value of assets which must remain in a company to meet creditors' claims. Essentially, ss 641–653 of the CA 2006 prohibit a company from returning the money paid for its shares to the shareholders (other than under very restricted circumstances), theoretically maintaining a minimum value of assets in the company to meet the demands of creditors. The amounts of paid-up share capital and premium are shown separately because the restrictions on disposing of assets representing the value of the latter are slightly less than for the former.

EXAMPLE 3

The rules outlined above can be illustrated using the figures from Example 2 (see **6.3.4**). On the current figures, the company may pay up to £3,515 to its shareholders because this figure simply represents profits that the directors decided not to distribute at an earlier date. However, the company must keep sufficient assets so that (once all its liabilities are paid off) there is £7,000 worth of assets remaining. Of that £7,000, however, £1,500 is share premium. In limited circumstances (see CA 2006, s 610), for example funding scrip issues (effectively turning premium into share capital), or writing off expenses of issuing shares (instead of reducing the retained profit reserve), assets representing that premium may be disposed of and, in the second example, the value of the company's assets may be reduced to £5,500.

Thus the different categories into which the capital and reserves are divided show the value of assets which cannot be returned to shareholders ('non-distributable' reserves) and the value which may be disposed of freely, or under restricted circumstances.

6.3.7   Miscellaneous

Having reviewed the fundamental aspects of the balance sheet, there are a number of other matters which commonly occur, and which may be conveniently dealt with at this point.

6.3.7.1   Revaluation

Tangible assets are initially recorded on the company's balance sheet at cost. In time, that value is likely to become inaccurate because the assets have depreciated (see **6.3.7.2**) or more rarely appreciated. If its tangible fixed assets have appreciated, a company is permitted, but not usually required, to revalue them at market value in the balance sheet. Upward revaluation on the balance sheet increases the net assets figure. This in turn means the shareholders' funds will increase, which must be shown under the capital and reserves. The increase cannot be included in the retained profit reserve in the balance sheet, however, because it is only an estimation of the assets' extra worth. It is shown as a separate line in the accounts labelled 'revaluation reserve', which indicates that it is not yet an amount of shareholders' funds which may be distributed. (The exception is if the gain reverses revaluation losses on the same asset which were previously deducted from the retained profit amount.)

The main advantage of upward revaluation to a company is that a higher net asset value usually increases borrowing power and improves the debt to equity ratio (see **7.4.3**). The disadvantage is that the shareholders might expect a higher return. Any charge to depreciation will be based on the increased asset value.

6.3.7.2 Depreciation

Whilst upward revaluation is optional, UK GAAP requires that all fixed assets which have a limited useful economic life must be depreciated. The exact method of depreciation, as well as the estimation of useful economic life, are decisions for the company (although fundamentally covered by FRS 15 – see **6.9.2**). The effect of depreciation is to reduce the net recorded value of the asset shown on the balance sheet. Charging depreciation will therefore reduce profits in the profit and loss account (see **6.4**), which in turn reduces the retained profit figure in the balance sheet.

6.3.7.3 Provisions

Provisions are amounts which are set aside out of a company's profits to cover 'a present obligation as a result of a past event for which it is probable that a transfer of economic benefits will be required' (FRS 12). They are used to ensure a cost is charged against the relevant period for calculating profit, even if it has not yet been paid. Provisions will commonly be made for deferred tax, pension costs and structural changes. They will appear in the balance sheet as a form of liability, usually as 'provisions for liabilities and charges'. Provisions will reduce the profits in the profit and loss account (see **6.4**), which in turn reduces the retained profit figure in the balance sheet.

6.3.8 'Snapshot'

The balance sheet is always given 'as at' a certain day. This is because a list of everything owned, and everything owed, can be accurate only at one given moment in time: the list will change each time an asset is disposed of, or a new liability incurred. The balance sheet is therefore often said to provide a 'snapshot' of the company's assets.

6.3.9 International Financial Reporting Standards

International Financial Reporting Standards also require a balance sheet to be drawn up with concepts similar to UK GAAP, although assets and liabilities are divided into 'current' and 'non-current', and they may be recorded at cost less depreciation and other losses or at their 'fair value' at each balance sheet date. Reduction in value of an asset is known as 'impairment'. The method for measuring ongoing 'fair value' will depend on the type of asset (eg, see IAS 39 for financial instruments, IAS 16 for property, plant and equipment). For property, plant and equipment, IAS 16 defines 'fair value' as 'The amount for which an asset could be exchanged, or a liability settled, between knowledgeable, willing parties in an arm's length transaction'.

6.4 PROFIT AND LOSS ACCOUNT

6.4.1 Introduction

The retained profit figure on a balance sheet has already been explained at **6.3.5**. Essentially, it shows profit that a company has made but which the directors have not distributed to the shareholders. This figure is a cumulative total of retained profit (less any losses) from year to year since the company started trading. A shareholder could compare a retained profit figure with the previous year to find any increase or decrease in the total. However, a shareholder really needs a breakdown to show exactly how the company made a profit, or loss, in a particular year. This gives rise to the second financial statement required by the CA 2006, the 'profit and loss account'. For brevity, the profit and loss accounting statement is referred to in the remainder of this chapter as the P&L account.

6.4.2   Period of a P&L account

Whilst the balance sheet is an inventory of assets and liabilities, and so has to be made at a specific date, the profit or loss that a company makes must be calculated over a specific period. The P&L account required by the CA 2006 calculates the profit, or loss, made over a period (generally 12 months) ending with the date of the balance sheet. There is, however, nothing to prevent a company's directors from drawing up a P&L account for a different period (see **6.5**).

6.4.3   Structure of a P&L account

The P&L account might be more accurately named the 'profit or loss' account, because it shows whether a company has made a profit or a loss over a period. The calculation is very straightforward: income less expenses. The income shown in a P&L account is income generated by the company's business activities, and does not include its share capital or loan monies. The expenses shown are expenses of a 'revenue' nature (ie, day-to-day costs of running the business), and do not include 'capital' expenses (such as plant and machinery).

In order to analyse a company's profit or loss, it is convenient to consider its trading in two stages:

(a)   The profit made on buying-in or manufacturing, and then selling the products of the business. This is essentially the money a company raises by selling its products over a period (its 'turnover'), less the price it paid for them. If the company manufactures its products, then the direct costs of producing the products as well as the cost of the raw materials must be deducted from turnover. This figure is known as the 'gross profit'. If a company is making a loss at this stage it is in serious trouble.

(b)   From gross profit, a company must then deduct all the general overheads of running the business, for example advertising costs, administration expenses, etc. This will produce a figure known as the 'net profit'.

The structure of a P&L account reflects the two stages outlined above. It will consist of:

(a)   *Trading (or manufacturing) account.* The first few lines of the P&L account, which calculate gross profit. The calculation is usually shown in more detail, particularly in the case of a manufacturing account, in a separate financial statement as part of the management accounts (see **6.8**); and

(b)   *Profit and loss account.* The main part of the P&L account showing the general expenses of the business to be deducted from gross profit to produce the net profit.

EXAMPLE 4

Profit and loss account for the year ended 31 December 2013

	£	£	£
Turnover	110,000		
Cost of sales	58,000		
Gross profit		52,000	
ADMINISTRATION			
Salaries	31,000		
Stationery	240		
Telephone	930		
Electricity	576		
Auditors	325		
General Expenses	925		
	33,996		
SALES			
Advertising	4,300		
Carriage	1,105		
	5,405		
FINANCIAL			
Interest	1,670		
Professional fees	215		
Bad debts	350		
Depreciation	645		
	2,880		
TOTAL EXPENSES		42,281	
NET PROFIT on ordinary activities before TAXATION		9,719	
TAXATION		2,517	
PROFIT on ordinary activities after TAXATION		7,202	
Extraordinary items		2,405	
		4,797	
Dividends			3,000
Retained profit for the year			1,797
Retained profit brought forward			1,718
Retained profit carried forward			3,515

6.4.4 Points to note on the P&L account

6.4.4.1 Turnover

Turnover is the total amount of money the business has taken from sales over the previous 12 months.

6.4.4.2 Cost of sales

Cost of sales is the basic cost to the company of buying the products which were sold during the year. To calculate the cost of the stock which was sold, the account will add the cost of stock held at the start of the year (opening stock) to the cost of stock acquired during the year, and then subtract any stock unsold at the end of the year (closing stock). For example, a company starts the year with stock costing £1,000, spends another £4,500 buying stock during the year, but has stock costing £2,300 left at the end of the year. The total cost of stock held *during* the year is:

$$£1,000 + £4,500 = £5,500.$$

However, the cost of stock *remaining* is £2,300. That means stock costing £5,500 – £2,300 = £3,200 was sold during the year.

If the business makes the products which it sells, the 'cost of sales' becomes 'cost of manufacture'. If the company is in the service industry, a similar calculation will be required to ascertain the cost of providing the service.

6.4.4.3   Net profit

In the P&L account, 'net profit' is gross profit less all expenses of the business. In one sense, this is a true measure of the profit the directors have managed to make for the year. The more efficiently the business is run, the lower expenses will be and the higher the net profit figure. Whilst tax deductions are still to be shown, those are effectively beyond the directors' control.

6.4.4.4   'Extraordinary' and 'exceptional' items

Historically, under SSAP 6 (see **6.9.2.1** for SSAPs), the P&L account had to reveal any 'extraordinary' and 'exceptional' items. 'Extraordinary' items were those outside the ordinary activities of the company and not expected to recur regularly or frequently; 'exceptional' items were those within the ordinary activities of the company which had to be disclosed as a separate item, due to their size or occurrence, to maintain a 'true and fair view' (see **6.5**). However, SSAP 6 has been superseded by FRS 3, and whilst the definitions of 'extraordinary' and 'exceptional' items remain largely the same, their interpretation has changed. Most items will now fall within the definition of 'ordinary' activities or 'exceptional' items, and the term 'extraordinary' items is practically redundant. Typical examples of 'exceptional' items include reorganisation costs, the disposal of a subsidiary, and profits or losses on disposal of material fixed assets.

6.4.4.5   Dividends and retained profit

Once any tax, extraordinary or exceptional items have been deducted from the net profit, there will be a final figure representing a profit or a loss made from the company's trading throughout the year. If the figure shows a profit, the directors must decide whether it should be used to pay a dividend to the shareholders, or retained in the company as investment.

The P&L account also shows a figure (either on the face of the accounts or in the notes) for 'retained profit carried forward'. This is the total of any profit which has been retained throughout the company's life, less any losses which have been absorbed. When this total is added to the profit (or absorbs the loss) for the year of the P&L account, the result is the figure appearing as the 'profit and loss account' at the bottom of a balance sheet (see **6.3.5**). It is the total retained profit as at the date of the balance sheet.

6.4.5   International Financial Reporting Standards

Under IFRS the P&L account is known as an 'income statement'. IFRS does not use the definitions 'extraordinary' or 'exceptional', but does require 'material items' (of income or expense) to be shown on a separate line of the income statement in order to draw attention to them. In most other respects IFRS is similar to UK GAAP in this area.

6.5   DIRECTORS' REPORT, AUDITOR'S REPORT, AND NOTES TO THE ACCOUNTS

The CA 2006 (s 415) requires the directors of a company to include a report with the annual accounts. This normally appears before the balance sheet and P&L account. There are prescribed items to be summarised in the directors' report, although they are usually dealt with in minimal detail. These items include the principal activities of the company, any changes in the business through the year, any anticipated changes in the business, recommended dividends, charitable and political donations, the directors' names and any interests they have in the company's shares or debentures.

Annual accounts will require certification by the company's auditors. This appears as a report to the members immediately after the directors' report. If the auditors are satisfied with the accounts (they will want to see more than just the P&L account and balance sheet – eg, a cash flow statement and statement of gains and losses) their report will be very brief, and their opinion for a UK listed company might typically be worded:

> In our opinion the financial statements give a true and fair view, in accordance with IFRS as adopted by the European Union as applied in accordance with the Companies Act 2006, of the state of affairs of the Company at ... (date of balance sheet) ... and cash flows for the financial year then ended and the financial statements and part of the directors' remuneration report to be audited have been properly prepared in accordance with the Companies Act 2006. The information given in the directors' report is consistent with the financial statements.

If the auditors are not happy with some aspect of the accounts, they must 'qualify' their report by clearly stating any problems they have discovered. Any such qualification is potentially damaging to a company because it will suggest the financial statements are not reliable. A bank may insist that a material qualification to the accounts will trigger an event of default (see **8.3**).

Lastly, the accounts will invariably include notes, cross-referring to a numbering system against certain entries in the P&L and balance sheet. These notes to the accounts break down the figures on the face of the accounts, providing detailed information on performance and accounting policies adopted by the company.

6.6 CASH FLOW STATEMENTS

As well as Companies Act requirements to produce a balance sheet and P&L account, FRS 1 (Revised 1996) requires companies to produce a cash flow statement. A cash flow statement will show the source of cash coming into a business (from operating activities, from investments and from raising share capital and borrowings), and the destination of cash going out, over a period (typically the accounting year). The cash flow statement is created by taking the net profit figure from the P&L account and adjusting it by adding back any non-cash deductions and then taking account of any other cash movements not reflected in that net profit figure. For example, the P&L account will have deducted depreciation on fixed assets to calculate the net profit figure. However, depreciation does not represent real cash spent, and so that amount will be added back to the net profit figure. Once all other items of cash inflow or outflow are included (that were not included in calculating the net profit figure), the end result shows whether the company generated more cash than it spent over the period, or vice versa. Lenders usually prefer using the cash flow statement to set financial covenants because it is a much better indicator of the company's 'health' than net profit which is subject to accounting fictions such as accruals and non-cash elements.

An IFRS-based cash flow statement should be near identical to the UK GAAP version.

6.7 CONSOLIDATED ACCOUNTS

When a company has one or more 'subsidiary undertakings', it must produce combined accounts for itself and its subsidiaries, known as 'consolidated accounts' (or 'group accounts'). Essentially, under s 1162 of the CA 2006, a 'subsidiary undertaking' is a company (or partnership, or unincorporated association) in which the parent:

(a)   has a majority of the voting rights; or

(b)   is a member and has the right to appoint or remove a majority of its board of directors; or

(c)   has the right to exercise a dominant influence:

    (i)   by virtue of provisions in the undertaking's memorandum or articles, or

    (ii)   by virtue of a control contract; or

(d)   is a member, and controls a majority of the voting rights through an agreement with other members; and

(e)   an undertaking is a parent undertaking in relation to another undertaking, a subsidiary undertaking, if:

    (i)   it has power to exercise or actually exercises a dominant influence or control over it, or

    (ii)   it is managed on a unified basis with the subsidiary undertaking.

The requirement for consolidated accounts is based on the premise that a parent company's business is likely to be closely linked with that of any subsidiary undertaking. The shareholders of the parent should therefore be provided with financial information on the whole group.

A subsidiary undertaking must continue to produce its own balance sheet and profit and loss account. A parent producing consolidated accounts must produce its own balance sheet, but is not obliged to (and usually will not) publish its own profit and loss account.

Consolidated accounts are usually produced by the parent company's directors to the same year end as the parent's accounts, and comprise a consolidated balance sheet, profit and loss account and cash flow statement. The parent and subsidiary undertakings must also reveal each other's identity in the notes to their individual accounts. The exemption from producing accounts which applies to small and medium-sized companies (see **6.9.1**) also applies to the obligation to produce consolidated accounts.

From 2005, European listed companies must produce their consolidated accounts in accordance with the IFRS (see **6.9.4** for more detail).

6.8   MANAGEMENT ACCOUNTS

Management accounts are financial summaries produced from time to time by a company's directors. They may be a breakdown of figures within the balance sheet and P&L accounts (eg, a manufacturing account), they may be financial projections, or they may be an interim balance sheet or P&L account drawn up over a period of one month or more. The board will use the management accounts to monitor the business through its financial year, and help it to make changes and predictions. They may, for example, use them to decide whether to declare an interim dividend.

Unlike final accounts, management accounts do not have to be shown to the shareholders, or lodged at the Companies Registry. Whether a bank has sight of management accounts will depend on the size of the borrower and its relationship with the bank. A borrower will usually be reluctant to provide management accounts: the detail they provide makes them very sensitive, since they may expose information which is hidden behind the broad approach of the published accounts. Any disclosure will often be subject to a confidentiality undertaking.

6.9   ACCOUNTING REGULATIONS

Having reviewed the basic form of company accounts, this chapter concludes with a summary of the regulations which govern them.

There are three main sources of UK regulation affecting company accounts:

(a)   the CA 2006;

(b)   SSAPs and FRSs; and

(c)   the UKLA's 'Listing Rules'.

Together with accepted accounting practices, these form 'UK GAAP' (Generally Accepted Accounting Practice).

6.9.1   Companies Act 2006

The CA 2006 requires the directors of every company to produce a balance sheet and P&L account for each financial year (ss 394–396). It also requires a directors' report (s 415) and auditors' report (s 495) to accompany the accounts (see also **6.5**). The Act then provides a range of rules relating to the content of those accounts, and the format in which they must be presented.

The CA 2006 also requires copies of the accounts and reports to be:

(a)   sent to every member, debenture holder, and anyone entitled to receive notice of general meetings (s 423). This must be done at least 21 days before (b) below,

(b)   laid before the company at a general meeting (unless, in the case of a private company, this requirement is dispensed with by elective resolution); and

(c)   delivered to the Registrar of Companies, for publication.

The requirements at (b) and (c) must both be satisfied within nine months of the financial year end in the case of a private company, and within six months if a public company (four months if a UK listed company).

From 1 April 2008, the CA 2006 also requires quoted companies to publish their annual accounts and reports on a website (s 430).

6.9.1.1   'Small' and 'medium-sized' companies

Delivering accounts

In the case of 'small' and 'medium-sized' companies, the requirement to deliver accounts to the Registrar is modified. 'Medium-sized' companies may provide the Registrar with an abbreviated P&L account. 'Small' companies need not provide the Registrar with a P&L account, and may send an abbreviated balance sheet. They may also have a reduced directors' report. The parameters for qualifying as a 'small or medium-sized' company (which is estimated to include around 90% of British companies) are currently (CA 2006, s 382 and s 466):

		'Small'	'Medium'
1.	'Turnover' not more than	£6.5m	£25.9m*
2.	'Balance sheet total' not more than	£3.26m	£12.9m*
3.	Average employees not more than	50	250

*net of group transactions

Any two criteria must be satisfied.

Auditing requirements

Some 'small' companies can also qualify for full or partial exemptions from auditing their accounts under the CA 2006. Under s 477, a company is totally exempt from auditing its accounts in a given financial year if:

(a)   it qualifies as a 'small' company for that year under s 382 of the CA 2006;

(b)   its 'turnover' for that year does not exceed £6.5m; and

(c)   its 'balance sheet total' for that year does not exceed £3.26m.

In addition, under s 482, a company which is a 'non-profit-making' company may enjoy exemption provided it is subject to a form of 'public' audit.

(Certain types of company are excluded from these exemptions, for example public companies, banking or insurance companies, and any company which is a parent company or subsidiary undertaking.)

6.9.1.2   True and fair view

There is a fundamental requirement under the CA 2006 that the accounts should provide a 'true and fair view'. This principle overrides all others. It is primarily the directors' responsibility to ensure that the accounts give a true and fair view, although it must also be addressed in the auditor's report (see **6.5**). Under the IFRS, the equivalent concept is 'fair presentation'.

6.9.2   SSAPs and FRSs

6.9.2.1   Harmonisation

Whilst the CA 2006 provides some regulation as to the content and format of company accounts, it still leaves companies with a wide choice in compiling the detail of their accounts. Apart from any other considerations, this makes comparison between companies' results very difficult. In order to overcome this problem, the largest accounting bodies decided to create a number of statements for particular areas of accounting which outlined the basis on which their members would prepare company accounts. The process began in 1971 with (prepare for acronym overload) the Accounting Standards Committee (ASC) producing Statements of Standard Accounting Practice (SSAPs). In 1990, the task of producing standards fell to the Accounting Standards Board (ASB) and from 1 July 2012 it moved to the Financial Reporting Council (FRC). The ASB, and now the FRC, adopted the original SSAPs, but are gradually updating or replacing them with their own standards, known as Financial Reporting Standards (FRSs).

6.9.2.2   Legal effect

A number of the SSAPs were considered so fundamental that they were given statutory effect by the Companies Acts. However, the SSAPs and FRSs do not generally have any authority other than with accountancy bodies requiring their members to follow them. Since every company must have its accounts audited, the auditor will be forced to record any variation from the SSAPs or FRSs in his report. Effectively, this ensures that a company usually follows the statements, with any deviation being made known in the accounts. In the international arena, the equivalents are 'International Accounting Standards' (IAS), originally created as an academic exercise to provide 'globally' applicable accounting standards, now being gradually replaced by IFRS.

6.9.3   The Listing, Disclosure and Transparency Rules

The UKLA's Listing, Disclosure and Transparency Rules impose some additional accounting requirements on London-listed companies. First, the Listing Rules require listed companies to prepare their annual report and accounts in accordance with the company's national law and in all material respects with national accounting standards or IFRS (LR 9.8.2R).

The information to be included in the listed company's annual report and accounts is outlined by LR 9.8.4. DTR 4.1 requires the annual report to be published within four months of the financial year end. DTR 4.2 requires a half-yearly (unaudited) financial report to be published no later than two months after the period to which it relates.

6.9.4   Summary accounts

Lastly, s 426 of the CA 2006 allows a listed company to substitute a summary of its full annual accounts for sending to consenting members. This is to avoid the expense of sending a full account, but the proviso is that the members retain the right to receive the full accounts on request.

SUMMARY

(1)   The balance sheet lists all a company's assets, and deducts all its liabilities. The value then remaining belongs to the shareholders. The assets and liabilities fluctuate, and so the calculation can be made only for a particular day (a 'snapshot'), usually the company's year end.

(2)   The P&L account, or 'Income Statement' under IFRS, shows a company's income over the 12 months immediately before the balance sheet date. It then subtracts all expenses of the business over that period to show the profit or loss the company has made. That figure is then combined with any previous retained profit and the total is the retained profit figure at the bottom of the balance sheet.

(3)   The cash flow statement shows all the cash brought into the company less all the cash spent by the company over the same period as the P&L account.

(4)   The balance sheet, P&L and cash flow statement must be prepared annually by the directors in order to show the shareholders how their company has been run. They are also deposited at the Companies Registry and are an invaluable source of information for lenders and creditors. The most useful analysis of company accounts comes from comparison with previous years and with results for similar businesses (see also **7.4.4**).

CHAPTER 7

UNDERTAKINGS

7.1	Introduction	75
7.2	What is an undertaking?	75
7.3	Financial covenants	76
7.4	Information undertakings	82
7.5	General undertakings	83
7.6	Undertakings – the bank's perspective	86
7.7	Undertakings – the borrower's perspective	87

> 'Why didst thou promise such a beauteous day,
> And make me travel forth without my cloak
> To let base clouds o'ertake me in my way,
> Hiding thy bravery in their rotten smoke?'
>
> William Shakespeare

7.1 INTRODUCTION

Representations are about information: undertakings are about control. The greater the control a bank has over a borrower, the better it can safeguard the money it has lent. Undertakings are one of the main provisions in a facility agreement which help a bank to monitor and control a borrower once the agreement is executed. As with representations and events of default, they may apply not just to the borrower, but also to other members of the borrower's group and to any guarantors.

7.2 WHAT IS AN UNDERTAKING?

7.2.1 Form and purpose

In a facility agreement, an undertaking (also known as a 'covenant') is simply a promise given by the borrower to the bank. It may involve a promise to do (or not to do) something, or to procure that something is (or is not) done by a third party within the borrower's control.

The purpose of the undertakings in a facility agreement is to protect the loan monies, as far as possible, by controlling the assets and activities of the borrower and, sometimes, group companies. Control is achieved using up to three different categories of undertaking:

(a) *Financial covenants* – traditionally known as financial *covenants* (not *undertakings*), these are financial targets which the borrower is required to meet during the life of the loan relating to profit, generation of cash or net worth. They are designed to check adherence to (and so are set with reference to) the borrower's projected performance under its business plan (see **Chapter 8**).

(b) *Information undertakings* – these are promises to provide the banks with information with which they can check the borrower's compliance with the provisions of the facility agreement.

(c) *General undertakings* – these are designed to control the business in general terms by, for example, prohibiting disposals, maintaining insurance and not diversifying from the key business.

These groups are examined more closely at **7.3–7.5** below.

An undertaking will require a borrower to meet certain standards (primarily financial) and to supply the bank with specific information in order to test those standards. Thus the undertakings allow the bank to monitor a borrower's status.

The undertakings are given 'teeth' by making breach of them an event of default (see **Chapter 8**). The bank will then have an opportunity, amongst other things, to cancel its commitment and demand repayment.

7.2.2   Undertaking or representation?

There is an overlap between undertakings and the representations dealt with in **Chapter 5**. Certain points may be covered using either type of clause.

> **EXAMPLE 1**
>
> A (repeated) representation such as:
>
> 'There are no encumbrances over the borrower's property'
>
> may be recast as an undertaking:
>
> 'The borrower will ensure at all times that there are no encumbrances over its property'.

> **EXAMPLE 2**
>
> An undertaking such as:
>
> 'The borrower will ensure it retains a majority shareholding in X Co'
>
> may be recast as a (repeated) representation:
>
> 'The borrower has a majority shareholding in X Co'.

The choice of whether to use a repeated representation or an undertaking will often depend on the drafting preference of the solicitor. In either case, the likely result of a breach is an event of default. However, some practitioners feel uncomfortable with deeming a borrower to repeat representations, and then relying on a deemed misrepresentation to call a default. They prefer a borrower to represent the position at signing and at the same time promise (undertake) that it will maintain the position throughout the term of the loan. Once that promise has been given, it will apply at all times (until the facility ends) and create a default immediately it is broken: in contrast, a repeating representation is tested only at the time of repetition (typically at the start of each interest period).

Note also that using a representation followed by an undertaking allows a strict initial test (the representation) followed by a more relaxed test (the undertaking) going forward. This ensures the banks elicit maximum information initially, but avoid a 'hair trigger' once the money has been lent.

In addition, a breach of a representation may give remedies under the Misrepresentation Act 1967 (see **5.5.1**), whereas a breach of an undertaking may give remedies of specific performance or an injunction (although note that specific performance is a discretionary remedy, and the courts will not order specific performance where damages are an adequate remedy (almost always the case for a facility agreement), and are particularly averse to granting specific performance of loan contracts).

7.3   FINANCIAL COVENANTS

7.3.1   What are financial covenants?

Financial covenants are undertakings which impose financial targets or limitations on a borrower. They are invariably seen in leveraged financings, may be used for cross-over credits, but are unusual for investment grade borrowers. The sections below concentrate on (maintenance) financial covenants seen in leveraged acquisition facilities, but project financing, real estate financing and some bond documents also use their own tailored forms of financial covenants. There are two broad types of financial covenant used in the London loan markets: maintenance covenants, and incurrence covenants.

Maintenance covenants

These are the most common form of financial covenant and are explained in a little more detail at **7.3.3**. They require the borrower to *maintain* a specified level of financial performance and are tested regularly over the life of the loan facility. The targets set in the financial covenants are based on the predictions for the borrower's performance shown in the directors' business plan (but usually allowing for a degree of underperformance against those predictions, known as 'headroom').

Maintenance covenants allow the banks to monitor the borrower's performance, to impose some control on what the borrower does with its money, and sometimes to incentivise the borrower. It is important to note, however that maintenance covenants measure *past* performance: the figures they use are for a period that has already taken place. They may indicate a positive or negative trend and so warn the bank of potential breach, but they will not tell the bank whether the borrower will meet its next interest payment.

The result of breaching the maintenance financial covenants is an event of default.

Incurrence covenants

Less common in the London market are 'incurrence' style financial covenants. Incurrence covenants also set financial targets, but the borrower has to show compliance only if it wants to do specified things, for example disposing of large assets, acquiring new companies or paying dividends. If the borrower does not do the specified things, it will not *incur* the covenants (ie they will not be tested). Incurrence covenants are currently found only in high yield bond financings, a US product which has found a foothold in the London market when bank liquidity has been reduced and is relatively expensive.

7.3.2 Form of financial covenants: limits and ratios

Some financial covenants simply set a financial limit which a borrower must attain, eg, net worth of at least £50 million. However, the most common type of financial covenant compares two figures obtained from the borrower's accounts. For example, comparing the level of debt to the amount of equity to determine 'gearing'; comparing cash flow to debt service to help determine liquidity. These comparisons are expressed as ratios, and set as limitations. For example, a borrower may promise to ensure that the ratio of debt to profit does not exceed 3:1.

7.3.3 Examples of financial covenants

7.3.3.1 Ratios

There are no 'rules' for computing ratios; however, there is little point in comparing figures which have no logical connection. For example, comparing a company's fixed assets to its share premium would produce a ratio, but a fairly meaningless one. The more common ratios used by banks in leveraged financing are set out below.

Leverage ratio

A leverage ratio compares the amount of debt a company has at a moment in time to the profit (or 'earnings') it has earned over a period (usually a year) leading up to that time. The ratio is typically written as:

Net Debt : EBITDA

'Debt' is usually defined as commercial borrowing (eg from loan facilities, bonds, finance leases and equivalents) and will not include short-term trade creditors (eg suppliers who give the borrower, say, 60 days to pay for goods). The amount of debt is typically reduced by the amount of freely available cash held in the borrower at that date (hence the term 'net' debt) on the basis that the cash is 'unused' borrowings and could in theory be used to pay back the debt. If the covenants are tested against the figures for a group of companies then the debt figure will come from consolidated accounts and be 'consolidated net debt'.

'EBITDA' stands for 'earnings before (taking into account) interest, tax, depreciation and amortisation' and is a measure of profit. Profit is seen as a clear measure of the success of a business, and EBITDA is an ingredient in most financial covenants, though it is not an accurate measure of how much cash a business is generating (see 'Fixed charge cover ratio' below). Exceptional profits or losses will typically be excluded from EBITDA to give a figure representing the trading performance of the borrower.

Banks will set the leverage ratio at a level which they know is acceptable to the loan market for particular borrowers and particular industries. In a buoyant market a highly-leveraged acquisition finance might see ratios as high as 8 or 9 to 1 for certain industries.

A leverage ratio is sometimes known as a 'debt cover' ratio, but note that 'gearing' is strictly the ratio of net debt to net worth.

Interest cover ratio

The interest cover ratio measure a borrower's ability to cover the interest payment and fee obligations under its borrowing. The ratio is typically written as:

EBITDA : Net Finance Charges

The term 'EBITDA' has been explained above.

Finance charges are fees and interest payments (but not capital repayments) due under the borrower's main debt obligations (commercial borrowing and equivalents). Any interest earned by the borrower from its investments is usually deducted from interest payable (hence the term 'net' finance charges).

Fixed charge cover ratio

A fixed charge cover ratio looks at the ability of a borrower to generate enough cash (rather than profit) to pay *all* amounts due under its borrowing. The ratio is typically written as:

Cashflow : Net Debt Service

Cashflow is, broadly, the amount of cash the borrower has generated from its business, less the amount it has spent, over a given period (typically a year). The definition usually starts with EBITDA but then adjusts the items included and excluded to represent cash movements more closely (EBITDA includes non-cash items and makes non-cash deductions). This is a similar concept to the cash flow statements discussed at **6.6**, though not quite as 'pure' (a strong borrower will negotiate out some cash expenditure from the cashflow definition, and it will not include cash from borrowing under loan facilities, bonds, etc).

Net debt service will include fees and interest payments due under the borrower's commercial borrowing and equivalents (like the interest cover ratio), but will also include any capital repayments due. The fixed charge cover ratio is typically set at 1:1.

In addition, the cashflow definition is used as a starting point for calculating whether the borrower has produced surplus cash over a period (ie more cash than the bank believes the borrower needs to run its business). This 'excess cash' is usually taken by the bank and used to prepay the loan, thereby reducing the leverage, under a provision known as a 'cash sweep'.

7.3.3.2 Limits

The following financial covenants may be set as minimum or maximum financial limits with which the borrower must comply.

Minimum net worth

A minimum net worth financial covenant aims to ensure the company maintains a minimum value of assets in the business. The definition of 'net worth' will vary slightly between agreements, but is intended to represent the difference between the borrower's assets (at their value in the latest accounts) and the borrower's liabilities. The starting point is therefore the paid-up share capital of the borrower together with any reserves (essentially the 'shareholders' funds' in the balance sheet (see **6.3.1**)).

If a bank has to look to a borrower's fixed assets to repay the loan, the borrower is almost certainly in severe financial difficulty and will probably be wound up. Most calculations of 'net worth' will therefore exclude any assets which may have little or no value if the borrower is in liquidation (these will generally be the so-called 'intangible assets'). The definition of 'net worth' is therefore likely to be headed 'tangible net worth' and (if otherwise included) exclude the following:

(a) *Goodwill.* Goodwill is the difference between the current book value of the assets of a company which could be sold off separately (its 'separable assets'), and the value of the company if it were to be sold as a whole. Under UK GAAP (and IFRS), only goodwill which has been 'acquired' when buying another company may be shown on a company's balance sheet (FRS 10 or IFRS 3). Since a business that is not trading successfully will probably be worth little more than the value of its tangible assets (unless there are particular items such as a brand name which can be identified and sold off separately), goodwill is usually excluded from the calculation.

(b) *Capitalised research and development costs.* Research and development costs are usually entered as an expense in the P&L account for the year in which the expense was incurred. However, in some circumstances, SSAP 13 allows these costs to be lumped together (capitalised) and treated as an asset in the balance sheet, if, amongst other things, it is reasonably certain that they will be recovered once the product to which they relate is developed. This capitalised amount is then 'amortised' (gradually deducted as an expense against profit over time) to spread the cost over a period as a form of accrual (see **6.3.8**). Most definitions of 'net worth' will require any costs capitalised in this way to be excluded because they do not represent a tangible asset.

(c) *Patents, copyrights, concessions, licences, etc.* Patents, copyrights and similar assets are likely to be excluded from a definition of 'net worth' because they are often not transferable (ie cannot be sold) or would be worth little or nothing on insolvency.

(d) *Payments on account.* Payments on account, where a borrower has received money in advance of providing any product or service, are also usually excluded from the net worth calculation since they would have to be repaid if the borrower did not perform.

(e) *Unaudited revaluation.* If the borrower has written up the value of fixed assets (eg, freehold or leasehold property) after the date of the last audited balance sheet, the increase may not be permitted to count towards 'net worth' until it is confirmed by the auditors. This is to avoid the borrower over-inflating the value in order to meet its financial covenants.

(f) *Tax provisions.* Any provisions for the payment of anticipated tax liability (see **6.3.7**) would usually be added back (ie, increasing net worth for the purpose of measuring compliance with the covenant).

Capital expenditure

This financial covenant is common in leveraged deals and puts a limit on the amount the borrower can spend on 'long-term' assets of the business (ie 'capital expenditure') over a given period. The aim of this covenant is to limit expansion of the business and help retain cash to service the debt. This covenant is known colloquially as the 'capex' covenant.

Borrowing

A bank will want to limit a borrower's exposure to other creditors, and this may be achieved through a financial covenant capping total borrowings. A borrower may ask for the cap to be linked to its tangible net worth, so that it remains relevant in the context of the borrower's size (and it then becomes a gearing ratio). Since there are many different ways for a corporate borrower to raise money, the definition of 'borrowings' (or 'financial indebtedness') must be fairly sophisticated. The following transactions are likely to be included in the definition because their commercial effect is similar to borrowing:

(a)   *Finance leases and instalment credit agreements.* Some leasing arrangements are structured to finance the use of the leased asset by one lessee (known as 'finance leases'). The lessee will usually be required, over the life of the lease, to pay instalments to the lessor equivalent to the full value of the leased asset together with a return on the capital value. The lessee is usually responsible for maintaining the asset, and early termination of the lease will incur a heavy penalty. The effect of these leases is very similar to borrowing a capital sum and paying it back in instalments (SSAP 21 actually requires the asset and capitalised obligation of 'finance leases' to be recorded in the lessee's balance sheet). Finance leases are used to fund assets such as computer hardware or heavy machinery, and frequently feature in aircraft financing.

Other types of agreements under which the borrower is effectively given credit and repays capital by instalments will also be defined as 'borrowing'. The most common example is a hire purchase agreement.

(b)   *Deferred purchase agreements.* Deferred purchase agreements allow for the purchase price of an asset or services to remain outstanding for a period of time, and will usually be defined as 'borrowings'.

(c)   *Capital instruments.* Capital instruments, for example bonds, notes and commercial paper, are borrowing methods explained in **Part III** of this book.

(d)   *Guarantees and indemnities.* Where the borrower has given a financial guarantee, indemnity or any other form of financial assurance in respect of any transaction, that will usually be included as 'borrowing'.

7.3.4   Using financial ratios

7.3.4.1   Defining terms

Accounting is certainly more akin to an art than a science. The CA 2006, SSAPs and FRSs allow the format and content of financial statements to vary widely between companies (see **6.9**). The financial covenants should therefore be carefully drafted so that they relate to the particular format used by the borrower. Any terminology should be specifically defined, rather than relying on accounting terms, to avoid ambiguity.

7.3.4.2   Information for testing

Under the CA 2006, all companies must produce some form of year end accounts, while (London) listed companies must also produce 'interims' – an unaudited report on their activities and profit and loss for the first six months of their financial year. These will provide figures with which a bank can test the financial covenants it has set for the borrower. However, even interims would provide a test of the financial covenants only twice a year, and a breach could be undiscovered for many months. If a bank wants to test a borrower's compliance more frequently than twice a year, what figures can it use? (Note that whilst banks will usually have a right to request financial information at any time (see **7.5**), they will not usually do so without suspicion that the borrower is in trouble.)

The directors of most companies produce their own set of accounts, which are more detailed than those published under Companies Act requirements. These 'management accounts' (see also **6.8**) will be produced at regular periods throughout the financial year (although they are not published). They will often include predictions as to future trends in the company's business, as well as historic performance figures and provide figures with which to test financial covenants; however, a borrower will not always be prepared to release them (a bank will usually insist on seeing management accounts of small borrowers, or in a 'rescue' situation). If a borrower is in a 'workout' situation, a bank may insist not only that it sees the management accounts, but also that they are produced more frequently than usual, say once every month (most companies produce quarterly management accounts), to allow for more regular testing.

7.3.4.3 Changes to GAAP and accounting policies

A bank will want to ensure that each new set of financial statements delivered by the borrower adopts the same accounting policies and practice used for the accounts the borrower originally supplied and on which the financial covenants were based. However, GAAP evolves from time to time and borrowers may legitimately wish to modify the policies they apply, for example with respect to depreciation. The usual solution to this problem is to allow the borrower to modify policies and follow changes to GAAP as long as its auditors provide a description of changes necessary to reflect the new financial statements as if written under the original policies and practice. This allows the bank still to check compliance with the financial covenants, and is known as a 'frozen GAAP' provision. To avoid the frozen GAAP provision becoming a long-term burden, there will also be provision for the bank and borrower to negotiate re-setting of the financial covenants to neutralise the accounting policy change (and, if they cannot agree, to use a third party 'expert' to advise on necessary changes).

PowerGen agrees terms for loan

By Antonia Sharpe

PowerGen, the UK electricity generator which has made an agreed £1.95bn bid for Midlands Electricity, the regional electricity company, will pay between 17.5 basis points and 22.5 basis points above the London interbank offered rate (Libor) when it draws on its £2.55bn acquisition facility.

The margin on the two-tranche facility will depend on the net gearing ratio of the combined group, according to PowerGen's offer document.

Tranche A, of £1.75bn, is a five-year term loan which can be drawn down over a nine-month period subject to PowerGen making the offer and it becoming unconditional.

Tranche B, of £800m, is a five-year multi-currency revolving credit facility available for purchases of Midlands shares and for refinancing.

● A $500m five-year revolving credit facility for **KLM**, the Dutch airline, has been over-subscribed, with more than 30 banks joining the transaction. KLM is now considering the size of the facility, which is due to be signed towards the end of this month.
● A £700m credit facility for **BTR**, the UK industrial group, was also oversubscribed but the borrower has decided not to increase the amount.

An example of a ratcheting margin by reference to gearing.
Source: *Financial Times*

7.3.4.4 Equity cure

Traditionally, borrowers could not cure a breach of a financial covenant: it was seen as a 'mathematical' test to be met at a given time, and failure to do so would require a waiver to avoid default. However, strong equity sponsors in acquisition financings have negotiated the right to inject cash into a borrower to help it meet its financial covenants. This right is known as 'equity cure' and works by reducing debt, either by actual prepayment or by leaving the money in an account which reduces 'net debt'.

Equity sponsors would prefer to treat the new cash as if it is profit made by the borrower (ie, increasing the borrower's EBITDA). Under this method, the ratio works for them (ie, they need inject less cash to get the same result) but it is rarely, if ever, given. Equity cure monies will, however, be treated as positive cashflow to help the borrower meet its fixed charge cover ratio.

7.4   INFORMATION UNDERTAKINGS

The effectiveness of most provisions in the facility agreement will depend on the bank receiving a regular supply of information from the borrower. The nature and extent of the information undertakings will depend on the type and size of loan, but might include those discussed below.

Syndicated facilities will require sufficient copies of any information to be delivered to the agent to supply the syndicate banks.

7.4.1   Financial information

The bank will require financial information to monitor the borrower's financial wellbeing and to check for any breach of the financial covenants. The main sources (not all of which are always required) are as follows:

(a)   Year end accounts (and interims, or possibly even pro forma quarterlies, if appropriate), including consolidated accounts if the borrower has subsidiary undertakings (see **6.6**). An investment grade borrower is typically given between 120 and 180 days (after its financial year end) to deliver its annual accounts, and up to 90 days to deliver interims.

(b)   Management accounts, which might include cash flow statements, income statements and a cash flow forecast. The frequency with which the management accounts are required will vary, but in extreme situations it might be as often as each month, with an overview every quarter. The bank will also want an undertaking specifying that the accounting principles used to prepare the management accounts are consistent with those used in the year end accounts.

(c)   A forecast of the borrower's performance, usually in the form of projected balance sheet, P&L account and cash flow statements for the financial year ahead. Sometimes a commentary of the borrower's actual performance as against its forecast performance is also required.

(d)   A certificate, provided on each covenant testing date, which shows compliance with all the financial covenants (a 'compliance certificate').

(e)   A 'sweep-up' provision requiring the borrower to provide any other information within its control, which relates to the financial condition or operation of the borrower, and which the bank requests. A well-advised borrower would negotiate this requirement subject to no material cost (at least prior to any default). A bank would not usually use this provision unless it suspected the borrower might be in breach.

7.4.2   Shareholder documents

A bank may ask for copies of all information sent to the borrower's shareholders, although a borrower might feel that this smacks of a 'trawling' process. A compromise might be to send the bank any information which the borrower is required, by statute, to send to its shareholders. This 'filter' should ensure the bank receives only the relatively important information.

7.4.3   'Know Your Customer'

Recent drives to combat money laundering have seen tighter monitoring of banks' clients, a process referred to as 'Know Your Customer' or 'KYC'. Banks will make initial KYC checks before the facility is executed. In addition, an undertaking to supply information reasonably requested by any lender in order to fulfil ongoing KYC obligations is now standard. Lenders will give a similar undertaking to each other.

Borrowers may, not unreasonably, ask to limit this undertaking to information within their possession or control, or which they can obtain with reasonable endeavours. This would avoid a breach of undertaking beyond their control (and leave the banks to rely on the illegality clause if necessary – see **9.9.3**).

7.4.4   Insurance

Most banks will require a borrower to maintain adequate insurance for its major assets, even if the loan is unsecured (see **7.5.1.1**). As a check to ensure the policies are renewed, a bank may include an undertaking requiring the borrower to produce an annual schedule of insurances. A periodic certification by one of the borrower's directors that the schedule is correct, the premiums have been paid, and there have been no substantial claims, is also usually required.

7.4.5   Notification of default

There will invariably be an undertaking requiring the borrower to notify the bank if it defaults under the loan. The undertaking may also require the borrower to notify the bank of any 'potential' events of default that might occur (note that failure to notify would therefore cause a default, even if the potential event of default itself has been, or might be, cured (see **8.6**)). The definition of 'potential event of default' is therefore critical, because it determines the sensitivity of the undertaking.

The undertaking will require written confirmation, to be given by the directors at the bank's request, confirming that there has been no default or potential event of default. This may be useful, to put pressure on the borrower if the bank fears it is in difficulty but has no evidence of default.

7.5   GENERAL UNDERTAKINGS

The final set of undertakings comprises those under which the borrower promises to do, or not to do, something. The aim of these positive (or 'affirmative') and negative undertakings is usually to preserve the borrower's assets, and to ensure there is not a fundamental change in the business on which the bank assessed its lending risk.

Once again, the exact form of these 'general' undertakings depends on the circumstances of each particular loan. However, it is possible to identify a number that are commonly used.

7.5.1   Positive undertakings

Positive undertakings require some sort of positive action by the borrower, or by an entity within the borrower's control.

7.5.1.1   Insurance

The bank will usually require the borrower to keep all its major assets insured. This may be because the bank holds some form of security over the assets, but it also avoids the borrower losing assets which it cannot replace, with a subsequent loss of income. In the case of very small borrowers, or in an acquisition finance, the borrower will sometimes employ one or more managers who the bank sees as crucial to the ongoing success of the business. In such a situation, the bank may make it a condition of lending that the borrower obtains, and maintains, 'Keyman' insurance over the life of these individuals. If the insured should die, a lump sum will be paid to the borrower, which will bolster the borrower through a potentially difficult time and help to fund a replacement for the 'key' man.

7.5.1.2   Consents, licences and laws

An undertaking will also usually be included requiring the borrower to ensure that it maintains all necessary consents, authorisations and licences to perform its obligations under the loan document. Similarly, a borrower must invariably undertake to comply with all laws if failure to do so might have a 'material adverse effect' (usually a defined term). Compliance with environmental laws is often covered in some detail in a separate undertaking.

7.5.1.3 Access to information and assistance

Very occasionally, an undertaking is included which requires a borrower to give the bank access to its books and records. The bank may also require the right to inspect the borrower's assets. In either case the borrower will want reasonable notice, and availability restricted to within office hours.

7.5.2 Negative undertakings

Negative undertakings prohibit the borrower from doing something, or require the borrower to ensure something is not done by an entity within the borrower's control.

7.5.2.1 Negative pledge

One of the most important negative undertakings is the so-called 'negative pledge'. This is an undertaking by the borrower not to create any security (other than to the bank) over its assets. Where the bank is unsecured, the purpose of this clause is self-evident. However, even if the bank has taken security, it may insist on a negative pledge to help protect its floating charge security (see **13.3**). Furthermore, a secured creditor is more able to pursue a debtor's assets than an unsecured creditor, and so the former may be more willing, or more able, to precipitate any action.

A borrower may want certain exceptions 'carved out' of the negative pledge to ensure that it can carry on business as usual, for example:

(a)   security that might be necessary under equipment leasing, or hire purchase arrangements. Control on this type of transaction should be achieved through specific undertakings if necessary;

(b)   liens arising under the common law, statute, and in the ordinary course of business. A trading company has little control over these occurring (eg, an asset which is retained by a third party until payment for services). The bank may want to restrict any carve-out to allow liens only on amounts overdue for a maximum of, say, 30 days;

(c)   cash collateralisation (ie depositing money by way of security) that may be necessary as part of the borrower's business arrangements;

(d)   security which pre-dates the facility;

(e)   security which the borrower acquires through purchasing an asset or business over which the security already exists (this may carry a proviso that the borrower obtains release of the security within a few months of acquiring the asset);

(f)   netting or 'set-off' arrangements between group companies, and any cash management arrangements with clearing banks;

(g)   retention of title clauses, allowing a creditor to recover assets from the borrower. If this carve-out is permitted, it should usually only be on the basis that the clause is not registered as a charge;

(h)   project finance, in which a borrower is lent money to finance a specific project, for example a factory. Banks to a project finance will want security over the asset being funded, but since that will not impinge on the existing assets of the borrower, there is an argument that it should be outside the negative pledge; and

(i)   a 'de minimis' amount (also known as a 'basket') allowing an aggregate amount of debt for which the borrower may create any security.

In addition, a borrower might ask for 'carve-outs', allowing security between companies in its group; new security which replaces existing security (eg, on a refinancing of existing debt); and security given in relation to 'factoring' (selling its debts).

Sometimes the negative pledge contains wording which attempts to create security for the bank automatically in the event that the undertaking is breached. This provides that, if the borrower gives security to a third party (so breaching the negative pledge), it is deemed to create equal security for the bank, at the same time and over the same assets. There are some doubts as to whether this type of provision is effective under English law, the fundamental problem being that the new security would probably fail for lack of registration.

7.5.2.2 Pari passu ranking

The negative pledge clause will often be accompanied by an undertaking under which the borrower is to ensure that:

> The claims of the bank rank at least pari passu with the claims of all other present or future unsecured and subordinated creditors, except for those preferred by bankruptcy, insolvency, liquidation or other similar laws.

Whilst the negative pledge ensures that the bank's right to repayment is not subordinated to secured creditors, a 'pari passu' undertaking tries to ensure that the bank is not subordinated to unsecured creditors. In fact, drafting this as an undertaking (ie, a promise to do it) arguably looks a little awkward, and some practitioners prefer to use a repeated representation or event of default instead (see **5.2.2**).

7.5.2.3 Disposals and acquisitions

Any substantial disposal of fixed assets may affect the borrower's ability to carry on making money to service the loan (it might also be an indication of cash flow problems). A bank will usually, therefore, restrict, if not prohibit, the disposal of fixed assets.

The undertaking preventing disposals must be carefully drafted to allow the borrower to continue its normal trade. Obviously, the clause should not prevent the sale of stock, nor the replacement or disposal of obsolete assets, in the ordinary course of business, though disposals of shares, cash or land may require the bank's consent (on the basis that even if the borrower does not 'need' them, they are likely to be of value). Alternatively, or in addition, the clause might allow disposals at arm's length up to a maximum aggregate annual value (a 'basket'), or be tied in to mandatory prepayment (see **9.2.3**).

A bank will have similar concerns with a borrower making substantial acquisitions: it will not want to risk the borrower buying a 'lemon', or trying to change its business. To prevent these, the financial covenants might limit the borrower's capital expenditure over the term of the loan.

7.5.2.4 Lending

Allowing a borrower to lend carries risk of non-repayment, and so a depletion of assets. The borrower will probably have to give an undertaking not to lend, other than in the ordinary course of its business (eg, trade credit) or within the group of companies 'controlled' by the facility agreement and any security.

7.5.2.5 Shares and dividends

With some small borrowers (and leveraged facilities) a bank may require an undertaking from the borrower not to make any distributions to its shareholders without the bank's consent or meeting a financial test. This is to avoid any money leaving the company, particularly as an interim dividend, before the bank is satisfied that the loan can be serviced. The bank may agree that the undertaking will not apply to the borrower's subsidiaries, since that would prevent profits being hived-up to the borrower to help it meet its obligations (sometimes known as 'dividend stripping').

Care must be taken if the borrower has issued any preference shares. Under the borrower's articles of association, these shares might provide the holder with a fixed rate of dividend which must be paid if the company's profits reach a pre-ordained amount. The undertaking should take account of any such obligations on the borrower to avoid inducing a breach of contract. Lastly, if the borrower has subsidiaries, then the bank may require that the borrower undertakes not to allow those subsidiaries to issue shares to third parties. This will prevent dilution of the borrower's holding, with the subsequent reduction in value.

7.5.2.6   Auditors

The bank may require a borrower to undertake that it will only appoint auditors whose size and status are satisfactory to the bank, although there is a danger that this type of clause is seen as anti-competitive and it is now very rare.

7.6   UNDERTAKINGS – THE BANK'S PERSPECTIVE

The decision to include a particular undertaking, and the level at which an undertaking is set, will be taken in light of a number of factors:

(a)   *The identity of the borrower.* Larger borrowers (eg, those within the FTSE 250) will generally have more power to negotiate which undertakings they will accept, and what information they will provide. These borrowers are perceived as being low risk and so banks will happily lend to them. Similarly, a borrower which has an established relationship with its bank may face less stringent undertakings.

(b)   *The type of loan.* Plain vanilla loans used for general corporate purposes will require only standard undertakings. More complex facilities, and those designed for specific purposes such as a project finance or acquisition finance, will require more specific undertakings. Overdraft facilities will not usually require any undertakings or financial covenants since they are on demand.

(c)   *Market conditions.* Probably the most important factor with regard to setting undertakings and financial covenants is the current market conditions. If there is a surplus of money in the loan market, the banks will be aware that a borrower may have other lenders to which it can turn. Equally, if the market is slow, and multiple banks are chasing a small number of deals, a borrower will have greater bargaining power. (See the article on p 88.)

When drafting undertakings for a bank (and advising on their enforcement), a solicitor should be aware of the provisions relating to 'shadow directorship' in the CA 2006, IA 1986, Company Directors Disqualification Act 1986 (CDDA 1986) and FSMA 2000. A 'shadow director' is, in broad terms, a person in accordance with whose directions or instructions the directors of the company are accustomed to act (the definition is almost identical in all four statutes – see ss 251, 251, 22 and 417 respectively), with an exception for professional advisers. If a bank uses the undertakings in its facility agreement to force a borrower to take certain action, it seems possible that the bank might be a 'shadow director'. The time of greatest risk is usually when a borrower is in financial difficulties: in an attempt to preserve its assets, a bank may be tempted to persuade the borrower's directors to take certain action under threat of enforcement of security, or even liquidation.

In *Re A Company (No 005009 of 1987)* [1989] BCLC 324, a company was allegedly managed in accordance with the bank's suggestions under threat of the bank otherwise appointing an administrative receiver. The judge held that this was arguably a case of shadow directorship, although the allegation was in fact dropped later in the case. In a more recent case *Re PFTZM Ltd* [1995] BCC 280, a company which could not meet its obligations under a secured loan was subject to weekly management meetings with the lending bank's staff in order to monitor the business. It was held that the bank was not acting as a shadow director, but simply trying 'to rescue what they could out of the company using their undoubted rights as secured creditors'.

The implications of being a shadow director include taking on the duties and responsibilities of an executive director (in so far as common law rules or equitable principles apply – see CA 2006, ss 170–177). Perhaps more seriously from a bank's perspective, a shadow director may be held liable for wrongful trading under the IA 1986, s 214(7), and may have to contribute to a company's assets on its liquidation. This is of particular concern to a bank involved in a workout or refinancing. Lastly, the provisions of the FSMA 2000 will apply equally to shadow directors as to executive directors (s 417).

7.7 UNDERTAKINGS – THE BORROWER'S PERSPECTIVE

A borrower is unlikely to be able to negotiate a loan that is 'undertaking free'. However, it is important to all parties that the facility agreement (in particular, a long-term loan) is workable in practice. In particular, the provision of financial projections and management accounts can be very time-consuming if they are not already part of the directors' remit. Furthermore, any failure to provide information on time may result in default, even if the information itself was satisfactory. The borrower's solicitor will therefore need to ensure that the undertakings are not too tight and, where possible, are subject to materiality or a de minimis. Any time limits for producing information, or for achieving a target, must be attainable. Requests for information should be 'reasonable' requests wherever possible. The borrower should also try to negotiate cure periods for as many breaches as possible (see **8.3** and **8.7**). Lastly, as with representations, the borrower will try to limit the number of companies subject to the undertaking, by, for example, referring only to 'Material Subsidiaries'.

Covenants in spotlight as banks reduce 'headroom' on company debt

By Anousha Sakoui

Mark Pain describes it as one of the most difficult periods of his 25-year career - involving round-the-clock work at an incredible intensity.

The finance director of Barratt Developments is referring to four months spent renegotiating the housebuilder's finances, at a time when the UK property market had nosedived.

It is an experience being lived by a growing number of companies having to face the fact that they can no longer refinance themselves out of trouble, unlike previous years, when debt financing was abundant and on easy terms.

"This is a turbulent river and we have crossed it, but there are still some on the other side," says Mr Pain.

Many companies are already in talks with lenders to ease debt terms, in particular waiving or resetting so-called covenants as earnings deteriorate.

The bad news is that banks have cut the margin for error they allow companies on meeting financial targets linked to earnings or other measures of ability to pay debt.

This so-called "headroom" has shrunk in bank lending terms this year by a third to about 20 per cent, according to research from analysts at Deloitte.

Covenants are financial ratios or limits that provide lenders with red flags warning of any sign that a company may start to struggle to meet debt repayments.

Advisers say more companies are struggling to meet these financing terms. Mike Duncan, chairman of the global banking practice at Allen & Overy, the law firm, believes this will worsen by the end of the year.

Barratt agreed with lenders to reset covenants, including swapping its interest cover-based covenant with a cash-flow covenant, highlighting banks' growing focus on the ability of companies to generate cash as they try to ride through the next few years, rather than profitability.

Barratt also had its leverage covenant and minimum tangible net worth covenants relaxed, which would allow it to make writedowns on its land bank.

Other covenants in the spotlight are based on the size of the loan relative to the value of the assets. Property companies are at risk of breaching these triggers as real estate prices plunge.

Mr Duncan says banks seem relatively relaxed about breaches for good quality commercial assets that still pay interest, but he expects them to be worried if rental income falls.

Banks balance the need to set these covenants tight enough to keep a grip on performance but loose enough to avoid breaches. Mr Duncan says initial breaches are more likely to be waived and covenants reset for a fee. A second breach is more of an issue

This year banks have, unsurprisingly, increased the

covenants they place on loan financings, reversing the pre-credit crunch trend of ever-loosening terms.

Once a company realises it is close to breaching, or has breached, tests it is thrown into talks with banks in an attempt to get waivers.

In the Barratt example, the board was taken aback by a big drop in orders in the first week of April. Concerned about a £400m debt refinancing due in 12 months, Mr Pain started talking to banks. As the sector remained under pressure into May, stress tests of finances started to indicate it could struggle to meet covenants.

The process can be fraught. After a series of meetings with banks and private placement noteholders, which had the same covenants as its bank debt, Mr Pain finalised the creditor sign-off on a restructuring of its finances mere hours before a trading update to the market early last month.

For banks, though, the growing concern is that many existing financings carry so few, or such loose, covenants that by the time a company is forced into talks it will be too late.

Because covenants and the negotiations around them are carried out behind closed doors, the scale of the problem is hidden. Some believe the number of companies struggling with covenants could be double what has been reported in the press.

Covenant measures

* **Leverage** - a measure of borrowings relative to earnings. For an investment grade company, debt divided by earnings before interest, tax, depreciation and amortisation (Ebitda) typically has to be kept below 3.5-3.75. For a leveraged buy-out for example, with more speculative grade debt, it can be much higher

* **Interest cover** - the ratio of interest cost to earnings before interest and tax. Generally set at about 3:1-3.5:1 for an investment grade company. Ensures that profitability is enough to ensure a company can meet interest payments

* **Capex** - places a restriction on the amount a company can spend on capital expenditure over a period of time. More common in buy-out financing

* **Debt service or cash flow** - monitors that a company has enough cash to cover both principal and interest repayments on debt. More common in buy-out financing

* **Tangible net worth** - measures the value of a company's tangible assets

An example of renegotiating breached covenants.
Source: *Financial Times*

CHAPTER 8

EVENTS OF DEFAULT

8.1	Introduction	89
8.2	Why have events of default?	89
8.3	Common events of default	90
8.4	Events of default and other clauses	95
8.5	Action on default	95
8.6	Potential events of default	96
8.7	LMA definition	97
8.8	Events of default – the bank's perspective	97
8.9	Events of default – the borrower's perspective	97

'It is impossible to live without failing at something, unless you live so cautiously that you might as well not have lived at all – in which case you will fail by default.'

JK Rowling

8.1 INTRODUCTION

The events of default dictate the circumstances in which a bank can terminate its loan early or take other action to reduce risk. Because of this, they will be among the most heavily negotiated clauses in the whole agreement. The events of default also dovetail with many other operative parts of a facility agreement.

8.2 WHY HAVE EVENTS OF DEFAULT?

If one party breaches the provisions of an agreement, an 'injured' party may seek a remedy for breach of contract. The type of remedy available for breach of contract (under English law) will depend on the type of term that has been breached:

(a) *Conditions*. Conditions are terms which are fundamental to a contract. Breach of a condition may allow the injured party to terminate the contract and claim damages, or to affirm the contract and claim damages.

(b) *Warranties*. Warranties are terms which are not considered fundamental to the contract (see also **5.5.2**). Breach of a warranty will not allow the injured party to terminate the contract, but merely to claim damages for any loss arising from the breach.

(c) *Intermediate (or innominate) terms*. Intermediate terms are a creature of judicial invention created to bridge the gap between conditions and warranties. They will usually be terms which are capable of being breached either in a trivial, or in a fundamental way. The remedy available on the breach of an intermediate term will be either damages, or damages and termination, depending on the effect of the breach on the contract.

In addition, if a party to the agreement makes a false representation to induce the other party to contract, the remedies for misrepresentation may be available (see **Chapter 5**).

However, if a borrower breaches a term of the facility agreement or is guilty of misrepresentation, a bank will not want to rely on common law or statutory remedies. If the breach is serious, a bank must be able to take immediate action. Events of default are events, specified in the facility agreement, which provide the bank with a contractual right to suspend or cancel any commitment, put the loan on demand, or immediately demand repayment of all outstanding principal and interest (known as 'acceleration').

8.3 COMMON EVENTS OF DEFAULT

In common with most of the other operative provisions, the events of default will be tailored to meet the requirements of each particular loan, bank and borrower. There are, however, certain events of default which will appear in most facility agreements, and these are explained below.

8.3.1 Late payment

Banks are highly sensitive about punctual payment by the borrower, not least because they themselves may have borrowed specifically to fund the loan (the bank will therefore have its own loan to service, matched with the income stream from its loan to the borrower – see **3.8**). Even if the bank has funded a loan from its own resources, it may conduct other business on the basis that the loan will be repaid on time and that it can re-invest the repayment. In either case, therefore, a bank will require default interest to be paid on the overdue amount (see **4.15**). There is usually also a general requirement to indemnify the bank against any costs associated with a default.

A further concern for the bank is that since a borrower's payment commitments are established in the facility agreement, those commitments should be accounted for in the borrower's projected cash flow requirements. A missed payment probably means a missed budget and may signal serious cash flow problems.

The inclusion of a default for late payment will be non-negotiable, and will usually cover late payment of any amount due under the agreement, including fees and expenses, as well as interest and repayments of principal. However, a borrower may argue, not unconvincingly, that accidental errors do occur. Furthermore, technical problems may also unavoidably delay payments, especially where financing is cross-border, or in a foreign currency. If, therefore, late payment is due to an administrative error or for technical reasons, a bank will sometimes allow a borrower three to five further business days in which to make payment (known as a 'cure period' or 'grace period'). The bank may, however, limit the errors to those of third parties and not the borrower. A bank's solicitor should ensure that any default interest and indemnity provisions are drafted so that they will run from the date when the payment is overdue, and not from the end of any grace period. A borrower may ask that any grace period should run only from when the bank notifies the borrower in writing that it has not received payment, though this is very rarely conceded.

Default for late payment is the most important event of default. The other events of default effectively play a 'supporting role': they are trying to predict situations which may lead to late payment.

8.3.2 Breach of representation

A bank will always want the option to call a default if one of the written representations proves to have been incorrect or misleading when made. The problem with this default is that it is often drafted very widely. A typical clause might provide for default if:

> Any representation or statement made or deemed to be made in, or in connection with, this agreement, or any document connected with this agreement, is incorrect or misleading when made or deemed to be made.

Thus, the default will cover statements made in connection with the document, as well as within the reps and warranties clauses. This might include anything from the inflated valuation of an important asset, to a mistake in the accounting reference date of a minor subsidiary.

A bank will therefore often concede some softening of this event of default. Usually this takes the form of a requirement for either the misstatement, or its consequences, to be 'material' or have a 'material adverse effect' (see also **11.5.3**). However, a bank will not want to start arguing over the meaning of 'material' at a time when it may want to pull the facility: it may insist that it will be the judge of 'materiality'.

8.3.3   Breach of undertaking

A breach of undertaking will be expressed as an explicit event of default in much the same way, and for the same reasons, as a breach of a representation. It is not uncommon to see a grace period in this event of default, and sometimes a materiality qualification too.

8.3.4   Breach of financial covenant

As mentioned at **7.3.4.4**, some equity sponsors in acquisition financings have negotiated 'equity cure' rights to avoid a default on breach of a financial covenant. A further concession sometimes requested by strong borrowers is a so-called 'Mulligan' provision. This works either:

(a)   to prevent the bank calling an event of default unless the borrower breaches a financial covenant on two consecutive testing dates (this is a 'true' Mulligan and is rarely, if ever, seen); or

(b)   to allow the bank to call a default on the first breach of a financial covenant, but to lose that right if it fails to call a default before the borrower meets the financial covenant on the subsequent test date (arguably not a true Mulligan and probably reflecting the commercial position in any event).

The term 'Mulligan' originates from a golfing expression, meaning a player is allowed a second tee shot without penalty.

8.3.5   Cross-default

Cross-default is a key event of default, and one which will be heavily negotiated. Imagine that a borrower defaults under another loan or financial contract (ie, other than the facility agreement). The other party to that contract may be in a very strong position to force terms on the borrower. These might include extra payment, additional security, or some other form of preferential treatment. The borrower may have done nothing to trigger a default of the facility agreement, and so the bank would have to sit and watch its position being eroded. A cross-default clause operates by automatically defaulting the borrower under the loan in the event that it defaults under certain other types of agreement (see also **5.2.2**). This ensures that the bank is also in a position to 'influence' the borrower and, if necessary, to protect its position by accelerating the loan. A cross-default clause also effectively gives a bank the benefit of the default provisions in other agreements to which the borrower is a party.

Because of the 'domino' effect which a cross-default might have, it is usually limited by:

(a)   being confined to defaults which occur under other documents providing 'financial indebtedness' (eg, loans, bonds, notes, acceptance credits, finance leases, guarantees, etc – see also **7.3.3**); and

(b)   including a threshold amount below which the default will not apply (a 'de minimis').

Other aspects that might be negotiated include the following:

(a)   A borrower will often argue that the cross-default should operate only if the other default will have a material effect on its ability to perform its obligations under the facility agreement.

(b)   A cross-default might be set to trigger at different points in the initial default, for example if:

(i)   the borrower simply fails to pay an amount due under another agreement; or

(ii)   the creditor under another agreement obtains a right to demand early repayment; or

(iii)   the creditor under another agreement actually exercises a right to demand early repayment (known as a 'cross-acceleration' clause).

A borrower would prefer option (iii) but banks will resist relying on just a cross-acceleration. Their concern is that the borrower will 'favour' the party with the benefit of a default (eg by paying fees, increased margin or giving them security) to persuade them not to accelerate.

(c)   Sometimes a borrower will ask for a carve-out (ie, an exception) for any defaults with respect to unpaid debts which the borrower is disputing in good faith. This is, however, strongly resisted by most banks. Pure debt disputes are seldom bona fides. Furthermore, a bank will not want to be arguing whether or not a dispute is in 'good faith' at a time when it might want to accelerate the loan. A bank will want a position where it can default the borrower if necessary, and the borrower will have to prove a dispute is in good faith to earn a waiver.

(d)   If the borrower is part of a group, a bank will often want the cross-default provision to extend to a default by any other companies in the group. A bank will argue that financial difficulties in a subsidiary will usually have an effect on the parent because of intra-group guarantees and letters of support. Furthermore, a bank will argue that a parent should not let a subsidiary default without good reason: if there is good reason then the event of default can be waived. However, a borrower will usually persuade a bank to limit any cross-default into its 'material' or 'principal' subsidiaries from time to time.

One issue for a bank is the evidential problem of finding out when a borrower has defaulted under another agreement. If a borrower knows that a default in another agreement will cross default into its loan then it has little incentive to reveal the first default. The fact that this in itself may cause the borrower to breach its representations when they are repeated is of little consequence; the bank will still be no wiser, and the borrower has simply defaulted twice instead of once. Furthermore, a bank is subject to an implied duty of confidentiality with regard to a customer's affairs (see *Tournier v National Provincial and Union Bank of England* [1924] 1 KB 461). This limits the availability of any information about defaulting borrowers 'in the marketplace'. A bank will therefore have to resort to its knowledge of the borrower's obligations under other agreements (through initial due diligence and subsequent information covenants), and its monitoring of the borrower's financial position.

8.3.6   Change of business

The type of business in which a borrower is involved plays a large part in the bank's initial risk assessment when agreeing to lend. A change in that business would entail a change in risk, and so be unacceptable to the bank without its consent. It will therefore usually be an event of default if the borrower makes any material change to its business, ceases to carry on any material part of its business, or disposes of a material part of its business ('material' may be defined, eg, with reference to net worth). The point at which outsourcing would trigger a 'change of business' is open to some debate.

8.3.7   Change of control

There are several reasons why a bank will be concerned about any change in control of the borrower. First, the parent of a borrowing subsidiary might have provided support which may be lost. Secondly, a bank may have a particular relationship with a parent which has been influential in its decision to lend to a subsidiary. Thirdly, a bank's original credit assessment (see **2.2.1**) may have been based on the group structure to which the borrower then belonged. Lastly, if the change of control is due to a listed borrower becoming privately owned (a 'public to private'), the original facility agreement terms may no longer be appropriate.

A change of control provision requires careful structuring. It might simply refer to any change in the shareholders, or include a change to the board of directors. Will a change of control occur if the original parent retains over 50%, or must it retain at least 75%? Note that a change of control is often drafted to trigger a mandatory prepayment of the facility rather than an event of default (see **9.2.3**).

8.3.8 Insolvency and related proceedings

The insolvency of a borrower will, without question, be an event of default. Any negotiation of this clause will simply relate to the timing of default. From a bank's perspective, an event of default should give it the ability to take action at the first sign of any problem. If a bank holds security, it will at least want the option to enforce it as early as possible to optimise its position with regard to other creditors and to preserve the borrower's assets. Typical triggers for this event of default are: 'inability to pay debts as they fall due' (see below), 'assets worth less than liabilities', 'ceasing to make payments on debts', 'negotiating with creditors to reschedule debts' (though borrowers might want to carve out negotiations with banks under the facility) and 'declaration of a debt moratorium'.

Some clauses may make reference to the two insolvency tests in s 123 of the IA 1986. Section 123(1) deems a company unable to pay its debts if it has not paid a debt three weeks after service of a statutory demand or court order (if the debt is over £750). Section 123(2) deems a company unable to pay its debts if the value of its assets is less than its liabilities. In *BNY Corporate Trustee Services Ltd v Eurosail-UK-2007-3BL Plc & Others* [2011] EWCA Civ 227, the Court of Appeal analysed the meaning of s 123(2) for the first time. The Court rejected the simple test that a company was insolvent merely because its 'liabilities (however assessed) exceed its assets (however assessed)'. It said that s 123(2) 'applies to a company whose assets and liabilities (including contingent and future liabilities) are such that it had reached a point of no return'. The case confirms that simply showing, at face value from a company's balance sheet, that its liabilities exceed its assets is not enough to satisfy the s 123(2) test.

In addition to insolvency itself, there will also be triggers related to insolvency *proceedings*. Typically this will include any corporate action, legal proceedings or other procedure or step (these last two being particularly important since the Enterprise Act 2002 introduced out of court appointment of an administrator) taken in relation to, for example:

(a) a moratorium, winding-up, dissolution, administration, reorganisation or arrangement with a creditor;

(b) the appointment of a liquidator, receiver, administrator, administrative receiver (or the equivalent in another jurisdiction); or

(c) the enforcement of any security over the borrower's assets.

From a borrower's perspective, once the bank 'pulls the plug' its problems are likely to get worse, especially if it is subject to cross default clauses in other documents. Ideally, therefore, a borrower wants any event of default to trigger as late as possible. A borrower might argue, therefore, that a creditor might 'take steps' to appoint an administrator as a method of forcing payment which the borrower disputes. It will typically ask for a remedy period, a carve-out for debts that are genuinely disputed (so long as proceedings are dismissed within, say, 30 days), or even a default limited to the actual appointment of an administrator, a receiver or similar officer.

8.3.9 Proceedings

If a borrower becomes involved in any material litigation, arbitration or similar proceedings, the bank will usually want the ability to call a default. A borrower will argue that this default should not be absolute but should be subject to a de minimis figure (see **11.5.5**). An alternative for the borrower is to draft the event of default so that it is only triggered by proceedings which will (the bank will want 'might') have a material adverse effect on the borrower's ability to perform its obligations under the loan.

8.3.10 Unlawful performance

A bank will invariably want to call a default if it becomes unlawful for a borrower to continue to perform its obligations under a facility agreement. The bank could not risk encouraging a borrower to break the law, and so the only option is to accelerate the loan. Similarly, a bank may also want an event of default if the borrower should lose any consents or authorisations necessary for it to perform its obligations under the loan. The borrower will want to introduce some element of materiality into both these clauses. A borrower may also argue that this should not be included as a default, since it has no control over the law, and ask instead for a provision for early termination for illegality.

8.3.11 General default

A provision will often be included in a facility agreement which makes it an event of default if the borrower fails to comply with any 'other obligations' (ie, other than representations and undertakings) under the facility agreement. This clause will invariably be drafted with a relatively long 'cure period' of perhaps 30 days. Specific events of default, which aim to pick up all the fundamental situations in which the bank may want to terminate the loan, will still stand, but the general default clause will 'sweep up' any minor defaults and make them actionable by the bank if the borrower cannot cure them.

8.3.12 Qualified accounts

In leveraged transactions it is not uncommon for a bank to include an event of default which is triggered if the borrower's accounts are qualified by the auditors (see **6.5**). A borrower will want to limit any default to a qualification which has a material adverse effect on its ability to perform its obligations under the loan facility.

8.3.13 Repudiation

Most facility agreements will make any actual, or attempted, repudiation by the borrower (ie words or conduct indicating it does not regard itself as being bound by the facility) an event of default. This provision is rarely negotiated.

8.3.14 Material adverse change

The material adverse change event of default, known colloquially as the 'MAC' clause, also acts as a 'sweep up' provision. It allows a bank to call a default if there is a material adverse change in the borrower's position or circumstances which might prevent it from complying with any provisions of the facility agreement. The potential breadth of this event of default means that many borrowers will try to exclude it, arguing that a detailed facility agreement which contains a raft of undertakings, financial covenants and events of default should not require such a 'catch all' provision. If a MAC clause is included (most banks' lending policies require it), it is always heavily negotiated.

A strong MAC clause might read as follows:

> Any event or circumstance occurs which the Majority Lenders reasonably believe might have a material adverse effect on the ability of the Borrower to perform or comply with its obligations under this Agreement

The first negotiation point for a borrower is to ensure the threshold for 'Majority Lenders' is as high as possible (commonly 66⅔%): the more banks that need to agree there is a MAC, the better. Borrowers might also ask for 'reasonably' (commonly accepted) and for 'might' to be replaced by 'will' (less common).

Negotiation will then turn to the phrase 'material adverse effect'. If this is left undefined, the uncertainty as to what it means might actually benefit the borrower in some circumstances. Equally, its breadth could be problematic, and so it is usual to have a definition of 'material adverse effect' along the following lines:

Material Adverse Effect means a material adverse effect on:

(a)   the business, operations, property, condition (financial or otherwise) or prospects of the borrower;

(b)   the ability of the borrower to perform its obligations under the finance documents; or

(c)   the validity or enforceability of the finance documents or the rights or remedies of any lender under the finance documents.

A strong borrower might argue for the removal of paragraph (a), on the basis that if it can perform its obligations under the document, and that document is valid and enforceable (ie paras (b) and (c)), then it should not be defaulted. It might also argue that (b) should refer to 'financial obligations'. If paragraph (a) is not negotiated out then a borrower might argue that it should be linked to (b) by 'and' being inserted between them. Focusing on (a) itself, the borrower might try to negotiate out the wider language, such as 'prospects', 'or otherwise' and maybe 'property'.

Lastly, there is a view that, as long as the borrower demonstrates that it can comply with all its obligations under the agreement (particularly any financial covenants – see **7.3**), it would be difficult for a bank to argue that any material change had been 'adverse'.

Such MAC clauses are not commonly used to default a borrower; a bank must be very sure of its case to use the MAC clause to demand repayment, but may be more willing to use it as a 'draw-stop' (ie to prevent new borrowing). The most common use for the MAC, therefore, is to threaten possible default and thereby persuade a borrower to start a dialogue with the bank (see **8.5** below). However, in *BNP Paribas v Yukos Oil Company* [2005] EWHC 1321 (Ch), the court upheld the validity of accelerating a loan based on a MAC event of default (it must be said the facts allowed a very clear argument for a MAC).

8.4   EVENTS OF DEFAULT AND OTHER CLAUSES

Ideally, the events of default should not overlap with any of the representations or undertakings. For example, if the borrower gives a repeating representation that there is no litigation, there should be no need for a litigation event of default (just a default on breach of representation). If for some reason there is both a repeating representation or undertaking and a specific event of default for the same circumstances, care should at least be taken that they are not contradictory: any carve-outs to the repeating representation or undertaking must be reflected in the event of default. Remember that a disclosure letter will circumvent a representation only with respect to breaches existing when the letter is accepted (see **5.2.3**).

8.5   ACTION ON DEFAULT

If an event of default occurs, a bank will want a number of different options, which might include:

(a)   cancelling any undrawn commitments if part of the loan has not been utilised; and/or

(b)   putting all or part of the facility 'on demand', and taking over the selection of interest periods (see **4.9**); and/or

(c)   demanding immediate repayment of part or all outstanding capital and interest, as well as any cash collateral for contingent liabilities (eg, bills of exchange or letters of credit); and/or

(d)   enforcing any security it holds.

The bank may choose not to exercise any of these options. It may feel that the event of default is not serious enough to terminate the loan, but that it justifies demanding additional fees from the borrower. Alternatively, the bank may use the default as an opportunity to insist that the borrower gets 'around the table' with the bank to discuss its business plans.

A bank will want these remedies available 'on or at any time after an Event of Default has occurred and until it is waived ...'; a borrower will want to add '... or remedied'. It is not unusual for banks to allow this request, but they should be aware that it has at least two implications. First, if the borrower can unilaterally remedy an event of default, he will have little incentive to disclose it when it occurs; if it must be waived, he is more likely to disclose. Secondly, what constitutes a remedy of certain types of default is not always clear, and ambiguity usually favours the borrower. Some facilities will try to specify what 'remedy' means for different events of default (but this is cumbersome) or else will say 'remedied to the satisfaction of the bank' (but this is less helpful to the borrower).

In the case of a syndicated loan, the agent will often be given discretion as to what action to take on an event of default, but with an overriding obligation to act in accordance with any instructions of the majority banks (either in number or value). Giving the agent this autonomy allows a faster response in time-critical situations, but at the price for the agent of taking on potential liability for wrong decisions (through action or inaction). Clearly, a borrower would want the most considered response possible, and so it may prefer that any default decision (and decisions in relation to a particular event of default) is taken by the entire syndicate, or a large majority of them.

If the loan is terminated and all outstanding amounts are immediately repayable, 'default interest' will apply until the amounts are settled in full (see **4.15**).

8.6 POTENTIAL EVENTS OF DEFAULT

Some events of default will include a specific 'grace period' (or 'cure period'), whereby the borrower is given a time period in which to remedy a 'default'. During this time, there is not a full event of default but simply a 'potential event of default'. A typical definition might be:

> ... an event which with the lapse of time, or giving of notice under the agreement, might constitute an event of default.

However, unless and until the default is remedied, the bank will not want to lend 'new' money to the borrower; thus, while a potential event of default is running, a bank's commitment to lend new money is suspended. This gives rise to a potential problem for a borrower under an RCF if a roll-over happens to fall within a grace period. A provision suspending further commitment will allow the bank to refuse to roll-over (ie, the borrower must repay the amount, but cannot then re-borrow). A borrower should therefore ensure that roll-overs are specifically allowed during a potential event of default. There is an argument that roll-overs should be allowed even if a full event of default is outstanding. The logic is that preventing a borrower from rolling over forces it to repay the revolving loan, which is 'de facto' acceleration. However, if an event of default is outstanding, the bank already has a remedy of acceleration; if it chooses not to accelerate, it should not do so 'by the back door' by preventing roll-over.

A borrower must usually undertake to tell the bank as soon as it is aware of any potential event of default.

Lastly, a borrower should never agree to give a repeating representation that there are no *potential* events of default, since if there are any the borrower will be unable to make the representation, which is, in itself, an event of default (effectively creating an event of default out of a potential event of default).

8.7   LMA DEFINITION

The Loan Market Association (LMA) facility agreements use the term 'event of default' in the traditional sense. However, they do not use the term 'potential event of default': they use the term 'default' to encompass both an 'event of default' and the equivalent of a 'potential event of default'. Thus the expression 'default which is not an event of default' is the LMA's way of expressing the equivalent concept of a 'potential event of default'.

8.8   EVENTS OF DEFAULT – THE BANK'S PERSPECTIVE

A bank will generally consider demanding early repayment of a loan as a 'last resort': recovering capital will usually involve selling assets, and this might mean winding up part or all of the borrower's business. However, the threat of recalling a loan can be used as a very potent negotiating tool. If a default occurs, the borrower is effectively at the bank's mercy, and the 'price' of not recalling the loan might be increased fees, a greater margin, tighter financial covenants or renegotiation of other terms. Any changes will be justified as consideration for the bank agreeing to continue despite the 'risk' of ignoring the default.

A borrower will sometimes argue that it should not be defaulted on the basis of events which are beyond its control, for example, a change in the law. Any such argument will be strongly resisted by the bank, because events of default are not based on 'fault' but on risk: they are situations in which a bank feels that the borrower's ability to perform the facility agreement may be compromised, and therefore it should have the right to terminate the facility agreement or take other appropriate action (see **8.5**).

Events of default do present some risk to the bank. The bank must ensure that it is justified in calling an event of default. Withdrawing a loan facility is likely to destroy a borrower's business, not least because of cross-default into other agreements. If a bank wrongly calls an event of default it may be sued by the borrower for breach of contract or in tort. In *Concord Trust v The Law Debenture Trust Corporation plc* [2005] UKHL 27, the House of Lords ruled that the wrongful calling of an event of default was not a breach of contract, but simply an ineffective action. However, the *Concord* decision was given in the context of default under a bond; it would not apply to a loan facility which was not fully utilised and where calling the default prevents further borrowing (see also **19.2.4.4**). Because of the consequences of calling a default, a bank will want the events of default drafted as clearly as possible (see also **Chapter 11**).

8.9   EVENTS OF DEFAULT – THE BORROWER'S PERSPECTIVE

The borrower must obviously be very cautious when agreeing to the events of default. To some extent, the events of default are intended to control how the borrower runs its business and what it does with the loan monies. If they are drafted too tightly, however, they will strangle the business.

Any breadth in the wording of the events of default will work for the borrower not just because it provides leeway, but also because a bank will be cautious about 'grey areas'. It is also true that a bank will not usually withdraw a loan without considerable provocation.

Wickes reaches deal on bank loans

By Andrew Taylor and Jim Kelly

Banks have renegotiated loan facilities made to Wickes, the troubled DIY retailer which last week warned that it had overstated profits due to accounting irregularities.

A syndicate of 11 banks and Trade Indemnity, the credit insurer, announced yesterday they had agreed to replace an £18m facility. Two other loan facilities for £50m and £30m have been capped, preventing Wickes from drawing further funds.

The deal will the ease worries of suppliers concerned about Wickes' ability to meet its obligations after lines of credit were temporarily frozen by the banks pending clarification of its financial position.

Barclays, which is leading the syndicate, said yesterday: "We believe that Wickes' problems can be resolved in the near future." It said bankers and accountants had worked over the weekend to "assess the cash flow position of Wickes' core UK operation".

Mr Michael von Brentano, who was appointed chairman of Wickes following the resignation of Mr Henry Sweetbaum, said: "We have made it plain that the accounting issues which have been uncovered should not detract from the fact that our operating businesses are sound."

Latest estimates suggest that Wickes' operating profits of £36.7m may have been overstated by £20m-£25m last year.

It is thought that the company, which normally pays suppliers at the start of each month, was facing a technical breach of its loan covenants. It was able to give the banks sufficient reassurance to allow loans to be renegotiated. The new £18m facility is thought to carry a higher interest rate than under the old agreement.

The company has said it will not pay its 1.5p final dividend, which had been due to be sent to shareholders today, because of uncertainty about its operating profits.

Price Waterhouse and Linklaters & Paines have been instructed to investigate the circumstances giving rise to the inaccuracies in Wickes' accounts, as well as the group's financial condition.

The inquiry is concentrating on the accounting treatment of rebates paid to Wickes by suppliers. In some instances, benefits to cover several years of trading were brought forward and included in a single year's profits.

The investigation is unlikely to be sufficiently advanced to allow the suspension of Wickes' shares to be lifted this week.

An example of loan agreement terms renegotiated after an event of default.
Source: *Financial Times*

CHAPTER 9

Boiler Plate, Mechanics and Miscellaneous Clauses

9.1	Introduction	99
9.2	Repayment, prepayment and cancellation	99
9.3	Margin protection	102
9.4	Costs and expenses	108
9.5	Fees	109
9.6	Remedies, waivers, partial invalidity and amendments	110
9.7	Force majeure	112
9.8	Governing law and jurisdiction	112
9.9	Miscellaneous	114
9.10	Schedules	116
9.11	Execution	116
9.12	US and English law loan facilities	118

'The fox knows a little about many things. The hedgehog knows only one thing, but it is a very big thing.'

Isaiah Berlin, Philosopher

9.1 INTRODUCTION

The preceding chapters have reviewed the main provisions of a loan facility in the order in which they will most usually be found in the agreement. Initial operative clauses will usually be followed by representations and warranties, undertakings and events of default (the only logic to this order is a vague chronology). The last three areas will be the most heavily negotiated, and unique to each facility agreement. In contrast, the remaining provisions are often seen as rather 'unglamorous', using standard clauses, and of minor consequence. The colloquial title for these clauses, the 'boiler plate', is far from inspiring, and many of them are in the back end of the document. Yet these provisions control some important areas: they seem unimportant only until something goes wrong. This chapter looks at the main 'boiler plate' clauses and funding mechanics, as well as at one or two miscellaneous items.

9.2 REPAYMENT, PREPAYMENT AND CANCELLATION

The following clauses are part of the mechanics of funding and settlement ('funding mechanics').

9.2.1 Repayment

The repayment clause is arguably the most important provision in the agreement. As part of the funding mechanics, it will appear before the representations, undertakings and events of default. The form of repayment will depend on the type of facility: a non-amortising loan will simply refer to a fixed date; if the loan is amortising, tables listing the amount to be repaid on specific dates are usually attached as schedules to the agreement. An overdraft is usually on demand and so does not strictly require a repayment date.

9.2.2   Prepayment

Some loans will allow (and in certain circumstances require) a borrower to repay capital before the dates envisaged by the facility agreement. This is known as 'prepayment'. Without some form of contractual provision, a borrower probably has no right to prepay a loan. (See *Hooper v Western Counties and South Wales Telephone Co Ltd* (1892) 68 LT 78: while this related to debt securities, at least one Commonwealth case has drawn the same conclusion for a loan facility.) From a borrower's perspective, the ability to pay down the loan as soon as spare capital is available will save interest payments. Furthermore, rates of both interest and margins will fluctuate: if there is a sustained downward movement, borrowers may refinance existing loans (either with their existing bank or a new one) part way through their term. Prepayment rights are usually also given against individual banks that have triggered payments under a gross-up clause (see **9.3.4.3**) or increased cost clause (see **9.3.2.6**).

A bank is usually happy for the borrower to prepay, but there are a number of points which the bank's solicitor will want to ensure are covered, and these are mentioned below.

9.2.2.1   Broken funding

As explained at **3.8**, large commercial loans may be funded by interbank lending ('matched funding'). If a borrower prepays part of the loan, the bank may be left to service an interbank loan without an equivalent interest stream from the borrower. Alternatively, the bank would have to terminate the interbank loan early and incur breakage fees (there is usually no provision for prepayment in interbank borrowing).

Facility agreements will therefore usually include an indemnity under which the borrower must reimburse the bank for any loss or liability it incurs as a result of prepayment (a 'break costs' clause – see **4.11**). Break costs will be avoided if the borrower can ensure that any prepayment is always made at the end of an interest period.

9.2.2.2   Prepayment fee

Sometimes a bank will want to charge a fee for prepayment (or a 'prepayment premium/ penalty') to cover any extra administration costs, particularly in the case of an agent taking prepayment on behalf of a syndicate.

In leveraged acquisition facilities (see **3.4**), the prepayment 'fee' may take the form of a 'call premium' (or 'call protection'), which is an additional amount payable by a borrower if it prepays the mezzanine lenders within a given period from first utilisation (see also **9.2.3**).

9.2.2.3   Order of application

In amortised loans, banks traditionally resist treating a partial prepayment as an early settlement of the next repayment amount due. This is primarily because the bank will want a borrower to continue to demonstrate the financial control necessary to maintain the steady repayment regime envisaged by the facility agreement. A bank may insist that any prepayment is treated as satisfying the final repayment obligations first (ie, prepayment will be applied against repayment obligations in inverse order of maturity), or else that the prepayment is spread across all the scheduled repayment amounts, reducing each one rateably. Taking the prepayment off the 'back end' of the loan reduces the life of the loan, which in turn reduces the bank's risk; using the rateable approach reduces exposure but maintains the relationship. Strong borrowers will be allowed to apply any prepayment as they choose.

In a syndicated facility, prepayments will usually be distributed to the banks in proportion to their advances ('pro rata').

9.2.2.4   Preference

If a corporate borrower is insolvent when it makes a prepayment, there is a danger that the prepayment might be a preference under the IA 1986, s 239. The bank could be required to repay any such 'preferred' prepayment to the insolvent company. A prepayment might also be a preference if it causes the borrower to become insolvent within six months of being made (or within 24 months if bank and borrower are 'connected', eg if the bank were a shadow director, or the two entities were under common control).

This might cause the bank a problem in two situations. If the bank's security is poorly drafted, the borrower (or its administrator, or receiver) might be able to claim that the secured debt is simply the amount of the outstanding loan when the borrower became insolvent. Any prepayment which has to be repaid as a preference will then become unsecured debt. Similarly, if the loan is fully repaid and the borrower becomes insolvent within six (or 24) months of a prepayment, the security might have fallen away and will no longer be available to secure a prepayment which has to be repaid as a preference. To avoid this, a bank might try to negotiate the right to retain security for a period after a prepayment (although often this is impractical and more a theoretical risk than a real one).

9.2.3 Mandatory prepayment

In some circumstances a borrower will be *required* to prepay the facility, known as 'mandatory repayment'. In an investment grade facility there are usually only two circumstances requiring mandatory prepayment:

(a) if it becomes unlawful for a bank to lend to the borrower. This is typically due to sanctions being imposed, for example the EU and US currently have wide-ranging sanctions against Cuba, Iran, Myanmar and others which may prevent banks lending to borrowers associated with the regimes. In a syndicated facility, the borrower is usually required to repay just the affected bank and not the whole syndicate; and

(b) if there is a change in control of the borrower. Control is typically defined as the ability to remove half or more of the directors, the ability to dictate how the company is run, the holding of a majority of the shares in the borrower, or the ability to cast more than half the shareholder votes. The bank's concern is that the borrower may be run differently or supported less by the new entity in control, and it will require prepayment of the whole amount outstanding.

In a leveraged facility there are likely to be additional mandatory prepayment events. In general terms, these are events which the banks see as an opportunity to take cash from the borrower to reduce the outstanding debt (reduce the 'leverage'), rather than repay completely, and typically include:

(a) if the borrower disposes of certain fundamental assets other than in the ordinary course of business (and assuming the proceeds are not required to purchase a replacement asset);

(b) if the borrower receives insurance monies for an asset it is not replacing;

(c) if the borrower generates more cash than it is deemed to require to run its business (this is known as an 'excess cash sweep');

(d) if the facility is required to fund an acquisition and the purchase price is subsequently adjusted downwards due to a revaluation event; and

(e) if the borrower subsequently raises funds through an issue of shares or debt securities.

These events usually result in repayment of part of the facility pro rata across the banks. In some acquisition financings, however, the mezzanine lenders (see **3.4**) are allowed to forgo their share of any prepayment (because they may be funds which do not have the flexibility of bank lenders to accept early repayment). Mandatory prepayment is a useful alternative to default since it will not usually trigger a cross-default.

9.2.4 Cancellation

If a loan provides a commitment period over which the borrower is allowed to utilise the facility (see **4.8.2** and **3.2.2**), the bank will almost certainly charge a fee for making the facility available during that period (known as a 'commitment fee' (see **9.5**)). However, a borrower may realise part way through the commitment period that it will not require the full amount of the available facility. Many loans allow the borrower to cancel any available amounts during the commitment period and so save on commitment fees (although sometimes a bank will charge cancellation fees!). The advantage to the bank is that it can use the cancelled commitments for other lending. A syndicate of banks will therefore want any cancellation to reduce their commitments rateably. A borrower must be sure that any cancellation fee is not prohibitive and that cancellation is available in the smallest multiples possible in order to give maximum flexibility.

Commitments may be mandatorily cancelled if there is an event of default during the commitment period, and will be automatically cancelled to the extent they are undrawn at the end of the commitment period.

The following clauses are usually considered part of the 'boiler plate'.

9.3 MARGIN PROTECTION

The interest rate charged by a bank on a syndicated loan is typically calculated by adding a margin to the estimated cost of lending (see **4.9**). If the cost of lending rises, the bank must be able to pass any increase to the borrower to protect its margin (thereby protecting its profit). This section looks at the main threats to the margin and how the bank might protect against them.

9.3.1 Funding rate

At **4.9.2**, the calculation of a bank's interest rate was expressed as:

(a)   funding rate (usually Libor); plus

(b)   margin (which must cover regulatory capital costs); and maybe

(c)   mandatory cost.

The 'funding rate' was explained at **4.9.2**, and accounts for a bank's major cost when making a loan. If a bank makes a loan with a floating rate of interest, any fluctuation in the funding rate is automatically passed on to the borrower at the start of each new interest period. If the loan is at a fixed rate, the bank cannot directly pass on any fluctuation, and so it tries to ensure that the rate is high enough to cover any likely rise in funding rates during the term of the loan.

9.3.2 Capital adequacy/regulatory capital

As explained in **Chapter 1**, banks are financial intermediaries: they lend money which they in turn have raised from depositors, investors and other banks. If a bank cannot recover the loans it makes in full, there is a danger that it would be unable to repay depositors or investors. Even a temporary inability to repay its debts is likely to panic depositors and cause a 'run' on the bank, as seen with Northern Rock's collapse and nationalisation in 2008. In an attempt to alleviate this threat, banks are required to maintain 'regulatory capital', essentially a minimum level of assets which can act as a 'buffer' to absorb any losses from the bank's lending activity. The requirement to maintain capital adds to the cost of making a loan, and any increase will threaten the margin. In 2013, the regulatory capital rules began a 10-year period of change, and so the following paragraphs briefly explain the origins, current status of and planned changes to, the regulatory capital requirements.

9.3.2.1 Origins of regulatory capital – the Basel Committee

In the mid-1980s, a group of 12 nations set up a committee to discuss creating a joint policy on regulatory capital (those involved were Luxembourg plus the 'G10' – the self-styled 'group of 10 most advanced economic nations', which actually number 11!). After several years the so-called 'Basel Committee' (they met in Basel, home to the Bank for International Settlements) came up with some 'Proposals for the International Convergence of Capital Measurement and Capital Standards'. Those proposals (known as the 'Basel Capital Accord') were adopted by all major banking jurisdictions, and implemented by 'local' legislation. More recently, a second, more sophisticated version of the Basel regime was adopted by most jurisdictions (the US being a notable exception). This new regime, commonly known as 'Basel II', was fully implemented in the UK from January 2008. However, the global banking crisis which began in late 2007 has prompted regulators to revisit the regulatory capital regime, and 'Basel III' is being implemented in stages from 2013 through to 2023 (see **9.3.2.5**).

9.3.2.2   Basic proposition of Basel regimes: assets backed by capital

The key proposition underpinning the Basel regimes is that a bank needs to recover its assets to repay its depositors: if there is a risk that an asset cannot be recovered in full, it must be backed by 'capital' to create a 'buffer'. This capital buffer is known as 'regulatory capital'. The starting point for the amount of regulatory capital a bank must hold is 8% of the value of each asset: so making a £100 loan would require a bank to have £8 of capital. However, this is just a minimum requirement. First, a regulator can increase the percentage for individual institutions or across the market if it feels it is necessary. (Institutions are understandably reluctant to publicise their individual percentages, but none is likely to be as low as 8% in the UK.) Secondly, the risk of a particular loan (or other asset) not being recovered will vary and so assets are 'risk weighted' to calculate whether more or less than 8% capital should be held.

9.3.2.3   Risk weightings

Basel II introduced a more sophisticated regime for risk weighting assets. A bank can use either the 'standardised approach' or the 'internal ratings based approach' ('IRB').

Under the standardised approach, the Basel II regulations provide a table of risk weightings to be applied to assets. For loan assets, the table looks to the credit rating of the borrower. For example, a loan to a company with an AAA rating would be risk weighted 20% (meaning 20% of £8, ie £1.60, of capital is needed to back a £100 loan). Risk weighting for a borrower with a BB rating would be 100% (£8) and, if rated B, 150% (so that £12 regulatory capital would be needed for a £100 loan). See **17.11** for more detail on credit rating.

The IRB approach actually has two versions, 'foundation' and 'advanced'. Both allow a bank to use its own (regulator-approved) model to calculate the risk of recovery of different assets. The foundation version relies in part on the regulator's risk assessment figures to populate the model, whereas the advanced approach allows a bank to use its own figures for the calculation. Large banks will usually use the IRB advanced approach to calculate their regulatory capital requirement.

9.3.2.4   Types of capital

So, a bank will use either the standardised or an IRB approach to calculate the amount of regulatory capital it requires. This then begs the question, 'what is capital'? The first notion to disabuse is that it is cash in an account: in fact, regulatory capital is made up of most assets a company holds from time to time. Basel II splits capital into three types: 'Tier 1, 2 and 3 capital'.

Tier 1 capital includes ordinary share capital, verified net profits and certain reserves (the idea is that these represent assets in the bank which are permanent, able to absorb losses, rank behind depositors, and do not carry an unavoidable maintenance cost such as interest or compulsory dividends).

Tier 2 capital has less 'permanence' than Tier 1 and/or may incur fixed costs, and includes cumulative perpetual shares, subordinated debt and revaluation reserves.

Tier 3 capital is the least 'stable' of all, for example short-term subordinated loans or non-verified profits.

It should be noted that Tier 1 capital may be further classified as 'core' and 'innovative', and Tier 2 may be 'upper' or 'lower'; there are limits on how much regulatory capital can be made up of each type. For example, at least half a bank's regulatory capital must be core Tier 1 capital, and Tier 3 capital can only be used to cover limited regulatory capital requirements.

9.3.2.5   Basel III

The collapse of Lehman Brothers bank in late 2008, and the banking crisis which followed, spurred regulators to look again at bank supervision and to tighten regulatory requirements, including regulatory capital, even further. As mentioned above, Basel III is being phased in from 2013 to 2023 and will be a much more stringent regime than Basel II. The details are beyond the scope of this book, but the key changes include the following:

(a)   Banks must have a greater percentage of Tier 1 capital and the regulatory capital must contain a greater degree of 'common equity' (ie ordinary shares and retained profits). So-called 'hybrid capital' (financial products designed to be treated as equity but behave more like debt) will be phased out.

(b)   Tier 2 capital will be simplified, whilst Tier 3 capital will be abolished.

(c)   Deductions from capital (certain assets that actually reduce a bank's capital, eg loans to other banks) will be increased.

(d)   The minimum ratio will stay at 8% (though see **9.3.2.2**), but the effect of the other changes mentioned here mean that it will probably be the equivalent of around 14% under the Basel II rules.

(e)   The IRB risk models (see **9.3.2.3**) will be tightened.

(f)   There will be two new buffers of capital introduced. The capital conservation buffer will be imposed if a bank is facing financial difficulties, in an attempt to prevent it from paying large dividends. The countercyclical buffer requires banks to build up extra reserves during periods of high economic growth, providing a 'grain store' for more straitened times.

(g)   There will be an increase in the capital requirement for global and domestic 'systematically important banks'. There will also be an increase in capital required to back loans to other financial institutions and certain derivatives.

(h)   There will be a liquidity requirement encouraging banks to hold enough liquid assets to deal with periods of high depositor withdrawal. (Northern Rock Bank required emergency loans from the Bank of England in 2007 because it suffered a liquidity crisis (a 'run on the bank'): it had one of the highest regulatory capital ratios of any bank at the time.)

(i)   There will be a new leverage ratio which compares the bank's assets *before* they are risk weighted to its Tier 1 capital.

Many of the proposals in Basel III are complex and not without controversy, and will require time to phase in, which is why they will not be in full effect until some time beyond 2020.

9.3.2.6   Increased costs clause

As a reminder, this section is looking at the key costs which might threaten the bank's margin and how they might be passed on to the borrower.

The requirement to maintain regulatory capital has a cost associated with it, and this cost is passed to the borrower as part of the margin on a loan. If regulations change and the cost of capital increases, that would eat into the margin and reduce the bank's profit. The increased costs clause in a facility agreement attempts to allow a bank to pass on any increase in regulatory costs to the borrower. It is a difficult provision for banks to use because calculating the cost of capital is not straightforward, and going 'cap in hand' to the borrower raises relationship and market perception issues. Borrowers will try to limit its application to changes which affect the banking market rather than individual bank changes (such as a regulator increasing a bank's capital ratio). One point to watch out for during the implementation of Basel III is that many increased costs clauses specifically exclude costs due to implementing Basel II, on the basis that banks should have already factored those costs into their margin. However, Basel III is technically an 'amendment' to Basel II and so arguably would fall within the exclusion: if a bank wishes to claim for Basel III increased costs, that should be mentioned specifically in the drafting.

9.3.3 Mandatory cost

The Bank of England was, historically, responsible for the regulation and supervision of the banking and insurance industries in the United Kingdom. On 1 June 1998, however, the Financial Services Authority (FSA) took over those regulatory and supervisory functions after the Bank of England was perceived to have mishandled various bank crises. Fifteen years later, on 1 April 2013, and again as a result of perceived failings in a banking crisis, the FSA was in turn forced to hand over its regulatory functions to two new entities, the FCA and the PRA (see **1.4**). There is a sense of déjà-vu: the PRA is part of the Bank of England.

Whoever is in charge, though, one element of bank regulation remains constant: banks must pay for the privilege. The costs of bank regulation are not straightforward since there are several components that might apply and at different rates, for example:

(a)   *Bank of England deposits.* The Bank of England may require banks lending out of a UK office to place various non-interest-bearing deposits with it, known as 'cash ratio deposits'. The size of deposit required relates to the size of sterling deposits that a bank has raised (known as its 'eligible liabilities').

(b)   *FCA and PRA fees.* The FCA and PRA charge a fee which also varies in amount and rate depending primarily on the size of the bank's (modified) eligible liabilities.

(b)   *European Central Bank (ECB) fees.* These might apply to banks lending out of a facility office based in a Participating Member State.

Until recently, most facility agreements gave banks the opportunity to recover these costs from the borrower. A formula attached as a schedule to the facility agreement converted the costs into a percentage, and this 'mandatory cost' could be added to the interest rate (see above). That meant any fluctuation in the costs could be passed to the borrower when interest was charged, protecting the banks' margin. However, since the level and applicability of mandatory cost varies between lenders, calculating and distributing costs for a large syndicate was complicated. The typical mandatory cost schedule required selected reference banks to supply average fee rates to the facility agent, and the average of those rates was then applied to each relevant lender depending on its commitment. As a result, from late April 2013, the Loan Market Association (LMA) withdrew the schedule calculating mandatory cost from its market documentation, and most banks stopped overtly calculating and charging it. If banks do want to charge mandatory cost, options include using the agent's own rate of Bank of England costs and FCA/PRA fees, or else using reference banks but simplifying the calculation method.

9.3.4 Withholding tax

Withholding tax is not a threat to the margin per se, but it is a potential threat to a bank recovering the full amount of interest it is expecting.

9.3.4.1 What is withholding tax?

Under the Income Tax Act 2007 (ITA 2007), there are certain circumstances in which a person paying interest must deduct tax from the payment before it is made. This is known as 'withholding tax' or 'deduction at source', and (like the more familiar PAYE) it is a tax imposed on the recipient of the payment but collected from the payer, providing a very efficient mechanism for tax collection. The withheld tax is either sent to HM Revenue and Customs (HMRC), or it may sometimes be netted off against any tax credit of the withholding party. Withholding tax does not apply to repayments of principal, nor on repayment of the discount element of a loan issued at a discount.

9.3.4.2   Withholding tax and banks

The section of the ITA 2007 which is of primary concern to a bank receiving interest payments is s 874. Under s 874, interest payments may be subject to UK withholding tax at a rate of 20% if they have a 'UK source'. Various factors will determine whether interest has a 'UK source', including the borrower being a UK resident, a loan being secured on assets in the UK, and payments being made from or through the UK.

There are, however, several exceptions to s 874 of particular relevance to commercial loans.

'Short' interest

Essentially, s 874 applies only to 'yearly' interest, which case law suggests is interest payable under a debt which is capable of having, and is intended to have, a term of at least 12 months. Interest on a debt for less than 12 months, known as 'short' interest, will not therefore be subject to withholding tax. This may be relevant for '364 day' facilities (see **3.2.4**) and bridging loans.

Some types of loan will be difficult to classify under this definition, for example, a loan which matures after six months but which may be rolled over by the borrower. HM Revenue and Customs therefore has some discretion, and may apply a 'hindsight test' which allows it to re-classify the type of interest once a loan has been running for a time. There is clear authority for the importance of intention (see Lord Denning MR in *Corinthian Securities v Cato* [1970] 1 QB 377). Paradoxically, the classification of 'annual' or 'short' interest depends only on the term (or intended term) of the loan, and has nothing to do with when the interest is actually paid.

Interest subject to corporation tax

Withholding tax will not apply to interest paid 'on an advance from a bank (as defined in ITA 2007, s 991) if, at the time when the payment is made, the person beneficially entitled to the interest is within the charge to corporation tax as respects the interest' (ITA 2007, s 879).

The requirement therefore has two elements to be satisfied before interest can be paid gross:

(a)   interest must be paid on an advance from a *bank* (essentially, an institution authorised as a deposit-taking institution under the Financial Services and Markets Act 2000); and

(b)   the person entitled to the interest is within the scope of *corporation tax* (at the time the interest is paid, and with respect to the interest).

Similarly, s 930 of the ITA 2007 exempts interest paid by a company if the payer reasonably believes that the beneficial owner of the interest is subject to UK corporation tax.

Interest paid by a bank

Section 878 of the ITA 2007 exempts interest paid by a bank in the ordinary course of its banking business.

The implications of withholding tax are discussed at **10.6**. If s 879 of the ITA 2007 applies, it imposes an obligation to withhold tax on anyone 'by or through whom' the payment is made. A syndicated loan will usually require the borrower to make interest payments to one of the banks as agent for the others (see **3.3.2**). When an agent bank pays the other syndicate members their share of the interest, it is someone 'through whom' the interest is paid. Will the agent be forced to deduct withholding tax a second time as it passes through its hands?

Remarkably, the ITA 2007 is silent on this point. In practice, however, the view is that the 'double hit' will not occur, and this is supported by judicial authority (on the ICTA 1988, predecessor to the ITA 2007) in *Grosvenor Place Estates v Roberts* (1960) 39 TC 433.

Double tax treaties

A bank can also avoid UK withholding tax if the interest is paid to a person resident overseas in a jurisdiction which enjoys a double tax treaty with the UK. The provisions and application of these treaties are complex, but in brief they may provide for most or all of the tax on interest payments to be levied in the country of the recipient. The country of the payer does not therefore tax the payment. UK treaties with the USA and many European countries provide for no tax to be collected in the payer's country. Treaties with some jurisdictions, eg Australia, reduce the amount of tax which must be withheld rather than extinguish completely.

These tax treaties do not apply automatically; treaty qualifying banks must complete an application form, and have it certified by their home tax authority and then filed with HMRC. It can take HMRC several months to process an application. However, banks may apply to HMRC for a 'passport'; if a UK entity borrows from a 'passported' bank, the treaty application will be expedited, with the time taken to process it reduced to a few weeks.

The residence of a bank that is not lending out of a UK facility office is therefore of great importance to a borrower. If it is resident outside the UK and not in a jurisdiction which has a double tax treaty with the UK, the borrower may have to withhold tax and so suffer the gross-up provisions (see **9.3.4.3**).

9.3.4.3 Provision for change in withholding tax – 'grossing-up'

Many banks will benefit from the exceptions under the ITA 2007, and will not suffer deduction of tax from interest payments. Furthermore, a borrower will usually be required to give a representation that all payments to be made under the loan will be free of any deductions. However, a bank will want to provide for any change in the situation, or for any unforeseen withholding tax, particularly if a loan has a non-UK element when interest might be paid from non-UK sources and be subject to withholding tax imposed by other jurisdictions. One solution is to provide for an indemnity from the borrower, under which it agrees to pay any withholding tax itself whilst paying the full amount due under the loan to the bank. However, in many jurisdictions the indemnity will not work, because the withholding tax will be levied on the amount indemnified.

A facility agreement will therefore usually include a 'gross-up clause', requiring all payments to be made 'free and clear' of withholding tax. If a deduction is required by law, the borrower will be obliged to gross up the payment so that the bank receives the full amount due after deduction of any tax. This is particularly important if a bank has match-funded its obligations (see **3.9**) because interest on interbank market loans is not subject to withholding tax (ITA 2007, s 878), and so any withholding by the borrower would leave a bank short of money to meet its interbank interest obligation.

Typical drafting for a gross-up clause would be:

> If a deduction is required by law to be made by an Obligor, the amount of the payment due from that Obligor shall be increased to an amount which (after making any deduction) leaves an amount equal to the payment which would have been due if no deduction had been required.

EXAMPLE

A UK borrower has to make an interest payment of £1,000. The bank receiving payment does not fall within the ITA 2007 exceptions, neither is it subject to a relevant double tax treaty, and the payment will be subject to withholding tax, currently at 20%. This would mean the bank receives only 80% of £1,000, or £800. If the loan contains a 'gross-up' provision, then the borrower must pay the bank an amount (X) sufficient to ensure that £1,000 remains after deducting 20% tax.

Thus 80% (or $^4/_5$) of X = 1,000

$X = 1,000 \times {}^5/_4$

$X = £1,250$

The borrower must make a payment of £1,250, of which £250 (20%) goes to HMRC, and £1,000 to the bank.

It should be understood that the gross-up clause is usually a 'last resort' provision: neither bank nor borrower wants to apply it because it will be costly for the borrower and strain its ability to meet regular loan payments.

Borrowers should ensure that the gross-up provisions only apply to banks that were exempt from withholding tax when they joined the syndicate. The borrower then only takes the risk of a change in tax law.

9.3.4.4   Tax credits

Withholding tax is simply a method of collecting tax on interest payments. If UK tax is withheld by a UK borrower, a UK bank can offset the tax against its corporation tax liability, and so the net result for a bank is simply a cash flow disadvantage. A borrower might then reasonably ask that once a bank gets tax credit for any withholding tax that has been paid, it reimburses the borrower. However, banks will strongly resist any borrower claim for an absolute right to reimbursement on the basis that it is in practice very difficult to allocate a tax credit to a particular facility and borrower. Any credit due back to the borrower is therefore usually left to the determination of the bank.

9.3.4.5   Other taxes

The borrower will usually be required to indemnify the bank against liability for any other taxes (apart from corporation tax in its jurisdiction of residence or the jurisdiction in which its relevant 'facility office' is located) which might be imposed on the bank after payment has been made.

9.3.5   Right to prepay

If the cost of the loan does increase, and a bank chooses to claim under one of the clauses outlined above, it is usual to give the borrower a right to prepay the loan. Whilst this might not always be practical for the borrower, it can be valuable in the case of a syndicated loan where one bank is subject to increased costs imposed in its own jurisdiction. In this case, the borrower usually has the option of just prepaying that one bank's commitment.

9.4   COSTS AND EXPENSES

A bank will usually require a borrower to indemnify it against the 'incidental' costs it incurs in setting-up and running the loan. These might include any costs in connection with the following:

(a)   The negotiation, preparation and execution of the loan document, any security documentation, and any supplemental documents.

(b)   The registration of the loan and ancillary documents, including any stamp duty or similar tax. In the UK, a straightforward facility agreement is not currently subject to stamp duty, although a nominal fixed duty is levied on instruments transferring property by way of security (eg, shares). The Stamp Act 1891 (SA 1891), on which the present system is based, does not actually state who is accountable for the duty, and the main sanction for non-payment is that the unstamped document will not be admissible in evidence in civil proceedings (SA 1891, s 14(1)). Many jurisdictions have much higher duties, particularly with regard to security documentation.

(c)   The preservation and enforcement of the bank's rights under the loan and ancillary documents. This may also include the costs of investigating any potential, or actual, event of default it believes may have occurred.

The bank should also include expense provisions in the mandate letter (or separate fee letter) (see **2.4.5**). In a syndicated loan, the arranger/agent will bear more expense than the other banks, since it will have taken the most active role in negotiating the loan and is the point of contact between the borrower and the syndicate. An agent will therefore want a provision requiring the other banks to indemnify it, in the proportion of their contributions to the facility, in the event that the borrower does not reimburse its expenses. A borrower will not want to provide a 'blank cheque' for the bank to spend on expenses. The best control it can probably hope to get is an obligation to repay only those expenses which the bank has 'reasonably incurred', with a requirement for the bank to produce full details of any amounts claimed.

9.5 FEES

9.5.1 Types of fee

In addition to paying interest and reimbursing certain of a bank's expenses, a borrower will also have to pay fees to the bank. The type of fees payable will depend on the nature of the facility. Fees are 'justified' as compensation for additional work or responsibility, and the widest range is found in syndicated facilities where the banks are required to take on a number of roles. A bank's fees can provide it with a very lucrative source of income. Common examples include the following.

9.5.1.1 Front end fees

Front end fees are usually paid shortly after signing or are recovered by withholding part of the initial utilisation. The bank in a bilateral loan may charge a 'front end fee' (also known as a 'facility' fee) in return for the initial work it must do to put the loan together (eg, due diligence and negotiation). It may be a lump sum, or be calculated as a percentage of the loan.

In a syndicated loan there may be several 'front end fees': the arranging bank is responsible for the initial work in constructing the facility, taking a leading role in due diligence and negotiation, and also for putting together the syndicate. The arranger's front end fee is usually larger than in a bilateral loan, and is known as the 'arrangement fee'. The arranger may have to use part of this fee in offering a 'participation fee' to attract other banks to the syndicate. The amount of management fees remaining once the arranger has paid any participation fees is traditionally known as the 'praecipium'.

9.5.1.2 Underwriting fee

A syndicated loan may involve a small initial group of banks who intend other banks to join the syndicate and take some or all of their commitment, but who agree to provide the entire loan between them if necessary. These initial banks underwrite the syndication, taking the risk that they may have to provide a larger part of the facility than they would want. Risk has its price, and the borrower will pay for this use of the underwriting bank's balance sheet by way of an underwriting fee (calculated as a percentage of the underwritten sum).

9.5.1.3   Commitment fee

The various costs that a bank must factor into pricing a loan were considered at **9.3.** They included a provision for regulatory capital which, essentially, requires a bank to back its lending with capital. The cost of meeting these requirements is covered by the margin a bank charges. However, regulatory capital provisions also apply, albeit on a reduced scale, to money which a bank is committed to lend but is as yet unutilised. A fee is therefore charged on any committed but undrawn money to cover the related regulatory capital costs. This 'commitment fee' is usually between 25% and 50% of the margin, and is charged in both bilateral and syndicated facilities on any unutilised (and uncancelled) commitment. The commitment fee is often drafted to run from signature of the facility agreement, even if the borrower has not yet satisfied the conditions precedent.

Some documents use a 'facility fee'. This is payable on both unutilised amounts (replacing a commitment fee) and utilised amounts, but with margin on utilised amounts reduced to compensate.

9.5.1.4   Agent's fee

A bank which takes on an agency role (eg, administrative or security agent – see **3.3.2**) will demand a fee to compensate for the extra responsibilities involved.

9.5.1.5   Cancellation fee

Some facilities are put in place but are never used. A common example is acquisition financing, where a company needs funding to bid for a target company. If the bid fails, the loan will never be utilised. If this is likely, the banks will usually incorporate a cancellation fee in the facility agreement (also known as a 'drop dead fee').

9.5.1.6   Utilisation fee

Facilities that are intended to be used only rarely, or not at all (eg, standby or swing-line facilities) may carry a utilisation fee. The utilisation fee will apply if the facility is used regularly, or borrowing under it exceeds a minimum amount.

9.5.2   Fee letter

A bank will usually want the details of its fees to be put in a letter separate from the loan facility (other than, usually, the commitment fee). The 'fee letter' provides confidentiality from syndicate members, other borrowers and the market generally.

The facility agreement should refer to the fee letter, and when the fees are payable, in order that non-payment carries the remedies of default under the facility.

An agent bank should also ensure that the facility agreement specifically refers to the fees payable to it (though not usually the amount) to avoid any argument that its fee letter arrangement with the borrower is a secret profit in breach of its fiduciary duties. Likewise, any individual fee to an agent should be expressed as payable to the bank individually, to demonstrate it is not a fee to be distributed among the banks in an agency role. Conversely, the facility agreement should specify when a fee is to be paid to the agent or lead manager to be split amongst the syndicate.

9.6   REMEDIES, WAIVERS, PARTIAL INVALIDITY AND AMENDMENTS

9.6.1   Remedies and waivers

Most facility agreements will contain a boiler plate clause along the following lines:

> The rights and remedies of the Bank under this agreement:
> (i)   shall not be waived by any failure, or delay, in their exercise;

(ii)   are cumulative, and shall not exclude or restrict its rights and remedies under any other agreement or the general law; and

(iii)   may be exercised in whole, in part, and as often as necessary.

Sub-clause (i) tries to avoid the borrower using the equitable doctrine of 'laches' (a form of estoppel) to preclude the bank exercising a right or remedy after unreasonable delay. Note, however, that case law suggests that continued performance of a contract will be inconsistent with a termination of a contract and result in the loss of a right to terminate (see *Tele2 International Card Company SA v Post Office Limited* [2009] EWCA Civ 9).

Sub-clause (ii) provides, first, that if the bank has more than one right or remedy under the agreement, it is not confined to using only one of them. This sub-clause also tries to avoid any merger of rights between, say, the facility agreement and a security document (there is authority that a superior security right will merge with an inferior one and the latter is effectively lost). Lastly, the sub-clause avoids any suggestion that the rights under the agreement should replace any rights under general law.

Sub-clause (iii) tries to avoid an argument that, in exercising any rights or remedies, the bank has only 'one bite at the cherry'.

The effectiveness of any of these clauses cannot be guaranteed, and the best advice to a bank is usually to act quickly and decisively, and to keep the borrower informed of any action it takes.

9.6.2 Partial invalidity

There is a danger, albeit remote, that an illegal or invalid clause might make an entire agreement unenforceable. The following type of clause is therefore commonly included in a facility agreement:

> If any provision of this agreement is prohibited, unenforceable, void or invalid, that shall not invalidate, or otherwise affect the enforceability of, the remaining provisions hereof.

This type of clause tries to enhance the possibility of a court severing an invalid section, allowing the other provisions to stand. Under English law there are two underlying principles in relation to severance:

(a)   a court will not construct a new contract: any severance must leave the original contract standing and not alter its basic scope or intention; and

(b)   a court will not sever if to do so is against public policy.

In *Goldsoll v Goldman* [1915] 1 Ch 292, the court formulated the 'blue pencil test': a provision may be severed only if it is possible to do so simply by 'running a blue pencil' through the invalid provisions. Whether or not the type of damage-limitation clause outlined above has any influence on a court's willingness to sever is open to debate.

9.6.3 Amendments and waivers

Under English contract law, no alterations to the provisions of an executed document will be effective without the agreement of all the parties. It is not difficult to imagine the logistical problems this might cause for a syndicated loan with numerous banks. In addition, a requirement for unanimity can result in the 'tail wagging the dog', since even banks with the smallest commitment will have a right of veto over a waiver or an amendment. Most syndicated facilities will therefore allow amendments and waivers to most of their clauses to be agreed by a majority of the syndicate. Until recently, investment grade facilities typically defined 'majority' as banks with more than $66\frac{2}{3}\%$ (sometimes 50%) of:

(a)   commitments to lend (if the facility is unutilised); or

(b)   actual money borrowed (once any utilisation has occurred).

However, investment grade facilities now usually follow the leveraged facility position, which typically defines 'majority' as banks with at least $66\frac{2}{3}$% of commitments, whether or nor utilised.

There are two provisions related to amendments and waivers that have become common in leveraged deals during the recent 'borrowers' market':

(a)   '*Yank the bank*' – this colloquial term refers to a clause allowing the borrower to take a bank out of the syndicate if the bank votes against an amendment or waiver which a requisite majority of banks voted to allow. Usually, the dissenting bank can be removed only if the borrower can find another lender to take the commitment, but sometimes the borrower is allowed to prepay the dissenting bank's commitment.

(b)   '*Use or lose*' – another colloquial term, a 'use or lose' (also known as 'snooze and lose') provision says that if a bank does not vote on an amendment or waiver decision within a given time (eg, 10 days) then that bank's commitment is disregarded in calculating whether the borrower gets the required majority. An even more aggressive (and therefore rarely, if ever, seen) version, known as 'delay and it's OK', deems a bank to have voted 'yes' to an amendment or waiver if it fails to vote within a specified number of days.

Whilst these clauses are borrower friendly, they are also popular with agents since they help with 'syndicate management'.

9.7   FORCE MAJEURE

There will be circumstances in which the parties to an agreement consider that performance of their obligations is, through no fault of any party, no longer possible. A 'force majeure' clause attempts to define those circumstances, typically natural disasters or war, but it might be any circumstance which the parties could neither foresee nor prevent. The clause might provide that the obligations under the contract are suspended until the circumstances have passed, or that the contract is immediately terminated. In either case, however, there will not usually be sanctions on either party since, by definition, there is no blame.

Most facility agreements do not include a specific force majeure clause but rely instead on provisions for increased costs (see **9.3**), illegality (see **9.2.3**), and material adverse change provisions (see **5.2.2** and **8.3**).

9.8   GOVERNING LAW AND JURISDICTION

In some countries, the evidence of a woman is worth only half the evidence of a man. In others, juries rather than judges will usually decide the level of a plaintiff's damages. Clearly, it is crucial to the parties to know and, if possible, control the law and jurisdiction which will apply on enforcement of a facility agreement. Normal conflict of law rules apply to facility agreements as in the case of any other commercial contract.

It is important to recognise two separate issues: the governing law of a document is different from the jurisdiction where a disputed document will be judged. If English courts have jurisdiction, they will rule on an agreement governed by Icelandic law: they must simply apply Icelandic law principles rather than English law principles.

9.8.1   Governing law

9.8.1.1   Common law rules

In English common law, the governing law of a contract (also known as its 'proper law') will determine issues which include the validity of the original document and any amendments (eg, sufficiency of consideration), interpretation of clauses and remoteness of any damages. The parties are free to choose the governing law provided their choice is bona fide and legal, and not contrary to public policy (see *Vita Food Products Inc v Unus Shipping Co Ltd (in Liquidation)*

[1939] AC 277). However, for most contracts, including facility agreements, the common law rules have been largely superseded by statute.

9.8.1.2 Rome I Regulation

The Rome I Regulation on the law applicable to contractual obligations (593/2008/EC) must be applied by EU Member States (except Denmark) to all contracts concluded on or after 17 December 2009 and determines which law is applicable to them. It replaced, with minor amendments, the Rome Convention with the same objective. The Regulation, like the Convention before it, allows complete freedom to choose the governing law of a contract (either expressly or impliedly), although the public policy, and certain 'mandatory rules' (eg, competition law, consumer protection) of the jurisdiction in which a dispute is heard, may supersede the governing law if necessary. If the choice of governing law is not express or reasonably certain, a court will attempt to identify the country with which the contract is 'most closely connected'.

9.8.1.3 Rome II Regulation

From 11 January 2009 the Rome II Regulation allows parties to choose the governing law of non-contractual obligations (eg, claims in tort). The choice will be upheld if: the claim falls within Rome II (some claims are excluded, eg those arising from voluntary trusts); the context is a commercial activity; and the choice of law was freely negotiated. In addition, if all the elements of a claim are outside the UK, non-English law provisions may still apply in limited circumstances. The usual election is for the governing law for non-contractual obligations to be the same as for contractual obligations.

9.8.1.4 Factors affecting choice

The party most likely to sue under a facility agreement is the bank, and so it is the bank which decides the governing law. It may choose the law of its own country, because it is familiar and accessible. Alternatively, it might consider using the law of the borrower's country, because that is where the contract will need to be enforced, and is probably the location of most of the borrower's assets. However, many overseas banks choose English law to govern loan documents because it is relatively sophisticated and stable, the legislation processes are (relatively) predictable, and it is considered 'creditor friendly'.

The jurisdiction in which the assets are situated will normally provide the governing law for any security documentation over those assets.

If the parties do not choose a governing law, the English courts will first look for any implied choice: the choice of jurisdiction will often be a strong influence. If no implied choice is evident, the courts will take a pragmatic view and look to factors such as nationality or residence of the parties, the currency of the loan contract and the place of execution or performance of the agreement. The issues of contractual capacity and authorisation of a party (see **4.6.2**) are determined by the law where it is domiciled.

9.8.2 Jurisdiction

A jurisdiction clause specifies the jurisdiction(s) in which the facility agreement may be enforced in court. The two main reasons for stipulating this are (i) to avoid litigation in unfavourable jurisdictions, and (ii) to enable the contract to be enforced as expected.

The three regimes that will usually apply if at least one party is domiciled in an EU or EFTA Member State (except Lichtenstein) are:

(a) the Brussels Regulation on jurisdiction and enforcement (Regulation No 44/2001), which binds all EU members;

(b) the 2007 Lugano Convention, which binds EU members (except Denmark) and Norway; and

(c)   the 1988 Lugano Convention, binding the EU, Switzerland and Iceland.

Which of these regimes applies (if any) can be a complex question. Broadly, however, if a party is domiciled in the EU, the Brussels Regulation applies; if domiciled in an EFTA State (except Lichtenstein), the relevant Lugano Convention applies. If a party is domiciled in Lichtenstein or outside the EU or EFTA then English domestic law will apply unless the parties have chosen exclusive jurisdiction of a Member State. Essentially, under English domestic law an English court will have jurisdiction if:

(a)   a company has a place of business in England, or has registered process agents at Companies House (see below) and is served with a claim form in England;

(b)   a company submits to the jurisdiction of the English courts; or

(c)   the English court gives authority to serve a claim form on an overseas company.

Similar considerations will apply to choosing jurisdiction as when choosing governing law. A bank might want to take advice from a solicitor as to which forum is likely to be quickest, or may be most sympathetic to its case (frequently, a clause will specify several jurisdictions in which any proceedings might be brought). The court which is given jurisdiction will enforce the agreement under the chosen governing law on the basis of evidence from local experts. It should be borne in mind that this is likely substantially to inflate any enforcement costs.

It is an ironic fact that the provisions for the governing law and jurisdiction are invariably the very last clauses in a document, and yet they are the very first things a draftsman should consider. More than one solicitor has forgotten to look at the back of the agreement he has been given to review until late in the day, only to discover that he is reviewing a document governed by the tribal law of Uzbekistan.

9.8.3   Agent for service of process

If any of the obligors in the facility is not an English registered company and does not have a branch or other place of business in Great Britain, the service of any English court documents on that obligor would require service 'out of jurisdiction' – a time-consuming process when time is of the essence. Fortunately, r 6.11 of the Civil Procedure Rules 1998 allows parties to use any contractually agreed method of service instead of serving out of jurisdiction:

(1)   Where—

(a)   a contract contains a term providing that, in the event of a claim being issued in relation to the contract, the claim form may be served by a method specified in the contract; and

(b)   a claim solely in respect of that contract is started,

the claim form may, subject to paragraph (2), be served on the defendant by the method or at the place specified in the contract.

The usual 'contractually agreed method' is to appoint a conveniently located third party to receive documents on the obligors' behalf, known as an 'agent for service of process'. Using an agent for service of process gives a certain address for service and will avoid a bank having to apply to court for leave to serve a foreign corporation. Several companies offer these services (for a fee), for example The Law Debenture Trust Corporation plc in the UK, and CT Corporation System in New York. Subsidiaries of the borrower are sometimes used, but this runs the risk that the subsidiary might be dissolved or sold. Using Consuls or Ambassadors is not a good idea either, in case they claim immunity to proceedings! Note that an 'agent for service of process' is different from a 'process agent' who is someone appointed to *serve* court documents.

9.9   MISCELLANEOUS

9.9.1   Inter-bank provisions

A syndicated facility agreement will contain a section dealing with the relationship between the various syndicate banks, appointing the agent bank(s) and specifying their powers to act on behalf of the other banks. It will usually contain provisions on matters such as monitoring defaults, liability for actions and information, resignation of agent banks, and indemnities. It will also deal with sharing of money in the event that some banks receive payment, or recover money, from a borrower and others do not. All of these matters need careful consideration by banks, borrowers and their solicitors.

9.9.2   Set-off

A facility agreement will usually contain a specific authority from the borrower giving the bank a right (but not an obligation) to set off credit balances in favour of the borrower against any amounts due but unpaid (see **13.5**). The borrower will be prohibited from exercising set-off. This is, in part, to prevent a defaulting borrower from making a counterclaim against the bank (eg for breach of duty) and then setting off the two claims as an excuse to delay repayment of the loan (note the counterclaim can still be made, but not set-off; see eg, *Credit Suisse International v Ramot Plana OOD* [2010] EWHC 2759 (Comm)). (See **9.9.5** for borrower set-off against a defaulting lender.)

9.9.3   Illegality

A bank will always want the ability to terminate the loan if it becomes 'illegal' for it to perform its obligations under the agreement (see also **9.2.3**). If a contract is illegal when entered into, it will not be enforceable. Similarly, if the performance of a contract becomes illegal after execution, a party which continues to perform the contract will generally be unable to enforce the contract. Without an express clause providing for repayment it might prove very difficult for a bank to be repaid in these circumstances.

A borrower might try to mitigate this clause by placing an obligation on the bank to avoid illegality wherever possible. For example, this might involve booking the loan to a facility office in another jurisdiction, or assigning the loan (see **Chapter 10**) to a bank unaffected by the illegality.

9.9.4   Notices

The boiler plate will contain the provisions under which a borrower and bank give notice to each other. Mundane as this might appear, it can be very important, since many of the rights under the document cannot be exercised without notice. Communications must be written, and sent either:

(a)   by post. Banks will sometimes want a notice sent to the borrower to be deemed to arrive a certain number of days after posting, but will never accept a reciprocal arrangement. Always beware of deemed receipt: it has led to litigation in times of postal strikes (see *Bradman v Trinity Estates plc* [1989] BCLC 757); or

(b)   by fax. Fax is almost instantaneous, but the problem is knowing whether it has been received: there is little that can be done if a borrower, suspicious of bad news, simply turns off his fax machine.

Perhaps surprisingly, e-mail has yet to be widely adopted as an acceptable medium for notices between bank and borrower, although posting information on a web page (eg, accounts) may be allowed in some circumstances.

9.9.5   Defaulting lender provisions

As a result of the chaos that ensued when Lehman Brothers bank collapsed in 2008, many borrowers and lenders now consider including provisions in the mechanics and boiler plate of the facility agreement which deal with a lender becoming insolvent (or otherwise defaulting on its obligation to lend), known as a 'defaulting lender'. The defaulting lender provisions typically cover some or all of the following:

(a)   Allowing the borrower to cancel any undrawn commitment of a defaulting lender. This is to avoid complications in dealing with an insolvent lender or its acting insolvency practitioner (eg administrator or liquidator). The borrower will hope that another bank will take up the commitment, but this will not be mandatory.

(b)   If the defaulting lender retains a commitment, no commitment fee is payable on the basis that it will almost certainly be unable to lend if required to do so.

(c)   If the defaulting lender retains a commitment it will not be allowed to vote on any decisions under the facility (it is 'disenfranchised'). This is because it may be very difficult to get a response from a defaulting lender (or its insolvency practitioner), and in any event its perspective on issues such as waiver requests is likely to be very different from that of the 'non-defaulting' banks.

(d)   The defaulting lender may be forced to transfer its participation (ie, money already advanced) in the facility to another lender at par (ie, face value rather than market value).

(e)   Any amount lent by a defaulting lender under a revolving credit facility is automatically turned into a term loan. This is to avoid the borrower having to repay that part of the revolver and then finding it is unable to re-draw from the defaulting lender.

(f)   The identity of a defaulting lender may be disclosed by the agent to the borrower.

(g)   If the defaulting lender is also the facility agent, payments and notices may be made directly between banks and borrower rather than through the agent. In addition, the defaulting agent can be removed by a majority vote of the remaining banks. This avoids the obvious problem of having an insolvent entity as the conduit for all payments and allows the loan mechanics to continue as smoothly as possible.

Some borrowers have suggested that they should be allowed to exercise set-off against defaulting lenders (usually a borrower is prohibited from doing so – see **9.9.2**). However, banks should strongly resist this since it causes issues with the pro-rata sharing provisions in the facility (see **9.9.1**), it can prevent Credit Default Swap (see **Glossary**) protection and makes the facility ineligible for certain central bank liquidity schemes (which, in essence, allow banks to temporarily swap illiquid assets (eg certain loans) for liquid ones (eg government securities) to aid bank liquidity).

9.10   SCHEDULES

The schedules appear at the very end of a document, after all the operative provisions but before the execution clause. They attach lists of information which could be included in the operative provisions but which would make them rather clumsy, for example, banks' commitments, condition precedent documents, repayment dates and amounts, as well as the mandatory costs formula. The schedules may also contain any agreed drafts of the documents required under the loan, such as utilisation requests, transfer certificates (see **Chapter 10**), compliance certificates, accession deeds, confidentiality undertaking and the form of any guarantee (if not built into the facility itself) and/or security to be provided, or sometimes the terms on which security will be given ('security principles').

9.11   EXECUTION

Where a syndicated loan requires a party to perform several defined roles, it is conventional for a bank to execute separately for each of those roles. For example, a bank would sign three times if it were a participating bank, the administrative agent and the security agent. If it signs only once, it must be made clear that this is in respect of all the bank's roles. Note that s 44(6) of the Companies Act 2006 requires that if a director is signing a document as director for more than one company (quite common for large groups), he must sign separately for each company.

If the loan involves a large syndicate, it may not be possible to find a date on which all the members are available to attend a signing meeting. There are three possible solutions:

(a)   the documents may be sent to each signatory in turn. This can be a rather cumbersome process, however, and may stretch the execution over several days;

(b)   the absent party may appoint someone to sign on its behalf under a power of attorney, which should be created by a deed. Section 7(1) of the Powers of Attorney Act 1971 (as amended) allows an attorney to sign in his own name, or that of the principal. The borrower's solicitor should check the power of attorney document for expiry, powers, and any conditions or limitations, before accepting an attorney's signature; or

(c)   the document may be executed in counterparts. This allows identical copies of the document to be signed simultaneously in as many different locations as necessary. This may be done in a number of ways, but care must be taken due to the judgment in R (*on the application of Mercury Tax Group and Another) v HM Revenue and Customs Commissioners and Others* [2008] EWHC 2721, which criticised poor practice in execution of deeds, and also because of the Law of Property (Miscellaneous Provisions) Act 1989. One of the following methods is therefore usually used for execution in counterparts:

(i)   The printed documents are sent to each party by post or courier. Each party signs its own document and confirms that it has done so (without any amendments) to the solicitor coordinating the documents. Once all parties have signed and confirmed, the facility is treated as executed and the parties then return their respective (whole) documents to the solicitor. The 'original agreement' is the composite of all the counterparts.

(ii)   The documents are circulated by e-mail with instructions to print off the full document and then proceed as for (i) above. Signatories may be asked to scan the signed document as a PDF and e-mail it back as proof of execution, though this PDF is evidential only and not an 'original'. As a practical matter, it is important to check that signatories have the facilities to print and scan large documents. Also, be aware that print sizes vary between some countries (eg the US and UK), and so the document will run to a different number of pages and the execution clauses will appear on different numbered pages (which can look odd when collating the originals). Solutions include sending documents by pdf (which has the added advantage that parties cannot alter the document), or removing the page numbers from the execution pages.

(iii)   The documents are circulated by e-mail with instructions to print off and sign the signature pages only, then to scan the signed pages into a PDF and return them together with an electronic copy of the (unsigned) document in a single e-mail. The true 'original' document is the electronic version and any hard copy is merely evidential. This method therefore cannot be used where hard copy originals are required, for example for registration.

(iv)   The documents are circulated by e-mail with instructions to print, sign and return just the signature pages to the solicitor coordinating the documents, as evidence of the document being signed. Strictly, this will mean that there is no 'original document'. This method cannot be used for executing deeds (due to the *Mercury Tax Group* ruling) or agreements with provisions for the sale or disposition of interests in land (because of s 2(1) and (3) of the Law of Property (Miscellaneous Provisions) Act 1989).

(v)   Just the signature pages are circulated (sometimes with a latest draft of the agreement) for signature in advance of the final documents being agreed. The pages are signed and returned to the solicitor coordinating the documents. When the documents are in agreed final form, the solicitor is authorised to affix the signature pages and the document treated as executed. As with method (iii), this method cannot be used for executing deeds or agreements with provisions for the sale or disposition of interests in land. The key issue, if using this method, is to ensure that there is clear authority from a party to attach its pre-signed signature pages to the relevant version of the document.

If executing in counterparts the document should ideally have a clause specifically allowing execution by counterparts to avoid any argument by a party that it did not realise that its signature alone could make the document 'live'.

The solicitor may produce 'conformed copies' (see **Glossary**) for each party or a CD containing copies of the original documents as appropriate.

Lastly, the location of execution may be important for tax purposes, with documents often needing to be executed 'offshore' (ie outside certain jurisdictions).

9.12   US AND ENGLISH LAW LOAN FACILITIES

The examination of loan facility provisions in the previous chapters is based on a document governed by English law to be used in the European syndicated loan market. Other jurisdictions and legal systems will have their own nuances which must be reflected in the loan document. By way of example, this section outlines some key differences between an English law facility agreement and one governed by US law and aimed at US lenders.

What drives the differences?

A number of factors will create differences between US and English law loan facilities and associated documents such as security agreements:

(1)   The insolvency regimes are different, although English law administration is quite similar to the US law equivalent ('Chapter 11') and both are far more 'creditor friendly' (they favour lenders) than most European regimes.

(2)   It is generally easier to take security over all of a borrower's assets under US law, and the registration and enforcement regimes are more standardised (under the Uniform Commercial Code). English security law is very flexible but relatively complex, having evolved over centuries of case law (although the recently simplified registration regime is helpful).

(3)   The US is a more litigious environment, which allows unconnected third parties to purchase and pursue legal claims and provides a more favourable costs regime for litigants.

(4)   The US market has more 'institutional investors' lending in the loan market, leading to greater liquidity and a convergence between loan and bond market terms. This last factor drives most of the points listed below.

Key differences in facility agreements

US institutional investors want more certainty of investment returns and loan duration than commercial bank lenders. This leads to different commercial terms and market conventions.

Call protection

Call protection is a US phrase for an early prepayment fee. It entitles the lenders to an extra fee if the loan is refinanced within a specified time of signing (usually 12 months). If incurred, call protection is typically payable as a fee of around 1% of the facility amount.

Libor floor

A Libor floor specifies that the Libor element of the interest rate calculation under the facility is treated as never less than a stated amount, even if the market rate is less. Libor floors are currently set at between 1% and 1.5%.

Limited amortisation

Another commercial term driven by institutional investors is that it is common to have an annual amortisation of around 1% per annum on the term loan 'B' (ie the term loan taken by institutional investors). This is simply to provide a current return on the facility.

'Covenant lite'

English leveraged loan facilities generally use 'maintenance' financial covenants: the borrower is obliged to show at regular intervals (usually every three months ('quarterly')) that it is maintaining the financial performance it predicted in its business plan. Within a given period of each testing date, the borrower must submit a compliance certificate to the agent bank confirming that it has met the financial covenants. This is quite onerous. US leveraged facilities generally contain just a single financial covenant or 'incurrence'-style covenants, which are only tested ('incurred') if the borrower wants to take certain specified actions (eg make further acquisitions or disposals). Cashflow covenants, which are common in London market leveraged facilities, are not typical in the US market. The US-style financial covenant packages are colloquially known as 'covenant lite' and are similar to those found in high yield bonds.

EBITDA equity cures

Many leveraged facilities allow the private equity owners of the borrower to inject money into the borrower to help it avoid a breach of its financial covenants. This process is known as 'equity cure'. In US facilities, the equity cure money can be treated as 'profit' of the borrower (also known as 'EBITDA'), which is particularly helpful to the borrower in curing a breach of its leverage covenant. In London market facilities governed by English law, equity cure monies would have to be treated as reducing the amount of debt for the purpose of testing the leverage covenant and could not be counted as EBITDA.

MAC event of default

US law facilities would typically not include a material adverse change (MAC) event of default. They would usually include a MAC representation, but breach would only usually prevent further utilisation of the revolving credit facility and could not be used to accelerate the loan.

Majority lender votes

Votes requiring consent of 'majority lenders' in US law facilities usually just require a simple majority. English law documents typically require two thirds.

Loan transfer

US facilities will typically allow the term loan to be freely transferred without borrower consent, although revolving credit facilities are more likely to require consent. English law facilities for the London market are more likely to require borrower consent, not to be unreasonably withheld or delayed, sometimes coupled with a 'white list' of institutions that lenders can transfer to freely.

CHAPTER 10

Novation, Assignment and Sub-participation

10.1	Introduction	121
10.2	Why sell a loan?	121
10.3	Moving rights and obligations	122
10.4	Selling assets	123
10.5	Global Transfer Agreement	130
10.6	Type of assets sold	130
10.7	Tax implications	130
10.8	Financial Services and Markets Act implications	131
10.9	Borrower transfers	131
10.10	Other jurisdictions	131
10.11	Securitisation	131
10.12	Asset sales – the bank's perspective	131
10.13	Asset sales – the borrower's perspective	131
10.14	Further reading	132

'The only permanent thing is change.'

Heraclitus

10.1 INTRODUCTION

Glance at a bank's balance sheet and it will contain the usual list of assets you might expect to find in a company: buildings, office equipment, and perhaps a few safes. The big difference is a large entry in the current assets under 'loans and advances' (see the sample balance sheet at **6.3.3**). As with other assets, a bank spends money to acquire loans, and they in turn produce money for the bank. However, once a bank has made a loan it might not keep it until it matures.

In one sense, a bank may use its loans like fixed assets: 'purchase' them, keep them for a time to earn an income, and then dispose of them. This chapter examines how banks dispose of their loans: an exercise known as 'asset sales'.

10.2 WHY SELL A LOAN?

Since the main purpose of a bank is to lend money, it might seem strange that it would want to dispose of its loans, but there are a number of common reasons for doing so.

10.2.1 Realising capital

A bank may want to realise some of the capital it has tied up in long-term loans in order to improve its liquidity. This would allow it to take advantage of any new lending opportunities which give a better return. Alternatively, a bank might decide to concentrate on a particular market and to sell any loans that do not 'fit the bill'.

10.2.2   Risk management

A bank may decide that its loan portfolio has become distorted. Too much emphasis on one type of loan or one type of borrower carries risk, and a bank may sell some existing loans to allow it to make others.

10.2.3   Balance sheet

A bank's ability to lend is subject to internal and external requirements to retain a percentage of its capital as cover for its loans ('regulatory capital' – see **9.3.3**). If a bank's capital is entirely allocated, it cannot participate in new loans (unless they carry a zero risk weighting), no matter how attractive or lucrative they might seem. Therefore, unless the bank can raise more capital, it must sell some existing loans to release capital for backing new ones.

10.2.4   Profit

A bank may see an opportunity to make some short-term profit by selling a loan. For example, if interest rates start to fall, an existing fixed interest loan might become very marketable. Conversely, if a borrower has defaulted or is performing badly, a lender may choose to sell its participation at a discount to crystallise any loss (see also **10.6**).

10.2.5   Prestige

A bank will sometimes want an initial involvement in a facility because it is particularly high-profile or important, for example the London 2012 Olympics financing. It may, however, choose to sell some or all of its share of the loan once it has derived any benefit to its market profile. Some forms of asset sale will allow a bank to keep its name to a loan but to lay off the lending risk.

10.2.6   Syndication

A bank may, either alone or with a small group of banks (Lead Arrangers), sometimes provide the full amount of a loan but bring in other banks to form a syndicate 'post-closing'. This 'postponement' of syndication allows large loans to be made quickly.

10.3   MOVING RIGHTS AND OBLIGATIONS

Before looking at how a bank might sell its assets, it is necessary briefly to consider the legal analysis of transferring a contractual role to another party. Most contracts operate by giving rights and obligations (liabilities) to each party. One party's rights will usually constitute another party's obligations. Under most facility agreements, a bank's fundamental obligation is to lend money (the borrower has a right to borrow), whilst its fundamental rights are usually to receive interest and eventual return of capital (the borrower is obliged to service and repay the loan). There are many other rights and obligations in a facility agreement, and since facility agreements are primarily designed to protect the bank, most rights are in favour of the bank and most obligations rest on the borrower.

In order to sell an asset, a bank must dispose of both its rights and its obligations, and this is where problems might arise. Under English law, rights under a contract (other than very personal rights) can be transferred at the instigation of the party entitled to them: contractual obligations can be moved only with the consent of the party to whom the obligation is owed. In other words, a borrower must agree to any change in a bank's obligations.

The rule is intended to prevent a party being prejudiced by the change in identity of an obligor. This can be illustrated by a simple example. Imagine that you lend your neighbour £500 on the understanding that she will pay you back in two weeks' time. You have known her for three years, she has a very well-paid job, and you obviously know where she lives. The chances of your neighbour fulfilling her obligation to pay back the money are good. Two weeks later your neighbour politely informs you that she had decided to lend the £500 to her brother who is a student in Spain, and so the obligation to repay you now rests with him. Not only have your chances of repayment probably fallen, but enforcing the obligation to repay has become much more difficult. It should now be clear why obligations cannot be transferred without the consent of the party to whom they are owed: you remain entitled to demand repayment of the £500 from your neighbour.

10.4 SELLING ASSETS

10.4.1 Summary

A bank can dispose of an asset in several different ways with different consequences. The most common methods are:

(a)   novation;

(b)   legal ('statutory' or 'disclosed') assignment;

(these two methods both result in the selling bank disposing of the asset completely)

(c)   equitable (or 'undisclosed') assignment;

(d)   sub-participation;

(e)   risk participation.

(Using any of these last three methods will entail the selling bank retaining some involvement in the asset.)

On examining all of these methods in more detail, it is important to keep in mind that the basic aim of a bank in selling an asset is to remove the risk associated with it.

10.4.2 Novation

10.4.2.1 What is novation?

The only way in which a party can effectively 'transfer' all its rights and obligations under a contract is with the consent of all the parties involved. This type of transaction is known as a 'novation', a term with its origins in Roman law. Novation involves one party's rights and obligations under a contract being cancelled and discharged, whilst a third party assumes identical new rights and obligations in their place. Novating a facility agreement simply means that a new bank is put in place of the old one. It is the most straightforward, and therefore most commonly used, transfer method under English law. This is set out in simplified terms in the figure below.

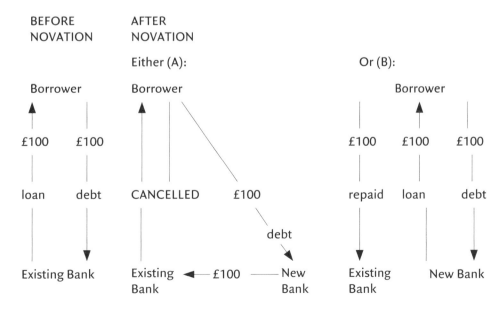

In method (A), the existing bank takes £100 from the new bank in return for releasing its rights and obligations under the loan (including its right to receive £100 repayment from the borrower). The new bank assumes identical rights and obligations with respect to the borrower as applied to the existing bank. This method is often contemplated in the original loan documentation, allowing the new bank to step into the facility agreement in place of the existing bank.

Method (B) has the same result as method (A), but it is achieved by the borrower effectively repaying the loan to the existing bank using a new loan from the new bank. This method will usually entail new loan documentation.

In strict legal terms, a novation does not transfer rights and liabilities: it cancels an existing contract and replaces it with another. The borrower's promise to perform its obligations in favour of a new bank is consideration for the existing bank releasing the old debt.

10.4.2.2   Advantages of novation

The main advantages in disposing of a loan by way of novation are as follows.

Moving obligations

Novation is the only proven method of moving contractual obligations as well as rights. In particular, this allows the existing bank to dispose of a loan which has an unutilised commitment (eg, under an RCF). Conversely, the new bank achieves a relationship with the borrower as if it were a party to the facility agreement.

Risk transfer

Novation can fully remove a loan (including any undrawn commitments) from the existing bank's balance sheet and so exclude it from any regulatory capital requirements.

Easy syndication

If the original facility agreement includes transfer certificates (see **10.4.2.3**), the existing (and any subsequent) bank can take on a large commitment without the delay of putting an underwriting syndicate together, knowing that it will easily be able to sell all or part of its commitment.

10.4.2.3   Disadvantages of novation

The main disadvantages of novating rights and obligations under a facility agreement are as follows.

Consent

The consent of all the parties involved in the original loan document is required, including any parties which have guaranteed the borrower's performance under the original facility agreement. This puts a great deal of power in the borrower's hands. Even if all parties are agreeable to a novation, a syndicated loan will present the logistical problems involved in organising the borrower, any obligors, and all the syndicate members to sign the document necessary to effect a novation.

One neat solution to the problem of consent, found predominantly in syndicated loans, is the use of 'transfer certificates'. The facility agreement will contain a clause under which the parties agree in advance that a bank may dispose of (by novation) any or all of its commitment. This is effectively an open offer to take a loan. To accept the offer, a new bank (together with the existing bank) must simply execute a transfer certificate, though the facility agreement may specify circumstances in which borrower consent is required (see **10.13**). A pro-forma certificate will usually be included as one of the schedules to the facility agreement. Transfer certificates can be used to dispose of all or part of both a bank's participation and/or its commitment.

A recent Australian case (*Goodridge v Macquarie Bank Limited* [2010] FCA 67) held that a prior agreement to novation in a loan agreement was invalid and simply an 'agreement to agree'. However, in *Habibsons Bank Ltd v Standard Chartered Bank (Hong Kong) Limited* [2010] EWCA Civ 1335, the Court of Appeal criticised the *Goodridge* decision. While this rebuttal was *obiter*, it is a very useful affirmation of the viability of standard transfer provisions in loan facilities, and so properly drafted transfer certificates should still be effective.

Note also that even if transfer certificates are used, the facility agreement may still require the borrower's consent to transfer in specified circumstances.

A system similar to the transfer certificate is the transferable loan certificate (TLC). The only significant difference is that the TLC operates through the agent bank issuing certificates and keeping a register of transfers. The TLC was originally devised to avoid stamp duties which are no longer in force, and so it is now relatively uncommon.

Secured loans

Since novation replaces existing obligations with new ones, it probably restarts the time periods ('hardening periods') during which the security might be set aside as a transaction at an undervalue, or preferred transaction, under the IA 1986, ss 238–241. The time limits for any floating charge being avoided under the IA 1986, s 245 might also be restarted (see **14.9** – although the likelihood of a liquidator using any of these provisions against a novation must be small). The other danger of security being re-dated to the time of each novation is that it might lose its priority over other security (see **14.3**). The favoured way to resolve these potential problems (in common law jurisdictions at least) is to appoint a security trustee to hold any security granted under the loan on trust for the banks. The banks participating in (or committed to) the facility will be beneficiaries of the security under the trust and may vary from time to time whilst the security remains. If the relevant jurisdiction does not recognise trusts, a 'parallel debt' structure might be used.

Disclosure

For obvious reasons, it is difficult to hide the identity of a transferee bank using novation.

10.4.3 Legal assignment

10.4.3.1 What is legal assignment?

Assignment is simply the transfer of rights. The Law of Property Act 1925 (LPA 1925), s 136 provides that a legal assignment of all debts and other choses in action (ie, rights enforceable by legal action rather than possession) must be:

(a) in writing and signed by the assignor;

(b) absolute (ie, unconditional); and

(c) notified in writing to any person(s) against whom the assignor could enforce the assigned rights.

In order to be 'absolute' in the context of loan transfers, an assignment must transfer the whole of the debt owed to the existing bank (see *Walter and Sullivan Ltd v Murphy (J) and Sons Ltd* [1955] 2 QB 584) (and cannot be 'by way of charge') (see **12.6**). If any one of the conditions for legal assignment is not fulfilled, the assignment will be an equitable one (see **10.4.4**). Legal assignments are also known as 'statutory assignments', or 'disclosed assignments'.

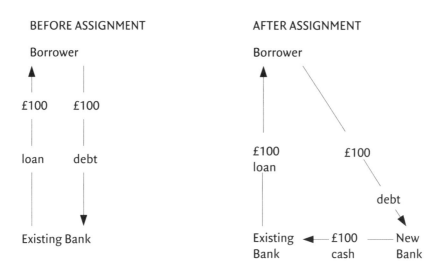

An assignment can transfer only rights and not obligations. The figure above shows an assignment in simplified terms. In the context of a facility agreement, a legal assignment will transfer to the new bank all the existing bank's rights under the facility agreement, the right to sue the borrower (and any guarantor), and the right to discharge the assigned debt. Any obligations of the bank can be transferred only if the borrower consents (ie by 'novation' – see **10.4.2**).

The assignment of some contracts is governed by legislation other than the LPA 1925. Of particular relevance in a banking context are bills of exchange and promissory notes (assignment of which is regulated under the Bills of Exchange Act 1882), and shares in registered companies, the rights under which are transferred in accordance with the CA 2006.

10.4.3.2   Advantages of legal assignment

Rights transferred

Subject to any restrictions in the loan facility and the 'disadvantages' discussed at **10.4.3.3**, legal assignment is an effective method of transferring rights under a facility agreement without requiring the borrower's consent.

Borrower's payments

On receiving notice of an assignment, the borrower is obliged to pay any monies due under the assigned loan to the new bank.

Secured loan

Any security, or a bank's rights as beneficiary of any security sharing agreement, may be assigned along with the debt, but is usually held by a Security Trustee or under a parallel debt structure (see **10.4.2.1**).

10.4.3.3   Disadvantages of legal assignment

Obligations not transferred

An assignment cannot transfer the assignor's obligations. Therefore, the existing bank cannot assign any undrawn commitments without the borrower's consent, which makes assigning a revolving credit facility problematic. In addition, any obligations the existing bank owes to its fellow syndicate members will not be transferred. Some facility documents therefore contain a proviso that an assignment will be effective only if the new bank gives an undertaking to perform the existing bank's obligations towards other syndicate banks. Others go further by purporting to assign the existing bank's rights and require the new bank to assume all the existing bank's obligations (including lending commitment to the borrower).

Rights not transferred

The rights under a contract can be assigned without consent only in 'cases where it can make no difference to the person on whom the obligation lies to which of two persons he is to discharge it' (*Tolhurst v Associated Portland Cement Manufacturers (1900) Ltd* [1902] 2 KB 660). The test is an objective one and so, for example, the character of an assignee will be ignored. In a banking context, there is a danger that any indemnity provisions for increased costs (see **9.3**) might be unassignable without consent because they are 'personal' (eg, they may vary substantially with the jurisdiction of a bank). The standard transfer provision will usually deal with this issue (see **10.13**).

10.4.3.4 Transferable loan instruments

Transferable loan instruments (TLIs) are simply a structured method of assigning a fully drawn commitment. They allow a bank to convert the repayment instalments due to it into debt instruments which mirror the terms of the facility agreement. These can be assigned by the new bank and existing bank executing a transfer Instrument. In a syndicated facility, the agent bank will usually keep a register of any commitments which are transferred.

The TLI (like any assignment) will transfer only rights and not obligations. Since the TLIs are debt instruments (ie, they evidence debt), they can be sued on by the buying bank without resort to the original facility agreement. The disadvantage of this is that the TLI is a 'debenture', which can cause problems under the FSMA 2000 (see **10.7**).

10.4.4 Equitable assignment

An assignment which does not meet any one (or more) of the provisions required for legal assignment under the LPA 1925, s 136 will (as long as there is an intention to assign) be an equitable assignment.

10.4.4.1 Differences between legal and equitable assignments

As a purely procedural matter, an equitable assignee (ie, the new bank) must join the assignor (the existing bank) in any action on the debt (*Three Rivers DC v Bank of England* [1995] 4 All ER 312). However, significant differences between legal and equitable assignments arise only if the obligor (ie, in the case of loan transfers, the borrower) is not given notice of an assignment (see **10.4.4.3**).

10.4.4.2 Advantages of equitable assignments

Partial assignment and non-disclosure

If a bank wants to assign part of an outstanding loan, it must use an equitable assignment. Likewise, if a bank wants to assign an outstanding loan without disclosing the identity of the new bank to the borrower, it must use an equitable assignment.

In all other material respects, equitable assignments share the advantages of legal assignments (see **10.4.3.2**).

10.4.4.3 Disadvantages of equitable assignments

Payments

If the equitable assignment is not notified to the borrower, it will not know the identity of the bank to which its debt has been assigned, and it is entitled to continue making payments through the existing bank. In some circumstances, this may be an advantage to the existing bank: some assignments allow the assignor to retain a percentage of the interest paid on the assigned loan. In that situation, the existing bank will be happy to receive payments from which it can skim its entitlement.

However, the new bank buying a non-disclosed assignment must rely on the borrower to pay its money, and on the existing bank to pass it on. It is therefore taking a double credit risk. Furthermore, if the borrower should become insolvent the new bank might have the near impossible task of tracing any monies which the existing bank received from the borrower but did not pass on.

Subject to equities

If the equitable assignment is unnotified, a new bank will be subject to all 'equities' (eg, mutual rights of set-off) which arise between the existing bank and the borrower, even *after* the loan is assigned (until notification of assignment).

10.4.4.4   Form of notice of assignment

The rights of a bank taking an assignment depend almost entirely on whether notice is given to the borrower. In light of the issues outlined above, a notice of assignment (legal or equitable) should require a borrower to confirm:

(a)   the amount of the existing bank's debt;

(b)   that it has no rights of set-off or counter-claim against the existing bank;

(c)   that it has no notice of other assignments of the same debt;

(d)   the facility agreement has not been varied; and

(e)   that it will pay amounts due and payable under the underlying contract to the new bank's order.

10.4.5   Sub-participation

10.4.5.1   What is sub-participation?

The main reason why a bank is interested in novation and assignment is that they both enable it to remove loans from its balance sheet. There is, however, a way to achieve the same objective whilst leaving the original loan in place, known as 'sub-participation' (or sometimes 'funded participation' (to differentiate from 'risk participation' – see **10.4.6**) or simply 'participation', although this is confusing because it is also the label for a bank's share of a loan).

Sub-participation (which has no technical legal meaning) is an arrangement under which an existing bank matches part or all of its loan to a borrower with a deposit it takes from a new bank (the 'sub-participant'). So far, this sounds like the inter-bank funding described at **4.9**. However, in a sub-participation the new bank agrees that its deposit will be serviced and repaid only when the borrower services and repays the loan from the existing bank. The sub-participant has effectively taken on the risk of the first loan: if the borrower fails to make a payment due under its loan from the existing bank, the existing bank will not have to pay the new bank. This is set out in simplified form in the figure below.

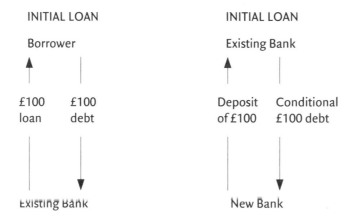

The existing bank's obligations to the new (sub-participant) bank match, and are conditional upon, the borrower's obligations to the existing bank.

There are two aspects to sub-participation which it is important to appreciate at this stage. First, the transaction does not involve any transfer of rights or obligations: the existing bank's contractual relationship with the borrower is unaffected. Secondly, since the sub-participation agreement is an entirely separate contract to the initial facility agreement, the new (sub-participant) bank will not have any rights directly against the borrower. This is known as a 'non-recourse' transaction. Any security provided by the borrower will remain with the existing bank.

10.4.5.2 Advantages of sub-participation

Risk transfer

Sub-participation will effectively remove a loan from inclusion in the existing bank's regulatory capital requirements, other than in respect of undrawn commitments (see **10.4.5.3**). The existing bank should ensure that any sub-participation agreement requires the new (sub-participant) bank to be subject to the terms of any re-financing of the borrower. Failure to do this will risk jeopardising an effective transfer of risk.

Consent

Unless there is a prohibition in the original facility agreement (which is unlikely), an existing bank may sub-participate without the consent of the borrower. The only problem the existing bank might face is in providing information about the borrower to a new bank, since all banks owe a duty of confidentiality to their clients (set out in *Tournier v National Provincial and Union Bank of England* [1924] 1 KB 461). An existing bank intending to sub-participate will therefore want to include a clause in the original facility agreement allowing it to release information about both the borrower and the loan, without a breach of duty.

Non-disclosure

An existing bank does not have to disclose a sub-participation to the borrower (unless it has a confidentiality issue – see above), and most sub-participations will be 'silent'. The advantage to both existing bank and borrower is that the relationship between them is maintained despite the risk being laid off.

10.4.5.3 Disadvantages of sub-participation

Sub-participant's credit risk

A new (sub-participant) bank must take a credit risk on both the existing bank and the borrower. If the borrower goes into liquidation, the new bank receives only what the existing bank can reclaim (because of the non-recourse nature); and if the existing bank goes into liquidation, the new bank will usually have to claim as an unsecured creditor. This double risk will be reflected in the new bank's fees for sub-participation.

Risk transfer

Funded sub-participation may not be fully effective to off-load the (entire) risk of undrawn commitments if it simply results in the existing bank taking a risk on the new bank instead of the borrower. The sub-participation agreement must ensure that the existing bank is put in funds in time to meet the borrower's demands for utilisation in order effectively to remove the risk.

10.4.6 Risk participation

Risk participation is a form of participation which acts like a guarantee. The risk participant bank will not immediately place any money with the existing bank, but will agree (for a fee) to put the existing bank in funds in certain circumstances (typically on any payment default by the borrower). Risk participation might be provided by a new bank as an interim measure before it takes full transfer of a loan.

A more common use for risk participation is to cover so-called 'unfunded' assets (ie, assets under which an existing bank has a potential outlay such as guarantees, letters of credit or swaps). If the existing bank's customer fails to meet its reimbursement obligations under these products, the new bank will put the existing bank in funds.

10.5 GLOBAL TRANSFER AGREEMENT

Sometimes a deal requires a large amount of simultaneous transfers, for example if a small number of banks initially underwrite the loan but then transfer to several dozen new banks after the closing. To avoid preparing a large number of transfer certificates, a Global Transfer Agreement may be used. This is simply a new contract which amends (and restates) the facility agreement to add a new schedule of commitments. The logistical advantages are obvious, though it is very transparent: all banks will see who else is lending and the 'level' of their commitment, and this will not suit all deals.

10.6 TYPE OF ASSETS SOLD

Originally, the main market for asset sales was for so-called 'distressed debt' (also known as 'impaired debt'). Distressed debt is corporate debt which a bank is prepared to sell at a price below the amount outstanding, usually because it believes the debt may be repaid late, or repaid only in part. Sales of distressed debt are typically from a syndicated loan, and may be one or more banks selling part or all of their commitments. The selling bank will free the distressed debt from its balance sheet, and avoid the time-consuming process of restructuring the debt. The buying bank takes the seller's entitlement to full repayment for a fraction of that amount. Therefore, whilst the buyer takes the risk of non-repayment, if the borrower makes a recovery his reward will be high.

At the end of 1996, however, a number of banks formed the 'Loan Market Association' (LMA), intending to enhance trading in (primarily) performing loans known as the 'par market'. The LMA, which now has a very substantial membership, has produced standardised documentation, settlement procedures, and agreed a code of practice for market activity, all of which has helped create a more active and efficient secondary market.

10.7 TAX IMPLICATIONS

Detailed analysis of the tax implications of asset sales is beyond the scope of this book. Briefly, there are usually two main types of tax which might affect asset sales: stamp duty (or stamp duty reserve tax (SDRT) payable on some undocumented transactions) and withholding tax.

Sub-participation does not involve any transfer of rights, and so will not attract stamp duty. Novation will not usually involve a transfer of property for stamp duty purposes and so will not normally attract the tax. If, however, the asset has rights other than those normally associated with a debt (eg, rights to acquire property) stamp duty or SDRT may apply. Assignment may prima facie attract stamp duty or SDRT; however, exemptions for transfer of loan capital (Finance Act 1986, ss 79(4) and 99(5)(a)) can often be used to avoid any duty.

In all asset sales between banks, and involving a UK resident/domiciled borrower, the relevance of withholding tax on interest payments will depend largely on whether the exemption under s 879 of the ITA 2007 applies (see **9.3.4**). The s 879 exemption will apply to loans which have been assigned as long as the advance was initially made by a 'bank' and the assignee is beneficially entitled to the interest and within the charge to UK incorporation tax at the time interest is paid. If the loan is novated (see **10.4.2**), however, this probably creates a new advance and so must be made to a 'bank' to ensure s 879 still applies.

10.8 FINANCIAL SERVICES AND MARKETS ACT IMPLICATIONS

Section 19 of the FSMA 2000 provides that:

> No person may carry on a regulated activity in the United Kingdom or purport to do so unless he is an authorised person or an exempt person.

This 'general prohibition' may impinge on some asset sales.

The only certain way for a bank to avoid the implications of the FSMA 2000 when selling participations, is probably to ensure that it is authorised to do so under the Act.

10.9 BORROWER TRANSFERS

Facility agreements will invariably prohibit a borrower from transferring any of its rights or obligations under the agreement without consent from the bank(s).

10.10 OTHER JURISDICTIONS

If a borrower (or any other obligor, such as a guarantor) is registered or domiciled in a jurisdiction other than England and Wales, there may be issues of local law which impinge on asset sales. Generally, sub-participations are unlikely to face problems because they use a contractual agreement completely outside the loan document and which will not affect the borrower. Novations and assignments may require consents of, or notices to, local regulatory bodies (or to the borrower) before being recognised. The golden rule is to get advice from a 'local' lawyer.

10.11 SECURITISATION

Sometimes a bank will want to sell not just one or two loans at a time but a whole group of loans together. Securitisation is a technique which allows banks to 'sell' a large portfolio of loans (or other income-producing assets), thereby freeing up capital to re-invest. In very basic terms, securitisation involves the owner of a pool of assets (the 'originator') transferring them to a specially formed company (a 'special purpose vehicle' or 'SPV'). The SPV funds its purchase of the assets by issuing debt securities (it is therefore known as the 'issuer'). Coupon and redemption of the debt securities are met with, and secured over, the asset pool.

10.12 ASSET SALES – THE BANK'S PERSPECTIVE

Most banks will require the flexibility to sell a loan if they decide it is necessary or desirable. They will, however, usually be receptive to a borrower's feelings towards maintaining some form of lending relationship during the term of the loan and allow some restrictions (see **10.12** below). In current markets, many entities other than traditional banks are involved in buying loans on the secondary market. A bank's solicitor should therefore ensure the facility transfer language allows transfer not just to other banks but also to trusts, funds, or other entities engaged in buying loans. (Some facilities restrict transferees to other 'financial institutions': in *Argo Fund Ltd v Essar Steel Ltd* [2005] EWHC 600 (Comm) the court gave a helpfully wide interpretation to the phrase 'financial institution'.) The facility agent will usually charge a fee of around £1,000 to £1,500 for each transfer.

10.13 ASSET SALES – THE BORROWER'S PERSPECTIVE

At first sight, the identity of the bank might appear to be of little importance to a borrower. After all, on novation, assignment and sub-participation the provisions of the facility agreement will apply to the existing bank(s) or any of their successors. However, whilst the provisions of the facility agreement will remain unchanged, some may affect the borrower more strictly (eg, the increased cost provisions). A borrower will usually enjoy a good relationship with its existing bank which it will be reluctant to lose. It might be a well-established relationship; a borrower might feel that the existing bank's involvement in due diligence and negotiating the loan give it a better insight into the borrower's business; a new bank might be less flexible.

It is unlikely that a bank will agree to a complete prohibition on transfer in the facility agreement. Moreover, a prohibition is probably not in the borrower's best interest: it would severely limit the number of banks willing to participate in the loan at syndication, and therefore result in higher fees or margin.

It is therefore common to see the borrower's consent required for transfer, but not to be unreasonably withheld or delayed. Even then, consent will not usually be required if the transferee bank is an existing lender (or an affiliate of an existing lender), and will not usually be required if an event of default has occurred and is continuing. Facility agreements also often prevent borrowers from withholding consent solely due to an increase in mandatory cost, and consent may be deemed given if the borrower fails to reply within a specified period (typically five days). Sometimes the agent will agree to maintain a minimum commitment, known as 'minimum hold', which gives the borrower the comfort of a continuing involvement by the existing bank. Other variations seen in leveraged deals include a 'white list' (a list of named institutions to which the bank may transfer) or on rare occasions a 'black list' (a list of named institutions to which the bank may *not* transfer).

Finally, the difficult credit conditions during 2008 and 2009 saw many loans trading at substantially less than their face value (below par). This has prompted borrowers to consider buying back portions of their own loan debt: buying the debt at a discount is a cheap way to prepay. Most facility agreements did not specifically address whether a borrower could buy back the loan, but there may be issues with prepayment restrictions, pro-rata sharing between lenders, restrictions on cash usage, and issues with novation. The LMA now offers specific mechanics to its facilities to deal with borrower debt buy-back. These mechanics either prohibit buy-back completely, or restrict which borrower-related entities might buy. Even if buy-back is allowed, the buying entity is usually required to allow all the syndicate banks a chance to sell (rather than approach specific banks). Furthermore, any debt they purchase will lose the associated voting rights to stop borrower entities interfering with votes.

10.14 FURTHER READING

Geoffrey Fuller, *Corporate Borrowing: Law and Practice* (4th edn, Jordans, 2009).

Debt buy-back sparks loans policy revision

Martin Arnold and Anousha Sakoui

Phones 4U has bought back some of its debt and with it joined a growing legion of companies capitalising on record-low debt prices.

The UK mobile phone retailer, owned by Providence Equity Partners, has bought £25m ($45m) of its debt at about 75 per cent of face value, according to a person familiar with the company.

Providence has already invested $2.5bn (£1.4bn) buying debt in its own and other buy-out deals, and recently hired Thomas Gahan from Deutsche Bank in the US to head its new capital markets group.

The news follows an ever-increasing number of mainly private equity-backed companies and their shareholders buying up their own debt either as an investment or in an attempt to reduce leverage as they navigate the global financial crisis.

However, lenders are not always supportive. One concern is that these debt buy-backs could allow shareholders or the company to build a blocking stake in the debt and influence future debt renegotiations or even block lenders from enforcing a default.

In response, the Loan Market Association, a trade body representing lenders, has published revised loan documentation that includes the ability to prohibit borrowers from buying back debt and stop shareholders or their affiliates voting debt they have bought back in negotiations with lenders - in a bid to avoid conflicts of interest. Borrowers can be allowed to buy back debt under certain conditions.

These buy-backs can happen in different ways.

The first is for a private equity company to buy its portfolio company's debt through a special purpose vehicle it owns, then consolidate it with the rest of the group - either selling the vehicle to the business or contributing it as equity ñ reducing leverage.

Another way is for the private equity group to use its own fund or a separate debt fund to buy the debt for investment purposes.

However, private equity groups with separate debt funds, such as KKR and Permira, say they have solid Chinese walls between their credit and buy-out teams.

Amadeus, the BC Partners and Cinven-owned travel IT company, has asked lenders' consent before doing a buy-back and has been negotiating the terms of it - a process investors generally prefer.

After discussion with lenders, the company has limited the size of the debt buy-back to €320m (£254m) and agreed not to vote in lender negotiations, according to a person familiar with the company.

Blackstone's German plastic film producer Klöckner Pentaplast has also been buying back debt, helping it reduce leverage. Earlier this year, it bought back about €25m of mezzanine, or subordinated, debt at about 20 to 30 per cent of face value, but has bought more since.

However, in spite of concerns, some banks may ultimately see these moves as a way to reduce the risk of a debt restructuring.

"Banks don't really want to end up owning the equity in these companies, so there is an alignment of interest between the debt and equity," said Peter Combe, chief executive of Permira Debt Managers, the €800m debt fund set up by the UK private equity group last year.

Source: *Financial Times*, 30 September 2008

CHAPTER 11

DRAFTING TIPS

11.1	Introduction	135
11.2	Creating the document	135
11.3	The aims of drafting	136
11.4	Templates and precedents	136
11.5	Drafting techniques	137
11.6	Key words	140
11.7	Time computations	142

> 'I am a bear of very little brain, and long words bother me.'
>
> Pooh Bear, in *Winnie-the-Pooh* by AA Milne

11.1 INTRODUCTION

Probably the hardest task of a banking solicitor is drafting the documentation. Having identified the issues which affect his client and having negotiated those issues (usually at some length), the solicitor must return to his office and create a document to reflect what the parties have agreed.

Most solicitors' firms have a house style of drafting documents to which they encourage adherence. Furthermore, like most skills, drafting legal documents is best learnt and perfected through practice. The aim of this chapter, therefore, is not to produce a set of drafting rules, but rather to highlight some of the issues and techniques which commonly arise in the context of drafting loan documentation. If there is a 'golden rule', however, it is this: work out what you want to achieve before putting pen to paper (or finger to key).

11.2 CREATING THE DOCUMENT

In order to put the techniques explained below into context, it is important to appreciate the way in which a facility agreement is created. Since a written facility agreement is primarily used to benefit the bank (see **3.7**), the drafting of the document starts and remains in the control of the bank's solicitor (although in some acquisition financings, where the sponsor's solicitor has drafted the term sheet, he may also draft the loan). The bank's solicitor will produce a first draft from the term sheet (see **2.3.2**), which will then be sent to all parties for comment. The borrower and his solicitor are likely to have a number of clauses which they want deleted or varied, and will annotate the first draft accordingly (this is usually the only time when the borrower's solicitor does any substantial drafting). Once the marked-up draft has been seen by all parties, a conference call or (more rarely) meeting is arranged to discuss the points that it raises. There then ensues a series of e-mail exchanges, telephone calls or meetings which will attempt to resolve all the issues, with the bank's solicitor periodically producing amended drafts of the agreement to reflect substantial changes.

The burden of drafting which the bank's solicitor must shoulder is partly offset by the fact that in creating the document he knows what he has, and has not, included. The borrower's solicitor must not only review the provisions that are in the draft agreement, but also identify any points which should be included for his client's protection but which are not. It is worth noting that the LMA (see **10.5**) has produced a series of widely-used term and revolving facilities for investment grade and leveraged deals, the former having been 'blessed' by both the LMA members and the Association of Corporate Treasurers (ACT – akin to a representative body for borrowers). These are widely used to provide conformity to the loan market and a first draft which eliminates some basic negotiation.

11.3   THE AIMS OF DRAFTING

There are a number of aims to bear in mind when creating or amending a facility agreement.

11.3.1   Certainty

The primary reason for having a written facility agreement is to create certainty between the parties. The document must be drafted to reflect what has been agreed.

Certainty may help to avoid litigation: in a case before the House of Lords (reviewing the interpretation of a guarantee), Lord Jauncey said:

> I find great difficulty in understanding the desire of commercial men to embody so simple an obligation in a document which is quite unnecessarily lengthy, which obfuscates its true purpose and which is likely to give rise to unnecessary arguments and litigation as to its meaning. (*Trafalgar House Construction (Regions) Ltd v General Surety & Guarantee Co Ltd* [1995] 3 WLR 204)

11.3.2   Ambiguity

Despite the general requirement for certainty, there are circumstances in which a party will want some ambiguity drafted into the facility agreement, for example, a requirement for 'reasonableness' when the bank exercises a right (see **11.5.6**). Any uncertainty will usually work in favour of the borrower and against the bank.

11.3.3   A workable document

There are two elements to a document being 'workable'. First, it must be reasonably user-friendly from the parties' point of view. A borrower in particular will not be happy with drafting which can only be understood by his solicitor. The borrower must be able to refer to the document from time to time in order to check what it can and cannot do. Whilst many facility agreements are long and complicated, the language need not be: the best documents are those which have simple language and are easily understood.

Attention to detail can also improve a document from the client's point of view. For example, putting a meaningful heading to each main clause and including a list of clauses at the front of the document is very helpful. When referring to a clause number, it is good practice to add the heading of the clause as well as the number. For example, 'subject to clause 16 (permitted disposals) the borrower may … '.

Secondly, the drafting must work in practice as well as in theory. For example, it is of little use drafting a clause which provides for interest payment dates to fall on a certain date each month if it does not also provide for what happens when that day is not a 'business day' when bank and borrower are open.

11.4   TEMPLATES AND PRECEDENTS

At some stage, most legal drafting will rely on the use of templates and/or precedents. Most firms have a set of template documents on their word-processing system which have been compiled over some years and which represent their most commonly used documents (eg, term loans, RCFs, guarantees and debentures). These templates can be used as a starting point for the bank's solicitor to create the first draft of the facility agreement. If the document to be drafted does not have a template, it is common practice to cannibalise precedent documents, ie those drafted for previous transactions, making alterations as required. The use of templates and precedents not only avoids 're-inventing the wheel', it also helps to maintain the house style of a particular firm.

There are two potential pitfalls in using precedents: first, failing to ensure conformity of terminology (for example, a precedent clause might define the borrower as 'the Borrower', whereas the document which is being created might use 'the Company'); secondly, precedents are negotiated documents, meaning standard clauses may have been changed or removed.

11.5 DRAFTING TECHNIQUES

Templates and precedents are particularly useful for boiler plate clauses, since these often require minimal alteration between documents. However, those clauses which are likely to require heavy negotiation (eg, representations, undertakings and events of default) are also likely to need substantial re-drafting. This section outlines some of the more common drafting techniques which can be used to achieve a compromise in these clauses.

11.5.1 Clause construction

When drafting a clause from scratch which must incorporate a right or obligation (eg, undertakings), it is worth remembering a principle of clause construction devised by George Coode, and outlined in **Skills for Lawyers**. In 1843, Coode suggested the following order for clause construction:

(1) Refer to any exceptions first: eg 'Subject to ... '.

(2) Next, set out the circumstances or conditions upon which the legal right or obligation depends, using the present tense: eg 'If X does [...] and Y does [...]'.

(3) Next, set out the right or obligation using the active and avoiding the passive: eg 'X must do 1, 2, 3, 4 and 5'.

(4) Finally, put the provision into paragraphs and give it a heading.

For example, a provision that the borrower can draw money only if the conditions precedent have been satisfied, notice has been given in the required form, and no event of default has occurred, might be drafted as:

4.1 Availability of loan

Subject to no event of default having occurred under clause 7, if the Borrower:

(a) satisfies all the conditions precedent listed in clause 3; and

(b) delivers to the Agent a notice of utilisation in accordance with clause 9;

the Banks will make available to the Borrower a term loan facility up to a maximum amount of £10,000,000 (ten million pounds).

The advantage of using this technique is that any provisos to the right (or obligation) created by the clause are clearly stated in the first part of the clause. However, many banking documents will not conform to this style. It is quite common to see the phrases 'subject to' or 'provided that' in the middle of a clause. For example:

The Banks will make available to the Borrower a term loan facility up to a maximum amount of £10,000,000 (ten million pounds) provided that no event of default has occurred under clause 7, the Borrower has satisfied all conditions precedent ...

11.5.2 Qualifying an obligation

Many obligations will be drafted as absolute. For example, an undertaking might provide: 'the borrower will not change the date of its financial year end without the bank's consent'. It would not be appropriate to draft this as 'the borrower will use its best endeavours not to change its financial year end without the bank's consent'.

However, a borrower may argue, particularly where an obligation involves a third party, that it is inappropriate to make an obligation absolute. The usual qualifiers are 'reasonable', 'all reasonable' or 'best' endeavours. For example:

The borrower will use *all reasonable endeavours* to prevent any circumstances occurring which would result in any person taking any action or making a claim against them under any environmental laws ...

What, then, is the difference between 'reasonable', 'all reasonable' and 'best' endeavours? Whilst there is plenty of pertinent case law, the meaning of each phrase will depend on its context. However, in general terms the case law can be summarised as follows:

'*Reasonable endeavours*' is the least onerous. It requires a party to adopt and pursue *one* reasonable course of action in order to achieve the result, bearing in mind its own commercial interests and the likelihood of success. It does not require the party to exhaust every course available to it.

'*All reasonable endeavours*' requires a party to explore *all* avenues reasonably open to it, and explore them all to the extent reasonable. However, the party is neither obliged to disregard its own commercial interests, nor required to continue trying to comply if it is clear that all further efforts would be futile.

'*Best endeavours*' is the most onerous and requires a party to take steps which a prudent, determined and reasonable obligee, acting in its own interests and desiring to achieve that result, would take. It is not an absolute obligation, though, and would not include actions which would lead to financial ruin, undermine commercial standing or goodwill, or have no likelihood of being successful.

It is worth noting that 'all reasonable' and 'best' endeavours are very similar, and some judges have held there is no practical difference (eg *Rhodia International Holdings v Huntsman International LLC* [2007] All ER (D) 264 and *Jet2.com Ltd v Blackpool Airport Ltd* [2011] EWHC 1529 (Comm)). What is common ground, however, is that the onus is on the obligor to show it has met the required level of 'endeavour'. Finally, 'endeavour' is sometimes replaced by 'efforts', but since most case law is based on 'endeavour', that is the more certain term to use.

Since the meaning of these phrases is inherently uncertain, it might be worth specifying parameters in some circumstances. For example, indicating acceptable expense, time limits, whether legal action is required or even any steps the party is not expected to take might be helpful. The downside is that these are yet more points to negotiate and so more often than not the generic wording is used.

11.5.3   Materiality

It is often the case that a borrower will not object to a clause (eg, an event of default) in principle, but finds that it is too tightly drafted. A common compromise for this sort of provision is to qualify the clause with 'materiality'. For example, an absolute provision under which the borrower will be defaulted in the event that it 'is in breach of any licence necessary for operation of its business' has no regard to the varying scale and consequences of any breach. A provision which defaults the borrower only in the event of a breach which 'may have a material adverse effect on its ability to perform its obligations under the facility agreement' is far more palatable for the borrower. A material adverse change event of default clause is an obvious example of the use of 'materiality' (see **5.2.2** and **8.3**).

Unfortunately, any clause which calls for a judgment may hold some danger for a bank. What does 'material' mean in the context of 'a material adverse effect'? A bank will be wary of calling a default only later to be proven to have acted negligently (see **8.8**). This is another case of uncertainty acting in the borrower's favour. The best solution from the bank's point of view is to define 'material'. However, quantifying 'material' might be very complicated, or even impossible. The next best solution for a bank is to be specifically entitled to make the decision as to what is 'material'. Thus wording such as 'material in the opinion of the bank' will avoid any argument. In a syndicated loan, the agent bank might prefer any discretion with respect to important decisions (eg, events of default) to be exercised by a 'majority' of the banks rather than the agent (see **9.6.3**). This may delay the process, but it relieves the agent of a difficult responsibility.

11.5.4 'Would' or 'might'

Some clauses (eg, certain events of default) will be drafted so that they are triggered by events which 'might' have particular consequences. For example, a borrower could be asked to give a representation that it:

> ... is not subject to any litigation, arbitration, or similar proceedings which might affect its ability to perform its obligations under the facility agreement.

From the borrower's point of view, this is clearly preferable to providing an absolute warranty that it is not subject to any such proceedings whatsoever. However, it is arguable that almost anything 'might' occur: the Earth might be overrun by aliens. A borrower will sometimes argue, therefore, that the word 'might' should be replaced by the word 'will' or 'would'. This can give a bank problems. To be certain that something will cause something else can be very difficult. The parties will usually agree to some form of compromise, such as 'is reasonably likely to ... ', or 'will in the bank's opinion'.

11.5.5 De minimis

De minimis non curat lex is the general legal principle that some breaches of duty or mistakes are too trivial to attract a legal remedy. In common parlance a 'de minimis provision' is one which excludes minor breaches of a term. It is another technique for softening the effect of a provision but, unlike some of the methods (eg, materiality) outlined above, without the risk for the bank of creating uncertainty. For example, a cross default clause (see **8.3.5**) might provide for a default '... if the Borrower fails to pay any indebtedness when it falls due'. This would mean the borrower could be defaulted for failing to pay the milk bill on time. A de minimis provision might add '... if the Borrower fails to pay any indebtedness in a principal amount exceeding £50,000'.

The level at which a de minimis is set is crucial; it must allow the borrower sufficient 'leeway' to run its day-to-day business, whilst not being so high as to prevent the provision which it modifies from operating effectively. The level of the de minimis provision will therefore largely depend on the nature of a borrower's business. One problem with de minimis provisions is that they can allow a multitude of minor breaches, which might together be as 'harmful' as a large breach. To overcome this problem, some de minimis provisions will set an aggregate outstanding maximum.

11.5.6 Reasonableness

The effect of most provisions can be altered substantially simply by inserting the word 'reasonable'. For example:

(a)   in the bank's reasonable opinion;

(b)   take all reasonable steps;

(c)   reasonably likely to have an effect;

(d)   use reasonable endeavours;

(e)   consent not to be unreasonably withheld.

This is a powerful tool for the borrower to reduce the severity of a provision. The real value for a borrower is the difficulty for the bank in making an objective decision about what is 'reasonable' in a given situation. Once again, the word introduces uncertainty into a provision, which will make a bank hesitate before calling a default.

11.6 KEY WORDS

Some of the words and phrases which occur in many loan documents, and which can cause some confusion, are explained below.

11.6.1 'Subsidiary'

It is quite common for a bank to require a parent company to guarantee any loans it has made to the parent's subsidiaries (and occasionally vice versa) (see **13.2**). Such 'cross guarantees' effectively breach the companies' status as separate legal entities vis-à-vis each other. Furthermore, a parent company may simply be a 'holding company', with most of the group's business being run through its subsidiaries and with no substantial assets of its own other than shareholdings. For these reasons many of the undertakings and events of default in a facility agreement may be drafted to take account of, or apply to, other companies in the borrower's group. The definition of 'subsidiary' in the facility agreement is therefore very important. Most agreements will usually refer to one of the two definitions in the CA 2006.

The CA 2006 uses two different concepts of 'subsidiary'.

11.6.1.1 Section 1159

For a company to be its subsidiary, the 'parent' company must:

(a)   hold a majority of the voting rights which can be exercised at a general meeting of the 'subsidiary'; or

(b)   be a member of the 'subsidiary' and have the right to appoint or remove its directors who together control more than half the voting rights at board meetings; or

(c)   be a member of the 'subsidiary' and control, pursuant to an agreement with other shareholders, a majority of the voting rights which can be exercised at a general meeting of the 'subsidiary'; or

(d)   be a holding company of another subsidiary which is itself the holding company of the 'subsidiary'.

In determining the voting rights, etc, of the 'holding company', the voting rights of its subsidiaries and certain nominees and trustees are taken into account.

11.6.1.2 Section 1162 and Sch 7

Section 1162 and Sch 7 provide a definition used in the CA 2006 in relation to financial statements (see full explanation at **6.6**). The important difference from s 1159 is the concept of 'subsidiary undertaking', whereby the ability to exercise a 'dominant influence' over a company (or partnership, or other unincorporated association) makes it a 'subsidiary undertaking' for accounting purposes. This might include joint-venture arrangements which a company would not usually consider to be a subsidiary.

A bank will always want as much control over the borrower as possible and so it will favour a wide definition of subsidiary in the facility agreement, usually the definition under s 1162 of the CA 2006. It is probably best to set out the definition in the loan document, rather than simply refer to the section number, in order to avoid any problems if the statutory definition is amended after the agreement is executed.

If a borrower is part of a large group of companies, it might ask that the provisions in the facility agreement apply only to its 'material subsidiaries' (ie, those worth over a certain amount). Subsidiaries may grow in size and importance, and so the bank will want the definition to embrace 'material subsidiaries from time to time', to catch any non-material subsidiary which becomes 'material' at a future date.

In *Enviroco Ltd v Farstad Supply A/S* [2009] EWCA Civ 1399, the Court of Appeal decided that a company ceased to be a subsidiary of its holding company when the subsidiary's shares were secured to a bank by way of legal mortgage. To prevent subsidiaries subject to a legal mortgage falling outside the controls of a facility agreement, it is worth considering amending the definition of 'subsidiary' to include companies which would qualify under s 1159 of the CA 2006 *but for* any legal mortgage of their shares (see also **15.2.2.6**).

The concept of 'subsidiary' varies widely internationally. It is therefore very important when dealing with foreign borrowers or foreign banks to be quite clear as to the scope of the 'subsidiary' definition.

11.6.2 Notwithstanding

'Notwithstanding' is most remarkable for the fact that it is one word and not three! It means 'in spite of', and so pushes aside the clause(s) to which it refers. For example: 'Notwithstanding the prohibition in clause 29 (giving security), the Borrower may provide a guarantee', means the borrower can give a guarantee whatever clause 29 might say.

The opposite effect can be achieved with the phrase 'Subject to...'. For example, 'Subject to the prohibition in clause 29 (giving security), the Borrower may provide a guarantee', means the borrower can give a guarantee only if clause 29 does not prevent it from doing so.

11.6.3 Definitions

Since, by its very nature, a definition will be repeated frequently throughout a document, it is particularly important to ensure that it is correct. Some of the points to watch out for include the following.

11.6.3.1 'Means' or 'includes'

Using the word 'means' will give a precise definition and avoid uncertainty. For example, '"Security" means a fixed charge or a floating charge'.

However, using the word 'includes' makes the definition much broader and less certain. For example, '"Security" includes a fixed charge or a floating charge'.

Imagine a facility agreement incorporating a negative pledge which prohibits the borrower from giving any 'security'. Under the first definition, the borrower could be safely advised that giving a mortgage, pledge or lien would not breach the agreement, but not under the second definition. This is an example of drafting which is deliberately imprecise in order to benefit the bank: a precise definition of 'security' carries a risk that the bank might not think of everything to be included, and it may not cover new products.

11.6.3.2 Law of Property Act 1925, s 61 and the Interpretation Act 1978

Section 61 of the LPA 1925 applies, amongst other things, to all deeds and contracts made after 1925 and, unless the context otherwise requires, will deem:

(a) 'month' to mean a calendar month;

(b) 'person' to include a corporation;

(c) the singular to include the plural (and vice versa);

(d) the masculine to include the feminine (and vice versa).

Under the Interpretation Act 1978, any reference to statutory provisions in a document will be deemed (subject to contrary intention) to be a reference to those provisions as amended or re-enacted from time to time. Curiously, but perhaps because most solicitors are cautious by training, many commercial documents explicitly state the provisions deemed by these two statutes. However, sometimes the 1978 Act provision is excluded to avoid amended legislation from bringing new meaning to a document (eg, if the definition of 'subsidiary' in the CA 2006 was changed under new legislation).

11.6.3.3 Eiusdem generis rule

The eiusdem generis rule of interpretation means that where general words follow a list of specific words, they are taken to be limited to categories of the same kind as the specific words. If a definition or other clause includes a list which is intended to be non-exclusive, the eiusdem generis rule can be avoided by the use of words such as 'whatsoever' to emphasise generality.

11.7 TIME COMPUTATIONS

Time limits are a crucial element in facility agreements. Most notice provisions and certain events of default will revolve around timing. Provisions dealing with timing will require careful drafting, and may be subject to certain statutory implied terms.

Unless specified otherwise, reference to a 'month' will mean a calendar month (LPA 1925, s 61). Furthermore, unless there is a contrary intention, the courts are likely to hold that:

(a)   the day on which an event occurs is not included when calculating a period which runs from the occurrence of that event (*Lester v Garland* (1808) 15 Ves 248). For example, the calculation of a period '21 days after giving notice', will not include the day on which notice is given (unless wording such as 'including' or 'commencing on' is used);

(b)   the period of a 'month' (or 'months') will end on the day which has the same date in the subsequent month (see *Dodds v Walker* [1981] 2 All ER 609). For example, two months from 20 March will be 20 May. If this rule would not yield a date (eg, one month from 31 August), the period is taken to end on the last day of the month in which it expires (eg, 30 September). The period will end at midnight on the appropriate day;

(c)   if a period is stated as 'not less than 3 months nor more than 6 months', the rule outlined in (b) above will apply. For example, if a notice is to be given 'not more than 3 months nor less than 2 months before cancellation', then cancellation on 30 November may be notified from 31 August to 30 September (inclusive);

(d)   notice of 'at least' or 'no fewer than' 21 days will usually exclude the day on which notice is given and the day on which it expires. The same effect is obtained by the expression '21 clear days';

(e)   'day' is a calendar day (ie, including all holidays, and not just a 'business day').

These implied rules will probably reflect the parties' intentions in most cases. However, since they are particularly critical in loan documents, timing provisions should be very specific. For example, a period of time should specify whether it is to include the day on which it begins or ends. A period should be stated as '21 clear days' if that is what is intended. Most documents will also specify that time limits or payment dates will always end by close of business on a 'business day' (usually defined as a day on which banks are generally open for business in London). If the end of a particular period will not fall on a 'business day', provision should be made for it to be deemed as falling on the 'business day' which immediately precedes it, or next follows it, as required. Loans which involve funding in currencies other than sterling will have to source those currencies in their country of origin (eg, a bank in London providing a US$ loan will have to borrow the dollars in, say, New York). This means that the 'business day' definition in the loan should specify that funds can be drawn only on a day on which both London and New York are open for business.

Repayment dates are usually contained in a schedule to the document, which specifies the exact date and time by which the money is to be received.

PART II

SECURED LENDING

CHAPTER 12

COMMON FORMS OF SECURITY

12.1	Introduction	145
12.2	Categorising security	145
12.3	Giving rights over assets	146
12.4	Transfer of ownership	149
12.5	Giving physical possession	150
12.6	Assignment	152
12.7	Some terminology	152
12.8	Further reading	153

'Protection is not a principle, but an expedient.'

Benjamin Disraeli

12.1 INTRODUCTION

What would you do if someone failed to repay money you had lent him? Your options might range from forgiving the debt to threatening bankruptcy, but ultimately your only effective sanction is probably to sue him for the unpaid amount. Litigation has its drawbacks: it is usually expensive, protracted, and obtaining enforcement of a judgment may take too long to be effective. Furthermore, if you have to litigate to recover a straightforward debt claim, it probably means the debtor cannot pay because he is insolvent. His assets must almost certainly be shared with other creditors, and the bottom line is that you will probably recover only part of the money due to you.

Taking security as a bank is all about increasing the likelihood of getting repaid. There are many ways to achieve this, but most rely on giving a bank direct recourse to a borrower's property in the event of the borrower's default. This will usually avoid the need for litigation, may ensure priority over other creditors, and will almost certainly hasten recovery of the debt. This chapter provides an introduction to some of the more common types of security, **Chapter 13** looks at 'quasi-security', **Chapter 14** develops some of the issues which can arise on taking security and **Chapter 15** briefly examines a typical security document.

Whilst security might be used to support almost any type of obligation, the following four chapters concentrate on security for loan transactions. For the sake of continuity, therefore, the text will generally refer to the giver of the security as the 'borrower', and the holder of the benefit of the security as the 'bank'.

12.2 CATEGORISING SECURITY

Security arrangements are sometimes categorised into 'consensual' (ie, agreed between the parties) and 'non-consensual' (ie, arising at law). It is probably more helpful, however, to categorise the main types of loan security according to their effect, that is:

(a) security which merely gives the bank rights over an asset (eg, fixed or floating charge – see **12.3**);

(b) security under which 'ownership' (ie, legal or equitable title: see below) in the secured asset is transferred to the bank (eg, a mortgage and assignment – see **12.4**); and

(c)   security under which the bank has actual (or 'constructive') possession of the secured asset (eg, pledge or lien – see **12.5**).

Each of these categories is examined below. At this stage, however, it is worth clarifying some terminology. In everyday language, the words 'ownership' and 'possession' are virtually interchangeable. However, in the context of security interests, the two terms have distinct meanings: 'ownership' means having title to an asset (legal or equitable); and 'possession' means having physical possession of an asset. These are the meanings attributed to 'ownership' and 'possession' in this book.

12.3   GIVING RIGHTS OVER ASSETS

The cornerstone of most loan security will be the charge. Charges may be 'fixed' or 'floating' and are always 'equitable' (other than the 'charge by deed expressed to be by way of legal mortgage' (LPA 1925, s 87) which is arguably not a true 'charge' anyway – see **12.4** – and other statutory charges, which are rarely seen).

12.3.1   Fixed charges conferring rights not possession

Probably the best way to ensure that a secured asset is available to meet unpaid monies is to take possession of it (known as a 'pledge' – see **12.5.1**). This will prevent the borrower disposing of the asset, or diminishing its value in any way. Consider, however, some typical assets of a trading company: machinery, vans, office equipment and premises. Giving a bank physical possession of those assets would simply prevent the borrower from running its business. If it is impractical, or impossible, for a bank to take possession of an asset, an alternative is to give it rights over the asset which:

(a)   prohibit the borrower from disposing of the asset without permission;

(b)   attempt to maintain the asset's value whilst it is in the borrower's hands; and

(c)   allow the bank recourse to the asset in the event of the borrower's default under the loan.

This is the aim of a fixed charge.

A fixed charge does not immediately transfer ownership or possession, but allows a borrower to use the charged assets (subject to conditions designed to maintain their value, and a prohibition on disposal) unless and until any 'enforcement event' occurs as specified in the charge document. On an 'enforcement event', under its contractual rights in the charge document, the bank may require the borrower to sell the asset, or the bank may take possession of, and sell, the asset, or appoint a receiver to do the same (this carries less risk for the bank since the receiver acts as the borrower's agent). The fixed charge simply gives the bank a claim over the charged assets in priority to other creditors. If the borrower sells an asset subject to a fixed charge, the rights created by the charge usually remain with the asset.

Some security documents will refer to fixed charges as 'specific equitable charges'.

12.3.2   Floating charges

12.3.2.1   What is a floating charge?

There will be certain of a borrower's assets for which a fixed charge is not an appropriate form of security. For example, any stock in trade subject to a fixed charge could not be sold without the bank's consent. This might not be a problem if the borrower is a boat-builder selling two or three boats a year. Consider, however, the problems that would be caused by taking a fixed charge over the stock in a sweet shop: clearly, it would be unworkable. The unsuitability of a fixed charge to secure assets which a borrower might want to deal with quickly and at some unspecified future date (ie, the borrower's current assets – see **6.3.2**), led to the development, from the late 19th century, of the floating charge.

A floating charge secures a group of assets which may fluctuate from time to time. The assets secured by a floating charge are identified generically, for example a borrower's 'trading stock' or its 'undertaking and assets' (fixed charges may also use generic descriptions, or alternatively refer to individual assets). Unlike a fixed charge, a floating charge specifically allows the borrower to deal with the charged assets in the ordinary course of business (which is very widely construed). This allows a borrower to sell its stock and dispose of its other current assets so that it may continue trading and make money which (in theory at least) it will eventually use to repay the secured loan. Conversely, any assets which are acquired after the floating charge is formed but which fall within the identified group will be subject to the charge.

The freedom to deal with assets, which is the very advantage of the floating charge, does give rise to a very important question: what is to stop a borrower from disposing of all its current assets, leaving the floating charge 'empty'? This is, in fact, a very real problem, and is one reason why a bank prefers to take a fixed charge over an asset whenever possible. The problem is minimised, however, through the concept of 'crystallisation'

12.3.2.2 Crystallisation

Each floating charge document will incorporate a mechanism through which the borrower's freedom to deal with the assets over which it floats can be frozen. This is known as 'crystallisation'. On the occurrence of certain events (see below), the floating charge will effectively become a fixed charge with respect to any of the assets over which it previously 'floated', and which remain in the borrower's ownership. The borrower will then be unable to dispose of those remaining assets without the bank's consent. Most charges provide for crystallisation to be simultaneously effective over all the assets secured by the charge. There is, however, no reason why a floating charge should not be partially crystallised (ie, preventing only a selection of the secured assets being dealt with) as long as the charge document specifically provides the power to do so.

The effectiveness of this mechanism is entirely dependent on the sensitivity of the trigger for crystallisation. There are two ways in which crystallisation might occur: under common law, or under the terms of the document creating the charge.

Crystallisation under common law

Case law has established a number of events which will cause a floating charge to crystallise, all of which are triggered by a cessation of the business as a going concern, or by a prohibition on the borrower using its charged assets:

(a) *The borrower's liquidation.* Crystallisation will occur when a winding-up order is made (including a voluntary winding-up, even if merely for reorganisation), but not simply when a petition to wind up is presented.

(b) *An administrative receiver, or receiver, is appointed by the bank.* If the bank appoints a receiver or an administrative receiver, this implies that the borrower's authority to deal with the asset has been withdrawn and thus it will crystallise a floating charge. There is authority that a floating charge will not be crystallised (under common law) merely by the crystallisation of another floating charge (since it does not necessarily signify the end of trading). The making of an administration order which is not intended to prevent the borrower continuing to run as a going concern will probably not crystallise a floating charge at common law.

(c) *The borrower ceases to carry on business.* A floating charge will crystallise if the borrower ceases trading for any reason (including where the borrower has disposed of its assets to such an extent that it can no longer carry on its business).

(d) *Intervention by the bank.* Most forms of intervention by a bank which prevent a borrower dealing with its charged assets will cause crystallisation at common law.

Under the charge document

Crystallisation will also occur in any of the circumstances agreed contractually between the borrower and bank in the charge document. These are important to alleviate any uncertainty about crystallisation at common law. These will usually consist of an immediate right to crystallise the floating charge at any time by giving notice to the borrower (a borrower may request the proviso 'if the bank reasonably believes the secured assets are in jeopardy ... ', etc), and a number of specified events which will crystallise the charge without any action by the bank, for example the appointment of an administrator. This second group of events is often referred to as 'automatic crystallisation' (somewhat confusing, since the term might be thought more applicable to the common law situations which cause crystallisation, outlined above). A lender may sometimes be asked to provide a certificate of non-crystallisation (eg, to a purchaser of the borrower's assets).

12.3.2.3   Post-crystallisation

The most widely accepted legal analysis of a floating charge is that it creates an immediate security interest, but does not attach to any individual asset until crystallisation (in contrast to a fixed charge, which attaches immediately – ie, it encumbers the charged assets with the rights it creates). However, crystallisation does not, in itself, create a new charge to be registered under the CA 2006 (*Re Manurewa Transport Ltd* [1971] NZLR 909).

The charge document will contain the powers which can be exercised by the bank (see **Chapter 15**) and will invariably include the power to appoint a receiver to run the business and realise the charged assets. Crystallising a floating charge will create an effective stranglehold on a borrower: without the use of its current assets it cannot usually make any money. A bank will therefore not take crystallisation lightly, and frequently it is a precursor to the appointment of a receiver.

On crystallisation, a floating charge effectively will become a fixed charge. However, this 'fixed charge' will rank behind any fixed security created before it crystallised and will be subject to any third party rights of set-off (see **13.5**), including legal or equitable rights, which accrued prior to the crystallisation.

12.3.2.4   Weaknesses of a floating charge

The floating charge suffers from a number of weaknesses to which the fixed charge is immune.

Fixed charges and administrator's costs

A floating charge is vulnerable to later fixed charges, although this may be alleviated by a prohibition on creating further security (see **14.2.2** and **14.3**). Floating charges also rank behind the costs and expenses of an administrator appointed to the borrower; the administrator can use any of the floating charge assets to fund the administration costs.

In addition, all liquidation expenses (other than litigation expenses) have automatic priority over floating charge holders, and are recoverable from the assets of the company (see the Insolvency (Amendment) Rules 2008 (SI 2008/737)).

Preferential creditors

Any proceeds realised from assets secured by a floating charge must be used to pay any 'preferential debts' of the company before meeting claims under the floating charge (IA 1986, s 40). 'Preferential debts' are defined at s 386, and specified fully in Sch 6 to the IA 1986, as modified from 15 September 2003 by the Enterprise Act 2002 (EA 2002) (s 251). The main preferential debts are now limited amounts of outstanding employees' wages and pension scheme contributions. The preferential status previously accorded to 'Crown creditors' (eg, PAYE contributions, VAT, social security contributions, etc) was abolished by the EA 2002.

These now rank as unsecured creditors. However, the Act also provides for an amount of the company's property which would otherwise go to floating charge-holders (the 'prescribed part'), to be set aside to pay unsecured creditors. The amount of this 'fund' is determined by statutory instrument from time to time. It is currently 50% of the first £10,000 of the prescribed part and 20% thereafter, subject to a maximum amount of £600,000 (see IA 1986, s 176A).

Avoidance of floating charge

As well as the provisions concerning transactions at an undervalue and preferences (see **14.9**) which can apply to all forms of security, the IA 1986 provides for specific circumstances in which a floating charge can be set aside by the court on the application of a liquidator or administrator (s 245). The degree of vulnerability of a floating charge will depend on whether or not it is granted to a 'connected person'.

12.3.2.5 Charge to connected person

If a company grants a floating charge to a 'connected person' (this includes a director, his close relatives, his business partners and their close relatives – see s 249 of the IA 1986) then it might be set aside if it was granted within two years of the onset of a company's insolvency.

12.3.2.6 Charge to unconnected person

A floating charge granted to a person not 'connected' with the company might be set aside if it was given within 12 months of the onset of the company's insolvency, provided that the company was either insolvent when it gave the charge, or became insolvent as a result.

However, a floating charge will not be invalid in either case to the extent that it is in return for valuable consideration (ie, money, goods, services or the reduction of any debt) given on or after the creation of the charge. The underlying debt will remain unsecured if the floating charge is set aside.

The concept of a 'floating charge' is very much a product of the English legal system (and derivative systems) and so may not be recognised or have an equivalent in other jurisdictions.

12.4 TRANSFER OF OWNERSHIP

12.4.1 Mortgages

A fixed charge creates an encumbrance over assets, giving the holder priority over other creditors. An alternative way to provide security over assets is by transferring ownership (ie, legal or equitable title) to the bank, along with a right to sell on default and an obligation to re-transfer title on satisfaction of the debt. This form of security interest is known as a 'mortgage'. The transfer of title may enhance a bank's ability to realise the security if necessary, and in the meantime prevents a borrower from selling the secured assets. A mortgage can therefore be thought of as an 'enhanced' charge, since it gives rights over an asset which are backed with a transfer of legal or equitable title. As Professor Goode explained in *Legal Problems of Credit and Security*, '... a mortgage is a right of appropriation (= charge) plus a transfer of ownership ...'. Subject to contrary intention (and statutory restrictions in the case of land), a (legal) mortgage entitles the bank to take immediate possession of the mortgaged asset. However, possession is not required to perfect the security (it is 'non-possessory' security) and, for reasons of practicality, most banks will not take possession of mortgaged assets before default.

12.4.2 Mortgages over land

Almost any asset can be secured by way of a mortgage, although many of us associate it with land because we give security over our homes. Under the LPA 1925 (as amended by the Land Registration Act 2002), the only way to create legal security over freehold or leasehold land is by way of 'a charge by deed expressed to be by way of legal mortgage' (LPA 1925, s 87). The terminology is not particularly helpful (it is not a 'true' charge, neither does it actually transfer legal title like most legal mortgages), but the net result is to provide the bank with rights equivalent to granting it a 3,000-year lease (or, for leasehold, a lease for one day less than the borrower's lease).

12.4.3   Legal and equitable mortgages

If a mortgage does not transfer *legal* title, it will be an equitable mortgage. Equitable mortgages can be created with less formality than their legal equivalent, and may result from any of the following, depending on the circumstances:

(a)   a written agreement by a borrower that the property is to be secured by way of equitable mortgage;

(b)   an agreement to provide a legal mortgage (once money has been lent, an agreement to provide a mortgage will take effect as an equitable mortgage);

(c)   a mortgage over an equitable interest;

(d)   a mortgage over property not yet owned by the borrower; or

(e)   a purported legal mortgage that does not comply with all the necessary formalities. For example, in the case of land, a failure to register the mortgage at the Land Registry (which may be accidental or intentional).

The fundamental difference between equitable and legal security interests is that the former can be ignored by a bona fide purchaser (or 'security taker') for value of the legal title to an asset without notice (actual or constructive) of the equitable security. However, the 'disadvantage' is largely overcome if the equitable security is registered under CA 2006, ss 860–894 (see **14.2**), because this provides notice of the security to anyone searching, or who is deemed to search, the register. An equitable mortgage may not benefit from the 'automatic' powers vested in legal mortgagees under LPA 1925, s 101, which include the power of sale (although these powers should be specifically given in the security document).

12.5   GIVING PHYSICAL POSSESSION

For the reasons of practicality explained at **12.3.1**, the most common forms of debt security are 'non-possessory': that is, the bank does not take immediate physical possession, but simply takes certain rights over the charged assets. However, there are circumstances in which a security interest involves possession of an asset from the outset.

12.5.1   Pledge

A pledge is a way of creating security by the actual (or constructive) delivery of a tangible movable asset to a creditor, to be held until the performance of an obligation (eg, repaying a debt). The bank will take possession while the borrower retains ownership. The best known example of a pledge is placing an article with a pawnbroker.

12.5.1.1   Rights of the pledgee

The security created by a pledge is essentially the possession of an asset. A pledged asset must therefore be 'delivered' by the borrower. This can be achieved by physical delivery, or by vesting control (sometimes known as 'constructive delivery' – eg, having the keys to a safe deposit box) with, in either case, an intention to create security. Some assets may be pledged by delivery of documents; however, the pledge will fail if the document does not effectively provide control. For example, simply holding the share certificate of a registered share does not give sufficient control (even if accompanied by a 'blank' stock transfer form) because the share certificate is not a document of title and it does not give the right to vote or receive dividends.

Since it does not transfer rights of ownership, a pledge will end as soon as the pledged asset is returned to the borrower. A pledge will confer certain implied rights, the most important of which is the right to sell the pledged assets to meet a defaulted debt.

12.5.1.2   Problems with taking a pledge

There are a number of practical difficulties with taking pledges. A bank will probably want to take a pledge only over valuable assets. This will lead to problems of keeping the pledged assets secure (imagine a pawnbroker taking a pledge over a Stradivarius violin) both on delivery to the bank and on return. Furthermore, the bank will probably be liable as bailee while it holds the pledged assets, and this may entail insurance costs.

There is no legal requirement to document a pledge. However, to avoid any argument that an asset has merely been deposited for safe-keeping, a 'letter of pledge' or 'memorandum of deposit' is usually provided by the borrower to evidence the terms of the pledge. One advantage of pledge security is that it does not require any form of registration: giving up possession is notice to third parties ('perfection').

12.5.1.3   What assets may be pledged?

A pledge involves the delivery of an asset into the possession of a creditor, therefore the asset must be capable of actual (or constructive) delivery. The most common types of asset to be pledged are therefore bearer instruments, such as bills of exchange, promissory notes and bearer bonds (see **18.2.2**). More substantial assets may be 'constructively pledged' by placing them in a location (eg, a warehouse) only accessible to the bank.

12.5.2   Lien

A lien is the right to retain possession of another person's property until he settles an obligation. The term 'lien' derives from the word 'ligamen', meaning 'binding'. Liens arise automatically under English law in certain types of commercial relationship. There are three main types of lien.

12.5.2.1   Common law (or particular) liens

A common law lien allows retention of the goods under which the debt arises. If, for example, a customer refuses to pay for his dry-cleaning, the cleaner has a right to retain the clothes in lieu of payment.

12.5.2.2   Statutory (or general) liens

Statutory liens allow certain persons to retain any goods in their possession against any obligation owed to them by the owner of those goods. Stockbrokers, bankers, solicitors and innkeepers all benefit from statutory liens, which arise by operation of law and without the need for any agreement.

Common law and statutory liens are both types of legal lien. Legal liens will usually require actual possession of the property which has been rightfully acquired. Unlike a mortgage or pledge, legal liens will not generally confer any right to sell the property. A banker's lien is an exception, however, allowing the retention and sale of any securities and cheques deposited by a customer.

12.5.2.3   Equitable liens

An equitable lien does not require possession of the property to which it attaches (usually land) and will give a right of sale through application to the court.

It is also possible for a lien to be created by contract. However, if the contract provided for any right of sale the 'lien' would be little different to a pledge.

12.6 ASSIGNMENT

Chapter 10 explained how a bank wanting to sell a loan could transfer its rights under the facility agreement by way of assignment. An assignment may also be used to create a mortgage over certain forms of asset.

The most common assets secured by assignment are a borrower's rights against a third party ('choses in action'), for example debts, and rights under various contracts. As with an assignment by way of sale, an assignment by way of security can be legal or equitable: it will in effect create a legal mortgage if it complies with s 136 of the LPA 1925 (a 'statutory assignment' – see **10.4.3**); otherwise it will create an equitable one (see **10.4.4**) (notice that assignment 'by way of charge' is expressly excluded from s 136 and so assigning rights by way of security will constitute a legal assignment only if it is an absolute assignment with a proviso for re-assignment on satisfaction of the secured obligation). Assignments by way of security will always include a provision (either explicit or implied) for reassignment on satisfaction of the debt. Priority between assignments depends on notice being given to the third party (see **14.3.3**).

12.7 SOME TERMINOLOGY

Unfortunately, the area of loan security suffers more than its fair share of overlapping and interchangeable terminology. Documents and statutes use identical terms to describe entirely different things, and the legal meaning of terms is often subtly different to their colloquial meaning. Some of the terms which have multiple meanings are explained below.

12.7.1 Debenture

At common law, a 'debenture' is any document which a company issues to acknowledge, or create, a debt.

But beware! In common banking parlance a 'debenture' is the name given to the document under which a borrower creates the security for a secured loan, usually incorporating fixed and floating charges along with other security interests (see **Chapter 15**).

12.7.2 Charge

A 'charge' is the appropriation of assets to the satisfaction of a debt. Strictly speaking, a charge does not transfer any ownership in property, but simply creates certain rights over it: in other words, it creates an equitable security interest. Used in this sense, there are only two forms of charge, fixed and floating (see **12.3).**

But beware! The term is used colloquially (even in statutes and case law) as a generic label for almost any type of security, including mortgages, liens and assignments.

12.7.3 Security/securities

The term 'security' refers to the provision of rights against a person's assets which are intended to enhance the probability of recovering a debt claim against him.

But beware! In common banking parlance the terms 'security', or 'securities' refer to the instrument (ie, the 'piece of paper') in which a borrower acknowledges debt, or to investments such as shares, debentures, stock, bonds, bills of exchange and other forms of tradeable debt (see **Part III**).

12.7.4 Statutory definitions

The confusion which can arise in terminology is illustrated by statutory definitions. In the LPA 1925, 'mortgage' is defined to include 'any charge or lien on any property for securing money or money's worth'. Under the IA 1986, 'security' means 'any mortgage, charge, lien or other security' (s 248(b)). In the CA 2006, the term 'charge' includes a 'mortgage'.

The statutory definitions are also often inclusive rather than specific. The 'moral' of this maze of terminology is that the label given to an instrument is not always a reliable indication of the type of security it provides; it is important to examine its substance.

12.8 FURTHER READING

Calnan, *Taking Security: Law and Practice* (2nd edn, Jordans, 2011).

Goode, *Commercial Law* (4th edn, Penguin, 2009).

Goode, *Legal Problems of Credit and Security* (4th edn, Sweet & Maxwell, 2008).

Fuller, *Corporate Borrowing: Law and Practice* (4th edn, Jordans, 2009).

CHAPTER 13

QUASI-SECURITY

13.1	Introduction	155
13.2	Third party support – guarantees and comfort letters	155
13.3	Negative pledge	159
13.4	Retention of title	159
13.5	Set-off	159
13.6	Why take security?	160
13.7	Security – the bank's perspective	162
13.8	Security – the borrower's perspective	163
13.9	Further reading	163

13.1 INTRODUCTION

Chapter 12 examined the most common methods by which a bank might take security in order to increase the likelihood of recovering a borrower's debt. However, there are various other ways a bank might choose to enhance its prospects of repayment, which are not strictly security interests because they do not create any rights 'in rem' (ie, rights over the asset). This chapter explains some of the more common types of 'quasi-security' before considering the main reasons for taking loan security.

13.2 THIRD PARTY SUPPORT – GUARANTEES AND COMFORT LETTERS

A bank will frequently look for a third party willing to support the borrower's repayment obligations. The generic name usually given to such third parties (together with the borrower) is 'obligor', and the two most common forms of third party support are the guarantee (which may be secured on the guarantor's assets) and the comfort letter. Guarantors are sometimes known as 'sureties'.

13.2.1 Guarantees

13.2.1.1 What is a guarantee?

A guarantee is a form of undertaking by one party to answer for another party's liabilities, usually on its default. In the context of a loan, the guarantor will frequently be a company in the same group as the borrower. For example, a bank might make a loan conditional on receiving a guarantee of the borrower's obligations from its parent company. Furthermore, the company which has given the guarantee may be required to give security over its own assets to support its potential liability under the guarantee. As well as providing a second source of repayment, a parent company will also guarantee punctual performance of the borrower's obligations under the facility, to encourage supervision of the borrower by the parent.

13.2.1.2 Guarantees and indemnities

Before considering guarantees further, the strict legal differences between the terms 'guarantee' and 'indemnity' should be appreciated (although the guarantee document will usually purport to contract out of these limitations – see **13.2.1.3**).

A guarantee must support a primary liability between two parties other than the guarantor: the guarantee agreement will be a secondary contract and will not create a 'stand alone' obligation. In other words, the validity of the obligation under a guarantee will be largely dependent on the guaranteed obligation (the main implications of which are explained at **13.2.1.3**).

An indemnity creates a binding obligation to indemnify a party for a specified loss which it may incur. Unlike a guarantee, an indemnity creates a 'stand alone' (or primary) obligation which is independent of the liability or default of another party. Furthermore, unlike a guarantee (see **13.2.1.4**), an indemnity does not need to be in writing to be enforceable. In general terms, an indemnity is more 'robust' than a guarantee: most loan facilities therefore contain a guarantee plus an indemnity, in case the guarantee fails.

13.2.1.3   Legal implications of a guarantee

Once a contract is legally classified as a guarantee there are a number of consequences at common law (some of which the bank will want to vary), including the following.

Consequences of being a secondary obligation

(a)   Since the guarantee is a 'secondary' contract, the guarantor will not be liable unless the default and liability of the borrower is proven. Most banks will therefore require that the 'guarantee' is 'on demand' and payable as if a 'principal debt': once the borrower defaults, the bank can immediately demand performance from the guarantor (ie, the bank does not need to prove the liability or default of the borrower; see eg, *McGuinness v Norwich and Peterborough Building Society* [2010] EWHC 2989 (Ch)).

(b)   If the contract between bank and borrower (the primary contract) is void (or if the borrower's obligation is discharged), the guarantor's obligation will fall away. A bank will therefore usually include a provision that the guarantee survives failure of the underlying obligation, as well as an indemnity within the guarantee document in order to create a primary obligation on the 'guarantor' if the guarantee fails.

(c)   If the contract between bank and borrower is varied in any material way without the guarantor's consent, the guarantor is released from the guarantee (even if the variation was not prejudicial to the guarantor). Similarly, certain acts which might be prejudicial to the guarantor (eg, if the bank fails to register security for the debt) will void the guarantee. This issue commonly arises where the facility which the guarantee supports is to be increased. In *Triodos Bank v Ashley Charles Dobbs* [2005] EWCA Civ 630, the Court of Appeal considered a guarantee which purported to allow 'any amendments, variation, waiver or release of an obligation' by the borrower, without reference to the guarantor. The Court held that any amendment or variation must be 'within the general purview of the original guarantee' (a test adopted in *Trade Indemnity Co Ltd v Workington Harbour and Dock Board* [1937] AC 1). In *Triodos* the guarantee was held not to survive an increase of the underlying facility, in part because the facility was to be used for a different purpose. The fact that the guarantor *knew* of the amendments made no difference – he had to *consent* with a clear understanding of the facts. Banks should therefore be aware that even with 'saving language' designed to bolster a guarantee, it might be jeopardised by refinancing the underlying facility.

Other key rights (usually waived or postponed)

(a)   A guarantor may use most rights of set-off or counter-claim which the borrower has against the bank (and which arose before the borrower defaulted) to reduce its liability under the guarantee.

(b)   Once it has paid out under the guarantee, a guarantor will be entitled to reimbursement from the borrower. This right will arise through an implied or actual indemnity between the borrower and guarantor.

(c) The guarantor will also be entitled to any security the bank holds for the borrower's debt, under the doctrine of subrogation. Subrogation arises only once a guarantor has paid the full amount to which it is liable under the guarantee (and does not arise automatically for an indemnity).

(d) If there is more than one guarantor of the debt, any guarantor that pays out will have a right to claim back a share of the payment from the co-guarantors (a right of 'contribution').

The problem with all these rights from a bank's perspective is that it may not want the guarantor to enforce them immediately (eg, if the subrogated security secures borrowings in addition to the guaranteed loan). The guarantee document should therefore postpone the rights until such time as the bank has been repaid in full and no longer requires the security. It will also want any obligation of contribution to be waived in respect of any subsidiary it wants to sell (eg, on enforcement of security).

13.2.1.4 General considerations for a bank's solicitor

In addition to the points mentioned above, a bank's solicitor should take account of the following:

(a) The governing law of a guarantee should, if possible, mirror that of the other loan documents as this will make enforcement easier.

(b) If the contract is legally a guarantee it must be evidenced in writing before it can be enforced (Statute of Frauds 1677, s 4). As with any other contract, a guarantee is enforceable only if it is given for consideration. In particular, there is a danger that a guarantee will be void for past consideration if it is pre-dated by the obligation it supports. The problem can be resolved by creating the guarantee document as a deed.

(c) A guarantee should be expressed as 'continuing' to avoid the rule in 'Clayton's case' (see **14.6**) and to help it to survive variations to the primary obligation (but see **13.2.1.3(c)**)

(d) The guarantee should provide that the bank's evidence of the borrower's liability is conclusive (at least in the first instance) to avoid any argument on enforcement.

(e) As with any other contract, a company must have the requisite power to enter into a guarantee, and its officers must be properly authorised. The CA 2006, s 172 requires a director to 'act in the way he considers, in good faith, would be most likely to promote the success of the company for the benefit of its members as a whole'. The section provides a (non-exhaustive) list of the factors to which directors must have regard in fulfilling this duty. In approving a guarantee, the directors must consider this duty together with the factors, and the board minutes should reflect that they have done so. Directors usually get comfortable with the s 172 duties (see **14.10** for more detail), but other jurisdictions will have different rules, and guarantees are often prohibited or limited to amounts actually received by the guarantor.

(f) A guarantee is capable of being 'financial assistance' under the provisions of CA 2006, ss 678–680 (see **14.11**).

13.2.1.5 Insolvency Act 1986

A guarantee is arguably capable of being a transaction at an undervalue (because, unlike a borrower granting security, it usually increases the guarantor's liabilities) and, in limited circumstances (eg, where the guarantor had previously only given third party security, with no guarantee), a preference, and so being set aside under IA 1986, ss 238 and 239 respectively (see **14.9**).

13.2.1.6 Counter-indemnity

A guarantor will usually want an express counter-indemnity from the borrower (ie, a contractual right to claim back any money it pays to the bank – see 'Guarantor's rights' at **13.2.1.3**).

13.2.1.7   Terminology

Terminology in this area is often used loosely. Watch out for documents referring to 'guarantees' which are actually warranties given by the borrower (see **5.2**). As mentioned at **13.2.1.2**, some 'guarantee' contracts are actually indemnities. The generic terms 'surety' and 'suretyship' are sometimes used; 'guarantor' and 'guarantee' should technically be used.

13.2.2   Comfort letters

Sometimes a parent company or other potential obligor will refuse to provide a guarantee. It may be contractually prevented from doing so (eg, by a negative pledge style undertaking; see **13.3**), or a company might not wish to create a contingency on its balance sheet. In such cases, the bank might demand a comfort letter from the company. Comfort letters (also known as 'support letters', or 'letters of intent') are usually given by a parent company in respect of a subsidiary. They range from a simple written acknowledgment of the fact that the subsidiary is undertaking the obligations created by the loan, to a statement of intention to maintain an interest in, and support for, a subsidiary, and to ensure it is capable of fulfilling those obligations (sometimes known as a 'keep-well' agreement).

Comfort letters are not normally intended to be legally binding but are used to reassure a bank that the parent company is aware of, and supports, its subsidiary's borrowing and other general or specific activities. They will require careful drafting. Statements of the comforter's 'intention' or 'policy' will not usually amount to an actionable undertaking. However, words such as 'guarantee' and 'undertake' may be binding. The general phrasing of comfort letters is usually deliberately vague so that the terms are not certain enough to be enforced under English contract law.

The test for determining whether a comfort letter has legal effect is to analyse it as though it were a contract. Was there offer and acceptance, intention to create legal relations and consideration? Did the issuer of the letter promise to do something? Has it failed to do that thing? Has the recipient of the letter suffered loss as a consequence of the failure? What is the measure of damages for the breach? In the seminal case of *Kleinwort Benson Ltd v Malaysia Mining Corpn* [1989] 1 All ER 785, a parent company's comfort letter stated: 'It is our policy to ensure that the business of [subsidiary] is at all times in a position to meet its liabilities to you under the above arrangements.' The Court of Appeal held this to be a statement of fact (ie, that this was the parent's policy) at the time rather than an undertaking actually to support the subsidiary going forward. However, the conclusion depended entirely on the facts – in this case, the parent had previously refused to give a guarantee or accept joint liability, which suggested that it did not intend the comfort letter to be binding. In contrast, the recent Australian case of *Gate Gourmet Australia (in liquidation) v Gate Gourmet Holding AG* [2004] NSWSC 149 found a 'comfort letter' to be legally binding. The key points were that the letter included technical language, was provided to reassure directors that their otherwise insolvent company could continue to trade, and made statements which were clearly promises, not just statements of fact.

In the case of *Re Atlantic Computers plc (in administration); National Australia Bank Ltd v Soden* [1995] BCC 696, it was held that the common intention of the parties to a comfort letter must be ascertained by reading it as a whole. The final paragraph of the letters in question, which asserted that they 'were not intended to be a guarantee' and that they were 'an expression of present intention by way of comfort only', was sufficient to show that they did not amount to a contractual promise.

A solicitor should be aware that even if the tests outlined above are not fulfilled, comfort letters may still be treated as binding in jurisdictions other than England and Wales.

13.3 NEGATIVE PLEDGE

There is a sense in which a negative pledge provision (one which prohibits a borrower granting security to third parties – see **7.5.2.1**) provides a form of security, because it is arguably a restriction on how the borrower may use its assets. There is, however, little doubt that a negative pledge clause is not technically a security interest (although a negative pledge might provide a claim in tort for damages against a third party which induces a borrower to breach the prohibition, and there is an argument that the third party (which cannot benefit from its own wrongdoing) holds any security on trust for the negative pledge holder). The negative pledge is usually included on the Companies Act registration form (see **Chapter 14**). This is a mandatory requirement for companies registered in Scotland under s 885(3) of the CA 2006.

13.4 RETENTION OF TITLE

Retention of title arrangements are dealt with in **Business Law and Practice**. In essence, a retention of title clause allows a seller to retain legal title to goods which have been supplied to a buyer until the buyer settles its account. If payment is not forthcoming, the seller can recover the goods from the buyer. A retention of title clause therefore acts as a type of security interest for the seller. This is clearly not of any use to 'secure' a loan. However, the existence of such a clause may undermine a bank's security: if a borrower does not have beneficial ownership of an asset, it cannot usually grant security over it. Where the borrower's business makes it appropriate, a bank should consider requiring representations and/or warranties to the effect that the borrower is not party to any agreements which contain a retention of title clause.

A bank should also check if any assets which are in a borrower's possession are actually subject to a finance lease (see **Glossary**), in which case ownership of the leased asset technically remains with the finance company (although usually subject to contractual rights of the borrower).

13.5 SET-OFF

13.5.1 What is 'set-off'?

Imagine that you take a loan from your bank for £1,500. You also have a current account with that bank into which your salary of £1,100 per month is paid. The money in that current account is owed to you by the bank. If you default on the loan repayment the bank will not want to let you draw your salary from the current account and then have to make a demand against you for the £1,500. It would prefer to keep the £1,100 towards payment of the loan, and then demand the balance of £400. This is known as 'set-off'. It is not strictly a security interest (and not so registrable) but a right to set a debt owed by a creditor to a debtor against the debtor's debt, and so reduce or extinguish that debt. A borrower should not be allowed to exercise set-off against the bank (see **9.9.2** and **9.9.5**).

13.5.2 When is set-off available?

The right of set-off is a complex area of law. In general terms, however, there are three ways in which a bank is *likely* to have a right of set-off against a borrower.

13.5.2.1 Equitable right of set-off

Broadly, a bank may set off a liquidated debt owed to it by a borrower against a liquidated debt owed by it to that borrower.

13.5.2.2 Contractual set-off

Most security documents supporting a loan will enhance the equitable right of set-off by allowing the bank to set off unliquidated (ie, contingent) claims.

13.5.2.3   Set-off on liquidation

Both equitable and contractual rights of set-off may be affected by the liquidation of a borrower when, in certain circumstances, r 4.90 of the Insolvency Rules 1986 (SI 1986/1925) provides for mandatory set-off. Basically, any 'mutual' credits, debts or dealings can be set off so long as the bank did not know of the petition for insolvency against the borrower when it gave credit. From 1 April 2005 the Insolvency (Amendment) Rules 2005 have rewritten r 4.90 and allowed set-off of contingent claims against a company.

There is a statutory right of set-off under the Statutes of Set-Off dating from the 1700s, but this is now of little real significance.

The right of set-off is particularly important if a debtor is in danger of becoming insolvent (but no petition has been lodged), since it allows access to the debtor's unsecured assets (ie, cash) without risk of being a transaction at an undervalue or a preference under IA 1986, ss 238 and 239.

13.5.3   Banker's right of combination

There is an implied right under common law which is peculiar to banks and which allows them, subject to contrary agreement, to combine two or more accounts of a borrower. If one account is in debit (ie, overdrawn), an account in credit can be used to 'repay' the overdraft. This is sometimes known as 'bankers' set-off', but is more correctly the right of 'combination'.

13.6   WHY TAKE SECURITY?

The introduction to **Chapter 12** stated that 'Taking security as a bank is all about increasing the likelihood of getting repaid'. There are a number of peripheral reasons for taking security.

13.6.1   Appointing an administrator or administrative receiver

If a bank wants to enforce security it will invariably do so through a third party, and usually when the borrower is, or is about to become, insolvent. Until late 2003, a bank with security (including a floating charge) over all (or substantially all) of the borrower's assets would usually appoint an administrative receiver with wide-ranging powers to manage the company and sell off assets to repay the bank. However, the EA 2002 has changed the insolvency landscape. To understand the current position, it is necessary briefly to consider two procedures both before and after the 2002 Act took effect.

13.6.1.1   Administration pre-Enterprise Act 2002

The administration procedure was introduced by the IA 1986. A court had to consider that one (or more) of four specific purposes would be achieved before making an administration order and appointing an administrator. The first, and key, purpose was to ensure 'the survival of the company, and the whole or any part of its undertaking, as a going concern'. To help achieve the purposes, an administrator was given wide powers to run the company and, crucially, a moratorium (or 'freeze') applied to the rights of all secured and unsecured creditors. This took effect immediately on presentation of the petition for administration.

The idea of a moratorium was unpopular with banks which, as the major creditors of a company, wanted the ability to enforce their security whenever they chose. They therefore lobbied for, and won, the right to block an administration order if they held security (which included a floating charge) over all, or substantially all, of a company's assets. This was achieved by appointing an administrative receiver under IA 1986 (s 9).

13.6.1.2   Administrative receivership pre-Enterprise Act 2002

An administrative receiver is defined in IA 1986, s 29(2), as:

(a)   a receiver or manager of the whole (or substantially the whole) of a company's property appointed by or on behalf of the holders of any debentures of the company secured by a charge which, as created, was a floating charge, or by such a charge and one or more other securities; or

(b)   a person who would be such a receiver or manager but for the appointment of some other person as the receiver of part of the company's property.

The term 'debenture' 'includes ... bonds and any other securities of a company ...' ('securities' is not defined).

Therefore, as long as a bank held security (which included a floating charge) over 'all or substantially all' of a borrower's assets, it could appoint an administrative receiver, with wide-ranging powers to manage the business and sell assets to repay the bank debt and, crucially, the power to block an administration order and moratorium. This was a critical part of a bank's security package, because it allowed the bank to take control if it wanted to realise its security.

13.6.1.3   Enterprise Act 2002

The EA 2002 is intended to assist small businesses and makes reforms to competition law, consumer protection law, personal bankruptcy law and corporate insolvency law. From 15 September 2003, it significantly amended the law relating to administration and administrative receivers; the key changes are explained below.

13.6.1.4   Administration post-Enterprise Act 2002

The four original purposes of administration were replaced by three new ones with more emphasis on corporate rescue. They essentially require the administrator to:

(a)   *attempt to rescue the company as a going concern* – if this is not reasonably practical, or would not produce the best result for the creditors as a whole;

(b)   *attempt to achieve a better result for creditors than if the company were wound up;* and (only if the administrator thinks the first two purposes are not reasonably practical)

(c)   *realise the company's property to distribute to secured or preferential creditors, so long as he does not unnecessarily harm the interests of the creditors as a whole.*

These purposes apply regardless of who appoints the administrator.

The appointment of an administrator was streamlined: as long as the company is or is likely to become insolvent, an administrator may be appointed:

(a)   by court order (as previously);

(b)   out of court by the holder of a 'qualifying floating charge'. This is essentially the same definition as under IA 1986, s 29(2) (see **13.6.1.2**), as long as the floating charge document also states that the EA 2002 applies to it, or it purports to allow the holder to appoint an administrator or administrative receiver; or

(c)   out of court by the company or its directors.

13.6.1.5   Administrative receivership post-Enterprise Act 2002

Perhaps the most significant change for banks is that the ability to appoint an administrative receiver, and so block an administration order, was abolished other than in limited circumstances. In addition to any floating charges created before 15 September 2003, there are eight 'exceptions' under which an administrative receiver *may* still be appointed: the 'capital market' exception, 'public–private partnership' exception, 'utilities projects' exception, 'urban regeneration projects' exception, 'project finance' exception, 'financial markets' exception, 'protected railways and other companies' exception and 'registered social landlord' exception. Suffice it to say these are intended to apply to 'specialised financing' and not to general commercial bank lending (see IA 1986, ss 72B–72G, inserted by EA 2002, s 250, for further details).

The EA 2002 does allow 'grand fathering'; in other words, if a bank was able to appoint an administrative receiver before the 2002 Act took effect (15 September 2003), it will retain the right (see IA 1986, s 72A, inserted by EA 2002, s 250).

In summary, where the bank holds a 'qualifying floating charge' created after 15 September 2003, but does not fall within one of the eight statutory exceptions, it will be permitted to appoint an administrator only to realise security on insolvency. The bank's administrator must consider the two prior purposes of administration before realising assets on the bank's behalf.

Further details on these procedures can be found in **Business Law and Practice**.

13.6.2   Asset control and stability

The primary aim of due diligence (see **2.2**) is to ensure that a borrower is capable of servicing a loan out of cash flow. A bank does not want to resort to a borrower's assets for repayment if it can be avoided. Taking a fixed charge over a borrower's assets will prevent it from disposing of them in normal circumstances, and this will at least help to ensure that the fixed assets on which forecasts were based in the due diligence remain in the company. The security therefore helps to maintain the borrower's stability.

13.6.3   Management

There are a number of ways in which a security interest can provide some degree of control over the management of a borrower even before it is enforced. First, it may prevent other banks from providing finance to the borrower if there is insufficient value in the assets to support any further security, effectively giving the secured bank a monopoly over a company's borrowing. Secondly, a bank will sometimes require the directors of a small company to provide security for the company's loan, usually in the form of personal guarantees. This does not just provide another source of repayment should anything go wrong, it also serves to concentrate the minds of the directors when making decisions crucial to the business. A bank may require a parent to guarantee the borrowings of its subsidiary for similar reasons. Thirdly, a security interest will sometimes allow a bank the right to take part in management decisions if the borrower defaults, even if the security is not realised (although this is more usually dealt with in the loan document). Any substantial involvement by a bank in the management of a corporate borrower will carry the danger of shadow directorship and subsequent liability (see **7.6**), although this is probably less of a risk for banks than for others.

13.6.4   Costs

Chapter 9 explained the requirement of regulatory capital imposed by central banks. Secured loans will carry less risk for a bank than unsecured loans, and compliance with regulatory capital requirements will make some types of secured loan 'cheaper' than unsecured loans.

13.6.5   Miscellaneous

Some of the points made above may not be a bank's primary reasons for taking security but merely the welcome consequences of doing so. There are many other consequences which might benefit the secured bank. For example, if all a borrower's assets are secured, an unsecured creditor might be less likely to wind up the company in pursuance of the debt, since he may find nothing left for him. Security interests may also give a creditor the right to pursue assets 'illegally' sold to third parties, and sometimes the right to trace proceeds.

13.7   SECURITY – THE BANK'S PERSPECTIVE

It is important to understand that not all loans are secured: taking security is expensive and time-consuming, and not usually necessary unless the bank thinks there is a real risk of insolvency or a specific need to preserve assets. Investment grade loans are unsecured; highly leveraged loans almost always secured. Whilst enforcement of most types of security will be a last resort, until that time a secured bank has greater control over the borrower and greater leverage to get the borrower 'around the table' to talk if a problem should arise.

A bank's solicitor should check that the borrower and any other party providing security has capacity to do so (see also **4.6.2**). For example, the articles of some companies will allow them to provide a guarantee only if it is matched by an indemnity from the guaranteed party. A check should also be made that there is no existing negative pledge.

13.8 SECURITY – THE BORROWER'S PERSPECTIVE

The borrower is invariably liable for all (reasonable) costs of providing security, which will include solicitors' fees, registration costs and, in some jurisdictions, notarial fees and stamp duty. As mentioned at **13.7** above, not all loans are secured, although more specialised lending for large assets (eg, for a ship or aircraft) or financing a project ('project finance') will always be secured over the asset or project in question. Leveraged loans are also secured, although borrowers have negotiated two 'concessions' in recent years. First, in most acquisition financings only share security is provided at 'closing' (ie, when the loan is available). The borrower is then given anything up to 120 days to provide the remaining asset security.

Secondly, it is now common to agree 'security principles' early in the negotiation. These are pre-agreed parameters for the type and extent of security to be given (particularly where multiple jurisdictions are involved), the costs that can be incurred, and any obligations on the borrower (eg, giving notice of an assignment).

13.9 FURTHER READING

Calnan, *Taking Security: Law and Practice* (2nd edn, Jordans, 2011).

Goode, *Commercial Law* (4th edn, Penguin, 2009).

Goode, *Legal Problems of Credit and Security* (4th edn, Sweet & Maxwell, 2008).

CHAPTER 14

FURTHER ISSUES ON TAKING SECURITY

14.1	Introduction	165
14.2	Perfection through registration	165
14.3	Priority of security	173
14.4	Contractual subordination	174
14.5	Tacking	175
14.6	Ruling off accounts	176
14.7	Fixed or floating charge?	177
14.8	Hardening periods	178
14.9	Capacity	179
14.10	Corporate benefit	179
14.11	Financial assistance	180
14.12	Applicable law	180
14.13	UNCITRAL Model Law	181
14.14	Other considerations on taking security	181
14.15	Further reading	182

'Borrow £1 million, and you are in trouble; borrow £1 billion, and the bank is in trouble.'

Old banking adage

14.1 INTRODUCTION

There are three key steps to creating a valid security interest:

(a) creation: that is, agreement to create a particular security interest between debtor and creditor (usually by executing a security document);

(b) attachment: that is, ensuring that the security interest binds on specific assets; and

(c) perfection: that is, ensuring the security interest is valid against third parties, giving priority (often achieved by registration).

The two previous chapters examined aspects of creation and attachment. This chapter looks at some of the issues associated with perfection and priority.

14.2 PERFECTION THROUGH REGISTRATION

14.2.1 The purpose of registration

The point has already been made that the safest way to secure an asset is to take possession of it (take a 'pledge'), but practical considerations dictate that the overwhelming majority of loan security is non-possessory. This gives rise to a problem: if a borrower retains the secured asset, what is to stop it, albeit fraudulently, selling or re-securing the asset to an unsuspecting third party? The problem is alleviated by a statutory requirement (under CA 2006) for the registration of security interests: placing the security contract on a public register creates a system of actual and deemed notice to third parties. In addition, the nature of the secured asset may entail registration under a different statutory regime (see **14.2.3**).

14.2.2 Companies Act provisions

14.2.2.1 The regime

The requirement for companies to register certain security interests at Companies House is longstanding. The primary aim is a mechanism to give third parties notice of the security and thereby make it valid against their claims (where relevant).

On 6 April 2013, after some years of consultation, an updated and simplified Companies Act security registration regime came into force. The new regime is found in ss 859A to 859Q of the CA 2006 and applies to companies and limited liability partnerships (LLPs) registered in the United Kingdom (ie England and Wales, Scotland and Northern Ireland). The key requirements are outlined below.

14.2.2.2 What must be registered?

Like the old regime, the new one applies to 'charges' created by companies and LLPs. The term 'charge' is defined to include mortgages (s 859A(7)), and 'charge' in this section (**14.2.2**) should be read to include 'mortgage'. By implication the regime does not apply to pledges or liens for which actual or constructive possession of the secured asset by the security holder operates as notice to third parties.

The old regime identified fixed charges which had to be registered by reference to the assets they secured (*all* floating charges were registrable), but its interpretation and application was ambiguous in places. As a result many practitioners registered every charge taken over any asset. The new regime starts from the premise that *all* charges (remember this includes mortgages) *may* be registered, with the following three (minor) exceptions (s 859A(6)):

(a)   a charge in favour of a landlord on a cash deposit given as security in connection with the lease of land;

(b)   a charge created by a member of Lloyd's to secure its obligations in connection with its underwriting business;

(c)   a charge excluded by any other Act.

The old language (s 860) *required* registration of certain charges. Whilst registration has technically now been made 'voluntary', the consequences of failure to register are such that chargeholders will almost always wish to do so (see **14.2.2.7**).

14.2.2.3 Who may effect registration?

Section 859A(2) allows either the company that created the charge or 'any person interested in the charge' to deliver the documents required for registration. A 'person interested' would include the chargeholder as well as the legal advisors to the company or chargeholder. In practice, it is almost invariably the chargeholder (or more specifically its solicitor) who applies for registration since it has most to lose from failure to do so (see **14.2.2.7**).

14.2.2.4 What is required for registration?

Registration is effected by delivering a 'section 859D statement of particulars' (s 859D), a certified copy of the instrument creating or evidencing the charge (if there is one) and the requisite fee. The 'statement of particulars' will usually be a form MR01 for a company (or MR08 where there is no charge instrument) or the equivalent forms LLMR01 and LLMR08 for a limited liability partnership. The form MR01 is much simpler than its predecessors (MG01 and Form 395), providing limited information about the company and security being registered. This is because, unlike previously, a copy of the entire security instrument is made available on the Companies House register. The form, copy of the instrument and fee should be sent with a covering letter with details of each document in the package and stating the company name, number, type of document and fee payable.

In recognition of the fact that the charge instrument may contain sensitive information and will appear as a public document, s 859G allows certain details to be obscured in the certified copy (known as 'redaction'). Information which can be redacted is essentially:

(a)   personal information relating to an individual (other than the name of the individual): for example, the date of birth, a residential address, mobile or personal telephone number, and in some circumstances the occupation or email address of the individual;

(b)   the number or other identifier of a bank or securities account of a company or an individual;

(c)   a signature.

Redaction usually involves obscuring the information in the certified copy using a black marker pen. The paragraph certifying it as a true copy of the original should state 'save for material redacted pursuant to s 859G'.

14.2.2.5   What is the time limit for registration?

The registration documents must be delivered before the end of 21 days beginning with the day after the date of creation of the charge (s 859A(4)). Weekends and public holidays will count towards the 21 days. The Companies House London Counter closes at 5pm, but packages delivered after that time are posted through a mailbox and stamped with the delivery time; postings up to midnight are treated as being received on that date.

If there is a defect with the submission, it must be corrected within the 21-day time limit for submission. The Registrar has power under the Companies Act to rectify incomplete or internally inconsistent submissions, and many firms pre-authorise Companies House to email them asking for instructions to make any necessary changes. For more serious errors, the forms will be returned to be resubmitted. In either case, the 21-day time limit keeps running, and so the best advice is to submit registration early and without errors! There is a useful checklist on the back page of the form MR01 highlighting the most common mistakes in submissions, which include (depressingly) entering the wrong company number, and forgetting to sign the form or include the fee.

Whilst there is provision at s 859F for the company (or a person interested) to apply to court for an extension to the 21-day period, there is no guarantee it will be granted and in practice this is never relied upon. If the registration deadline is missed, it is usually resolved by re-taking new security: an expensive and highly embarrassing situation to explain to the client.

14.2.2.6   What is the effect of valid registration?

A validly registered charge is valid against a liquidator, administrator and any creditor of the company that created the charge, although it will not prevent the terms of a charge being challenged (eg as floating not fixed) or challenge as a preference, transaction at undervalue or similar process.

The form MR01 also has a 'tick box' for noting whether the terms of the charge include a negative pledge. The intention is to put anyone who searches the register on notice of the negative pledge. The theory is that if a subsequent fixed charge is created over assets subject to a prior floating charge, the fixed chargeholder would have knowingly breached the negative pledge and would be forced to hand over any proceeds of the fixed charge. This has not been tested in court.

14.2.2.7   What is the effect of invalid registration?

Failure to register a charge within the 21-day period has the following consequences (s 859H):

(a)   the security is void against a liquidator, administrator and any creditor of the company; and

(b)   the amount secured by the void security becomes immediately payable.

In accordance with
Sections 859A and
859J of the Companies
Act 2006.

MR01

Particulars of a charge

Companies House

A fee is payable with this form. Please see 'How to pay' on the last page.	You can use the WebFiling service to file this form online. Please go to www.companieshouse.gov.uk	
✓ **What this form is for** You may use this form to register a charge created or evidenced by an instrument.	✗ **What this form is NOT for** You may not use this form to register a charge where there is no instrument. Use form MR08.	For further information, please refer to our guidance at: www.companieshouse.gov.uk

This form **must be delivered to the Registrar for registration within 21 days** beginning with the day after the date of creation of the charge. If delivered outside of the 21 days it will be rejected unless it is accompanied by a court order extending the time for delivery.

You **must** enclose a certified copy of the instrument with this form. This will be scanned and placed on the public record.

1   Company details

For official use

Company number

Company name in full

→ **Filling in this form**
Please complete in typescript or in bold black capitals.

All fields are mandatory unless specified or indicated by *

2   Charge creation date

Charge creation date   d d   m m   y y y y

3   Names of persons, security agents or trustees entitled to the charge

Please show the names of each of the persons, security agents or trustees entitled to the charge.

Name

Name

Name

Name

If there are more than four names, please supply any four of these names then tick the statement below.

☐ I confirm that there are more than four persons, security agents or trustees entitled to the charge.

| MR01 |
| Particulars of a charge |

4   **Description**

Please give a short description of any land (including buildings), ship, aircraft or intellectual property registered (or required to be registered) in the UK which is subject to this fixed charge or fixed security.

Continuation page
Please use a continuation page if you need to enter more details.

Description

5   **Fixed charge or fixed security**

Does the instrument include a fixed charge or fixed security over any tangible or intangible (or in Scotland) corporeal or incorporeal property not described above? Please tick the appropriate box.

☐   **Yes**

☐   **No**

6   **Floating charge**

Is the instrument expressed to contain a floating charge? Please tick the appropriate box.

☐   **Yes** Continue

☐   **No**   Go to **Section 7**

Is the floating charge expressed to cover all the property and undertaking of the company?

☐   **Yes**

7   **Negative Pledge**

Do any of the terms of the charge prohibit or restrict the chargor from creating any further security that will rank equally with or ahead of the charge? Please tick the appropriate box.

☐   **Yes**

☐   **No**

04/13 Version 1.0

MR01
Particulars of a charge

8	**Trustee statement** ❶

You may tick the box if the company named in Section 1 is acting as trustee of the property or undertaking which is the subject of the charge. ☐	❶ This statement may be filed after the registration of the charge (use form MR06).

9	**Signature**

Please sign the form here.

Signature

Signature

X   X

This form must be signed by a person with an interest in the charge.

MR01
Particulars of a charge

Presenter information

We will send the certificate to the address entered below. All details given here will be available on the public record. You do not have to show any details here but, if none are given, we will send the certificate to the company's Registered Office address.

Contact name

Company name

Address

Post town

County/Region

Postcode

Country

DX

Telephone

Certificate

We will send your certificate to the presenter's address if given above or to the company's Registered Office if you have left the presenter's information blank.

Checklist

We may return forms completed incorrectly or with information missing.

Please make sure you have remembered the following:
- ☐ The company name and number match the information held on the public Register.
- ☐ You have included a certified copy of the instrument with this form.
- ☐ You have entered the date on which the charge was created.
- ☐ You have shown the names of persons entitled to the charge.
- ☐ You have ticked any appropriate boxes in Sections 3, 5, 6, 7 & 8.
- ☐ You have given a description in Section 4, if appropriate.
- ☐ You have signed the form.
- ☐ You have enclosed the correct fee.
- ☐ Please do not send the original instrument; it must be a certified copy.

Important information

Please note that all information on this form will appear on the public record.

How to pay

A fee of £13 is payable to Companies House in respect of each mortgage or charge filed on paper.

Make cheques or postal orders payable to 'Companies House.'

Where to send

You may return this form to any Companies House address. However, for expediency, we advise you to return it to the appropriate address below:

For companies registered in England and Wales:
The Registrar of Companies, Companies House,
Crown Way, Cardiff, Wales, CF14 3UZ.
DX 33050 Cardiff.

For companies registered in Scotland:
The Registrar of Companies, Companies House,
Fourth floor, Edinburgh Quay 2,
139 Fountainbridge, Edinburgh, Scotland, EH3 9FF.
DX ED235 Edinburgh 1
or LP - 4 Edinburgh 2 (Legal Post).

For companies registered in Northern Ireland:
The Registrar of Companies, Companies House,
Second Floor, The Linenhall, 32-38 Linenhall Street,
Belfast, Northern Ireland, BT2 8BG.
DX 481 N.R. Belfast 1.

Further information

For further information, please see the guidance notes on the website at www.companieshouse.gov.uk or email enquiries@companieshouse.gov.uk

This form is available in an alternative format. Please visit the forms page on the website at www.companieshouse.gov.uk

04/13 Version 1.0

This form has been provided free of charge by Companies House.

The charge remains valid against the company creating it unless and until that company goes into liquidation or administration. The old regime made failure to register a criminal offence (the company and every officer who was in default was liable to a fine), but the new regime has repealed that provision.

14.2.2.8 Documents to be kept by the company

The old regime required the company to keep its own register of charges, but that will not apply for charges created after 6 April 2013. There is still an obligation on the company to keep the following documents available for inspection at its registered office (s 859P) or acceptable alternative location (s 859Q(2)):

(a)   a copy of every instrument creating a charge capable of registration under the CA 2006;

(b)   a copy of every instrument that amends or varies a charge capable of registration under the CA 2006;

(c)   a copy of any documents containing particulars required for registration if those particulars are not in the charge instrument;

(d)   a copy of any translation required as part of the registration (see CA 2006, s 1105).

The documents may be certified copies (other than the translation) and be available without charge to a creditor or shareholder, and to any other person on payment of a prescribed fee.

14.2.2.9 Security release and memorandum of satisfaction

At some point, all or part of the secured debt will be repaid and the security will be wholly or partially released (some security documents purport to allow a bank to retain the security for a period even after repayment as 'insurance' against the repayment being clawed back under the IA 1986 (see **14.9**), though in practice these provisions are highly unlikely to apply). Security might also be released to allow for disposal of a particular asset. Release is usually achieved by a deed of release drawn up by the borrower's solicitor. Whilst there is no statutory requirement to notify Companies House of security release, the borrower will want to keep the register up to date for third parties and creditors. Form MR04 can be used to update the register for partial or full satisfaction of a charge.

14.2.2.10 Property acquired already subject to a charge

Under the old regime, if a company acquired property subject to a charge, registration was required within 21 days of acquiring the property. Failure to comply was an offence, although it would not make the charge void. The new regime simply allows a company (or person interested) to register a charge which already exists on property it acquires (assuming the charge would have been capable of registration if the company had created it) – see s 859C. There is no time limit, and non-registration does not constitute an offence or make the acquired charge void.

14.2.2.11 Overseas companies

The Companies Act registration requirements apply to companies and limited liability partnerships registered in the United Kingdom. Previous iterations of the regime left ambiguity as to whether they also applied to overseas companies in some circumstances. The uncertainty was aided and abetted by an unhelpful judgment in *Slavenburg's Bank NV v Intercontinental National Resources Ltd* [1980] 1 All ER 955, leading to attempted registration of security apparently unconnected to the UK (known as 'Slavenburg registrations'). However, the Overseas Companies (Execution of Documents and Registration of Charges) (Amendment) Regulations 2011 (SI 2011/2194) helpfully determine that any charge created by an overseas company on or after 1 October 2011 will not require registration at Companies House. This applies even if the secured asset is within the UK or the security document is governed by English law. Note, however, that there remains an obligation on overseas companies to register charges at 'specialist' asset registries such as Land Registry, the UK

Intellectual Property Office, the Aircraft Mortgage Register and the relevant port of registry for any UK registered ship.

14.2.3 Registration requirements for specific assets

Brief mention must be made of certain registration requirements for specific assets sited in England or Wales, or registered under English law. The most notable statutory regimes for registration of non-possessory security are:

(a) land – registered land (under the Land Registration Act 2002 (LRA 2002) and Land Registration Rules 2003, SI 2003/1417 (from 13 October 2003)) at District Land Registry;

(b) ships – (under the Merchant Shipping Act 1894) registered at the ship's port of registration;

(c) aircraft – (under the Mortgaging of Aircraft Order 1972, SI 1972/1268) in the UK Aircraft Mortgage Register maintained by the Civil Aviation Authority; and

(d) intellectual property, for example patents and copyrights – under various statutory provisions.

14.2.4 Security created by individuals: Bills of Sale Acts 1878 and 1882

The Bills of Sale Acts 1878 and 1882 impose registration requirements on security created by individuals. The Acts require most written, non-possessory charges given by an individual or a partnership over tangible property to be registered in prescribed form at the Supreme Court as a bill of sale (the Bills of Sale Acts require each charged asset to be identified in the register, which is the main reason why it is impracticable for individuals or partnerships to give floating charges). Furthermore, IA 1986, s 344 requires most forms of assignment of a trader's book debts to be registered as a bill of sale if they are to be valid against a trustee in bankruptcy.

14.3 PRIORITY OF SECURITY

This is a complex area, and what follows is therefore a summary of the main rules.

14.3.1 Priority between charges and mortgages

Fixed charges and mortgages

Generally, fixed charges and mortgages rank in order of creation (provided they are properly registered). At common law, a legal mortgage will take priority over an existing equitable security interest, only if the legal mortgage was taken bona fide, for value and without notice of the prior equitable security. Registration in accordance with s 860 of the CA 2006 gives notice to anyone who has, or ought to have, searched the register, which will usually protect a prior registered equitable security.

Fixed and floating charges

A fixed charge (and a mortgage) will rank in priority to a floating charge. This is because a floating charge, ostensibly, allows the chargor to deal with the charged asset, and this will include granting security over it. However, this vulnerability might be avoided if the floating charge contains a negative pledge and the later fixed charge-holder has notice of the prohibition (constructive notice is probably achieved through registration – see **14.2.2.6**). (In the case of *Griffiths v Yorkshire Bank plc* [1994] 1 WLR 1427, the judge ruled that a negative pledge in a floating charge was not effective to prevent later security being created with priority, although details of the restriction were registered in the Companies Registry. This decision also seems to suggest that a crystallised floating charge might sometimes rank ahead of preferential creditors. However, both conclusions fly in the face of previously long-accepted principles and seem contrary to the Companies Act provisions.)

Priority between floating charges is (subject to contrary agreement) governed by their time of creation (if properly registered): an earlier charge will take priority even if the later one has crystallised.

Remember that registration simply perfects a security by giving notice to third parties. The date of the charge from which priority can be calculated is not the date it is registered but the date it is created. This means that a search made on the day of registering a charge might not show a charge created within the last 21 days, which would have priority over a charge created more recently.

14.3.2 Priority for security over land

The priority between interests in security over land is a complicated area. Of primary importance, however, is the priority between registered mortgages. Under the registered land system, the bank proposing to take a legal mortgage must first complete a 'priority search' at Land Registry. The priority search will show any existing encumbrances over the registered land as well as any recent actual or proposed dealings with the land. Assuming the priority search does not reveal other encumbrances, dealings or existing priority searches, the bank will have a period of 30 working days within which to register the new legal mortgage and take priority. Registration within that period will ensure priority even over an earlier dated unregistered legal mortgage if it does not have the benefit of a priority search.

14.3.3 Priority between assignments – the rule in Dearle v Hall

The case of *Dearle v Hall* (1828) 3 Russ 1 established a rule of priorities between assignments over choses in action. In order to ensure priority, notice of assignment must be given to the third party which owes the obligation. For example, if C is owed £1,000 by D, and C assigns the debt to its bank B as security for a loan, B can perfect the assignment by notifying D that his debt is assigned. However, if B fails to notify D, and C later assigns D's debt to E, then E's assignment will gain priority over B's if E notifies D first. The rule will not apply, however, where a subsequent assignee (ie, E) knows of the earlier assignment (ie, to B) when taking his assignment. Thus, registration of the security at the Companies Registry will usually defeat the rule.

14.4 CONTRACTUAL SUBORDINATION

14.4.1 Contractual priority arrangements

The previous section discussed the order of priority between various security interests and nothing can be done directly to vary that order. It is possible, however, for creditors to decide between themselves on the order in which they will benefit from claims against a defaulting debtor. Such priority arrangements are frequently used in large financings which involve several 'layers' of debt: if the borrower defaults, the order in which the banks will have their loans repaid is contractually prearranged. The document creating these rights is usually known as an 'intercreditor agreement', 'subordination agreement' or 'deed of priorities'. These are complex documents and the legal issues surrounding the effect and effectiveness of contractual subordination are unsettled. However, the key provisions are outlined below.

14.4.2 A typical arrangement

How do these subordination arrangements work? A typical intercreditor agreement will restrict its participants so that:

(a)   the participating lenders are divided into an agreed order of priority for repayment of their credit. 'Senior creditors' enjoy top priority, whilst 'subordinated creditors' rank below them. Subordinated creditors are further subdivided, for example 'mezzanine', 'loan notes' and 'high yield', all of which enjoy different levels of priority among the subordinated group;

(b) no participating bank may enforce any security or otherwise proceed against the borrower without the agreement of the senior banks (or occasionally only with majority consent);

(c) when any security is enforced, or any money received after a specified event (eg, a potential default by the borrower), either:

(i) subordinated creditors agree contractually not to claim against the borrower until the senior creditors are repaid, thereby maximising the assets available to satisfy senior debt (usually known as 'contingent debt subordination'), or

(ii) subordinated creditors agree to hold any money they receive on trust for senior creditors (known as a 'turnover trust'). This is more robust than contingent debt subordination and maximises return in all circumstances. Some practitioners take the view that this type of subordination creates a proprietory interest over the debt which requires registration as a charge under the CA 2006. However, the court in *SSSL Realisations Limited* [2004] EWHC (Ch) 1760 held that the turnover trust in that case did not create a charge: it did create a proprietory right, but since it was limited to the debt owed there was no charge over the 'junior' creditor's property.

(d) the pooled money will then be distributed in accordance with the agreement. Thus the 'senior' banks will be paid back first. Once they have been repaid in full, any remaining money will be used to repay the 'mezzanine' and other subordinated creditors, as appropriate.

Subordination occurs in other ways. For example, ordinary shareholders (equity) will be automatically subordinated to all other creditors (debt), because they cannot usually distribute the company's assets and realise their capital until all creditors of the company are repaid (known as 'structural subordination'). Subordination between shareholders can be achieved by issuing preferential shares which carry rights to participate in the distribution of assets before other shareholders.

14.4.3 When is contractual subordination used?

Why would a bank agree to postpone its claim to, and even share its security with, other banks? The main incentive is that, generally, the greater the risk, the larger the share of the syndicate fees (or the greater the margin). Provided the borrower does not default, the subordinated banks will ultimately get a better return on their loans. All banks will want to diversify their lending to create a mixture of risk and, when a syndicate is formed, some banks will be looking to make less risky loans and will participate only as senior banks: other banks will accept subordinated positions because they can take more risk (see also **9.3.3**).

Contractual subordination might also be used where an unsecured bank requires any debts to a borrower's directors or parent company to be subordinated to its own. Alternatively, an existing bank might benefit by allowing new finance into the borrower to enhance the business. The only way to attract new finance might be to release some existing security, or to agree subordination to the new bank.

Subordination agreements are usually executed as deeds. The borrower is usually a party.

14.5 TACKING

Tacking is the ability to secure new advances under existing security. It will depend on whether the secured asset is unregistered land, registered land or personalty.

14.5.1 Unregistered land

New advances relating to unregistered land can be 'tacked' onto an existing mortgage (or charge) under s 94 of the LPA 1925 if:

(a)   an arrangement has been made to that effect with the subsequent mortgagees; or

(b)   the mortgagee had no notice of subsequent mortgages when it made the new advance; or

(c)   where the mortgage imposes an obligation on the first mortgagee to make further advances.

14.5.2   Registered land

In the case of registered land, there are specific provisions brought in by the LRA 2002, s 49. In outline, these allow a mortgage (or charge) holder to tack if:

(a)   he has not received notice of the subsequent security; or

(b)   the new advance is under an obligation already on the register when the subsequent charge was created; or

(c)   the maximum amount of the first charge was agreed and on the register when the subsequent charge was created.

14.5.3   Personalty

Mortgaged/charged personalty is subject to the provisions of LPA 1925, s 94. Thus any actual or constructive notice of a subsequent mortgage/charge will end a prior mortgagee's/chargee's right to tack unless the conditions in (a) or (c) at **14.5.1** are fulfilled.

14.6   RULING OFF ACCOUNTS

When a borrower makes a payment to a bank, the borrower may (subject to any contrary agreement) instruct the bank as to which account it should be appropriated (although see the banker's right of combination at **13.5.3**), or which loan should be repaid (but see **9.2.2**). However, in the absence of instructions or specific agreement, the rule laid down in *Devaynes v Noble* (1816) 1 Mer 572 (known as '*Clayton's case*') will apply. In a banking context the rule says that money paid to the bank will discharge the borrower's debt in the chronological order in which the debt was incurred. If this rule applied, there might be circumstances in which a bank would be disadvantaged, particularly if it was providing a secured revolving account (eg, an overdraft or RCF). This is best explained by way of example:

EXAMPLE

Bank provides a secured RCF for Borrower. Borrower draws two tranches as follows:

1 January – £2,000

1 March – £4,000

On 1 February, Bank also provides Borrower with an unsecured overdraft of up to £5,000. On 1 April, Borrower makes a payment of £2,000 to Bank, with no instructions as to whether it should reduce the overdraft, the RCF, or be put into a new account. If there is no other agreement between them, the rule in *Clayton's case* means that the £2,000 will be treated as repaying the debt which was incurred earliest – it will reduce the secured RCF.

There are several reasons why this might disadvantage Bank:

(a)   If Borrower is in financial difficulty, Bank might prefer the £2,000 to reduce the unsecured overdraft rather than the RCF which has the benefit of security.

(b)   Even if the overdraft was secured, new security may be more vulnerable to being set aside than older 'hardened' security (see **14.9**): Bank may prefer newer secured loans to be repaid first.

(c)   Finally, if Bank learns that Borrower has organised a loan from another lender secured by second ranking security, in certain circumstances new advances would rank behind the second loan. Therefore, as the RCF was repaid and re-drawn, it would lose priority to the new loan.

To avoid problems (a) and (b), banks may insist that they can choose where payments are appropriated in some circumstances (eg, where payments are not received in full). The third problem is usually dealt with by allowing a bank to 'rule off' an account if it learns that a borrower has taken a second secured loan. This means that the original secured loan (which has priority to the new secured loan) is preserved ('ruled-off') and not treated as repaid by any amounts received from the borrower until the first bank can ensure that any new advances it makes will rank ahead. In addition, security should be specified as securing all amounts due from time to time from the borrower to the bank, and banks should include a negative pledge in their loan facility and debenture.

The rule in *Clayton's case* may also affect guarantees. Subject to contrary agreement, once a guaranteed liability has been fixed in value, any payment by the borrower to the bank will be deemed to reduce the guaranteed debt, placing any other debts which are outstanding beyond the guarantee. This can be avoided by specifying the guarantee to be 'continuing', or alternatively an 'all monies guarantee'.

14.7 FIXED OR FLOATING CHARGE?

14.7.1 Which is preferable?

Chapter 12 outlined the main differences between fixed and floating charges, but which is preferable if the bank has a choice? The principal advantages of the floating charge are:

(a)   it allows the borrower to deal freely with the charged assets in the ordinary course of business;

(b)   in restricted circumstances, it allows the bank to appoint an administrative receiver (see **13.6.1**), who may manage the borrower's business, and also block an administration order (a floating charge taken primarily for this reason is known as a 'lightweight' or a 'phantom' floating charge). After changes made by the EA 2002, this is relevant only to 'specialised' financial structures (eg, project finance, housing finance and capital markets – see **13.6.1.5**);

(c)   the holder of a 'qualifying floating charge' (as defined by IA 1986, Sch B1, para 14) can appoint an administrator using an out of court procedure. It can also choose the identity of an administrator by intervening in a third party's court application.

The main disadvantages are:

(a)   a floating charge will be subordinated to any preferential creditors (see **12.3.2**);

(b)   a floating charge might be vulnerable to later fixed charges, even if it contains a negative pledge which is registered (see **14.3**);

(c)   a floating charge can be set aside under wider circumstances than a fixed charge (see **12.3.2**);

(d)   some of the proceeds realised from a floating charge may be allocated to unsecured creditors (see **12.3.2**);

(e)   the proceeds of a floating charge may be taken by a liquidator to cover his expenses.

The flexibility of the floating charge would almost certainly score points with a borrower and, arguably, the trading freedom it gives the borrower is also good for the bank. However, that freedom and the general vulnerability of the floating charge mean that it will always be second choice for the bank where a fixed charge is available. The protection of a fixed charge is more certain. Banks are inclined to take a floating charge where 'necessary' (eg, for stock), giving them the right to appoint an administrative receiver in some circumstances (see above), and to declare all other charges as fixed. However, as explained below, the nature of a charge is not determined by its label, but by its effect.

14.7.2   Recognising a floating charge

If the name of a charge is not conclusive proof of its nature, how is it determined as fixed or floating? The most commonly quoted description of a floating charge is that of Romer LJ in *Re Yorkshire Woolcombers Association Ltd* [1903] 2 Ch 284:

> I certainly do not intend to attempt to give an exact definition of the term 'floating charge', nor am I prepared to say that there will not be a floating charge within the meaning of the Companies Act 1900, which does not contain all the three characteristics that I am about to mention, but I certainly think that if a charge has the three characteristics that I am about to mention it is a floating charge. (1) If it is a charge on a class of assets of a company present and future; (2) If that class is one which, in the ordinary course of the business of the company, would be changing from time to time; and (3) If you find that by the charge it is contemplated that, until some future step is taken by or on behalf of those interested in the charge, the company may carry on its business in the ordinary way as far as concerns the particular class of assets I am dealing with.

Subsequent cases have emphasised the third characteristic identified by Romer LJ: the security must allow a company to deal with its assets in the ordinary course of business. Put another way, if a charge allows a borrower to deal with the charged assets without the bank's consent, it almost certainly will not be a fixed charge, even if it is called a 'fixed charge'. A fixed charge requires the bank to exhibit control over the charged asset (see also *Chalk v Kahn and Another* [2000] 2 BCLC 361).

14.8   HARDENING PERIODS

When new security is granted, there is often a reference made to its 'hardening period'. This refers to a period during which the security is vulnerable to provisions in the IA 1986 for setting aside certain transactions. The primary concerns are as follows.

14.8.1   Transactions at an undervalue (IA 1986, s 238)

An administrator or a liquidator can apply to court to set aside a transaction in which a company received either no consideration, or significantly less consideration than it provided (a 'transaction at an undervalue'), and which was entered into within two years of winding-up. The transaction must either have been made when the company was insolvent, or have resulted in the company's insolvency (this is presumed if with a connected person). Furthermore, if the directors can show the transaction was entered into in good faith, and with reasonable grounds to believe it would benefit the company, it cannot be set aside.

14.8.2   Preferences (IA 1986, s 239)

A 'preference' is a transaction in which a company intentionally benefits a creditor (or a surety or guarantor) by enhancing its position in the event that the company becomes insolvent. Providing new or enhanced security can be a preference. As under s 238, a transaction will be set aside only if it was made when the company was insolvent, or results in insolvency. A liquidator or an administrator can apply for a transaction to be set aside if it was made within six months of winding-up, although if the transaction was with a 'connected' person (this includes a director, his close relatives, his business partners and their close relatives – see s 249) the time limit is extended to two years. A transaction will not be a preference unless the company was influenced by a desire to put the preferred person in a better position on winding-up (this is a rebuttable presumption in the case of a connected person). Granting security in an attempt to ensure 'survival' is therefore probably not a preference.

A director might also be warned that any involvement in an insolvent company giving a transaction at an undervalue or a preference may lead to his disqualification under the CDDA 1986.

14.8.3 Floating charges (IA 1986, s 245)

Floating charges can be set aside if not granted for valuable consideration, and if granted within a given period before the company's insolvency (see **12.3.2**).

14.8.4 Summary

The important periods for hardening of security are therefore six months, 12 months (setting aside a floating charge) and two years, depending on the circumstances.

14.9 CAPACITY

One of the first things that should be checked by the bank's (and strictly, the borrower's) solicitor is the capacity of a borrower to provide security (if lack of capacity is discovered early enough it can usually be rectified). The issues as to a company's capacity to give security are largely the same as those which apply to its capacity to borrow, discussed at **4.6.2**.

Trustees are something of a 'special case'. Most of their powers and limitations will be found in the deed creating the trust, which will need careful review. Under the Trustee Act 1925, s 16, trustees (including personal representatives) are given the power to grant security, provided that the borrowing is for the purposes of the trust and is authorised by the trust deed, or under general law. This power applies whatever the trust deed might provide, but does not apply to trustees of charitable property.

14.10 CORPORATE BENEFIT

It is not uncommon for a bank to require additional security from a borrower's parent, subsidiary or sister company. This might be necessary to make up for a deficiency in the borrower's assets and reduce an otherwise unacceptable risk of lending. Alternatively, it might reduce the cost of the loan. However, it is necessary for a company providing a guarantee, indemnity or real security to prove it derives sufficient 'corporate benefit' from granting the security. From 1 October 2007, this duty derives from the CA 2006, s 172, which requires a director to 'act in the way he considers, in good faith, would be most likely to promote the success of the company for the benefit of its members as a whole'. The section provides a (non-exhaustive) list of the factors to which directors must have regard in fulfilling this duty. In approving a guarantee or security, the directors must consider this duty together with the factors, and the board minutes should reflect that they have done so.

At first sight, it might seem difficult to justify a company giving a guarantee or security for another company's loan as being in its best interests. When can a director justify his company securing another's obligations? This is really a commercial question of substance: what are the benefits and risks of providing the security? In crude terms, the greater the risk, the more benefit the company must derive as a consequence thereof. A parent company might justify supporting a subsidiary because directly or indirectly it will normally receive dividends from its shareholding. A subsidiary securing its parent (eg, an 'up-stream' guarantee) could argue that the support from its parent (eg, financial, marketing, product development) provides sufficient corporate benefit. This argument is more tenuous if the company is a small fish in a large group pond, but can be strengthened by a down-stream support letter (see **13.2.2**).

If a company believes there is insufficient corporate benefit to provide security, there is authority to suggest that it may still be given, provided that:

(a) the company's shareholders unanimously direct the security to be given; and

(b) the company is not insolvent either at the time of giving the security, or immediately following the giving of the security.

Remember that other jurisdictions will have different rules which might limit or prohibit guarantees and security given to group companies, particularly upstream.

14.11 FINANCIAL ASSISTANCE

Under the CA 2006, s 678, a public company and any of its subsidiaries are generally prohibited from directly or indirectly providing financial assistance (which includes giving guarantees and security) to any person in order to purchase the public company's shares.

14.12 APPLICABLE LAW

The legal system which governs a security interest will dictate how the security will be perfected (eg, notice, registration, etc) and how it may be enforced. Under the provisions of English law (and most other jurisdictions) the legal system applicable to a security interest will depend on whether the secured assets are movable or immovable. Security over immovable assets will, for purely practical reasons, be governed by the legal system of the place where the assets are physically situated (known as the 'lex situs'). The most common types of immovable assets include land, buildings, and heavy plant and machinery.

Ascertaining the legal system applicable to tangible movable assets is slightly more complicated. Generally, the *lex situs* of the asset when the security is created will determine the validity of its creation and perfection. However, if the asset is moved into another jurisdiction then the rules of that legal system may supersede the original lex situs with regard to perfection and enforcement. Local lawyers must therefore be instructed to ensure that any necessary steps are taken to maintain the validity of the security. These issues are of particular importance for valuable assets which regularly move between jurisdictions, such as ships and aircraft.

Security over intangible assets (eg, debts) is usually subject to the governing law of the contract creating the asset, but the law of the place of performance of the asset (eg, where the debt is to be paid) is also relevant.

From 31 May 2002, the EU Insolvency Regulation (EUIR) came into force in all EU Member States except Denmark. The EUIR provides rules that dictate which system of insolvency law applies in a 'cross-border' insolvency situation: in other words, it resolves conflicts of law situations but does not change the substantive insolvency laws currently in existence.

Under the EUIR, the main insolvency proceedings will be opened in the jurisdiction of the entity's Centre of Main Interest (COMI). The rather vague definition of COMI is where an entity 'conducts the administration of his interests on a regular basis' (Preamble 13). More helpfully, there is a rebuttable presumption that the COMI is in the jurisdiction of an entity's registered office (Article 3(1)), although factors such as location of employees, head office, board meetings and where the company does most of its business can influence the COMI. There can only be one COMI, but it can change over time.

There are two main circumstances in which assets may be subject to insolvency proceedings in jurisdictions other than the COMI. First, assets outside the COMI which are subject to 'rights in rem' (broadly, security interests) are basically unaffected by the COMI proceedings. Secondly, supplemental proceedings may be brought in a jurisdiction where a company has an 'establishment'. An 'establishment' is defined, in best euro-speak, as 'any place of operations where the debtor carries out non-transitory economic activity with human means and goods' – in essence a branch. Any supplemental proceedings will only apply to assets within the jurisdiction of the establishment.

The EUIR applies to companies, partnerships and individuals with their COMI in an EU Member State (other than Denmark), but not to most regulated entities (eg, banks, insurance companies) which have separate regimes. Once the definitions have benefited from the clarity brought by litigation, the EUIR should prove a positive tool for banking lawyers assessing insolvency risk in a cross-border transaction.

14.13 UNCITRAL MODEL LAW

In April 2006, the Cross-Border Insolvency Regulations 2006 (SI 2006/1030) came into force in England and Wales. These Regulations implemented the main provisions of the 'Model Law' on Cross-Border Insolvency devised by UNCITRAL (the United Nations Commission on International Trade Law). The Model Law aims to facilitate cross border insolvencies by providing a framework for dealing with problematic issues, for example where creditors, debtors and assets are located in different jurisdictions. Where the Model Law covers the same ground as the EUIR then the EUIR takes precedence.

14.14 OTHER CONSIDERATIONS ON TAKING SECURITY

When a solicitor is advising on security issues, there are a number of peripheral points to be covered, including the following.

14.14.1 Prior security

Copies of any existing charges (and other security interests) should be checked to ascertain the extent of their influence, and also to check for negative pledges. A subordination agreement may be necessary (see **14.4**).

14.14.2 Notification requirements

It may be necessary to notify third parties such as licensing authorities and landlords.

14.14.3 Overseas registration

Security interests over property situated overseas may need to be registered in the jurisdiction in which it is situated: some property may be incapable of being the subject of security, and rules about enforcement and insolvency may be very different from those of English law. Local lawyers should be instructed.

14.14.4 Parallel debt structures

In common law jurisdictions, security for a syndicated loan will be held by a security trustee (usually one of the lenders): legal title to the security is held on trust and the syndicate banks are the beneficiaries. This allows the syndicate members to change (as the loan participation is traded) without danger of the security being treated as renewed (and so losing priority or hardening periods).

Civil law jurisdictions do not recognise trust structures, and so a 'parallel debt' structure may be used instead. In a parallel debt structure, a security *agent* will hold the security on behalf of the syndicate. However, most jurisdictions will only allow a party to hold security to the extent it is owed a debt. A parallel debt structure therefore creates a debt owed to the security agent in the same amount as the debt owed to the bank syndicate. At first sight it looks as though the borrower has to repay its loan twice, but the two debts run in parallel. Thus, in normal circumstances, the borrower repays the syndicate, and any amount he repays is deemed to reduce the debt to the security agent at the same time. If the syndicate is repaid in full, the security agent debt is treated as repaid in full. On a default, however, the security agent becomes entitled to demand repayment of the debt owed to him and enforce the security if necessary. For every amount the security agent recovers, the syndicated debt will be deemed to reduce by the same. Therefore the borrower only ever has to repay the amount he borrowed, because the debts reduce 'in parallel'.

Most civil law jurisdictions recognise some form of parallel debt structure. They are still not quite as effective as a trust structure, however: the syndicate takes a risk on the security agent becoming insolvent (think Lehmans!), whereas if a security trustee became insolvent the trust assets would not be part of its estate.

14.15 FURTHER READING

Calnan, *Taking Security: Law and Practice* (2nd edn, Jordans, 2011).

Goode, *Commercial Law* (4th edn, Penguin, 2009).

Goode, *Legal Problems of Credit and Security* (4th edn, Sweet & Maxwell, 2008).

CHAPTER 15

SECURITY DOCUMENTATION – DEBENTURES

15.1	Introduction	183
15.2	Structure of a typical debenture	183
15.3	Execution	189

'Men lend their money to traders on mortgages or consignments of goods because they suspect their circumstances and they will not run the risk of their general credit.'

Lord Mansfield (*Foxcroft v Devonshire* (1760))

15.1 INTRODUCTION

In broad terms, a debenture is 'a document which either creates a debt or acknowledges it' (see *Levy v Abercorris Slate and Slab Co* (1887) 37 Ch D 260). The document creating security for a secured loan is commonly known as a 'mortgage debenture', or simply a 'debenture'. The label is slightly misleading: these documents will usually create charges as well as mortgages, and they are only created as 'debentures' for one particular reason (see **15.2.1**). This chapter briefly examines the typical structure of a mortgage debenture (hereinafter 'debenture').

15.2 STRUCTURE OF A TYPICAL DEBENTURE

Most banks have their own short standard form debenture, consisting of two or three pages of closely typed terms which are not usually open to negotiation. They will use these debentures for creating security over small, straightforward loans. However, more complex secured loan facilities will require a longer and more sophisticated debenture, which is usually drafted by the bank's solicitor. The broad structure of most debentures is similar to other commercial documents, ie: date, title and parties; preamble; definitions; operative provisions; schedules; and execution. The main operative provisions are explained below.

15.2.1 Covenant to pay

The first clause in the operative part of a debenture is invariably the 'covenant to pay'. This clause acknowledges the debt obligation of the borrower to the bank (making the document a 'debenture' to comply with IA 1986, s 29(2) if it is able to appoint an administrative receiver – **13.6.1**). The covenant to pay may refer to a specific debt obligation, or to all debts between the bank and borrower, known as an 'all monies' clause (a debenture securing an overdraft facility will usually use an 'all monies clause'). A typical 'all monies' covenant to pay is:

> The Borrower agrees to discharge on demand, each and every liability which the Borrower may have to the Bank, whether under sole or joint liability, whether under this Debenture or otherwise, and whether as principal or surety, and to pay to the Bank every sum now or hereafter due, owing or incurred by the Borrower to the Bank in respect of such liabilities.

The phrase 'on demand' is intended to prevent the Limitation Act 1939 operating against the bank until it makes a demand. It does not, and should not, alter the payment obligations in any facility agreement which it secures (see *Cryne v Barclays Bank plc* [1987] BCLC 548 in which it was held that the words 'due, owing or incurred' meant that demand under the debenture could be made only when the loan was due under the facility agreement which it secured).

Some debentures refer to monies owing or incurred 'on any account whatsoever', but this wording may be inadvisable because there is a danger that it would not include certain types of obligation (eg, loan stock – see *Re Quest Cae Limited* [1985] BCLC 266).

15.2.2 Charging clause

The second clause in a debenture is usually the charging clause. This clause specifies which of the borrower's assets are charged to repay the debts acknowledged in the covenant to pay, as well as how each type of asset is secured. The following paragraphs examine some of the issues which arise with respect to charging particular assets.

15.2.2.1 Land

A debenture will usually secure leasehold and freehold land by way of a 'charge by way of legal mortgage' (see **12.4**). Details of any registered land which is to be secured will be included in a schedule to the debenture, so that the security can be registered at Land Registry under the LRA 2002 (the schedule will also usually list details of unregistered land for ease of reference). The terms of any leases to be secured should be checked to ensure they do not prohibit particular forms of security interest being granted over them (eg, a prohibition on assignment or sub-letting). Future acquired land cannot be secured by legal mortgage, and is therefore secured by an equitable mortgage over the property once acquired. (The borrower may then be required to give a legal mortgage – see **15.2.3**.)

Some practitioners put security over land in a separate 'stand-alone' document to avoid having to register and disclose 'incorporated documents' (eg, the facility agreement) under Land Registry, Rule 139.

15.2.2.2 Fixed plant and machinery

A mortgage of land will automatically secure any assets which are, or become, permanently fixed to the secured property (known as 'fixtures'), and it is not strictly necessary to list these individually. There may, however, be other assets which will not be 'fixtures' but are nevertheless fixed assets (eg, certain plant and machinery), and so the charging clause should specifically mention 'buildings, trade and other fixtures, and fixed plant and machinery' if these are to be secured.

15.2.2.3 Cash deposits (bank accounts)

There are circumstances in which a bank may want to take security over a cash deposit made with it. For example, the bank might have provided a performance guarantee in return for which it demands a cash deposit from the guaranteed party. 'Cash deposit' does not entail a suitcase full of used banknotes; rather it involves the borrower opening an account with the bank into which it credits the required amount. The obvious way to secure the account is for the depositor to create a mortgage or charge over it in favour of the bank. However, in 1987, a controversial first instance decision by Millett J in *Re Charge Card Services* [1987] Ch 150 included the following statements (emphasis added):

> [a debt] ... cannot be made the subject of a *legal* or *equitable mortgage* in favour of the debtor, since this requires a conveyance or assignment by way of security, and this operates as a conditional release;

and

> a *charge* in favour of a debtor of his own indebtedness to the chargor is conceptually impossible.

In other words, a depositor could not *charge* or *mortgage* (ie, assign by way of security) its account with a bank to that bank. The argument for this proposition was based on the fact that an account is a debt owed by a bank to a depositor, and a debt is simply a right to sue the debtor for the amount owed. If that right were charged, or mortgaged, in favour of the debtor it would be giving the debtor the right to sue himself: this would simply cancel (or reduce) the debt. Millett J's judgment (at least with respect to the invalidity of a charge in these circumstances) was criticised by practitioners and legal commentators.

In October 1997, in *Morris v Agrichemicals Ltd* [1997] 3 WLR 909 (also known as 'BCCI No 8'), the House of Lords, led by Lord Hoffmann, declared that a *charge* in favour of a person over the benefit of a deposit made with that person, by another, is not a conceptual impossibility. It must be assumed, since Lord Hoffmann did not opine otherwise, that an assignment (mortgage) of the account to the bank remains ineffective.

How should a depositor provide a bank with security ('cash collateral') over a deposit (ie, an account) with that bank? It is important that the means of enforcing a cash collateral arrangement is by set-off – contractual set-off prior to winding-up, and mandatory set-off after winding-up (see **13.5**): any security granted over the account is intended to ensure that the money is in the account when the bank needs to set off. Therefore, the bank should usually require (assuming the depositor will not have unhindered access to the account – otherwise (b) will probably be a floating charge and (d) will not usually be appropriate):

(a)   an express (contractual) right of set-off;

(b)   a fixed charge over the account (assuming the depositor will not be allowed to withdraw any money without the bank's prior consent);

(c)   a prohibition on the depositor assigning the account (to deal with the fact that a bona fide purchaser, for value, without notice could defeat the fixed charge); and

(d)   if the depositor's obligation is contingent, a 'flawed asset' arrangement (that is, the deposit only becomes repayable at the same time that the depositor's debt becomes due and unpaid). This protects the account from a liquidator until the bank can exercise its rights of set-off.

Note that an assignment (mortgage) will usually be possible if security over an account is given to a security trustee or an agent bank on behalf of a syndicate, and that none of these issues will apply if a borrower gives security over an account held with a third party bank.

15.2.2.4   Goodwill

The goodwill of a borrower is probably automatically secured as an inseparable part of the borrower's secured 'undertaking'. However, to avoid any uncertainty, a debenture will usually specifically secure the borrower's goodwill (as well as other intellectual property rights) by way of a fixed charge.

15.2.2.5   Book debts

Book debts (also known as 'receivables') are the monies owed to a borrower by its debtors, and a bank will want to secure them with a fixed charge or, for single large debts, possibly an assignment (see **12.6**). The fact that book debts are usually a valuable asset means there has been considerable litigation over what constitutes fixed security (remember, if security is deemed floating not fixed, it will increase the amount available to preferential creditors). Most cases suggest that book debts have two elements, the debt and the proceeds of the debt, and that a bank must show control over both elements to achieve fixed security over either (eg, *Re Brightlife* [1987] Ch 200; *Re Keenan Bros* [1986] BCLC 242). Taking control over the debt element is usually uncontroversial: the bank must prevent the borrower doing anything other than collecting in the debt (eg, not allowing any discounting, factoring or assigning of the debt). Controlling the proceeds, however, is more difficult, because the borrower usually needs access to them to run its business.

In the early 1990s there was a run of judgments which moved against the previous cases and was much more in favour of the banks. The leading case was *Re New Bullas Trading* [1994] 1 BCLC 485, where the Court of Appeal blessed a debenture allowing fixed security over the unrealised debt and floating security over the proceeds (the New Bullas debenture required the realised debts to be paid into a specified account and then released under the directions of the creditor (ie, fixed security), but with the proviso that an absence of creditor's directions would automatically release the account monies from the fixed charge into a floating charge).

Many debentures subsequently used the *New Bullas* approach; however, the decision was subject to judicial criticism (see *Re Westmaze Ltd* (1998) *The Times*, 15 July, *Chalk v Kahn and Another* [2000] 2 BCLC 361 and *Agnew and Another v Commissioner of Inland Revenue* [2001] UKPC 28, [2001] 3 WLR 454 ('Brumark')). Most recently, the House of Lords in *National Westminster Bank plc v Spectrum Plus Limited* [2005] UKHL 41 held that to create a fixed charge over book debts, the chargee must control both the debt and its proceeds; the exact degree of control required to avoid recharacterisation remains unclear. Furthermore, the Lords suggested that the same principles would apply to security over assets other than book debts. This has led to concern that security over shares, insurance policies and even land may be recharacterised if control is not taken over the proceeds of those assets.

In summary, while total control over both debt and proceeds will definitely give fixed security, such tight restrictions are usually commercially unworkable. The vexed question for practitioners, still unanswered by the courts, is how much control (if any) may be given to the borrower without fixed security being lost.

Take note that bank accounts may not be considered 'book debts' and so the charge should refer to them expressly if they are to be secured.

15.2.2.6   Shares

Shares may be in registered form (in which a register of legal owners is maintained by the company), in bearer form (where legal ownership is generally determined by possession of the share certificate, or, in English companies, by possession of a 'share warrant' – see CA 2006, s 79) or 'dematerialised' (where they are held and traded electronically – see below). Registered shares are the most common form, and they are usually secured in one of two ways (for companies incorporated in England and Wales):

(a)   Creating a legal mortgage by transferring the shares into the bank's name and issuing a new share certificate to that effect. This method is not common because it creates greater administration issues and potential liabilities for the bank as owner of the company (eg, under the Pensions Act 2004). In *Enviroco Ltd v Farstad Supply A/S* [2009] EWCA Civ 1399, the Court of Appeal decided that a company ceased to be a subsidiary of its holding company if the holding company gave a legal mortgage over the subsidiary's shares. However, there was no suggestion that the company then became a subsidiary of the mortgagee (the bank). The debenture will allow the bank to sell the shares on default of the borrower and provide for re-transfer when the loan is repaid.

(b)   Creating an equitable mortgage (or charge) by taking custody of the share certificate together with a stock transfer form executed by the borrower, but with the transferee's name and other details left blank. The security document should also contain a power of attorney allowing the bank to complete the stock transfer form and submit it, with the share certificates, to register a new owner (see **15.2.8**). The bank can then enforce the security by completing the transfer form with its own name, or that of any purchaser. The advantage of this method is that the bank does not have the 'inconvenience' of ownership pre-enforcement (eg, voting, passing dividend and shareholder information back to the borrower, etc) and does not run the risk of the company whose shares are secured becoming a subsidiary of the bank (before enforcement).

In either case, enforcement of the security will not require further involvement of the borrower. The bank's solicitor should ensure that the shares are fully paid up, that (in the case of (a) above) any stamp duty payable on the transfer form has been paid, and that there are no restrictions on transfer in the articles (eg, pre-emption rights). In the case of bearer shares, security is usually achieved simply by taking delivery of the share certificate and a memorandum of deposit (ie, a pledge). The matter is more complex if the shares are held in a depository or clearing system (see also **19.2.7**), or are traded on an electronic transfer system, and details are beyond the scope of this book.

15.2.2.7 Stock in trade and sundry assets

The main asset which is specifically subject to a floating charge is the borrower's stock in trade (see **12.3.2**). However, there will be other 'grey areas' where purported 'fixed charges' may not effectively secure assets (eg, book debts or insurance proceeds). Control might be demonstrated by requiring segregation of assets, restrictions on dealing with assets, or an obligation to account for any proceeds of disposal. There is, however, no absolute guarantee that these methods will be sufficient in all circumstances. Most debentures will therefore declare any assets within these 'grey areas' to be secured by a fixed charge, but then use a floating charge to secure any property not effectively secured by the fixed charge. The floating charge acts as a type of 'safety net'.

15.2.2.8 Choses in action

Various choses in action will be secured by way of legal or equitable assignment. These might include rental or leasing rights, debts, property rights, insurance proceeds, investments and any uncalled capital contributions on the borrower's shares. The assignment should be specified as subject to redemption to avoid any question of permanence which would attract stamp duty.

15.2.3 Further assurance clause

A debenture will usually include an undertaking by the borrower to do anything necessary in order to perfect the security (this is sometimes known as a 'further assurance' clause). This might include execution of any documents required by the bank, the conversion of equitable mortgage to legal mortgage, the deposit of any documents of title, or even the provision of additional security to ensure that the bank obtains the full security anticipated in the debenture.

15.2.4 Undertakings

Most debentures will contain a number of undertakings, the most common being:

(a) a negative pledge. This may be included even if the facility agreement contains a negative pledge to help ensure registration at the Companies Registry (and therefore notification) of its terms;

(b) an undertaking to execute, at the bank's request, a legal mortgage in place of an equitable one (ie, perfection of security);

(c) an undertaking to provide the bank with any documents of title it might request;

(d) an undertaking to repair and maintain land, and insure all assets, together with a power of attorney allowing the bank to do these things (and recover any expenses it incurs) if the borrower does not.

Care should be taken not to duplicate (except in the case of (a) above), or conflict with, similar clauses in any loan documentation.

15.2.5 Crystallisation clause

If it creates a floating charge, the debenture will specify when the floating charge crystallises (see **12.3.2**). This will usually be:

(a)   at any time the bank notifies the borrower in writing (although a borrower may resist the bank being able to crystallise the floating charge at will, and insist that it is linked to a default under the facility agreement, or at least a perception that the assets secured by the charge are in jeopardy); and

(b)   automatically on specified events, for example on any demand by the bank for repayment, on a petition for the winding-up of, or an administration order in relation to, the borrower, or if the borrower ceases to carry on a substantial part of its business.

15.2.6 Appointment of a receiver, administrator or administrative receiver

The bank will have a right (subject to contrary agreement) to immediate possession of any assets over which it has a legal mortgage. However, this right of possession does not extend to assets over which the bank has merely an equitable mortgage or charge. The debenture should therefore give the bank an express contractual right to take possession of the charged assets on specified 'enforcement events' (ie, events of default).

The bank should also be given the right, on an enforcement event, to appoint a receiver of the secured property, an administrator and, if permitted, an administrative receiver – see **13.6.1**. These individuals are licensed insolvency practitioners and are usually appointed as agents of the borrower, selling assets to meet the borrower's obligations to the lender, to avoid the bank being liable for any of their acts or omissions. The debenture will contain any powers the office-holder is to have beyond his normal statutory powers.

15.2.7 Collection of debts

A debenture will usually require the borrower to collect in any debts and claims of the business 'promptly', and to pay them into specified accounts (see **15.2.2.5**).

15.2.8 Power of attorney

A debenture will invariably provide the bank and any receiver it appoints with a power of attorney. This will allow the bank to carry out any of the borrower's obligations under the debenture which the borrower fails to honour, for example, conveying legal title for any assets over which it has only equitable security, or enforcing equitable security over shares (see **15.2.2**). The instrument creating a power of attorney must be executed as a deed and, provided it is also expressed to be 'irrevocable', it will survive the borrower's liquidation (Powers of Attorney Act 1971, s 4). Powers of attorney are strictly construed and therefore will need to be widely drafted to cover the bank's needs.

15.2.9 Redemption of the security

The debenture must provide for the release of the security once the secured obligations are satisfied. However, the bank may require the right to retain the security for a period of at least six months after satisfaction of the debt, in case the monies used to repay the loan are reclaimed by the courts as a preference (see **14.9**). There are no strict formalities for the discharge of security, other than for registered land for which the requisite form should be filed with the Registrar. The borrower will usually be made liable for any costs involved in discharging the security.

15.2.10 Administrative provisions

As with any other commercial agreement, a debenture will contain a number of boiler plate clauses concerning administrative matters, such as notice periods, interpretation, service of documents, and costs and expenses.

15.3 EXECUTION

Debentures should be made by way of deed. Under the Law of Property (Miscellaneous Provisions) Act 1989, a document will not be a deed unless:

> it makes clear on its face that it is intended to be a deed ... whether by describing itself as a deed or expressing itself to be executed or signed as a deed or otherwise.

The introduction or execution (or preferably both) of a debenture should be drafted accordingly. A debenture should be created as a deed because:

(a) it avoids any doubt as to sufficiency of consideration;

(b) it is necessary because debentures invariably create a power of attorney (see the Power of Attorney Act 1971, s 1);

(c) it is necessary if a debenture conveys or creates a legal estate in land (LPA 1925, s 52); and

(d) it is necessary if the bank is to take powers under LPA 1925, s 101.

A debenture should also be expressed as being made by the borrower 'in favour of the bank' (rather than 'between' borrower and bank) to ensure that it can be enforced by a party other than the bank (eg, a receiver or attorney).

Note that, from 6 April 2008, a company can execute a deed by the signature of one director whose signature is witnessed (CA 2006, s 44).

CHAPTER 16

LEGAL OPINIONS

16.1	Introduction	191
16.2	What are legal opinions?	191
16.3	Preamble	192
16.4	Assumptions	193
16.5	Opinion	193
16.6	Qualifications	194
16.7	Foreign counsel legal opinions	195
16.8	Conclusion	196

'There is nothing in the world so easy as giving an opinion; consequently, in general, there are few things so utterly valueless.'

Charles William Day, *The Maxims, Experiences, and Observations of Agogos*

16.1 INTRODUCTION

Legal opinions were first introduced in the USA, where they were required by banks' auditors in order to confirm the enforceability of loan documentation inter-state. It is now usual for banks in the UK, making either substantial loans or capital market investments (see **Chapter 17**), to require a legal opinion. This chapter briefly explains the typical structure and content of a legal opinion relating to loan documentation.

16.2 WHAT ARE LEGAL OPINIONS?

16.2.1 Purpose

Legal opinions relate only to matters of law and not to matters of fact. In a banking context, legal opinions will usually confirm that all the documents associated with the loan are legally valid and enforceable. The opinion will also highlight areas which may be problematic (eg, on enforcement), helping the bank to assess any associated risk. The opinion does not, however, provide a guarantee that the borrower will service or repay the loan, a confirmation of commercial efficacy for a transaction, or a complete risk assessment. In one sense, a legal opinion is simply a written statement by a solicitor that he has done his job properly.

16.2.2 Who provides the opinion?

The opinion is usually provided by the bank's solicitor (who will have created and negotiated the loan documentation) and is addressed to the bank. Generally, only an addressee may sue the solicitor if the opinion proves wrong, although the solicitor will owe a general responsibility to anyone he knows has relied on his advice. If the transaction involves a syndicate (or underwriters), the opinion may be addressed to the agent bank on their behalf, or be addressed to each of them individually (so that they can each sue on it individually).

A lawyer can only opine on the law of the jurisdiction in which he is qualified. Therefore, if an opinion is required on an overseas matter, it will be necessary to instruct local lawyers.

16.2.3 When are opinions used?

There are three situations in which legal opinions will almost always be required:

(a) *Large loans.* If a bank makes a large loan with complex documentation, and external lawyers are involved, the bank will want an opinion, (usually) given by the bank's lawyers, that the documents are legal, valid and binding. Banks will not usually require legal opinions for small, unsecured loan transactions: the fact that a bank's in-house legal department has 'signed off' on the loan may be sufficient for the bank's internal procedures.

(b) *Secured lending.* Where a bank takes security for a loan, it will usually want an opinion to confirm the priority and enforceability of the security, and to outline any risks associated with those issues.

(c) *Overseas jurisdictions.* If a bank is providing money to a borrower incorporated outside England and Wales, or is taking security falling under an overseas jurisdiction (see **14.12**), it will invariably require a legal opinion from a local lawyer with respect to the enforceability, legality, priority, etc, of the relevant documents.

Even if the loan is a repeat of an earlier one (a re-financing), the bank may still require a new opinion (even if the opinion is identical to the previous one) in order to update its effect (see below).

A bank will usually make the delivery of a satisfactory legal opinion a condition precedent to the loan being drawn down (see **4.7.4**). If this is the case, a borrower ideally should insist that the bank and the opining solicitors agree the form of the opinion in advance of executing the facility agreement (it will then appear as a schedule to the facility agreement). Unfortunately, this does not always happen, and many 'eleventh hour' problems are due to disagreement over the content of legal opinions.

16.2.4 Form of the opinion

Legal opinions are invariably written in the form of a letter on the solicitor's headed notepaper, addressed to the bank and signed in the firm's name (it is common policy that only partners may sign legal opinions). The date of the letter is very important, since a legal opinion can be given only at a particular date, taking account of the law as it stands at that time.

Most legal opinions will follow a similar format:

(a) preamble;

(b) assumptions;

(c) opinion; and

(d) qualifications.

Some firms will put the assumptions and qualifications into a schedule in order to emphasise the actual 'opinion'.

More detail on each section is given below.

16.3 PREAMBLE

The first section of the opinion will specify the addressees and then briefly outline the form of the loan transaction (eg, the parties, the type of loan, the maturity date, etc). The opinion will then usually provide two lists: the first will be a list of all the documents in respect of which the opinion is given (in addition to the facility agreement, this will normally include any security documents and guarantees); the second list will specify the documents which the solicitor has reviewed in order to give the opinion (which, in addition to the documents opined upon, will probably include board and shareholders' resolutions, memorandum and articles, security registration forms, etc).

Usually, the legal opinion will be delivered after the documents to which it refers have been executed. However, the timing of some transactions may make this impossible, and the opinion will need to refer to unexecuted documents. In this case, the opinion should be clear that it refers to a specific draft and assumes the executed document is unchanged from that draft.

Lastly, the preamble to the opinion will also contain a record of any searches (eg, at the Companies Registry and Companies Court) on which the opinion relies, together with the dates on which they are made.

16.4 ASSUMPTIONS

All opinions will be based on certain assumptions of fact (remember, the opinion only addresses the law) which the opining solicitor must make. The most common assumptions include:

(a) that all signatures appearing on the reviewed documents are genuine;

(b) that the documents submitted to the solicitor as originals are authentic and complete;

(c) that the documents submitted to the solicitor as copies are complete and conform to the original document (which was itself authentic);

(d) that any resolutions were properly passed at quorate meetings which were duly convened and held;

(e) that the documents on which the opinion relies (as listed) remain accurate;

(f) if the opinion predates the execution of the documents on which it opines, that those documents are executed unchanged;

(g) that any searches (see above) remain unchanged;

(h) that (since the date of the relevant search) the companies to which the opinion relates have not become subject to any type of insolvency procedure;

(i) that no foreign law would affect the conclusions reached in the opinion;

and, if the opinion covers security documents:

(j) that the bank had no notice of any prohibition or restriction on creating the security, or notice of any other security in the same assets;

(k) that immediately after providing any guarantee (or other security), each obligor was fully solvent, and that the provision of the guarantee (or security) was in good faith, for the benefit of the obligor and did not constitute financial assistance.

The assumptions will also often be followed by a list of limitations, for example that the opinion is based solely upon the law of England and Wales, that no opinion is expressed as to the title of any obligor with respect to the secured assets, and that no opinion is expressed as to matters of fact.

16.5 OPINION

At this point the actual opinion appears, usually in the form of a series of numbered statements. The actual opinion will be quite short by comparison with the overall length of the letter: the vast majority of the paragraphs are assumptions and qualifications. The exact form of a legal opinion will be a matter for negotiation between the bank and its solicitor. It might relate only to the borrower and the facility agreement, or it might include some or all of the obligors and other transaction documents. However, for a straightforward domestic loan facility, the matters which are most commonly opined upon (either by the bank's, or sometimes the borrower's, solicitors) are as follows:

(a) That the borrower was properly incorporated and is not in liquidation. If the loan is secured, the bank might want this opinion to cover any main obligors. In the USA, it is common to opine that a company is of 'good standing', meaning it has paid all due taxes and other substantial levies necessary for it to continue in business; however, this phrase has no technical meaning in English law.

(b)   The borrower has the requisite power to enter into and perform the facility agreement, and has taken any action necessary to authorise execution of the facility agreement. The first part is essentially a statement that borrowing under the facility agreement is intra vires for the borrower. Once again, this will occasionally be worded to include main obligors, with respect to their security. The second part covers any procedural matters which were necessary, such as board meetings. The opinion will usually assume that the necessary procedures were validly performed.

(c)   The execution, delivery and performance of the facility agreement will not contravene English law, any regulation applicable to companies (incorporated in England and Wales), and will not violate any provision of the borrower's memorandum and articles. This is essentially a declaration that the facility agreement is not illegal, is properly constituted so as to bind the borrower, and would be upheld in the courts if sued upon (although the remedy cannot be predicted with any certainty). Under English contract law, an agreement which is illegal at the time it is formed will not be enforced by the court. One of the functions of the legal opinion, therefore, is to ensure the loan documents are not illegal ab initio. The consequences of a contract which becomes illegal after execution can be dealt with in the contract itself (see **9.9.3**).

(d)   Payments made by the borrower will not be subject to UK taxes (ie, withholding tax), and no taxes are payable on execution or registration of the facility agreement. The implications of withholding tax and grossing-up provisions are dealt with at **9.3.4**. The second part refers primarily to stamp duty (the result of non-payment being non-enforceability of the document on which the stamp duty is due).

(e)   All necessary registration, filings, licences and consents have been obtained in order to validate the loan document. Some jurisdictions may impose exchange controls or other requirements. Almost all jurisdictions will have a registration system for non-possessory security.

16.6 QUALIFICATIONS

The statements made in a legal opinion will never be unequivocal. They will always be subject to a number of qualifications or provisos. In a similar way to the disclosures against warranties (see **5.2.4**), the qualifications to an opinion allow the opining solicitor to modify general declarations. The most common qualifications are as follows:

(a)   The validity, performance and enforcement of the facility agreement may be affected by insolvency proceedings (and similar processes). The opinion may give particular examples, such as the powers of administrators and administrative receivers under IA 1986 (as modified by the EA 2002), and the provisions for setting aside transactions at an undervalue and preferences under IA 1986, s 423 and ss 238–239 respectively.

(b)   Any declaration in the opinion that the facility agreement is enforceable must be read on the basis that equitable remedies are at the discretion of the court (eg, specific performance and injunctions are not usually available if damages would be an adequate alternative).

(c)   A provision purporting to create a fixed charge may be construed as creating a floating charge (see **14.7**).

(d)   The enforcement of some security rights is controlled by law. For example, a mortgagee has duties to both the borrower and any prior mortgagees.

(e)   Any claims under the loan may be affected by lapse of time (ie, under the Limitation Acts), by any rights of set-off or counter-claim. Provisions in the facility agreement absolving the bank of liability for default may not be effective in court.

(f)   The opinion can only take account of the law of England and Wales.

(g) A court may refuse to entertain proceedings if a claim has been, or is being, brought elsewhere.

(h) Certain specific provisions may not be upheld by a court, most notably default interest (which may be declared penal – see **4.9**), provisions for severability (see **9.6**), and provisions requiring a borrower to pay the costs of litigation on enforcement. Evidence which might be held as conclusive under the facility agreement will not necessarily be acceptable to a court.

16.7 FOREIGN COUNSEL LEGAL OPINIONS

If the facility agreement is governed by English law but a borrower (or guarantor) is incorporated outside of England and Wales, the banks will usually require a legal opinion from counsel in that jurisdiction. Ideally, any foreign counsel opinion should be similar to the English law opinion: following the layout and using similar assumptions and reservations helps the client to review and understand the opinions.

16.7.1 What should the opinion cover?

Focusing on the opinion, the following issues should usually be covered:

(a) *Borrower's status*: confirmation that the borrower is duly incorporated, duly organised and validly exists in its jurisdiction. Specific terms may be appropriate in certain jurisdictions, such as 'good standing' (see **16.5** at (a)).

(b) *Authorisation*: that the borrower has the power and authority to execute the transaction documents and perform the obligations they contain.

(c) *No legal conflict*: that there is no breach of law, regulation, treaty, etc, nor any conflict with the constitutional documents of the borrower. Sometimes the opinion will be provided by the borrower's own internal counsel, in which case the opinion should cover conflict with existing contracts to which the borrower is party.

(d) *Legal, valid, binding and enforceable*: that the transaction documents bind the borrower and are not contrary to public policy.

(e) *Filings, registrations and consent*: confirmation that it is not necessary or desirable to file, register, notarise (which usually involves reading and executing the documents in front of a notary – quite common in civil law jurisdictions), stamp (a type of document tax) or take any other action to make the documents legal, valid, enforceable and admissible in evidence.

(f) *Withholding tax*: lenders are very sensitive to withholding tax being imposed (see **9.3.4**) and so will want confirmation that it is not applied in the local jurisdiction.

(g) *Domicile*: confirmation that the lenders will not become domiciled in the local jurisdiction by virtue of the transaction documentation, and conversely that it is not necessary for the lenders to take domicile or establish a place of business in the jurisdiction to enforce the documents.

(h) *Choice of law*: that the choice of governing law for the documents (eg English law) would be recognised and enforced if the lenders needed to enforce the documents or take proceedings in the local jurisdiction. Also, that any *judgment* obtained under the governing law of the document would be enforced.

(i) *Lender's claims rank pari passu*: it is unusual for opinions to be given on ranking among secured parties, but usually a statement that the debt will rank at least *pari passu* (equally) with unsecured and unsubordinated creditors will be given.

(j) *Jurisdiction and agent for service of process*: confirmation that the borrower's submission to jurisdiction (that is, agreeing that claims under the documents will be heard in a specific jurisdiction) is valid and cannot be revoked. Also, confirmation that the appointment of an agent in the jurisdiction of the governing law (an 'agent for service of process') is valid and cannot be revoked.

And if it is a secured loan:

(k)   *Valid security*: that the borrower has created a valid and effective security interest over the relevant assets, and that it covers future as well as current advances.

16.7.2   Additional issues

Other issues that may be covered in the foreign counsel's opinion include:

(a)   no limitation on paying interest (prohibited in some Middle-Eastern countries);

(b)   no exchange control (preventing recovery of security or debt from the jurisdiction);

(c)   that the borrower is solvent; and

(d)   that the borrower cannot claim immunity to proceedings.

And if guarantees or security are being taken:

(e)   whether there are any restrictions on providing guarantees and security (for example, the amount of guarantees is often limited by law); and

(f)   whether there are issues with financial assistance (most jurisdictions prohibit or limit a company assisting the purchase of its parent's shares).

It is probably also worth asking whether any documents need translating into the local language (eg to be enforceable or notarised).

Foreign counsel will need as much information as possible, both at the start of the transaction and as it progresses, and details inevitably change. It is important, therefore, to keep a dialogue open throughout the transaction, notifying the counsel of new information and, in particular, of any delay to closing.

16.8   CONCLUSION

The examples of matters opined upon, and the assumptions and qualifications given above, are designed to provide an idea of the areas commonly covered. All of these will vary between transactions, depending on the nature of the loan, the documents involved in the transaction, any international aspects of the deal and the requirements of the bank. The format of most legal opinions will, however, closely follow that outlined above.

Lastly, on the basis that it is a necessary expense in providing the loan, it is invariably the borrower who must pay the solicitor's fees for producing any opinions.

PART III

CAPITAL MARKETS

CHAPTER 17

INTRODUCTION TO INTERNATIONAL CAPITAL MARKETS

17.1	Introduction	199
17.2	What is a capital market?	199
17.3	Domestic and euromarkets	200
17.4	Debt and equity securities	203
17.5	Bonds and notes	203
17.6	Other debt securities	207
17.7	Primary and secondary markets	210
17.8	Clearing systems	210
17.9	International Capital Markets Association	211
17.10	The issuers	212
17.11	Credit rating	212
17.12	Further reading	214

'When investing money, the amount of interest you want should depend on whether you want to eat well or sleep well.'

Wall Street dictum

17.1 INTRODUCTION

The preceding two parts of this book have dealt with aspects of raising finance by way of a commercial loan. In certain circumstances, however, entities with substantial borrowing requirements may turn to a different source of funds known as the 'capital markets'. This part of the book introduces the capital markets, the most common instruments that are used to raise finance on those markets, and the process of issuing one such instrument, the eurobond (also known as 'International Bonds' or just 'bonds').

17.2 WHAT IS A CAPITAL MARKET?

17.2.1 Investment capital

A capital market is not a marketplace in the sense of a physical place, such as a trading floor with people waving their arms and trading in securities. It refers instead to the vast amount of capital available from financial institutions, pension funds and investment funds (and a few high-net-worth individuals) which want to buy securities, either to hold as an investment or to trade. References to the 'market' are more accurately references to the borrowing requirements of potential issuers, and the funds available from investors. The 'size' of a market refers to the amount of funds available from the participants and the tradeability of the securities issued. An 'illiquid' market means that the participants are unwilling to buy new or trade in issued securities.

The international capital markets are subject to an even more confusing array of terminology than commercial bank lending. The terms used in this section of the book are given their most common meaning, but different participants in the capital markets may have different terminology for the same thing or process, and no terminology should be thought of as definitive (eg, strictly speaking, commercial bank lending is a 'capital market', but colloquially the phrase refers to debt and equity securities only).

17.2.2 Comparing debt securities to loan facilities

There are some fundamental differences between raising money through the capital markets and borrowing by way of a loan facility. The main differences include:

(a)   In a capital markets issue a borrower traditionally issues a document (or documents) evidencing the debt obligation (known as 'debt securities', 'instruments' or more colloquially 'bonds') in return for the money it receives from lenders. The borrower is therefore known as the 'issuer'.

(b)   Whilst the vast majority of loan facilities are (at least initially) provided by banks, a wide variety of institutions, and some individuals, 'lend' by purchasing securities on the capital markets. The lenders in the capital markets are known as 'investors' (although they are not just investors in the traditional sense of holding on to the investment until it matures, but also speculators who buy securities hoping to sell them at a profit prior to their maturity).

(c)   Since the potential number of investors is far greater than lenders offering commercial loans, the amount of funds available to an issuer is potentially much larger and interest rates lower. This wide investor base allows a borrower's debt (and therefore any risk) to be spread among numerous 'investors'. Furthermore, the regulatory capital costs associated with most commercial loan facilities (see **9.3.2** and **9.3.3**) will not apply to capital markets investors. These factors help reduce the cost of raising money on capital markets.

(d)   **Chapter 10** explained how loan facilities can be sold, but despite the advent of the LMA most 'asset sales' have a limited market. In contrast, the capital markets are well established and geared towards the relatively quick and simple trading of debt. The ability to sell securities easily and quickly provides liquidity to the market: more investors are prepared to buy knowing that they can sell prior to maturity and realise their capital if necessary. The liquidity of the market means investors are prepared to accept lower yields, which reduces the cost of borrowing for the issuer.

(e)   The more extensive market means that the size and maturities of the debt can be more varied than for most commercial loans. An investor can usually invest in smaller 'participations' in a capital markets issue than in a loan facility. Certain debt securities can be significantly longer term than commercial loans, for example 30-year Gilt-edged securities (government bonds).

(f)   A listed bond issue inevitably involves 'publicity', whereas a syndicated loan can remain confidential.

(g)   Generally speaking, the undertakings and events of default in the terms and conditions of capital markets securities are less onerous and restrictive than in a facility agreement. There is no specific relationship bank monitoring compliance with wide-ranging financial covenants as there would be in a loan facility, although a trustee will have a basic role of overseeing standard undertakings (see **19.2.4**).

17.3 DOMESTIC AND EUROMARKETS

Capital markets may be either 'domestic' markets, or 'euro' markets (also known as international markets).

17.3.1 Domestic markets

A 'domestic' market is the market in a currency in its country of origin. Raising sterling in the UK, euros in France or US dollars in the United States are all examples of using domestic markets. When currencies are raised in their domestic markets, they are usually subject to control by that country's central bank or relevant central monetary authority (eg, the FSA and the Bank of England in the UK, or the Securities Exchange Commission and Federal Reserve Bank in the USA). The largest domestic capital market is the USA.

17.3.2   Euromarkets

17.3.2.1   The meaning of 'euro'

'Euro' is a prefix used very frequently in capital markets terminology: there are 'eurobonds', 'euronotes' and 'eurocurrencies'. 'Euro' does not imply the involvement of European currencies, money deposited in Europe or, indeed, necessarily indicate any 'European' connection. The term 'euro' simply refers to a currency held outside the currency's country of origin.

17.3.2.2   Eurocurrencies

Imagine a large UK exporter, such as Jaguar cars, which receives several millions of US dollars every year in payment for the cars it sells in the USA. If Jaguar invests those dollars outside their country of origin (eg, in an issue of securities in the UK) they are 'eurodollars'. There is a large number of exporters in this country earning currencies from all over the world, as well as many financial institutions which find themselves holding foreign currencies as a result of various transactions (these are sometimes known colloquially as currencies 'on holiday'). In London, therefore, as in any financial centre of a country which has a modicum of international trade, there is ownership of a large pool of the most common foreign currencies. The organisations owning these currencies will invest them by lending them to other institutions which require dollars, yen, sterling, etc. This creates the eurocurrency market.

17.3.2.3   Eurosecurities

Securities issued to attract the pool of eurocurrencies are known as 'euro' securities or, sometimes, 'international securities'. For example, if Tesco plc issues dollar denominated bonds in London, they are 'eurobonds'. A bond issued in London to raise sterling from *overseas* investors (rather than *domestic* investors) may also be regarded as a eurobond. The euromarkets 'globalised' the world's capital markets, providing an issuer with access to a much greater source of funds than in its domestic market alone. Any currency which is held outside its 'natural' country in sufficient quantity is likely to be targeted by the euromarkets.

(Note that the 'euro' prefix is sometimes still used colloquially, but will not appear on the face of the instrument. Furthermore, most practitioners will simply refer to 'bonds' or 'notes' (rather than 'eurobonds' or 'euronotes') and for simplicity the term 'bond' will generally be used below.)

17.3.2.4   Why use eurocurrencies?

Why should an issuer be particularly interested in the eurocurrency markets? What is wrong with borrowing dollars from US investors, or yen from the Japanese? Why do institutions keep foreign currency to invest instead of exchanging it for the currency of their own country? The answer to these questions lies within the origins of the euromarkets. In the late 1960s and early 1970s, the US Government put strict controls on interest rates and levied taxes on non-nationals issuing bonds in the USA (a form of exchange control). Investors avoided the interest rate restrictions by lending dollars outside the USA, and companies issued dollar denominated bonds outside the USA to avoid the US Government tax. The dollar and other euromarkets evolved, therefore, because they were immune to any domestic restrictions. Today, there are fewer domestic controls, and eurocurrencies are no longer 'refugees' from monetary restraints. However, having established an abundant (and therefore relatively cheap) source of funds, the euromarkets continue to flourish. Even if, for example, a borrower does not require Czech koruna, it will often be cheaper, and easier, to issue koruna eurobonds and exchange the eurodollars into a currency it requires, than to borrow that currency direct.

17.3.2.5 'Foreign' securities

A eurocurrency instrument taps into money which is held outside of its country of origin. This is not the same as tapping into money held outside the *issuer's* country. For example, if a German company issues sterling securities in Germany (or France, Switzerland, Japan, etc – ie anywhere outside the UK) it is a 'euro' issue, since it is aimed at sterling owned outside the UK. However, if a *non-British* company issues a sterling instrument (to 'domestic' investors) in the UK, this will raise currency in its country of origin, and so it is not a 'euro' issue but rather a 'foreign' issue. Foreign issues are known in the markets by highly colloquial names: an instrument issued by a non-British company in the UK to raise sterling from the UK domestic market is known as a 'bulldog'. Likewise, if a foreign company issues a dollar instrument in the US domestic market it is known as a 'yankee', and a yen instrument in Japan raising local yen is a 'samurai', etc.

Europe leads way for Yankee bond sales
By Richard Milne and Anousha Sakoui

Non-US companies have issued record volumes of US bonds this year, as they turn to dollar markets to access cheap funding.

The rush has been led by European companies, which have favoured the US over their domestic debt markets due to a combination of lower rates and higher activity. In total, European groups have accounted for more than half of this year's issuance of so-called 'Yankee' bonds – dollar-denominated bonds sold by non-American companies into the US.

So far this year, 773 have been issued, raising $412.9bn – beating the $378.1bn raised up to this point last year, according to data provider Dealogic.

Nearly 20 per cent of all bond issuance by European companies has been in the form of Yankee bonds, the highest percentage of total issuance in the past 10 years.

Statoil, the Norwegian oil company, and ArcelorMittal, the world's biggest steelmaker,

are two of the European groups to tap the US bond markets this month.

European companies have raised $236bn in the US so far this year – the same amount as last year but through a record 501 issues. This is the highest number of Yankee bonds to be sold in any year since the euro was created and more than double the number issued over the same period last year.

While the US corporate bond market has had its busiest August on record, Europe has been relatively quiet. 'The dollar market looks attractive and is busy and active for European issuers. We expect this trend will continue,' said Mark Lewellen, head of European corporate origination at Barclays Capital.

Among the non-US issuers making debut bond offerings in the dollar market this year are Russian Railways, Anglo Gold Ashanti, Brambles of Australia and Qatari Diar.

'Much of our corporate pipeline is in the dollar market. US

investors are very keen on non-US names,' said Mr Lewellen.

Companies are being attracted to the market by low interest rates. For example, US technology group IBM has issued bonds paying 1 per cent – the lowest coupon ever on a three-year corporate bond.

But the biggest rise in European dollar issuance has been among banks, which have sold more Yankee bonds in the year to date than in any year since 2000. Royal Bank of Scotland, the UK state-backed bank, raised $3.6bn last week in its biggest US dollar unguaranteed senior bond offering.

For European companies, the decision over where to issue bonds has been made easier by lower costs for swapping the proceeds of dollar bond issues back into euros.

'Yankee bonds are helping European banks' fill their so-called "funding gap", said Jean-Marc Mercier, head of European syndicate at HSBC. 'They are securing fantastic cost of funding levels in the US.'

An article from 22 August 2010.
Source: *Financial Times at* <http://www.ft.com>

17.4 DEBT AND EQUITY SECURITIES

'Securities' were defined at **12.7** as instruments in which a borrower (or more accurately an 'issuer') acknowledges a debt or an investment. The best-known securities are probably shares in listed companies which are traded on the stock market. Raising finance through share issues (known as 'equity' securities, since they provide equity in the issuer) is the subject of **Public Companies and Equity Finance**. This book is primarily concerned with debt securities which, in legal terms, are more similar to a straightforward debt obligation under a loan than to a share (although certain equity linked securities (see **17.5.5**) initially have the characteristics of a debt obligation but may be exchanged or converted into equity securities). There are a number of important differences between typical debt and equity securities.

17.4.1 Equity securities (ordinary shares)

In general terms:

(a) they are essentially a non-returnable investment. An investor can realise its investment capital only by selling the shares or winding up the company;

(b) an investor has no absolute right to receive a return on its investment (a 'dividend');

(c) an investor will rank behind all other creditors of the company (ie, those owed 'debts') in the event of a winding-up;

(d) an investor will take equity (a share) in the issuer, and is usually (although not always) given the power to vote on major issues at shareholders' meetings.

17.4.2 Debt securities (bonds)

In general terms:

(a) the investment will have a maturity date on which the issuer must redeem the security by repaying the investor. Most debt securities are tradeable on established markets, allowing an investor easily and quickly to realise the capital value of the instrument prior to its maturity;

(b) under the terms and conditions of the security it holds, an investor will have the right to receive a regular return on its investment (an interest payment or 'coupon'), or the investment may be issued at a 'discount' to its face value on redemption at maturity (see below);

(c) the investment may occasionally be secured, although it will more commonly be unsecured and rank behind all secured and preferred creditors and pari passu with all other unsecured creditors (but ahead of the equity investors) in the event of the winding-up of the issuer;

(d) with the exception of equity linked securities where the original debt obligation may be exchanged for equity (see **17.5.5**), an investor does not take any equity in the issuer, or have any rights over the issuer other than basic rights to call an event of default if coupon or principal are not paid or undertakings (which are very basic) are breached.

The following section explains the characteristics of the most common debt security structures found in the capital markets.

17.5 BONDS AND NOTES

A bond is a certificate of debt under which the issuer obligates itself to pay the principal to the bondholder on a specified date, usually (there is no hard and fast rule) three years or more after the date of issue.

The main characteristics of a bond are:

(a)   it is a debt obligation (although some bonds may have conversion rights into equity) made by way of a transferable instrument (see **18.3.1**) with a medium- or long-term maturity;

(b)   initially, it is sold by way of marketing to a wide number of investors through a syndicate of financial institutions, or it is sold to a small group of specifically targeted investors (known as a 'private placement');

(c)   it is a marketable instrument (ie, it has an established secondary market);

(d)   it may or may not be listed on a recognised stock exchange (see **21.8**);

(e)   it will bear interest (usually payable semi-annually), or be issued at a discount to its face value on redemption.

Until relatively recently, the term 'note' was reserved for securities with a short maturity (eg less than three years) or with a floating rate coupon: everything else was a 'bond'. However, the terms are now almost interchangeable and 'note' is probably used more commonly than 'bond'. Confusingly, there are no written rules; the cognoscenti just know which terms are used in the market. As a rule of thumb you should refer to:

(a)   'floating rate notes', not 'floating rate bonds' (see **17.5.2**);

(b)   a 'global note', rather than a 'global bond' (see **18.2.1**);

(c)   securities issued under a programme as 'notes', not 'bonds' (see **17.6**);

(d)   securities issued under a securitisation as 'notes', not 'bonds'.

If in doubt, use the term 'note' rather than 'bond'.

Bonds are probably the most widely used debt security on the capital markets. They can take a number of different forms, the most common of which are explained below.

17.5.1   Fixed rate bonds

Many bonds are issued on a 'fixed rate' basis. This means that the rate of interest (known as the 'coupon': see **17.5.4**) they yield for the investor is fixed at the time of issue and will not change during the life of the bond. The interest is usually payable annually (or semi-annually in the case of some 'emerging markets' issuers) in arrear, an infrequent return on investment compared with most loan facilities. The rate of interest will depend primarily on the market conditions prevailing at the time of issue, the credit rating of the issuer (see **17.11**), and the length of maturity of the bond. The starting point of the interest calculation will be based on the rate offered at that time on a government security (eg, a treasury bill) of similar maturity. A margin will be added to reflect the issuer's creditworthiness and the maturity of the bond (the longer the maturity, the higher the interest rate, since investors must wait longer for the return of their capital), and the composite rate is then shown on the bond as a single figure. Fixed interest bonds without any special features are known as 'straight bonds' or 'plain vanilla bonds'.

17.5.2   Floating rate notes

Floating rate notes ('FRNs') pay interest which fluctuates in accordance with a variable benchmark rate, which (if it is issued in London) is usually the LIBOR (see **4.9**) for the currency in which the bond is issued. The interest rate payable on the FRN is the benchmark rate plus a margin (in a similar way to floating rate loan facilities – see **4.9**), for example US$ LIBOR plus 50 basis points (0.5%). The rate is recalculated each time the interest is paid in order to reflect the then current benchmark rate. Floating rate notes will usually pay interest more frequently than fixed rate bonds (eg, quarterly) in order to reflect the changing market rate.

Floating rate notes appeal to issuers such as financial institutions which lend at a floating rate and so want to borrow at a floating rate to achieve 'matched funding' (ie, when the interest rate falls, they will receive less money from their lending, but will also be paying less for their borrowing).

17.5.2.1 Reverse FRNs

Under a reverse FRN, the interest rate payable on the bond rises or falls in the opposite direction to a benchmark level of market interest rates. This type of bond might appeal to investors who believe that general interest rates are likely to fall from the current level and want to speculate. Alternatively, they may be used to hedge an exposure that an investor has in a particular currency.

17.5.3 Variable rate bonds

Some bonds have a rate of interest which varies throughout their term, although, unlike FRNs, the rate does not vary freely in accordance with an underlying benchmark. Under a variable rate bond, the variation of interest rates is restricted, or is designed to alter in accordance with a pre-determined schedule. This type of bond can be structured in a variety of ways.

17.5.3.1 'Step-up' or 'step-down' bonds

In a 'step-up' bond, the initial fixed interest rate moves up to another (pre-determined) fixed rate after a given time. For example, a 10-year bond with a fixed rate of 3% for the first five years and 5% for the remaining five years (there may be more than one step). In a 'step-down' bond, the interest rate reduces rather than increases.

17.5.3.2 Collars

A bond which is subject to a 'collar' is similar to an FRN in that its rate of interest will vary in accordance with a benchmark rate (eg, LIBOR); however, the rate of interest payable is subject to an upper and a lower limit. These limits are known as the 'cap' and 'floor' respectively, and turn the underlying FRN into a variable rate bond. The advantages of a collar are that it guarantees a minimum return for the investor, and a maximum outlay for the issuer.

17.5.4 Zero coupon bonds

Zero coupon bonds do not pay any interest. The term 'coupon' refers to the interest on a bond and is derived from the fact that interest on definitive bearer bonds is claimed by tearing off perforated coupons at the side of the bond instrument and presenting them for payment. It might be thought strange that any investor would purchase an instrument which bears no interest. However, the amount which the investor pays for a zero coupon bond on its issue is less than its face value (ie, the value printed on the bond) on redemption. The bond is said to be issued at a 'discount' (a bond issued at substantially less than its face value is known as a 'deep discount bond'). The investor's return is achieved on maturity, when the issuer will redeem the bond at its face value.

> **EXAMPLE**
> Imagine that an instrument with a face value of $100, and a maturity of 12 months, is sold on issue at a discount of 10%, ie at $90. On maturity, one year later, the investor can claim $100 from the issuer. The investor will have made a return of $10 on a one-year investment of $90 – equivalent to an interest rate of a little over 11%.

The investor's return is represented by the difference between the cost of the bond at issue and its value when redeemed, spread over the term of the bond. There is therefore a gradual appreciation in the amount for which the bond might be sold as the date of maturity becomes closer. The investor can therefore make a partial return on its investment even if it sells the bond before it matures. The size of discount given on the issue of a zero coupon bond will reflect the return available to an investor purchasing interest-bearing bonds at the same time as the issue of the zero coupon bond (otherwise the bonds would not be attractive to investors). Furthermore, as interest rates fall, the price of a zero coupon bond already in issue will rise since the yield it offers to maturity can be lower yet still compete with equivalent interest-bearing bonds. Zero coupon bonds are usually favoured by investors who prefer to be taxed on a capital gain than on income.

17.5.5   Equity linked bonds

Although this section of the book is focusing on debt instruments, it is important to recognise that some bonds are linked to the equity (ie, the share capital) of the issuer. These are known as 'equity linked bonds' and they provide an investor with the opportunity to obtain some form of equity interest in the issuer (in which case the issuer must clearly be a company), or a related company. There are three main types of equity linked bond:

(a)   convertible bonds;

(b)   bonds with warrants; and

(c)   exchangeable bonds.

The typical characteristics of these instruments are explained below.

17.5.5.1   Convertible bonds

Convertible bonds provide the bondholder with an option to convert (or sometimes the issuer with an option to force conversion of) the bond into shares in the issuer, at some stage after issue. The bondholder's option to convert usually exists throughout the life of the bond. However, the bond may include a condition that the option is available only during a specific period, or expires after a given date.

Once a bondholder converts, the issuer will create new shares to be given in exchange for the bond, which is then redeemed in consideration for the issue of shares (thereby extinguishing the debt obligation of the issuer). The directors should ensure that there are no restrictions on allotment in the company's articles (see CA 2006, s 550); and, since the new shares are effectively issued for cash consideration, the existing shareholders may have pre-emption rights to be disapplied (under CA 2006, ss 561–573).

A convertible bond will also specify the 'conversion price'. This is the price at which the shares a bondholder receives in exchange for its bond will be valued upon conversion. For example, if the bondholder converts its convertible bonds with a total face value of $10,000 at a conversion price of $25 per share, it will receive 400 shares. The conversion price of the shares is invariably higher than their market value at the time the convertible bond is issued. The difference between the two is known as the 'conversion premium'.

The main attraction of convertible bonds from an investor's point of view is that they provide a potential high return with a limited risk. The bondholder may be happy simply to retain the steady fixed income from the unconverted bond (although this will usually be less than a similar non-convertible bond issued at the same time), particularly if the issuer appears to have a policy of not paying dividends. However, if the issuer performs well, the bondholder can take advantage of any resultant rise in its share price by exercising its conversion rights and selling some or all of the shares it has received on conversion.

From an issuer's perspective, the interest rate it must offer on a convertible bond will be less than an equivalent non-convertible bond, due to the added attraction of convertibility. The convertible bond also allows an issuer effectively to defer equity financing if it feels that its share price is currently undervalued and is therefore reluctant to raise equity finance at that time.

17.5.5.2   Bonds with warrants

Bonds with warrants are bonds which are issued as two securities: an interest-bearing security (the 'bond'), and an option to purchase shares in the issuer which can be exercised by the bondholder (the 'warrants'). The bond element will pay a fixed rate of interest and have a specified maturity, and will always remain as a debt obligation whether or not the warrants are exercised. The warrants provide the bondholder with a right to buy shares at a pre-determined price, either within a specified time period (a 'narrow exercise period', found in most European-style warrants), or at any time (a 'wide exercise period', found in US-style warrants).

The warrants are intended to provide an incentive for investors to purchase the bond and also allow the issuer to have a lower coupon (as for convertibles – see **17.5.5.1**). The warrants are detachable instruments, allowing a bondholder to trade them (as a right to buy shares in the issuer) separately from the bonds. Like convertible bonds, bonds with warrants are, to some degree, a speculative investment since the value of the right to take equity depends on the future market value of the issuer's shares.

17.5.5.3   Exchangeable bonds

Exchangeable bonds are similar in nature to convertible bonds, sharing the characteristics of an option to convert the debt into an equity interest. The difference is that the shares for which the bond can be exchanged are not shares in the issuer of the bonds but shares in a related company, such as a parent or subsidiary. Exchangeable bonds are less common than convertible bonds.

17.5.5.4   Conclusion

Equity linked bonds are debt instruments when they are issued and do not confer any 'shareholder' type rights on the investor until such time as the debt instrument converts or changes, in accordance with its terms and conditions, into some form of equity instrument.

17.6   OTHER DEBT SECURITIES

17.6.1   Medium term notes

Medium term notes (usually referred to as 'MTNs') are very similar in form to bonds or FRNs, other than the way in which they are issued. Bonds and FRNs are usually issued as a 'one off' issue for that issuer (a 'stand-alone' issue), for example 5,000 bonds at US$10,000 each, with a five-year maturity to raise US$50,000,000 for ABC Plc: MTNs, however, are issued in several series (ie, separate sets of issues) through a 'programme'. Essentially, an MTN programme involves the issuer and an arranger agreeing a set of legal documentation under which the issuer can issue notes of varying currencies and maturities (usually between one and 30 years), and bearing fixed, floating or variable rates of interest. The MTN programme may provide that the notes are issued in either bearer or registered form; and if in bearer form, they may be held as global notes or in definitive form (see **18.2**). The agreed documentation will specify the terms and conditions of any series of notes which are issued, as well as provide an information memorandum to be used for selling the notes to investors (this will need updating periodically). The programme will state an initial aggregate amount which it intends to raise through the series of issues.

The programme will also appoint a number of 'dealers', one of whom (although not always the same one) acts as a lead manager to each separate issue of notes. The advantage of an MTN programme is that it allows an issuer to issue a wide variety of notes at very short notice (since the majority of the necessary documentation is already in place).

17.6.2   Commercial paper

Commercial paper is a type of security providing issuers (which include large companies, banks and building societies) with short-term borrowing in the capital markets. It is issued through a programme, in a similar way to MTNs. An entity wishing to issue commercial paper must first find a bank willing to set up a programme for an agreed maximum amount of borrowing. The bank will then usually appoint a number of dealers, who will be responsible for finding buyers for the commercial paper in return for a commission. Commercial paper issues are not usually underwritten (ie, there is no guarantee that an issue will be sold), but conversely the issuer is not under any obligation to issue.

Commercial paper is usually unsecured, sold at a discount rather than being interest bearing (for withholding tax reasons), may be issued with varying maturities and is almost always in global form (see **18.2.2**). Commercial paper is usually available in various maturities of up to 365 days, although in practice, maturities will often be just one or two months. When the issuer wants to raise money, the dealers will sell the requisite amount of commercial paper under the programme (the dealers will sometimes suggest to the issuer that it is a good time to issue paper of a certain maturity under the programme). Whilst the programme specifies a maximum amount of paper which may be issued, it is a 'rolling' maximum limiting the amount which can be outstanding at any one time. The British Bankers' Association produces guidelines for the London Commercial paper market specifying standards which are a prerequisite for issuing paper in the UK.

17.6.3 Certificates of deposit

Certificates of deposit (known as 'CDs') are quite literally certificates (ie, receipts) issued by a bank or building society in return for a deposit of money made with them in the form of a loan. They are negotiable instruments issued in bearer form. CDs issued and payable in the UK (known as 'London CDs') usually have a maturity of no more than five years and may bear interest (which is more common), or be issued at a discount. The advantage to a lender of investing spare cash in a CD is that it receives a very good rate of interest (because the loan is not repayable until the CD matures), but it can recover capital at any time by selling the CD in the market. The issuer, meanwhile, has the advantage of a deposit which it knows is not repayable until maturity. CDs are unsecured obligations and, like commercial paper, any issue, if it is intended to trade in the London market, is bound to follow British Bankers' Association guidelines.

Ten-year gilt yields touch record low

By Robin Wigglesworth and Mary Watkins in London

The UK's 10-year borrowing costs touched a record low of just 1.407 per cent as fears over Spain's economic and financial malaise caused investors to head for highly rated assets outside the eurozone.

While the UK's bond yields fell across the curve, the 10-year benchmark bond yield of Germany, another haven asset in the eurozone crisis, edged up slightly to 1.17 per cent. The move indicated that investors are concerned that its creditworthiness may be impaired by possible rescues of the single currency area's stricken members.

Yields on US Treasuries were also lower, with five-, 10 - and 30-year bond yields hitting record lows in US intraday trade. By early afternoon in the US, five-year Treasuries were trading at 0.56 per cent, 10-year bonds at 1.43 per cent and 30-year Treasuries at 2.51 per cent.

While gilts later moved back to 1.47 per cent, analysts said the fact that Treasuries, gilts and Bunds continued to flirt with record lows

reflected investors' rush into the few remaining bond markets seen as relatively safe.

Government bonds of Europe's "soft core" countries have also rallied since the European Central Bank stopped paying interest on deposits held by banks at the ECB, but investors have continued to flee the eurozone's struggling periphery.

Analysts say that many investors have lost faith with eurozone policy makers and their ability to get to grips with problems in Spain and Italy.

Divyang Shah, global strategist at IFR Markets, said the latest bout of market volatility reflected the view that "eurozone negative tail-risk scenarios are now back on the radar screens".

Investors are weighing up a range of possible scenarios, from an early exit of the eurozone by Greece to a full sovereign bailout for Spain.

Mr Shah said the lack of stimulus for the eurozone economy

would do little to keep investors from putting "their funds anywhere else but the safety of the safest of sovereign bonds of Bunds, core eurozone, gilts and Treasuries".

Other so-called semi-core members of the eurozone have also benefited from the flight away from southern European economies.

But the 10-year bond yields of Finland, the Netherlands, Austria and France – eurozone countries that have enjoyed a strong rally in their government debt markets in recent weeks – all climbed higher on Monday. The 10-year bond yields of Norway and Sweden, two highly rated non-euro countries, eased slightly.

The euro fell against the US dollar and Japanese yen, underlining the "flight to safety", but edged up against most other currencies, particularly those of emerging markets, which are smaller and less liquid than the major global currencies.

Source: *Financial Times*, 23 July 2012

17.6.4   Bills of exchange

A bill of exchange was, originally, simply an instrument recognising a trade debt. Rather than demanding immediate payment for goods, a seller draws up a document under which the buyer of the goods promises to pay for them after a specified period, such as three months. This form of credit is a 'trade bill of exchange'. Trade bills of exchange may be sold, at a discount, in the capital markets. Whilst the seller gets slightly less money than if he had waited for the buyer to pay under the trade bill, he gets the money earlier. Some bills of exchange will have payment of the amount due under them guaranteed (or 'accepted') by a bank. These are known as 'bank bills' or 'accepted bills'. Because they carry less risk of non-repayment, accepted bills will be sold at a higher price (ie, less discount) than identical non-accepted trade bills.

Accepted bills also provide large companies with a form of very short-term finance. A company can establish an agreement with a bank allowing it to issue bills of exchange (up to an aggregate amount) which the bank will 'accept' (ie, undertake the payment obligations) in return for a fee. This is known as an 'acceptance credit facility': there is no underlying trade debt. The company can then sell the accepted bills to raise short-term money.

17.6.5   Treasury bills

Treasury bills are capital markets instruments which work in a similar way to bills of exchange and are used by governments for short-term borrowing in order to balance their cash flow. In London, the Government auctions treasury bills to banks and other financial institutions every Friday. The treasury bills do not bear interest, but are sold at a discount.

17.7 PRIMARY AND SECONDARY MARKETS

When a security is issued, it is offered on what is known as the 'primary market'. The primary market involves the sale of securities by an issuer to investors in order for the issuer to raise the money it requires. If the investor holds the security until it matures, the transaction will have been confined to the primary market. However, most investors will want the ability to sell a security before it matures, allowing them to realise its capital value early. This is known as the 'secondary market', in which investors and traders can buy and sell securities already in issue.

Certain investors will buy securities to hold as a 'long-term' investment, ie until the security matures. Other investors buy securities in order to 'play' the market, ie to sell them when their value rises. These investors may hold a selection (or 'book') of securities (in the same way as an equity investor holds a portfolio of shares in various companies), which they trade on the market (some financial institutions act as brokers, buying and selling securities on behalf of their client investors). These investors are generally known as 'traders'. An instrument with an established secondary market is usually known as a 'marketable instrument'.

Whilst an issuer usually has no direct part to play in it, the secondary market will have an effect on its ability to issue in the primary market. This is because one of the most important features of any security instrument, both at and after issue, is its marketability. Some of the factors affecting marketability include:

(a)   the identity of the issuer and its credit rating;

(b)   the type of security being issued;

(c)   the number of potential investors that can be offered the issue (ie, are there any regulatory or practical restrictions?).

Marketability may also be enhanced if the securities are listed on a regulated market. For example, many domestic and eurosecurities are listed on the London Stock Exchange which provides regulated information about the issuer (in the form of listing particulars). This encourages investors to take the securities on issue, and provides an indication of market interest and value of particular securities which is helpful in launching and pricing a new issue. Although the securities may be listed on a stock exchange, they may (particularly in the case of bonds) still be traded in the secondary market 'off exchange' (see **21.8.1**).

17.8 CLEARING SYSTEMS

17.8.1 What is a clearing system?

Originally all eurobonds took the form (known as 'definitive form') of paper certificates which represented a debt to be paid by the issuer to whoever possessed the bond (the 'bearer') at maturity. However, these definitive 'bearer bonds' are difficult to trade rapidly in large numbers and are vulnerable to theft or loss in the same way as cash. To speed trading and improve security, 'clearing systems' were developed which allowed the bonds to be left safely in a vault and for trading to take place through accounts. There are a number of clearing systems worldwide which deal with trading bearer (and other) securities. However, in the international eurosecurities markets, there are two systems of paramount importance: the Euroclear system and the Clearstream Service (which is part of the Deutsche Börse Group), commonly referred to as 'Euroclear' and 'Clearstream'.

Euroclear was created by Morgan Guaranty Trust Company of New York in 1968. It is now owned largely by 'user shareholders' with a core operation in Brussels and subsidiary operations in Paris, Amsterdam and London. Clearstream was created (originally as 'Cedel') in 1970, and operates primarily from Luxembourg and Frankfurt.

17.8.2   Operation of the clearing systems

Euroclear and Clearstream are not confined to dealing with bonds. Both clearing systems will accept most common forms of securities which are actively traded in the international capital markets, for example bonds, notes, debenture stock, commercial paper, certain certificates of deposit (depending on their place of issue) and some types of shares. However, in order to explain the clearing systems' processes, this section concentrates on bond issues.

Euroclear and Clearstream operate in similar ways. The primary purpose of a clearing system is to avoid the physical handling of bearer instruments on issue and on subsequent trading. Therefore, the actual bond certificates (which may be in definitive bearer form or global form – see **18.2**) are invariably passed on to a bank known as a 'depositary' (see **19.2.7**) for safekeeping, and the clearing system works through a series of 'book entries' (akin to depositing cash with your bank and debiting your account to pay debts rather than withdrawing cash). In order to participate in a clearing system, an investor will have two accounts with the system (although some investors will use accounts held by their bank or broker who act as nominee for them):

(a)   a securities clearance account to and from which the securities are credited (the account does not usually allocate the holder specific bonds, ie the bonds in a particular issue are fungible); and

(b)   a cash account (like a current account) through which all payments from the sale or purchase of securities must pass.

Each issue of securities is allocated a unique code number, known as its ISIN (International Securities Identification Number), from which is derived the 'Common Code'. The Common Code is used as a label to identify the particular *issue* each time the clearing system is instructed to deal in securities, and it should not be mistaken for a security device, nor a way of identifying individual bonds within an issue (other issue identification numbers are sometimes seen, eg 'sedol' – used by the London Stock Exchange). If a bondholder wants to sell some bonds on the secondary market, it instructs the clearer, which reduces the seller's securities clearance account by the requisite number of securities and credits them to the securities clearance account of the purchaser. At the same time, the cash account of the purchaser is debited, and the cash account of the seller credited, to represent payment for the securities. Euroclear and Clearstream also allow trading between their two systems since each has securities and cash accounts with the other (this is known as the 'bridge').

Clearing systems have a function in both the primary and secondary markets. In the primary market, they will accept a new issue of bonds onto their systems, so long as it has complied with any regulations applicable to it (eg, selling restrictions – see **18.2.1**). On the closing date of a new issue, the requisite number of bonds will be credited to the securities clearance accounts of the syndicate members and can then be transferred to the accounts of the investors (see **21.10**).

The clearing systems also keep a record of interest payment dates and redemption dates for each issue, and will 'present' the securities for payment when appropriate. The bondholders therefore avoid the need to present the coupons or certificates themselves. The clearing systems will also act on investors' instructions with respect to any options or conversion rights which might be attached to the securities. The legal position of securities held in a clearing system is discussed in **Chapter 18**.

17.9   INTERNATIONAL CAPITAL MARKETS ASSOCIATION

The International Capital Markets Association (ICMA) was formed in July 2005 by the merger of the International Primary Markets Association (IPMA) and the International Securities Markets Association (ISMA). ICMA is the association for financial institutions which play an active role, usually as managers, underwriters and traders, in the primary and secondary bond markets. ICMA is a trade association, as opposed to a statutory body, created by participants in the international capital markets with a view to establishing recognised standards of market practice. Membership of ICMA brings a financial institution the status and recognition, from other institutions and issuers, necessary to take a major part in large euromarket deals. Members of ICMA include banks, members of recognised stock exchanges, licensed dealers in securities and affiliated organisations.

ICMA is a self-regulating body, and the ultimate sanction for non-compliance with its recommendations is expulsion from the Association. In order to appreciate the gravity of expulsion, it is important to understand that the euromarket works with something of the aura of a 'members' club'. An institution which breaches ICMA rules will soon become known to other euromarket institutions, and they may become reluctant to deal with the offender. Persistent or serious breaches will eventually result in an offender being unable to raise a syndicate, and being left out of invitations to join other syndicates.

ICMA publishes, and periodically updates, recommendations to its members in relation to both debt and equity issues in the form of a handbook (non-members must comply with the recommendations if they hope to join the institution). The areas typically covered include the following:

(a)   The timing of a bond issue. In particular, ICMA regulates the time which must elapse between the various stages of the issuing process (eg, the minimum time which managers should be allowed to review documentation prepared by the lead manager – see **21.5**).

(b)   The minimum content of certain documents (eg, the invitation telex).

(c)   The timescale to be allowed for payment of fees and commissions to the managers.

These, and other ICMA regulations, are dealt with in more detail in **Chapter 19**, which explains the process of issuing a bond.

17.10   THE ISSUERS

The following types of entity use capital markets for raising money:

(a)   companies, including banks and financial institutions (recent examples include EADS, the Airbus manufacturer (€1bn, due 2016), Volkswagen (€956m, average life 4.1 years), Standard Chartered Bank ($1.5bn, callable from 2015);

(b)   governments/sovereign (ie, government-owned) entities (eg, Republic of Portugal (€3bn, due 2015));

(c)   public authorities (eg, City of Berne (SFr 180m, due 2025);

(d)   supranationals (eg, the European Investment Bank (€75m, due 2030)).

Each entity will need the authority to issue bonds. English companies should be authorised in their constitutive documents to issue debt securities; whilst governments and public bodies are likely to be authorised by statute or statutory instrument.

17.11   CREDIT RATING

When an investor is deciding whether to purchase or make a particular investment, the most important factor affecting its decision is the risk of non-payment. The higher the risk that an issue may not be serviced or repaid, the greater the return an investor will demand. Some institutions, such as pension funds and investment funds, are limited by their constitution as to the risk they can take when investing their funds.

Investors in the international capital markets are particularly sensitive to risk, and most issuers and/or their individual debt security issues will therefore be given a credit rating. Official ratings for the euromarkets are provided by specialist independent rating organisations, the best known of which are the US firms, Moody's Investors Service, Standard and Poor's, and Fitch Ratings, Duff & Phelps. A credit rating is an opinion on the risk of default on payment, and will be based on a number of different factors, including an issuer's current financial statements, past and projected performance, management, market position and operating environment.

The ratings are split into two broad categories: 'investment grade' and 'speculative grade'. The range of Standard and Poor's long-term debt ratings (which are very similar to those used by Fitch), together with their brief explanation of each grade, are shown below.

Standard and Poor's ratings

AAA Highest rating, ability to repay interest and principal extremely strong.

AA Very strong capacity to repay interest and principal.

A Strong ability to pay, but somewhat susceptible to adverse economic conditions.

BBB Adequate capacity to repay debt, but more subject to bad economic conditions. Lowest investment-grade rating.

BB Any debt rated this grade or below has significant speculative characteristics.

B Has vulnerability to default but presently has the capacity to meet interest payments and principal repayments.

CCC Vulnerable to non-payment.

CC Currently highly vulnerable to non-payment.

C Typically in arrears on payment or liquidation petition filed, but payments still continuing.

D Debt is in default.

Moody's ratings

Aaa Bonds of the best quality.

Aa

A

Baa Lowest form of investment grade.

Ba Speculative elements.

B

Caa

Ca

C Lowest rated class of bonds.

If a bond issue is to be individually rated, a rating will be assigned at launch of the issue (there is an appeals procedure for issuers who are unhappy with the proposed rating). The rating given to an issue is then periodically reviewed: if the risk has increased, the rating will fall (and vice versa). Ratings of issuers themselves are also periodically reviewed. A rating above the dotted line (ie, BBB or Baa) is known as 'investment grade', but anything below the line carries an increasing degree of speculation as to whether the issuer will be able to meet its obligations. To provide greater flexibility within their main gradings, Standard and Poor's may modify grades between AA to CCC by adding a + or – symbol to show relative standing within the main grade (eg, AA– or BBB+). Moody's achieve a similar effect by applying 'numerical modifiers', 1, 2, and 3 ('1' being better than '2', etc) to classifications between Aa and Caa inclusive (eg, A2 or Baa1).

There is only a limited European market for bonds issued at below investment grade; indeed, the constitution of some types of financial institution will only allow them to invest in securities graded AA (or Aa) or above. Issues with a rating below 'Investment Grade' must try harder to attract investors, and so generally pay a higher coupon; hence, they are known as 'high yield' (or, in the 1980s, as 'junk bonds'). Credit ratings are not only available on fixed income securities; they are also provided for short-term investments, and even some syndicated loans.

The recent financial crisis has led to a new focus on rating agencies and the way ratings are produced. The agencies attracted criticism from some quarters when bonds given high quality ratings became worthless. This was less prevalent with plain vanilla bonds raising corporate debt, but more so among notes issued as part of complex, securitisation-based structures. Critics claimed that investors made decisions to buy paper based on the credit rating of a product, rather than fully understanding the structure and risks explained in the prospectus. In addition, the rating agencies are paid by the issuer (or originator) to give a rating, and the issuer wants the best rating possible to keep the coupon low. Some felt this gave rise to a conflict of interest. Lastly, rating agencies have also been criticised for exacerbating recent government financial crises, for example by suddenly downgrading bonds for countries such as Greece, Spain and Portugal.

As a result, the rating agencies have been subject to some litigation, and during 2010 regulators across Europe and in the US looked to regulate the rating agencies more closely. This ranged from requiring agencies to hold licences, to requiring more transparency as to their rating methods and documentation. Meanwhile, in August 2011, Standard and Poors controversially downgraded US credit from AAA to AA+.

17.12 FURTHER READING

Valdez, *An Introduction to Global Financial Markets* (6th edn, Macmillan, 2010).

CHAPTER 18

THE FORMS AND LEGAL CHARACTERISTICS OF A BOND

18.1	Introduction	215
18.2	The form of a bond	215
18.3	Legal nature of a bond	218
18.4	Comparing registered and bearer bonds	219
18.5	The legal effect on bearer bonds held in clearing systems	221
18.6	Further reading	222

'Within three months – that's a month before this bond expires – I do expect return of thrice three times the value of this bond.'

William Shakespeare, *The Merchant of Venice*

18.1 INTRODUCTION

Chapter 17 explained the concept of raising finance on the capital markets and examined the characteristics and structures of various debt securities. The remainder of this part of the book concentrates on bonds, since they are probably the most common form of debt security issued on the capital markets.

18.2 THE FORM OF A BOND

The first eurobond issue is generally accredited to Autostrade, the Italian motorway operator, and was launched in 1963. As was mentioned in **Chapter 17**, early investors in the eurobond market held printed bearer certificates with tear-off coupons attached which were used to claim interest. These certificates are known as 'definitive bearer bonds'. As the eurobond market grew, holding and trading these physical certificates became impractical. In 1968 Euroclear was created to store the definitive bonds safely and to record transfers between investors through an account system. As this 'clearing system' grew in size and sophistication (Clearstream, then known as 'Cedel' started in 1971), printing definitive bonds was seen as largely unnecessary other than in specific circumstances. Thus definitive certificates are rare today and bonds take on other forms, most typically:

(a) temporary global form, followed by either:
  (i) permanent global form, or
  (ii) definitive form (which may be bearer or registered); or
(b) permanent global form from the outset.

This chapter explains what these terms mean and when the different forms of a bond are used.

18.2.1 Temporary global form

18.2.1.1 What is a temporary global note?

When a bond is first issued, it will almost certainly not be in the form of certificates. The total debt obligation of the issuer will, instead, usually start life as a single document known as a 'temporary global note'.

The temporary global note document is a wordprocessed document, prepared by the lead manager's solicitor, and which represents all the bonds to be offered under that particular issue. It will be executed by an authorised officer of the issuer and 'authenticated' by the fiscal agent (or principal paying agent) (see **19.2**). All the terms and conditions which apply to the bonds (see **19.4**) will be attached to, or incorporated in, the temporary global note. The document will also have a schedule attached to it on which the fiscal agent (or principal paying agent) can record all exchanges of the temporary global note for definitive bonds, as well as interest payments (if any) which are made during the life of the temporary global note.

18.2.1.2 Why use a temporary global note?

As the name suggests, the temporary global note exists only for a short time. There are two reasons why bonds are initially issued as a single document in temporary global form.

Time constraints

Once an entity has decided to raise money through a bond issue, the process of issue will usually proceed relatively quickly. Many bond issues (in particular, eurobond issues) have a time scale of three to five weeks between launch (ie, when the offer is announced) and closing (ie, issue of the bonds). This timetable is primarily driven by market practice: issuing a bond is intended to be a relatively quick way for a borrower to raise finance, and the markets therefore have an expectation to fulfil (a short period between launch and issue also minimises the risk that the market moves and the price of the bonds becomes unattractive to potential investors). However, such a short timetable makes it difficult to complete the security printing and necessary 'authentication' of the certificates which represents the final definitive form of a bearer bond. Producing a temporary global note allows the issue to close, and be placed in a clearing system, before the final certificates are ready.

Selling restrictions

In order to understand the second reason for producing a bond in a temporary global form, it is necessary to appreciate the concept of 'selling restrictions'. Most jurisdictions impose restrictions on securities being offered or sold within that jurisdiction. Many of these restrictions are imposed on issues made to the public in order to protect unsophisticated investors. However, they may also be driven by policies of investment control or taxation (a detailed analysis of these restrictions is beyond the scope of this book).

In order to avoid contravening any restrictions which might apply to it, a bond will include contractual restrictions on the institutions selling the issue (the 'syndicate'). These are known as 'selling restrictions'. For example, the syndicate might be contractually prohibited from selling bonds to 'US persons' if this would require registration of the issue with the Securities Exchange Commission (an elaborate and costly procedure) (there are exceptions to these rules and procedures to follow in order to benefit from those exceptions, commonly known as 'safe harbours').

The most commonly applicable selling restrictions are those imposed under US tax and securities laws. Some of these require that definitive bonds cannot be delivered for a period (usually 40 days) after issue (known as a 'lock-up' period). More commonly, there will be a restricted period during which definitive bonds may be offered only to certain investors. In either case, the use of a temporary global note helps to ensure compliance with the restrictions.

18.2.2 Permanent global and definitive forms

Once any lock-up period expires, the temporary global note must be exchanged for either a permanent global note (as the name suggests, this is a permanent version of the temporary global note), or bonds in definitive form (in other words, separate certificates representing each bond).

18.2.2.1 Permanent global note

As with the temporary global note, this is a wordprocessed document (as opposed to being security printed) prepared by the lead manager's solicitor, and which represents all the bonds in issue. The permanent global note is issued on the closing date of the issue (see **21.10**), and is usually held by a bank known as the 'common depository' for safe-keeping on behalf of the clearing systems (but see 'New Global Notes' at **19.2.7**).

The main advantage of using a permanent global note rather than definitive bonds is cost, since the permanent global note is not security printed. However, it does prima facie leave bondholders without a bearer instrument with which to prove ownership. In circumstances where it is important that the investor has legal ownership of the debt obligation represented by the bond, the terms and conditions require the issuer to print definitive bearer bonds and distribute them to the investors. The permanent global notes state the circumstances in which definitives should be printed, most commonly:

(a)   if any bondholder requires a definitive bond, in order to prove his legal entitlement to the bond in which he has invested, in connection with legal proceedings, eg in a tax dispute;

(b)   if the bondholder requires definitive forms in order to trade the bonds (ie, physically to deliver the bond certificates) because the clearing systems have for some reason ceased to operate, preventing trading through the clearing systems with reference to the global note; and

(c)   on or following a default by the issuer (where the bondholder might need to sue the issuer).

However, even if the global note states that the issuer must print definitive bonds (providing the investor with legal ownership), the issuer may refuse to comply with that condition. There are various methods which practitioners use to avoid this problem. The first solution is to provide investors with direct rights of enforcement in the text of the global note itself, which is executed by the issuer. The second is for the issuer to execute a unilateral deed of covenant (a 'deed poll') in favour of the bondholders from time to time. This contains a declaration by the issuer to pay those persons shown as investors on the relevant accounts at the clearing systems, and provides a contractual link between the issuer and the investors on which an investor can sue the issuer for breach of the terms of the bonds. A third solution is to appoint a trustee to the issue which holds the issuer covenant to pay on trust for the bondholders: the trustee can then enforce on the bondholders' behalf. Whichever solution is used, the documents make it clear that they are 'alternatives': the debt is paid only once.

18.2.2.2 Definitive form

A bond issued in 'definitive form' can be either a 'bearer' or 'registered' instrument.

Bearer bonds

The most familiar bearer instrument to most people is currency (eg, a £5 note), and bearer bonds share similar characteristics. They are security printed documents in order to make forgery very difficult, the issuer's debt obligation is printed on the bond itself and ownership can be transferred by physical delivery. A bearer bond has the following basic features:

(a)   *A promise to pay.* The face of the bond will include a simple statement to pay principal (and, if relevant, interest). For example:

I promise to pay the bearer $US10,000 on the 12th November 2017, in accordance with the terms and conditions contained herein.

The bearer bond will be signed by at least one officer of the issuer, although the signature is part of the security printing rather than being an original on each definitive bond instrument. However, each instrument is individually 'authenticated' (ie, signed) by the fiscal agent (or paying agent), and will not be valid until this is done.

(b)   *Terms and conditions.* The terms and conditions of the bearer bond will be printed on the reverse of the bond itself, together with the addresses of the relevant paying agents. The main terms and conditions are reviewed in **Chapter 19.**

(c)   *Coupons.* If the bond bears interest, coupons will be printed on the right-hand side of a bearer bond which must be torn off and surrendered to the paying agents in order to claim each interest payment as it falls due (the coupon is probably a bearer document itself). The name and address of the paying agents will be printed on the reverse side of each coupon.

(e)   *Talons.* The maximum number of coupons which can be attached to a eurobond is 27 (under ICMA rules). If a bond carries more than 27 interest payment dates (eg, a bond paying semi-annual interest with a maturity of 14 years), the final coupon (at the top left of the coupon sheet next to the bond) will be known as a 'talon'. The talon can be exchanged for a further sheet of coupons in relation to the remaining interest payments once all the coupons on the first sheet have been claimed.

Registered bonds

Registered bonds create a promise to pay the person whose name appears on a register of bondholders held by the issuer (or its agent for this purpose) rather than the holder of the actual bond certificate. Registered bonds can be transferred only by an entry on the register; title will not pass by physical delivery of the bond instrument. The terms and conditions of the bond will be printed on the reverse of the instrument.

Most bonds are issued in bearer form and registered bonds are rare. However, bond issues which are intended to be placed in the US but not registered with the Securities Exchange Commission are usually in registered form to take advantage of registration exemptions.

18.3   LEGAL NATURE OF A BOND

18.3.1   Transferability

In order to attract investors, the debt obligation of a bond must be easily transferable. Bonds will achieve transferability in one of two ways:

(a)   creating the bond as a bearer instrument, allowing transfer by simple physical delivery. This is the most straightforward way to achieve transfer, although the vulnerability this creates means that bearer bonds will usually be traded through a clearing system; and

(b)   making the bond a registrable instrument so that transfer is effected by a document of transfer and an entry on the register confirming that transfer has taken place (in a similar way to registered shares).

There is, however, an important legal difference between bearer bonds and registered bonds. Only bearer bonds can be 'negotiable'.

18.3.2 Negotiability

Negotiability of a bond is of paramount importance in order to ensure that it is freely marketable (and should be distinguished from transferability or assignability (see **10.4.3**)).

18.3.2.1 Achieving negotiability

In deciding on negotiability it is first necessary to decide which jurisdiction is applicable. Usually, the jurisdiction in which the 'negotiation' takes place is relevant: in the case of a bearer bond this will be the place where the bond is delivered. In a conflict of laws situation, negotiable instruments are usually treated as chattels because the debt claim is represented by a tangible document rather than a simple 'book entry'.

Under English law, there are two ways in which negotiability can be achieved.

By statute

The Bills of Exchange Act 1882 confers negotiability on bills of exchange, promissory notes and cheques. However, the Act requires conditions as to amount and unconditionality of an instrument before they can be negotiable, and bonds invariably fall foul of those conditions (eg, a floating rate of interest or grossing-up provisions will make bonds 'uncertain' and therefore outside the provisions of the Act).

By mercantile custom

It is an established principle of English common law that an instrument can achieve negotiability simply because it is customarily treated as negotiable in the 'markets' in which it is usually traded. The financial community treats definitive bearer bonds (but not registered bonds) as negotiable, and therefore definitive bearer bonds have achieved negotiability by mercantile custom.

18.3.2.2 Consequences of negotiability

The consequences of negotiability work in favour of a transferee who purchases the bond bona fide, for value and without any actual notice of a defect in title (known as a 'holder in due course'). A negotiable bond purchased by a 'holder in due course' will have the following benefits:

(a) the purchaser can obtain better title than the seller (eg, if the seller obtained the bond dishonestly);

(b) the purchaser will take a clean legal title to the bond and is entitled to payment in full, notwithstanding any claims of set-off or other defence which the issuer may have had against any previous holder;

(c) the purchaser can sue the issuer directly in the case of a dispute over the bond, and does not need to join the transferor in a claim (although a bond issued under a trust deed will usually give the trustee the power to act on behalf of the bondholders);

(d) if a 'holder in due course' presents a stolen bond, the issuer must pay out on that bond as well as on any replacement bond it has issued to the original bondholder. Because of this risk, an issuer will not usually provide a replacement bond without first obtaining an indemnity from the original bondholder to the effect that he will recompense the issuer if it has to pay out on the original bond.

18.4 COMPARING REGISTERED AND BEARER BONDS

Having examined the legal consequences of negotiability, the differences between registered and bearer bonds can be examined.

18.4.1 Title

A bona fide purchaser for value without notice (of defects in title) of a bearer bond can obtain better title than the seller; but the purchaser of a registered bond, which is not a negotiable instrument, will not obtain good title if the seller stole the bond certificate and was able to obtain a transfer in the register.

18.4.2 Claims and defences of an issuer

Negotiable bearer bonds will always be sold free from any claim the issuer might have against a previous holder. The purchaser of a registered bond is, in principle at least (although this may be varied under contract), subject to the rights the issuer might have against the transferor, such as set-off.

18.4.3 Priorities

A purchaser of a bearer bond will usually take the bond free of any equities (ie, third party claims), for example a person for whom the bond was held on trust. A purchaser of a registered bond will only take the bond free of competing interests of which he had no actual or constructive notice.

18.4.4 Anonymity

Bearer bonds can be held anonymously since the issuer will not know at any time who owns the bond. An issuer will know the identity of the registered holder of a registered bond, although the true beneficial ownership may lie behind a nominee holder.

18.4.5 Transfer

Bearer bonds are transferred by delivery. The similarity to cash of bearer bonds makes them vulnerable to theft if they are transferred by physical delivery, and most bearer bonds are therefore traded through clearing systems (see **17.8**). The transfer of a registered bond requires the execution of an instrument of transfer, and the filing of the instrument and the original bond certificate with the issuer or his agent for that purpose (whoever maintains the register of bondholders), and finally an amendment to the register. This whole process can take some time and is a lengthier process than the physical delivery of a bearer bond, or its transfer within a clearing system which is effected by book entries.

Rate shift poses a risk for Yankee trade

By Robin Wigglesworth in London and Nicole Bullock in New York

A shift in a key financial rate risks damping the 'Yankee trade' of European companies selling US dollar-denominated bonds and swapping the proceeds into euros, a popular funding strategy.

The five year euro-dollar basis swap, effectively the annual cost for European companies when they borrow dollars and exchange them for euros, has moved from a negative 67 basis points at the start of the year to a negative 37bp on Thursday.

That means that the effective annual cost for a European company selling a five-year bond yielding 3 per cent and swapping the proceeds from the sale into euros has increased from 2.33 per cent late last year to 2.63 per cent.

The fall in the basis swap rate reflects the improvement in market sentiment surrounding the eurozone debt crisis, which has eased funding conditions for European companies.

Although the rate is still favourable for dollar issuance, if the cost of entering into a swap with banks is factored in, euro-denominated bond issuance has

become more enticing, bankers said.

"Swapping euros into dollars is now much more attractive than it has been for a long time," said Chris Marrow, head of European corporate debt markets at Credit Suisse. "Over the next few weeks and months this could encourage more European borrowers to stick to euros."

Longer-dated swap rates have also moved sharply this year. The 10-year euro-dollar swap rate is now a negative 25bp, versus a negative 47bp at the start of the year.

"European issuers are still getting a discount to issue in the US," said Ryan Preclaw, a US-based credit strategist at Barclays. "It is just not quite as much of a discount."

Euro-denominated debt issuance has soared this year, but the 'Yankee trade' has remained popular, particularly with multinational companies that have operations in the US or those whose borrowing needs are so big that the US remains the most viable market.

European companies have sold $42.3bn of bonds in the US in the first three months of the year, the most active quarter for the funding strategy since the first quarter of 2011, according to Dealogic data. Overall, European companies sold $106bn of Yankee bonds last year, according to the data provider.

A top debt syndicate banker based in London doubted that the recent move in the swap rate would slow the 'Yankee trade' Once companies have done the initial paperwork required, it is relatively easy to be a repeat bond issuer in the US

"It's getting more competitive, but it's still cheaper to borrow in dollars," he said. "Even after two doses of [European Central Bank loans to banks] it's still quite a difference."

The banker estimated that euro issuance would become more attractive if the five-year swap rate hit a negative 20 bp. Given the cost, and complexity, of entering into currency swaps with banks, more companies would at that level eschew dollars for euros, he said.

Source: *Financial Times*, 22 March 2012

18.5 THE LEGAL EFFECT ON BEARER BONDS HELD IN CLEARING SYSTEMS

As explained at **18.2** above, it is now unusual for definitive bearer bonds to be printed and held in a depositary. However, if they are, it is important to understand the legal rights of the various parties with respect to the bonds. Some investors may not actually be 'participants' in a clearing system (ie, they will not have their own accounts in a system) but will rely on a financial institution which is a participant to act as their nominee. In that case, a definitive bearer bond transaction will involve a chain of parties:

Investor ——→ Participant ——→ Clearing System ——→ Depository

In basic terms the investors (ie, bondholders) give the bond to a participant (ie, an entity holding accounts with the clearing system – assuming the investor is not a participant itself), which must give the bond to the clearing system (eg, Euroclear or Clearstream), which in turn gives the instrument to a depositary bank for safekeeping. The danger for an investor is that if any of these parties goes into liquidation in possession of his bearer securities, the investor will be left to claim as an unsecured creditor. The way to avoid this risk is to ensure that the proprietary rights over the securities remain with the investor and are not vested in any of the other parties in the chain. In the event of another party's liquidation, the investor can therefore simply reclaim the bonds. The following sections examine each relationship in turn.

18.5.1   Investor – Participant

The law governing the relationship between the investor and the participant will usually be the governing law they have chosen in the documentation acknowledging their transaction (see also **9.8**). Under English law, the deposit of bearer securities with a participant will result in the investor passing legal title to the participant, but the investor retaining beneficial ownership. The participant therefore takes all the rights against the issuer such as payment of coupon and principal, and any conversion rights. However, the participant must account for any payments it receives, must comply with the investor's instructions as to any rights under the security, and must transfer the securities back to the investor at his request. The investor can also demand the return of the bonds in the event of the participant's liquidation and they will not become part of the participant's general pool of assets.

18.5.2   Participant – Clearing system

The two main clearing systems for bonds, Euroclear and Clearstream (see **17.8.1**), are (respectively) Belgian and Luxembourg entities, and the terms and conditions of the clearing systems will be construed in accordance with the local law. For the sake of simplicity, we will assume that the clearing system being used is Euroclear in Belgium.

Under general Belgian law, participants depositing bearer securities in Euroclear would have contractual rights against Euroclear for the return of their securities. However, general Belgian law is modified under a specific decree, so that the participants retain a proprietary right of ownership in the securities credited to their securities clearance account. Therefore, if Euroclear should become insolvent, the participants will not be unsecured creditors but will have the right to the return of the securities which are credited to their securities account.

18.5.3   Clearing systems – Depository

The final link in the chain is that between the clearing system and the depositary bank where the bearer instruments are held for safekeeping. This relationship is subject not only to the local law of the relevant clearing system, but also to the law of the jurisdiction in which the depository is situated. It is therefore important for the participant to ensure that the proprietory rights in the bearer securities are not in any way transferred to the depositary bank. The clearing systems will usually ensure that this is the case before using a depository; however, some participants may want a legal opinion from local lawyers to confirm that this is the case.

With careful planning and legal advice, therefore, an investor with bearer securities can avoid taking a credit risk on any of the other parties involved in the clearing system process.

18.6   FURTHER READING

This chapter has provided a brief overview of the legal 'chain' of rights over a bond: for a more thorough examination, see the excellent *Interests in Securities* (Oxford University Press, 2000) by Dr Joanna Benjamin.

CHAPTER 19

ISSUING A BOND – THE PARTIES AND DOCUMENTATION

19.1	Introduction	223
19.2	Parties to a bond issue	223
19.3	Documentation of a bond issue	227
19.4	Terms and conditions of a bond	232

19.1 INTRODUCTION

The next three chapters concentrate on the parties, documents and process involved in the issue of a eurobond. The reason for examining a eurobond is that they are among the most common form of debt security and something of a paradigm for debt securities issued in the London markets. Many of the matters which are dealt with will, however, also apply to issues of other types of bond and other debt securities.

The characteristics of a bond were explained at **17.5**, and the concept of eurocurrencies was explained at **17.3.2**: a eurobond is a bond which is issued to attract eurocurrencies. In other words, it is a bond denominated in a globally recognised currency which is not the currency of the country in which the bond is issued. It is generally agreed that the very first eurobond was issued in 1963 by Autostrade (the Italian motorway authority) in London, arranged by SG Warburg (now part of UBS) for US$15,000,000. However, the real increase in these bond issues came in the early 1980s, reflecting a reduction in the size of the syndicated loan market caused by the imposition of more severe regulatory capital requirements (see **9.3.3**). Banks facing restrictions on lending turned instead to the lucrative fees available from underwriting bond issues.

19.2 PARTIES TO A BOND ISSUE

19.2.1 The issuer

The various entities which might issue debt securities on the capital markets were listed at **17.10**. The key question for a lawyer is whether the issuer is a 'debut issuer', in which case the prospectus will need drafting from scratch, or has issued before, when the existing prospectus can probably just be updated. By definition, eurobonds will raise a currency that is not 'indigenous' to the country in which they are issued. If the issuer does not have a specific requirement for that currency, it will enter into a derivative or foreign exchange transaction to exchange the money for a currency it can use.

19.2.2 Lead manager

The lead manager to an issue will be a financial institution such as an investment bank, and it will have a role similar to the arranger in a syndicated loan (see **3.3.2**). It will be responsible for arranging the bond issue and managing the issue process, from receiving its mandate through to the issuer receiving funds. The lead manager will advise the issuer on the structure, timing and pricing of the issue, and so takes the credit for success and responsibility for the failure of the issue to sell. If the issue is to be listed, the lead manager will usually be the 'sponsor' required by the UKLA to provide confirmations (eg, of compliance with the Listing Rules) for listing. Bond issues of sovereign, supranational or frequent issuers are sometimes identified with reference to the lead manager (eg, the Nomura International plc World Bank Euroyen Global Note).

19.2.3   Syndicate

The lead manager will recruit a number of 'co-managers' to join him in a 'syndicate'. The syndicate are effectively a distribution network for the issue, using their contacts and knowledge of the market to find investors ('book building'). In most bond issues on the London market, the syndicate agree with the issuer to take all the bonds, even if they cannot find investors. This gives the issuer the reassurance of knowing the exact amount of the funds it will receive. The syndicate (in return for a fee) take the risk that the issue is not fully subscribed by investors, in which case they will buy the unsold bonds (they may sell any such bonds in the secondary market at a lower price in order to clear their books, or they may retain the bonds in the hope that demand for them increases and they make a profit on a sale). The names of the syndicate will appear on the prospectus in order of contribution to the amount of the issue that they have sold, and if equal in alphabetical order. In some US issues and some high-yield UK issues, the syndicate will only have to use 'reasonable endeavours' to sell the securities, and a separate group of banks will 'underwrite' (ie, purchase) any unsold bonds to give the issuer certainty of funds.

19.2.4   Fiscal agent and trustee

A bond issue will use either a fiscal agent (under a fiscal agency agreement), or a trustee (under a trust deed). The legal effect of each arrangement is quite different.

19.2.4.1   Fiscal agent

The fiscal agent is appointed by, and is the representative and agent of, the issuer and not the bondholders. He is primarily responsible for paying principal and interest to the bondholders. The fiscal agent will also have certain administrative functions, including the publication of notices to the bondholders and acting as a depository for the issuer's accounts and other financial information which is open to inspection by the bondholders (although he has no duty to review or investigate such information). The fiscal agency agreement will appoint the fiscal agent and explicitly state that he does not owe the bondholders any duty of care.

19.2.4.2   Trustee

A trustee is initially chosen and appointed by the issuer (through its advisers) but represents the interests of the bondholders. The property held on trust is the issuer's covenant to pay the bondholders. The trustee's powers and duties are recorded in a trust deed, but he will also owe the bondholders a duty of care under common law trust principles. The trustee can act on behalf of bondholders in certain situations (see below for more details). Trust arrangements are a concept peculiar to common law jurisdictions and will not usually be recognised by civil law jurisdictions. In a bond transaction, the trustee is likely to be either a professional trust association (eg, The Law Debenture Trust Corporation), or a subsidiary of a bank or other financial institution, whose sole function is to act as a trust corporation.

19.2.4.3   Choosing between a trustee and a fiscal agency

The majority of bond issues will use a fiscal agency rather than a trustee, primarily because of cost considerations. However, there are specific circumstances in which a fiscal agent is insufficient and a trustee must be appointed. These include the following.

Secured issues

If the bonds are secured, a trustee is required to hold the security. This is primarily due to the impracticality of providing individual bondholders with a right to part of the security, which would have to be transferred every time the bond changed hands. Any such transfer may restart 'hardening periods' (see **14.9**). Therefore, the trustee holds the security on trust for all the bondholders from time to time. A fiscal agent cannot perform this function since he is the agent of the issuer and so acts in the issuer's interests.

Subordinated issues

If bonds are to be issued which are subordinated to (ie, ranking behind) the repayment of another bond issue, the same trustee may be appointed to both senior and junior issues to ensure effective subordination (although it is now quite common to achieve subordination contractually through the terms of the issue, creating 'contingent debt').

19.2.4.4 Advantages of using a trust arrangement

Under a trust arrangement, the trustee has legal ownership of any claims that the bondholders (ie, the beneficiaries) have against the issuer. There are advantages of using a trust arrangement for both the issuer and the bondholders.

Advantages for the issuer

The advantages of using a trust arrangement from the issuer's perspective are based on the possibility of dealing with one sophisticated party representing the bondholders, rather than dealing with a group of individuals. For example:

(a) Only the trustee can act in the event of a default by the issuer (albeit that he can act only within the terms of the trust deed under which he is appointed, or on the direction of a specific majority of bondholders). This will usually lead to a more considered approach towards a default than might be the case if the bondholders could precipitate action individually. The issuer can deal with a professional trustee rather than a disparate group of potentially less sophisticated bondholders with varying views and requirements. Furthermore, many trust deeds will provide the trustee with authority to waive technical events of default where he sees fit. The trustee therefore protects the issuer from 'rogue' bondholders.

Interestingly, in *Concord Trust v The Law Debenture Trust Corporation plc* [2005] UKHL 27, the House of Lords held that if a trustee mistakenly called an event of default (ie when no event of default had actually occurred), this was not a breach of contract, but simply an 'ineffective action'. This is some comfort to trustees who had feared they might be sued for wrongfully calling a default; however, an action in tort (for negligence or interference by unlawful means) may lie in some circumstances (though not on the facts in *Concord*).

(b) A trustee can be given power to agree certain amendments to the terms of a bond without calling a meeting of bondholders (eg, to approve a restructuring of the issuer's group), providing the issuer with greater flexibility.

Advantages for the bondholders

There are a number of important advantages for a bondholder in creating an issue with a trust arrangement:

(a) If an event of default occurs, the bondholders can rely on a professional entity (the trustee) to pursue the situation on their behalf. Individual action by each bondholder, which can be expensive and difficult to pursue, is not necessary since the trustee will act on their behalf. Class actions are fraught with difficulties because of the variety and disparity of bondholders.

(b) Most bond issues are unsecured, and so if an issuer is facing financial difficulties, the bondholders are very vulnerable. A trustee acting on behalf of all the bondholders is more likely to achieve a moratorium, or a negotiated resolution with other creditors, than bondholders would if they acted as individuals.

(c)   If the bondholders need to make a collective decision, the trustee can chair any meetings and make recommendations.

(d)   After a default, an issuer must make any payment through the trustee rather than to individual bondholders. This avoids a powerful bondholder negotiating himself a good deal at the expense of minority bondholders.

(e)   A trustee will have investigative and monitoring powers which a fiscal agent will not. It is not, however, usual practice in bond issues for the trust deed to create any specific duties of investigation for the trustee: he will usually act simply as a medium for receiving certain information, such as the issuer's annual accounts, notices and certificates of compliance which must be available for inspection by the bondholders. The common law duty to act with due diligence in the best interests of the beneficiaries (ie, the bondholders) is still applicable irrespective of the contractual requirements of the trust deed, for example, if the trustee is given the power in the trust deed to request financial information from the issuer then he has a positive duty to do so if it would be in the best interests of the bondholders.

19.2.4.5   Advantages of using a fiscal agent

The primary advantage to the issuer of appointing a fiscal agent rather than a trustee is cost. A trustee will require his own solicitor (whose fees must be met by the issuer) to advise on the trust documentation, and a trustee's fees during the life of the bond will reflect the substantial responsibilities he must undertake. By way of contrast, there is considerable competition to take the high profile and prestigious role of fiscal agent. This drives down the fiscal agent's fees, and it is not unknown for institutions to take on the fiscal agency role for no remuneration provided that they are also awarded another role in the issue (eg, as the common depositary bank).

19.2.5   Listing agent

When listing on certain exchanges a listing agent must be appointed by an issuer to communicate with the listing authority on its behalf, to lodge the necessary documents with the listing authority, and to advise the issuer on the listing rules and process (see also **21.8**). The concept of Listing Agent for the UKLA was removed with the introduction of the FSMA 2000 on 1 December 2001.

19.2.6   Principal paying agent and paying agents

A paying agent is an agent of the issuer responsible for co-ordinating payments of principal and interest under the bond. It will receive payment monies from the issuer and distribute them to the appropriate paying agents, who pay the bondholders resident in their jurisdictions. If an issuer uses a fiscal agent, it will usually take the role of principal paying agent. However, if the issuer uses a trustee structure (or if the fiscal agent does not have a 'presence' in a jurisdiction in which interest payments must be made) a principal paying agent (or further paying agents) will be appointed.

19.2.7   Depository and common depository

A depository is a bank appointed on behalf of a clearing system dealing with a particular issue to act as 'safe keeper' of the temporary global note, the permanent global note, and any definitive bearer bonds traded through a clearing system. If an issue uses more than one clearing system, each system must use the same depository and it will be known as the 'common depository'. There are only a limited number of international commercial banks which have been approved by the clearing systems to perform the role of depository. The common depository will hold part of an issue for Euroclear and part for Clearstream, and transfers can be made between the two systems (see **17.8**).

As well as providing a 'hole in the ground', using a depository also allows the bonds to be kept in jurisdictions other than those of the clearing systems, giving rise to tax and other advantages. The use of a depository to hold the bonds is sometimes known as 'immobilisation' (not to be confused with 'dematerialisation', whereby paper securities are dispensed with altogether, and the rights are recorded and traded electronically).

There is one circumstance in which a global note cannot be placed with a common depository. Some issuers will want their securities to be recognised by the European Central Bank as 'eligible collateral' for the euro central banking system (known as 'Eurosystem'). These securities can be used to support exposure in Eurosystem and so are popular with certain investors. From July 2006, securities are only eligible as Eurosystem collateral if their global form is held by the clearing system themselves and not at a common depository. This is known as a 'New Global Note' structure (or 'NGN').

19.2.8 Legal advisers

Separate legal advisers will be appointed by the issuer and the lead manager. If the issue involves a trust arrangement, the trustee will also instruct solicitors, although they will sometimes use the same firm as the lead manager with a Chinese wall between the two sets of solicitors. Most bond issues are governed by English law. However, if the issue involves an overseas jurisdiction, irrespective of whether the bonds themselves are governed by English law, lawyers from that jurisdiction must be instructed to ensure compliance with local laws and regulations.

The role of legal advisers in an issue primarily involves the preparation of documentation (the principal documents will be produced initially by the solicitors to the lead manager – see **Chapter 21**). The solicitors will also be involved in the due diligence process, and will have to produce a legal opinion for the transaction.

19.2.9 Auditors

Auditors will be involved in the issue process whenever the issuer is an entity which produces accounts (primarily companies and certain quasi-governmental entities). The lead manager and its legal advisers will want to review the issuer's accounts for at least the previous three years. If the issue is to be listed, the audited accounts may have to be published, or incorporated by reference, in the prospectus (or listing particulars). The issuer's auditors will be asked to provide a comfort letter addressed to the lead manager and the syndicate, confirming that there has been no material change in the issuer's financial condition since the last published accounts, and a 'consent letter' consenting to the publication of their report in the offering document (see **19.3**).

19.3 DOCUMENTATION OF A BOND ISSUE

19.3.1 List of required documents

A typical bond issue involves a substantial number of documents. The principal documents required are listed below in two sections:

(a)   documents relating to the underwriting, subscription and distribution of the bonds; and

(b)   documents which relate to and constitute the bonds themselves.

19.3.1.1 Underwriting, subscription and distribution

(a)   mandate letter;

(b)   invitation 'telex';

(c)   allotment 'telex';

(d)   prospectus or other offering document;

(e)   subscription agreement (or underwriting agreement);

(f)   agreement among managers;

(g)   auditor's report and consent letter;

(h)   auditor's comfort letters;

(i)   legal opinions.

19.3.1.2   Bonds and related documents

(a)   fiscal agency agreement (including paying agency agreement) (or trust deed);

(b)   paying agency agreement (if no fiscal agent);

(c)   temporary global note;

(d)   permanent global note (or definitive form bond);

(e)   deed of guarantee (if the issue is guaranteed and there is no trust deed);

(f)   deed of covenant (if no trustee, and bonds are in permanent global form).

19.3.2   Mandate letter

Once the issuer has awarded an institution the mandate to act as lead manager for the proposed bond issue, there will be a series of meetings and/or an exchange of correspondence which results in a letter (or sometimes telex or fax) which confirms the fundamental terms of the issue. This is known as the 'mandate letter'. It will also authorise the lead manager to announce the issue and allow him to invite other institutions (co-managers) to form a syndicate which will distribute the issue. The mandate letter is usually prepared by the lead manager.

19.3.3   Invitation telex

The invitation telex is the document sent by the lead manager to prospective co-managers (lead managers and co-managers together form the 'syndicate') inviting them to participate in the issue by subscribing for the bonds on their issue. If the issue is being underwritten (see **19.3.6**) the invitation telex will also request the co-managers to give an underwriting commitment. The invitation telex is prepared and sent by the lead manager (having usually been checked by its solicitors) on the day the issue is launched (see **21.7**). Note that the invitation telex (and allotment telex) is usually a fax or an e-mail rather than a telex.

The requirement to send an invitation telex, and its minimum content, are governed by ICMA rules. The telex must provide summary information about the issue and its basic terms and conditions. It may also provide a brief description of the issuer and its business, as well as any guarantor. The invitation telex will also outline the timetable of the issue.

19.3.4   Allotment telex

The invitation telex will have asked the co-managers to notify the lead manager of the maximum value of bonds for which they are prepared to subscribe on issue. Once he has received a response from all the co-managers, the lead manager will decide exactly how to divide the issue between them and will notify the co-managers by sending an allotment telex. The allocation is at the sole discretion of the lead manager, and is subject to the issue actually completing. The allotment telex will also contain a request for each co-manager's payment and transfer instructions for the bonds to which they are subscribing, which the lead manager will give to the clearing system at closing (see **21.10**).

ICMA rules require that allotments are made within 24 hours after the launch of the issue.

19.3.5   Prospectus or listing particulars

The prospectus is the document which provides detailed information about an issue for potential investors. If the issue is to be listed on the London Stock Exchange Professional Securities Market ('PSM') then this document is known as the 'listing particulars'. Since these 'selling documents' are at the heart of any bond issue, they are examined separately in **Chapter 20**.

19.3.6 Subscription agreement/underwriting agreement

The subscription agreement is a contract between the issuer, the lead manager and the co-managers which records the basis on which the issuer will sell, and the managers will buy, the bonds on issue. The syndicate members will be subscribing for the bonds on the basis that they will keep very few, or none, of those bonds for themselves ('for their own book'). Before they agree to subscribe (ie, before they sign the subscription agreement) the syndicate members will have lined up investors who want to take the bonds.

As explained at **19.2.3**, most (UK) bonds work on the basis that the syndicate will subscribe for all of the bonds between them, even if they cannot place them with investors. Under the terms of the subscription agreement, the liability of the syndicate members to the issuer of an issue is joint and several (compare this with a syndicated loan in which each bank's liability is restricted to its commitment). Therefore, whilst the managers will agree between themselves how many bonds they will each subscribe for (in the 'agreement among managers'), the subscription agreement allows an issuer to require any one manager to subscribe for the entire bond issue if necessary. If the issue uses underwriting banks instead, the subscription agreement will contain the terms of the underwriting (and may be called an 'underwriting agreement').

The subscription agreement will also cover the following matters:

(a) Conditions precedent to the issue. These might include legal opinions to the managers, auditors' consent and comfort letters, and a closing certificate confirming there has been no material adverse change to the issuer's representations and warranties.

(b) The pricing of the issue (ie, the interest rate payable on the bonds and, if appropriate, the price at which convertible bonds can be converted into shares).

(c) Fees and commissions payable to the managers. These will usually include a 'selling commission' (also known as a 'selling concession') and a 'management/underwriting commission', both calculated as a percentage of the principal amount of the bonds.

(d) Costs and expenses to be paid by the issuer. These are likely to include costs in connection with preparing and printing the bonds and documentation of the issue, any costs of listing, advertising costs, and the fees and expenses of the trustee (if one is used). There is also likely to be a provision under which the issuer pays for all or part of the syndicate's legal costs.

(e) Representations and warranties given by the issuer to each of the managers. These will include representations of fact, for example that any (material) information supplied by the issuer in connection with the issue (particularly with respect to the offering circular) is true and accurate in all material respects, as well as representations of law, for example that the issuer is validly existing and incorporated (the subscription agreement will also contain indemnities given by the issuer to the managers in respect of any misrepresentation).

(f) A representation from the managers that they will comply with all applicable selling restrictions (see **18.2.1**).

(g) A force majeure clause (see **9.7**), allowing the lead manager to terminate the syndicate's obligations under the subscription agreement (other than pre-existing liabilities). Force majeure is typically triggered when financial, political or economic conditions change such that the lead manager believes they are likely materially to prejudice the success of the issue. There is a standard ICMA force majeure clause which is usually used.

19.3.7   Agreement among managers

The agreement among managers is a contract between the lead manager and the co-managers. Its main purpose is to record the number of bonds which each member of the syndicate has agreed to take. However, the agreement also covers payment and allocation of the managers' commission (these are governed by ICMA rules). The agreement among managers also delegates power to the lead manager to act on behalf of the syndicate in certain circumstances. ICMA has produced a standard form of agreement among managers which is incorporated by reference in most bond issues.

19.3.8   Auditor's report, consent letter and comfort letters

The prospectus or other offering document may include extracts from the latest set of accounts for the issuer, but not necessarily the entire set of statutory accounts filed at Companies House. The issuer's auditors will therefore be required to 'sign off' on the extract to confirm it is consistent with the annual accounts. This is sometimes contained in an 'auditor's report', which may be in the prospectus, and a typical format is given below.

> The Directors
> Issuer plc,
> (address)
>
> 15 August 2013
>
> Dear Sirs
>
> Issuer plc (the 'Company')
>
> We have examined the financial information set out on pages 15 to 19 of the Prospectus dated 15 August 2013 issued by the Company in respect of US$50,000,000 bonds due 2017.
>
> In our opinion the financial information is consistent with the annual accounts of the Company for the three years ended 31 December 2012, which we audited in accordance with Auditing Standards and on which we reported without qualification.
>
> Yours faithfully
>
> Auditors

The auditors will be asked to provide a consent letter, consenting to the printing of their report in the prospectus (or listing particulars), and comfort letters, addressed to the managers, which essentially confirm:

(a)   that there has been no material adverse change in the issuer's financial position since the latest audited accounts; and

(b)   that any unaudited financial information contained in the offering document is correct.

There will usually be two comfort letters, the first given at the execution of the subscription agreement (the 'signing'), and the second, updating the first, at the time of the closing. The comfort letters are as important to the managers as the legal opinions, and will be legally binding on the auditors (although auditors will often attempt to limit their liability).

19.3.9   Legal opinions

Legal opinions are required by the lead manager and (usually) the co-managers and the trustee. One legal opinion will be required from the lead manager's solicitors with respect to the binding nature of the documentation, and a second will be required from the issuer's solicitors confirming the due incorporation of the issuer, that all necessary consents have been obtained, the position regarding taxation, and enforceability of the contractual documents against the issuer. Opinions from local lawyers will be required if the issue involves other jurisdictions.

19.3.10 Fiscal agency agreement

The fiscal agency agreement is a contract between the issuer, the fiscal agent (as fiscal agent and principal paying agent), and any other paying agents which have been appointed. The fiscal agency agreement records the structure through which the bondholders will receive payment of coupon and principal. Payments to bondholders are made through paying agents, because the issuer will not have the administrative capability to make the payments itself. If the issue uses a trust arrangement then it will require a 'principal paying agent' (usually a bank); if a fiscal agent is used, he will perform the function of a principal paying agent. Further paying agents will need to be appointed if an issue requires payments to be made in jurisdictions outside that of the principal paying agent (although they will often be branch offices of the principal paying agent).

Bonds will usually be held in a clearing system, and so payment will involve funds flowing through that system.

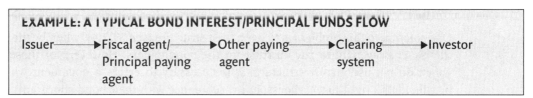

EXAMPLE: A TYPICAL BOND INTEREST/PRINCIPAL FUNDS FLOW

Issuer ——▶ Fiscal agent/ ——▶ Other paying ——▶ Clearing ——▶ Investor
Principal paying   agent   system
agent

The fiscal agency agreement will also document the following matters:

(a)   the procedure for authentication of the temporary global note and definitive bonds;

(b)   the process necessary to exchange the temporary global note for definitive bonds;

(c)   the issue of replacement bonds (eg, on loss or theft of the original);

(d)   the procedures for convening the bondholders' meetings;

(e)   fees and expenses of the paying agents.

The fiscal agency agreement will also contain the full terms and conditions of the bonds, as well as the forms (if any) of temporary global notes, permanent global notes and definitive bonds, which will appear in a schedule to the agreement.

19.3.11 Paying agency agreement

If a bond issue uses a trust arrangement, the trustee is not responsible for making any payments of coupon or principal. A 'principal paying agent' (together with any other paying agents if necessary) must be appointed under a separate agreement with the issuer. This is known as the 'paying agency agreement', and it will cover similar payment matters to the fiscal agency agreement (see **19.3.10**).

19.3.12 Trust deed

If a trustee is employed as opposed to a fiscal agent (see **19.2.4**), a trust deed will be required to cover the following matters:

(a)   creation of the trust relationship;

(b)   the trust property (the issuer's covenant to pay);

(c)   the trustee's powers and duties;

(d)   appointment and removal of the trustee;

(e)   the requirements for, and organisation of, bondholders' meetings;

(f)   some monitoring of the issuer's financial position.

19.3.13 Deed of guarantee

Some corporate issuers (usually for tax reasons) may use a subsidiary company to issue securities and thereby raise finance for the parent or group. These subsidiaries may be formed solely for the purpose of the issue (often known as 'special purpose vehicles' or 'SPVs'), or they may be general finance vehicles through which the group does most, or all, of its financing. In either case they are often little more than shell companies with few assets. Such a company is unlikely to attain 'investment grade' status (see **17.11**), and therefore the parent company will need to guarantee the SPV's (or the finance vehicle's) obligations under the bond in order to lift the credit rating of the issue. The guarantee may be endorsed on the bond itself, or it may be made as a unilateral declaration of guarantee, by the parent company, in a deed of guarantee.

19.3.14 Deed of covenant

If a note is in permanent global form (ie, there are no definitive bonds) then the legal owner of the note is the common depositary bank since it is the bearer (holding the note on behalf of the clearing system). However, in the event of non-payment, the common depositary will not bring a claim against the issuer on the bondholders' behalf. Furthermore, whilst the global note is exchangeable for definitives, the issuer may be unwilling to comply with this condition if it is in a non-payment situation. The bondholders are left unable to enforce their claim.

One solution to this problem is to use a trust structure (see **19.2.4**), whereby the trustee holds the issuer's covenant to pay on trust for the bondholders. However, for those bond issues which do not use a trust structure, it is necessary to create a document which gives the bondholders a right to sue the issuer in accordance with their bond allocations shown in the clearing systems. That document is known as a deed of covenant: a promise to pay executed by the issuer in a deed poll (ie, a unilateral document), and which gives bondholders the right to claim against the issuer in accordance with their bond allocation shown on clearing system accounts.

19.4 TERMS AND CONDITIONS OF A BOND

19.4.1 Comparison with a facility agreement

The terms in a bond are generally both fewer and shorter than the terms in most commercial facility agreements. There are also standard terms for bonds which are used in international capital markets, and substantial variation from, or heavy negotiation of, the standard terms is unusual. The reason for this standardisation is to provide instruments which are familiar to investors, without complex terms, making them easily tradeable.

A bondholder will usually have five main concerns:

(a)   the issuer's and the issue's credit rating;

(b)   the amount of its investment;

(c)   the return it will receive on its investment;

(d)   when it is able to redeem its investment;

(e)   its rights on the issuer's default ranking pari passu with any other holders of the same or similar debt instruments of the issuer.

A bondholder will not be concerned with the detailed business of the issuer, or with intricate financial covenants unless it is a 'high yield' bond. Unlike the borrower in a loan transaction, the issuer of a bond will not make detailed representations and warranties to the investor. The issuer will provide information about itself and its finances in the prospectus (or listing particulars), and investors will normally rely on this in making their decision to invest. Liability for the content of these documents is discussed in **Chapter 20**.

19.4.2 Where are the terms and conditions found?

The terms and conditions of a bond govern how the instrument operates once it has been issued. Unlike most commercial loan transactions, a bond issue involves numerous documents relating to the funding. Several of those documents will contain a complete set of terms and conditions of the bond, for example:

(a)   in the temporary global note;

(b)   on the back of the definitive bearer (or registered) bond, or in the permanent global note;

(c)   as a schedule to the fiscal agency agreement (or trust deed);

(d)   sometimes in the paying agency agreement (if there is a trustee);

(e)   in the prospectus (or listing particulars).

The debt obligation is evident in the bond itself (whether in temporary global, definitive, or permanent global form) and is the property held on trust if a trustee is appointed (see the covenant to pay in the trust deed).

19.4.3   Specific terms and conditions of a bond

19.4.3.1   Preamble

The preamble is a short initial paragraph which may confirm the authorisation of the issue by the board (or other authorising body) of the issuer, and which lists the parties to, and dates of, all relevant contractual documents entered into in respect of the issue. This list will include the trust deed, fiscal agency agreement and paying agency agreement.

19.4.3.2   Form, denomination and title

This short clause will state the form (eg, bearer, registered or global) the bonds will take, the amounts in which they are issued (eg, US$10,000 and US$100,000 and also known as 'par value' or 'denomination'), and a statement as to how title to the bonds will pass (eg, for bearer bonds, title will pass by delivery).

19.4.3.3   Status

The status clause will specify the characteristic of the debt obligation and its ranking amongst other debt obligations of the issuer, indicating to the bondholder how it stands vis-à-vis other creditors of the issuer. Bonds are usually unsecured and rank pari passu with all other unsecured creditors. However, bonds may be secured or subordinated. (Banks may issue subordinated bonds so that the proceeds of the issue will supplement their 'Tier 2 Capital' for regulatory capital purposes: see **9.3.3**.)

19.4.3.4   Negative pledge

The negative pledge in a standard bond transaction will almost always be less onerous than the negative pledge required by the lenders in a commercial banking transaction (see **7.5.2.1**).

EXAMPLE

So long as any of the Bonds or Coupons remains outstanding, the issuer will not create or permit to subsist any mortgage, charge, lien or other form of security interest or encumbrance upon the whole or any part of its undertaking, assets or revenues present or future to secure any present or future indebtedness in the form of bonds, notes, debentures, loan stock or other securities, or any guarantee of or indemnity in respect of such indebtedness, unless the Issuer's obligations under the Bonds and the Coupons are secured equally and rateably therewith or have the benefit of such other security, guarantee, indemnity or other arrangement as shall be approved by an Extraordinary Resolution of the Bondholders.

This form of negative pledge simply ensures that the issuer will not issue debt securities ranking higher than the current issue, unless the bondholders of this current issue receive identical rights. Any stronger form of negative pledge would be unworkable, since (unlike restrictive terms in a facility agreement) it would require a bondholders' meeting to obtain a waiver of this term.

19.4.3.5 Coupon

If a bond carries a fixed coupon, the rate will be determined on or before the launch date, and the coupon will be payable annually in arrear. If the coupon is at a floating rate, the method of calculation is explained in the interest clause, and the coupon payment dates are specified. The coupon payment dates will usually be the same dates in the appropriate months depending on the commencement date of the issue itself (eg, if quarterly – 15 August, 15 November, 15 February and 15 May). Since those days may not be days on which banks are open, a 'business day' definition must be introduced into this condition (see **11.7**).

The 365/365 basis for calculating domestic loan interest was explained at **4.9**. For fixed rate bonds issued *before* 1 January 1999, the convention was to use the '360/360' basis in which each calendar month is treated as having 30 days, so that one-twelfth of the annual interest rate will accrue for each month irrespective of the actual number of days in that month. However, fixed rate bonds issued *after* 1 January 1999 usually use the 'Actual/Actual' convention. Unfortunately, there are at least three different interpretations of this convention, but the most commonly adopted will probably be the ICMA method (r 251), ie actual days elapsed over the product of the number of days in a coupon period and the number of coupon periods. For floating rate notes (and syndicated loans, for most currencies other than sterling), the 'Actual/360' or '365/360' basis is usually used. This applies the 'annual' rate (x%) to the principal sum as if it were x% per 360 days. Over a calendar year, therefore, the interest charged is actually slightly more than the 'annual' rate and is different for months of different lengths.

> **EXAMPLE**
>
> If the annual coupon is 6%, and the principal sum is £200, then the '365/360' basis requires interest of £12 to be paid every 360 days: ie 3.33p per day or approximately £12.17 per calendar year.

19.4.3.6 Payments

The mechanics for payment under a definitive bearer bond are relatively simple, requiring surrender of the bond for payment of principal, and surrender of the relevant coupon for interest. Surrender and payment are effected through the paying agents, who are agents of the issuer (in contrast with facility agreements where payments are made through the agent which is an agent of the lenders). Most bonds, however, will be held in clearing systems, and so payments will be made from the paying agents directly to the clearing systems which credit the money to the relevant cash account of each bondholder.

19.4.3.7 Redemption and purchase

The bond will usually specify three occasions on which it may be redeemed:

(a) On maturity (usually 'at par', ie at face value).

(b) For tax reasons. As with a facility agreement, an issuer will not want to maintain a bond issue if a change in tax law or practice renders its borrowing more expensive. A bond will therefore include a 'tax redemption clause' permitting redemption of the entire issue if, as a result of a change in tax laws, the issuer is required to gross up payments of interest or principal. The issuer must redeem the whole issue, and not just part.

(c) Re-purchase. There is no legal reason why an issuer should not purchase its own bonds in the secondary market, and the terms will specifically permit this. However, if the bonds are listed on the London Stock Exchange, the Listing Rules generally require the issuer to notify all the bondholders of its intentions, through a Regulatory Information Service (RIS) – see Rule 12.5). Any purchases which are made by tender offer to the bondholders generally must be made to all the bondholders.

19.4.3.8 Taxation

An issuer will be required to gross up payments to investors in very limited circumstances, since the issuer has little control over the bondholder's identity and tax domicile. Any grossing-up obligation is usually restricted to taxes imposed by the issuer's own jurisdiction and would benefit only 'non-domestic' investors (see also **9.3.4**).

19.4.3.9 Events of default

The events of default in a bond issue are almost invariably less onerous and less detailed than in a facility agreement. Any default for non-payment of interest will have a grace period (often as much as 14 days) as a matter of course. Cross-default clauses are often subject to a high minimum threshold (ie, de minimis).

19.4.3.10 Prescription

The prescription period is the time in which a bondholder must claim principal and coupon, usually 10 years and five years respectively, from the due date for payment. The prescription periods avoid the issuer looking to statutes of limitation to limit its liability. At the end of the prescription period, the debt is actually extinguished not just action barred. (This is important to avoid the situation where an investor may search for an applicable jurisdiction with a limitation period which only views action barring as procedural, and with a longer limitation period than the prescription period.)

19.4.3.11 Replacement of bonds and coupons

This provision deals with lost, stolen, defaced or destroyed bonds. The risk to an issuer of simply replacing a 'lost' bearer instrument has already been mentioned: if the original bond is presented for payment, the issuer will have to honour the payment obligations on both original and replacement (this also applies to replacement coupons). The condition for replacement of bonds and coupons therefore provides that the bondholder claiming a replacement must indemnify the issuer in respect of any payments the issuer has to make on the original bond or coupon and pay all expenses of the issuer in making such a replacement (including any tax). Any mutilated or defaced bonds will have to be surrendered before a replacement is issued.

19.4.3.12 Meetings of bondholders and modification

The procedure for convening bondholders' meetings and the conducting of business thereat is provided for in the fiscal agency agreement (or trust deed). The trustee (or, if no trustee, the issuer) convenes meetings, either on its own initiative or at the request of bondholders holding at least 10% in aggregate of the principal amount of the bonds. Bondholder meetings are usually convened only when there is a problem with the issue or the issuer, or if any modifications of the terms and conditions are required. The conditions governing meetings are usually in standard form. Notice must generally be given to all bondholders through publication in an appropriate newspaper (eg, the *Financial Times*), and strict quorum requirements must be met for meetings to modify the terms and conditions. Matters on which bondholders might be asked to vote include the following:

(a)   a postponement, reduction or cancellation of principal or interest;

(b)   the release of any security or guarantee;

(c)   a change in the currency of the bonds;

(d)   waiver of any event of default;

(e)   appointment of a new trustee;

(f)   reorganisation of the issuer (eg, on a merger);

(g)   if there is no trustee, the appointment of a bondholders' committee to represent bondholders in a liquidation or reorganisation.

Under English law, there are no specific statutory requirements as to when a majority can bind a minority of bondholders. However, in order to protect the minority, English euromarket practice dictates that the majority of bondholders required to pass an extraordinary resolution is 75% (the matters listed above will usually require an extraordinary resolution). Certain civil law jurisdictions have precise statutory requirements as to which matters require a majority vote. A trustee is usually given power to approve minor modifications, or waive a minor breach of the terms and conditions, provided that such action is not materially prejudicial to the bondholders.

19.4.3.13 Notices

In a commercial loan transaction, the lenders' names and addresses appear in the parties clause, a schedule and on the signing pages of the loan document. However, the identity of bond investors will not be known, and therefore notice can be given only by one or more of an RIS, the FSA or a national newspaper (usually the *Financial Times* and, for issues listed on the Luxembourg Stock Exchange, the *Luxemburger Wort*) (see Rule 9.6). If bonds are listed on the London Stock Exchange, copies of any notices to bondholders must also be given to the Exchange. Notices of meetings for holders of London listed debt securities in bearer form must usually be placed in a leading national newspaper circulating in the UK, and a copy of the notice must be sent to the Company Announcements Office of the London Stock Exchange. When bonds are held in clearing systems, notices must also be sent to the systems, which have a duty to notify the relevant securities account holders.

19.4.3.14 Further issues

An issuer is usually permitted to issue further bonds with the same terms and conditions as the bonds in the issue: in other words, it may increase the size of the issue. Any such further issue will be allowed without the consent of the bondholders (which would be a time-consuming and difficult process). Any further issue will have the same ISIN number in the clearing systems and will be treated as part of the original issue once it has gone through the same 'lock up' provisions. In order for a further issue to be treated by the clearing systems as 'fully fungible' (ie, the new instruments are indistinct from those of the original issue), it must have exactly the same terms and conditions in all respects as the original issue.

19.4.3.15 Governing law and jurisdiction

These are standard boiler plate clauses (see **9.8**). The governing law will usually be English, with a submission to the non-exclusive jurisdiction of the English courts. For certainty and ease of enforcement, all documents in the issue process should have the same governing law.

50-year Swiss bond unlikely to set pulses racing

Lack of liquidity may restrict appeal of new sovereign issue, writes **William Hall**

The Swiss government's decision to issue a 50-year government bond breaks new ground in the maturity of debt issued by sovereign borrowers. But its initial reception suggests that Switzerland's "half-century" bond is unlikely to capture the imagination of the investment community.

Most governments in industrialised countries issue bonds of up to 30 years maturity. But Switzerland is the first country in recent memory to issue a 50-year bond. It carries a 4 per cent coupon and was priced to yield 4.095 per cent.

It is not Switzerland's first attempt to tap this segment of the market. In 1909 it issued a 50-year bond with a 3.5 per cent coupon. However, the gap between Switzerland's last 50-year bond and its latest issue suggests that demand for this maturity is limited, despite the country's triple-A credit rating. It is understood that the Swiss government took SFr200m of the new bond and total bids of SFr265m at the auction resulted in just SFr189m being sold.

The Swiss government has issued around SFr40bn of bond issues, so the SFr189m raised this week will not make much of a dent in its appetite for funds to finance a government debt which now tops SFr100bn.

The new bond is targeted at those Swiss investors which are required by law to earn a minimum 4 per cent on their funds under management. However, analysts questioned whether there would be much demand for the paper given its limited liquidity. Normally, investors prefer issues of between SFr2bn to SFr4bn.

Peter Thomann, who heads the Swiss government's treasury operations, admits that this week's issue is an experiment. Until recently Swiss government issues ranged between eight and 15 years. However, it now has issues ranging from two years to 30 years in its fund-raising armoury, and the latest bond fixes a new point on the yield curve.

Beat Schwab, of Credit Suisse First Boston, said the issue highlighted the steepness of the yield curve at the short end. The average yield on Swiss government bonds is 2.42 per cent and the gap between 10-year and 30-year

The new bond is targeted at those Swiss investors that are required by law to earn a minimum 4 per cent on their funds under management

government paper is around 120 basis points. By contrast, the 50-year bond is only yielding 35 basis points more than the 30-year bond.

Mr Schwab said the new bond might appeal to euro-sceptic foreign investors bearish about the prospects for the single currency. The Swiss franc is a traditional safe haven, and short-term Swiss interest rates are 200 basis points below comparable German rates. But lack of liquidity will severely restrict its appeal.

Analysts are split on whether the Swiss franc will assume greater importance as investors seek to diversify their portfolios or will be marginalised by the Euro. But clearly the Swiss government at least believes its currency will still be circulating in 50 years' time.

Source: Financial Times

CHAPTER 20

BOND PROSPECTUS AND LISTING PARTICULARS

20.1	Introduction	239
20.2	Obtaining a London listing	239
20.3	When is an approved prospectus required?	240
20.4	Contents of a prospectus	241
20.5	General duty of disclosure	244
20.6	Omission of information	244
20.7	Liability for prospectus and listing particulars	245
20.8	Other jurisdictions	247

20.1 INTRODUCTION

International bonds are usually listed, primarily for tax efficiency and because of investor demand (see **21.8.1**). The jurisdictions most commonly used for listing a London-based bond issue are Ireland, Luxembourg and of course London itself. All three of these bourses are subject to the EU penchant for market harmonisation in the guise of the Financial Services Action Plan, which focused most recently on issuers' disclosure requirements by way of the Prospectus Directive. This chapter looks primarily at a London listing for a stand-alone bond, and the requirements for producing a disclosure document to inform potential investors about the issue and issuer.

20.2 OBTAINING A LONDON LISTING

Listing a bond in London actually involves two (closely connected) separate events:

(a) admission to the 'Official List'; and

(b) admission to trading on one of two markets, one 'regulated' and one 'unregulated'.

These stages are described below.

20.2.1 Admission to the Official List

The phrase 'admission to the "Official List"' means satisfying the legal requirements for a London listing.

There is a veritable 'regulatory waterfall' which eventually ends in the 'pool' of listing rules: at the top sits the Prospectus Directive (2003/71/EC), as amended by Directive 2010/73/EU under the European Commission's 'five-year review'. The Directive is implemented in the UK by the Prospectus Regulations 2005 and two further Regulations in 2011 and 2012. The Prospectus Regulations in turn required modifications and extensions to Part VI of the Financial Services and Markets Act 2000 (and certain derivative regulations). The modified FSMA 2000 empowers the Financial Conduct Authority (as the 'competent authority') to implement the Listing Rules. The FCA delegates this task to a division known as the United Kingdom Listing Authority (the UKLA). Finally, the UKLA's implementation of the Listing Rules take the form of the 'Listing, Prospectus and Disclosure and Transparency Rules', found in three sourcebooks of the same name within the FSA Handbook.

If a bond issue complies with the Listing Rules, it will be eligible for admission to trading.

20.2.2 Admission to trading

The phrase 'admission to trading' means placing the bond on one of the markets for listed securities run by the London Stock Exchange (LSE). There are two main markets for bonds:

(a) The London Stock Exchange's 'Main Market' (sometimes known as the 'LSE Regulated Market' or, historically, the 'gilt-edged and fixed interest market'): this is an EEA 'regulated market', for the purposes of many EU Directives. It has stricter rules than the Professional Securities Market (see below) and requires publication of a UKLA-approved disclosure document known as a 'prospectus' – see further below.

(b) The Professional Securities Market (PSM), which is sometimes referred to as an 'unregulated market', that is one with 'locally created' rules. It has a slightly more relaxed regime than the Main Market and requires publication of a UKLA-approved disclosure document known as 'listing particulars' rather than a prospectus (although note that there is considerable overlap in the requirements).

20.3 WHEN IS AN APPROVED PROSPECTUS REQUIRED?

A prospectus approved by the UKLA is essentially required (as a prerequisite) if a bond issue is to be offered to the public or admitted to trading on the Main Market. If the issuer's 'home state' (usually the jurisdiction of the issuer's incorporation in the case of equity, but subject to a case-by-case choice for many types of debt issue – see FSMA 2000, s 102) is not the UK but the prospectus has been approved by another EEA 'competent' authority as satisfying disclosure requirements, the prospectus will be accepted by the 'host state' listing authority (eg the UKLA in the UK). This 'mutual recognition' or 'passporting' of a prospectus is usually subject to a few additional requirements such as a translation of the transaction summary (see **20.4.1.3**).

There are two groups of exceptions to producing an approved prospectus, one relating to the type of bonds and the other relating to the type of offer.

20.3.1 Bonds which are exempt from producing an approved prospectus

Certain exempt securities are listed in the Prospectus Rules and also in Sch 11A to the FSMA 2000. These exemptions relate to very specific types of issue (for example, one guaranteed by an EEA government or local authority, or where the offer is for less than €5 million or equivalent) and most are not usually relevant for a corporate bond issue.

20.3.2 Offer types which are exempt from producing an approved prospectus

Even if the bond is offered to the public, in the UK there are exemptions from producing an approved prospectus provided that the bond is not admitted to trading on a regulated market (eg if it is admitted to trading on the PSM rather than the Main Market in the UK). These exemptions are found in s 86 of the FSMA 2000 (PR 1.2.1) and focus on offers which are not targeting the 'general public'. For a corporate issuer, the main exemptions from July 2012 (in line with the amending Directive 2010/73/EU) are:

(a) an offer which is made to or directed at 'qualified investors' (for example, governments, central banks and entities authorised or regulated to operate in financial markets);

(b) an offer which is made to or directed at fewer than 150 persons (other than 'qualified investors') per EEA State;

(c) the minimum consideration which may be paid by any person pursuant to the securities offer is €100,000 (or equivalent);

(d) where the securities have a minimum denomination of €100,000 (or equivalent), often referred to as a 'wholesale' offer;

(e) where the total consideration for the securities is less than €100,000.

20.4 CONTENTS OF A PROSPECTUS

20.4.1 Authority, format and general content

20.4.1.1 Authority

The UKLA derives its authority to insist upon the issue and publication of a prospectus or listing particulars from s 79 of the FSMA 2000, which provides that the Listing Rules can require that securities may not be admitted to the official list unless:

(a) listing particulars have been submitted to, and approved by, the competent authority and published, or

(b) in such cases as may be specified by listing rules, such document ... as may be so specified has been published.

20.4.1.2 General content

Assuming the bond issue requires a prospectus (see **20.3.1** and **20.3.2** for exceptions), Prospectus Rule 2.1 dictates the general content requirement by quoting three subsections of s 87A of the FSMA 2000 on the 'necessary information' to be contained in the prospectus:

(2) The necessary information is the information necessary to enable investors to make an informed assessment of —

    (a) the assets and liabilities, financial position, profits and losses, and prospects of the issuer of the transferable securities and of any guarantor; and

    (b) the rights attaching to the transferable securities.

(3) The necessary information must be presented in a form which is comprehensible and easy to analyse.

(4) The necessary information must be prepared having regard to the particular nature of the transferable securities and their issuer.

The level of detail required in a prospectus will depend on whether it is a 'retail' (ie 'non-exempt') or 'wholesale' (ie 'exempt') offer. The 'wholesale' regime requires less detailed disclosure, but applies only if the securities are denominated at or above €100,000 or equivalent.

20.4.1.3 Prospectus format

The format of a prospectus is outlined at Prospectus Rule 2.2. There are two options for stand-alone bond issues: either a single document or as three separate documents. The three separate documents are:

(a) a 'registration document', which contains information relating to the issuer;

(b) a 'securities note', which contains the information relating to the bonds; and

(c) for retail deals, a 'summary', which, currently, 'must convey concisely, in non-technical language and in an appropriate structure, the key information relevant to the securities' (FSMA 2000, s 87A(6)). The summary should not exceed 7% of the length of a prospectus or 15 pages, whichever is the longer. The requirement for an 'appropriate structure' was introduced from 1 July 2012 and there are now detailed provisions mandating content and layout of summaries.

The advantage in using the three documents is that the registration document is valid for 12 months and so can be re-used for any number of issues during that period. However, most stand-alone issues since July 2005 have used a single document format.

Lastly, Prospectus Rule 2.2.7 allows the issuer of a debt programme (eg an MTN programme) to use a 'base prospectus' (containing the main information on issuer and programme) and a 'final terms' document (which contains information on each particular securities issue under the programme).

20.4.1.4   Listing particulars

If a bond issue is to be admitted to trading on the PSM (this tends to be a minority), or is being admitted to trading on the LSE but does not require a prospectus under the Prospectus Directive, then listing particulars must be prepared. Listing Rule 4 details the content and format of listing particulars, and does so largely by incorporating selected parts of the Prospectus Rules. Listing particulars will therefore usually look like a 'low fat' version of a prospectus.

20.4.2   Responsibility for information

Section 84(1)(d) of the FSMA 2000 allows the Prospectus Rules to specify who is responsible for a prospectus, and this is covered by Prospectus Rule 5.5. For a bond (see Prospectus Rule 5.5.4) this includes:

(a)   the issuer;

(b)   anyone who accepts (and the prospectus states as accepting) responsibility;

(c)   the offeror (if this is not the issuer);

(d)   the person requesting admission to trading (if this is not the issuer);

(e)   any guarantor (in relation to information on them or the guarantee); and

(f)   anyone else who has authorised the contents of the prospectus.

In the case of a bond (and most other non-equity related securities) the issuer's directors are *not* required to take responsibility for the prospectus. After market consultation, the UK used its Member State discretion to ensure this was the case, thereby maintaining the status quo with the previous regime.

The Prospectus Rules require each of those responsible to make a declaration in the prospectus in the following form (see Prospectus Rules, Annex V, Appendix 3):

> [   ] accepts responsibility for the information contained in this document. To the best of their knowledge and belief (having taken all reasonable care to ensure that such is the case) the information contained in this document is in accordance with the facts and does not omit anything likely to affect the import of such information.

Liability for errors and omissions is considered in more detail at **20.7**.

20.4.3   Key information relating to the issuer

For prospectus disclosure, the Prospectus Directive Regulation (and therefore the UK Prospectus Rules) makes a distinction based on the type of securities, the type of issuer and the denomination of securities. For bonds, different disclosure Annexes apply for 'wholesale' or 'retail' debt. For wholesale (or 'exempt') debt securities – that is, with a minimum denomination of €100,000 or equivalent – the relevant disclosure annexes in PR Appendix 3 are Annexes IX and XIII. For retail (or 'non-exempt') securities – that is, with a denomination of less than €100,000 or equivalent – the relevant disclosure annexes in PR Appendix 3 are IV and V. Additional or alternative disclosure annexes may apply depending on whether bonds are convertible, asset-backed or derivatives, or, for example, if the issuer is a bank or sovereign entity.

For the purposes of this chapter, the retail regime is used to illustrate the sort of information to be disclosed. The content requirements for wholesale debt are fairly similar, although, as might be anticipated, they are slightly less detailed (requiring fewer explanatory sections, in view of the greater experience of the investors likely to be buying larger denominations) and less stringent about the basis on which financial information must be prepared. Similarly, in most circumstances, there is no need to include a summary section at the front of the prospectus for wholesale debt.

The minimum disclosure requirements for information relating to the issuer under the more onerous 'retail' regime include the following:

20.4.3.1 Persons responsible

The responsibility statement mentioned at **20.4.2** above.

20.4.3.2 Financial information

Audited accounts covering the last two financial years (unless the issuer is under two years old) to include a balance sheet, income statement (ie profit and loss account), cash flow statement and accounting policies. If the issuer prepares consolidated accounts it must use those in the registration document.

In a major change from the previous regime, all financial information must now be prepared in accordance with International Financial Reporting Standards (IFRS – see **6.9.5**) or an 'equivalent'. Pursuant to EU Regulation No 1289/2008 and delegated Regulation (EU) No 311/2012, 'equivalent' includes US, Japanese, Canadian, South Korean and Chinese GAAP. In addition, Indian GAAP may be used for financial years starting prior to 1 January 2015. For some issues, IFRS will not be required.

20.4.3.3 Risk factors

Another new requirement is the 'prominent disclosure of risk factors that may affect the issuer's liability to fulfil its obligations under the securities to investors'. These will be factors specific to the issuer or maybe to its industry, for example risks relating to business cycles, competition, reliance on raw materials or product liability.

20.4.3.4 Information about the issuer

Unsurprisingly, and in accordance with the previous rules, information about the issuer itself is considered vital. So the name, registration number, place and date of registration, registered office address and any 'recent events particular to the issuer which are to a material extent relevant to the evaluation of the issuer's solvency' must all be included.

20.4.3.5 Business overview

The prospectus must describe the issuer's activities, new products and markets. It must also include a statement that there has been no material adverse change in the prospects of the issuer since its last published audited accounts (or explanation why this statement cannot be made). Any profits forecasts or estimates are strictly regulated.

20.4.3.6 Administrative, management, supervisory bodies and shareholders

Names, business addresses and functions of directors (or equivalent) must be disclosed and, to the extent known to the issuer, the identity of any 'controlling' shareholders.

20.4.3.7 Material contracts and displaying documents

The prospectus must summarise any material contracts 'not entered into in the ordinary course of the issuer's business' which could result in any member of the group being under an obligation or entitlement that is material to the issuer's obligations under the securities. Finally, the prospectus must indicate where certain 'display documents' (eg the memorandum and articles, reports, valuations, historical accounts etc) may be inspected.

This 'issuer information' appears in the registration document if a three-part prospectus is used.

20.4.4 Key information relating to the bonds

The minimum disclosure requirements for information relating to the bonds (where securities are denominated less than €100,000) are outlined in Annex V, Appendix 3 to the Prospectus Rules. They include the following:

20.4.4.1 Use of proceeds

The document must disclose why the money is being raised, the estimated total cost of the issue and some detail as to each principal intended use of the proceeds.

20.4.4.2 Information about the securities

Details as to the type (eg registered or bearer), currency, ranking, coupon, maturity and governing law of the securities must be included. The securities document must also give details of the terms and conditions of the offer, for example, the total amount, methods for paying up the securities and delivery back, pricing details, and the name and address of any paying agents.

20.4.4.3 Repeated information

Remember that the securities and registration documents may be issued as stand-alone documents, and so some of the information is common to both, for example the responsibility statement and risk factors.

Lastly, Prospectus Rule 2.4 brings another departure from the previous rules in allowing an issuer to incorporate information by reference into the prospectus. However, incorporated information must first have been approved by the competent authority of the Home Member State, or filed with or notified to the FSA in accordance with the Prospectus Directive. The summary document must not incorporate information by reference (Prospectus Rule 2.4.4).

This 'bond information' appears in the securities document if a three-part prospectus is used.

20.5 GENERAL DUTY OF DISCLOSURE

In drafting the prospectus it is important to remember the general disclosure obligation contained in s 87A of the FSMA 2000. This provides that the prospectus must contain all information which is:

> necessary to enable investors to make an informed assessment of:
>
> (a)   the assets and liabilities, financial position, profits and losses, and prospects of the issuer of the transferable securities and of any guarantor; and
>
> (b)   the rights attaching to the transferable securities.

The prospectus must therefore contain information which the market reasonably needs and expects to receive so as to make an 'informed assessment' of the issuer's general position and the rights attached to the securities.

Section 87A also states that in determining what information is required to comply with this obligation, account must be taken of 'the nature of the transferable securities and their issuer.'

There is a similar general disclosure obligation for listing particulars in s 80 of the FSMA 2000, which also requires consideration of:

(a)   the nature of the persons who are likely to consider acquiring the securities;

(b)   the fact that certain matters may reasonably be expected to be within the knowledge of professional advisers of any kind which those persons may reasonably be expected to consult; and

(c)   any information available to investors or their professional advisers by virtue of requirements imposed by listing rules, by any other legislation or by a recognised investment exchange.

20.6 OMISSION OF INFORMATION

In most cases, if the Listing or Prospectus Rules require disclosure of information, the issuer's directors have little choice but to comply, however difficult or unpalatable that may be. The requirements for bonds are, however, generally less wide-ranging than for equity issues, reflecting the more sophisticated investor base of the former. The Rules list limited circumstances in which the UKLA can authorise the omission of information. Under Prospectus Rule 2.5, exemption from the duty to disclose (whether that duty arises under the Rules, s 87A or s 80) may be granted if:

(a) disclosure would be contrary to the public interest, for example, information relating to important defence contracts;

(b) disclosure would be seriously detrimental to the issuer of the securities (provided that omitting the information would not be likely to mislead a potential investor as to any facts the knowledge of which is essential in order to make an informed assessment); or

(c) the information is of minor importance only and not such as to influence the assessment of the assets and liabilities, financial position, profits and losses and prospects of the issuer.

Since one of the issuer's responsibilities is to ensure compliance with the Listing and Prospectus Rules requirements, and to submit the listing particulars to the UKLA, both he and his solicitors will prepare the annotated copy of the listing particulars and the 'non-applicable' letter (see **21.8.3**). If it is within the specific requirements of the Listing or Prospectus Rules, or within the general duty under the FSMA 2000, the information must be included unless the UKLA allows omission. The consequences of failing to include the required information are examined at **20.7**.

20.7 LIABILITY FOR PROSPECTUS AND LISTING PARTICULARS

Misstatements in, and omissions from, the prospectus or listing particulars can give rise to both civil and criminal liability on the part of those responsible. All of the procedures outlined below apply to both a prospectus and listing particulars, but for simplicity this section refers only to 'prospectus'.

20.7.1 Civil liability

20.7.1.1 The Financial Services and Markets Act 2000

Compensation under s 90

Section 90 of the FSMA 2000 applies to both a prospectus and any supplementary prospectus (or listing particulars and supplementary listing particulars). It provides that anyone responsible for those documents is liable to compensate any person who acquires any of the securities and suffers loss in respect of them 'as a result of any untrue or misleading statement in the [prospectus] or any omission from them of any matter required to be included' under the general disclosure obligation. Certain defences are available, however.

Liability under the section is far-reaching. In this context, two points are particularly worthy of note. First, the section is concerned with a loss suffered by a person who has 'acquired' any of the securities. This may include not only the original investors on the marketing of the securities, but also subsequent purchasers on the secondary market. Secondly, the person concerned must establish that he suffered loss in respect of the securities 'as a result of' the offending statement or omission. Most commentators consider that this condition is satisfied if, for example, the price paid for the securities is higher than it would be but for the error or omission. It is not necessary for the investor to have relied on the prospectus in deciding to invest, or, indeed, even to have read them. That said, if the investor knows of the error or omission at the time of investing, his loss cannot be said to arise as a result of it.

Defences

A number of defences are available to a person facing a claim for compensation (see Sch 10 to the FSMA 2000):

(a)   That at the time the prospectus was submitted to the UKLA he reasonably believed, having made such enquiries (if any) as were reasonable, that the statement was true and not misleading, or that the matter the omission of which caused the loss was properly omitted. This is not sufficient on its own, however. The person must also establish one of four other facts, namely that:

   (i)   he continued in that belief until the time when the securities were acquired; or

   (ii)   they were acquired before it was reasonably practical to bring a correction to the attention of persons likely to acquire the securities in question; or

   (iii) before the securities were acquired he had taken all such steps as were reasonable for him to have taken to ensure that a correction was brought to the attention of those persons; or

   (iv)   he continued in that belief until after the commencement of dealings in the securities following listing, and the securities were acquired after such a lapse of time that he ought in the circumstances to be excused.

(b)   Where the alleged loss arises as a result of an expert's statement, and that the person defending the claim reasonably believed that the expert was competent to make or authorise the statement in the prospectus and had consented to its inclusion in the form and context in which it was included. Again, this defence is available only if one of four facts, broadly similar to those referred to in paras (i)–(iv) above, is also established. This is not a defence for the expert in question. It is a defence for the issuer if confronted with a claim arising out of some error contained in an expert's report which forms part of the prospectus (eg, the accountants' report).

(c)   That before the securities were acquired he had published a correction 'in a manner calculated to bring it to the attention of persons likely to acquire the securities' (or, as the case may be, a statement that the expert was not competent or had not consented); or, at the very least, that he had taken all such steps as were reasonable for him to secure such publication, which he reasonably believed had taken place before the acquisition.

(d)   That the loss arose from an official statement or one contained in a public official document, which had been accurately and fairly reproduced in the prospectus.

(e)   That the investor knew that the statement was false or misleading, or knew the matter which had been omitted.

(f)   Where the potential liability arose from a failure to provide a supplementary prospectus, and that he reasonably believed that the change or new matter did not warrant them.

20.7.1.2   *Hedley Byrne v Heller: negligent misstatement*

Misstatements in a prospectus may give rise to liability in tort under the rule in *Hedley Byrne & Co Ltd v Heller & Partners Ltd* [1964] AC 465. Liability arises if a person suffers loss having relied upon a misstatement and the person who made the misstatement owed a duty of care to the one suffering loss on the faith of it. For a duty of care to arise in these circumstances, a special relationship must exist between the person giving the information and the person relying on its accuracy.

Applying the principle to misstatements in a prospectus, it is thought that those assuming responsibility for the prospectus owe a duty of care to those applying for securities in the company on the marketing of those securities, but not to subsequent trading on the secondary market (see *Caparo Industries v Dickman* [1990] 1 All ER 568 and *Al Nakib Investments (Jersey) v Longcroft* [1990] 3 All ER 321). The inability of a subsequent purchaser to bring a claim for negligent misstatement contrasts with the position in relation to liability under the FSMA 2000 (see **20.6.1.1**); so too does the requirement that the claimant must have relied on the misstatement to his detriment.

20.7.1.3   The Misrepresentation Act 1967

A person may be able to rescind the contract for the acquisition of the securities and/or claim damages under the Misrepresentation Act 1967 if he acted upon an incorrect or misleading statement contained in the prospectus, or an omission from them. Under the 1967 Act, a claim for damages may be made only against the other party to the contract. So, for example, a manager, but not a purchaser in the secondary market, would have a claim against the issuer under the Act (see also **5.5.1**).

20.7.1.4   Contract

If an investor subscribes for and receives securities at the time of their issue (ie, in the primary market), he will have entered into a contract and the prospectus will form part of that contract because of the representations and warranties in the subscription agreement. If the prospectus is wrong or misleading, the investor may be entitled, under normal contractual principles, to rescind the contract and/or sue the other contracting party for damages.

As part of the subscription arrangements, the syndicate of managers generally obtain a number of warranties from the issuer (see **19.3.6**). These warranties are usually supported by appropriate indemnities. If an investor, who does not have the benefit of those warranties, brings a claim against a member of the syndicate, that syndicate member may seek recompense from the issuer under the terms of the warranties and indemnities.

20.7.2   Criminal liability

20.7.2.1   The Financial Services Act 2012 (FSA 2012), ss 89 and 90

Section 397 of the FSMA 2000 was repealed in April 2013 and replaced by new, similar offences in ss 89 and 90 of the FSA 2012. These sections make it a criminal offence for any person knowingly or recklessly to make a misleading, false or deceptive statement, promise or forecast, or dishonestly to conceal any material facts, if he does so for the purpose of inducing another person to enter, or offer to enter into a 'relevant agreement' (or refrain from doing so), or to exercise or refrain from exercising rights conferred by a relevant investment. Liability also attaches if the person is reckless as to whether such actions will produce this effect.

Section 90 of the FSA 2012 provides that a person is guilty of an offence if he 'does any act or engages in any course of conduct which creates a false or misleading impression as to the market in or the price or value of any relevant investments' if he intends to create that impression and thereby to induce another person to acquire, dispose of, subscribe for or underwrite those investments. It is also an offence recklessly or knowingly to create such an impression with a view to creating a gain for oneself or a loss for someone else.

A person charged with an offence under s 397(3) has a defence if *inter alia* he can prove that he reasonably believed that his act or conduct would not create such an impression.

Depending on the circumstances, a misstatement in the prospectus might give rise to charges on both counts. Each offence is punishable by imprisonment and/or a fine.

20.7.2.2   Other provisions

Errors in, and omissions from, the prospectus may also give rise to criminal penalties under other provisions, for example the Theft Act 1968 (misleading statements by a company's officers with intent to deceive the members or creditors) or the Fraud Act 2006 (fraud by false representation or by failure to disclose information where there is a legal duty to do so).

20.8   OTHER JURISDICTIONS

This chapter discusses liability for the information contained in listing particulars under English law only. Other jurisdictions may impose different liabilities, either statutory or common law, which may also apply to an issue irrespective of what law the issue is governed by as a result of the nationality of the investor. On 1 March 2013, the European Securities and Markets Authority (ESMA) published a review of liability regimes in Europe. Liabilities imposed by US law can be particularly onerous.

CHAPTER 21

ISSUING A BOND – THE PROCESS

21.1	Introduction	249
21.2	The stages of a bond issue	249
21.3	Mandate	251
21.4	Due diligence	251
21.5	Documentation	252
21.6	Marketing	252
21.7	Launch and syndication	252
21.8	Listing	253
21.9	Signing	255
21.10	Closing	255

Thank goodness for that . . . the last chapter! David Adams

21.1 INTRODUCTION

Having briefly examined the parties and documents involved in a bond issue, this chapter concentrates on the actual process which an issuer must go through to issue the bonds.

One of the reasons why an issuer might choose to raise money on the euromarkets is the speed of the fund-raising process. The time between the issuer first instructing an investment bank to arrange the issue ('mandate') and when the issuer receives the money ('closing') may be as little as three weeks for a stand-alone bond (although five to six weeks is more usual). In order that an issue can be achieved this quickly, the bond market (through ICMA recommendations) has developed a guideline timetable for the issue process. Each party involved in the issue must be aware of the timetable, but it is usually the responsibility of the lead manager and its solicitors to monitor and 'police' the process.

21.2 THE STAGES OF A BOND ISSUE

The basic stages of a bond issue are as follows:

(a) Mandate.

(b) Due diligence.

(c) Documentation process begins.

(d) Marketing.

(e) Launch and syndication.

(f) Listing (both application to the UKLA and to the relevant exchange).

(g) Signing.

(h) Closing.

See Figure **21.1** below. This is the usual order in which each stage of the issue process occurs, although not every stage will be completed before the next one begins. The substance of each stage is explained below.

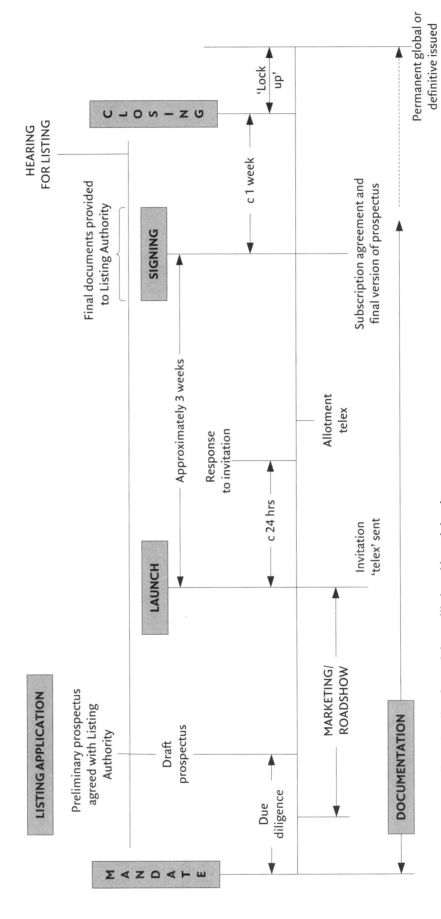

Figure 21.1   Paradigm timeline for a plain vanilla bond by a debut issuer

21.3 MANDATE

It should by now be clear that the question of the best way for a particular company to raise finance is a complex one. The company's directors will usually have lengthy meetings with investment banks and its own accountants before deciding whether an issue of debt securities is appropriate. Once the decision has been made, however, the first stage is for the company to instruct an investment bank to lead-manage the issue. This is known as the 'mandate'.

Once appointed, the lead manager will first advise as to the most appropriate structure for an issue (ie, which type of security) and the best market to target. For example, the lead manager may know that Japanese investors are particularly interested in the type of business the company runs, and suggest that the issue is targeted towards them. The lead manager will therefore approach its Japanese clients within its investor base, and will choose syndicate members which can 'bring in' Japanese investors.

The issuer and lead manager must first agree a number of important matters. These will include the marketing strategy, the decision whether to list, the identity of the fiscal agent (or trustee) and paying agents, and the fee structure. Once agreed, they will be recorded in the 'mandate letter' or 'term sheet', which is drafted by the lead manager. The basic terms and conditions of the bonds (such as price and status) will also be included in the mandate letter. The legal advisers will often have had little or no involvement up until the end of this mandate process.

21.4 DUE DILIGENCE

The due diligence process for a loan facility was explained in **Chapter 2**. Bond issues will also require a due diligence process in which the lead manager ascertains and verifies the information it needs for the issue (which is driven primarily by the information required to be included in the prospectus or listing particulars). The extent of the due diligence process will depend on a number of factors, including:

(a)   whether the lead manager already has a working relationship with the issuer;

(b)   the date of the issuer's latest audited accounts;

(c)   whether the issuer has previously issued euromarket securities and, if so, how recently;

(d)   the intended market for the issue (eg, an issue involving US investors will tend to require a more detailed due diligence process, since US investors are more litigious than most!);

(e)   the term of the bond (ie, the length of time until maturity);

(f)   whether the issue is rated: an unrated issue may require more due diligence than one which is fully rated; and

(g)   whether the issue is equity linked (eg, the debt is convertible into shares).

As a general rule, the due diligence process for an issue of equity linked securities will be more 'in depth' than for a straight debt issue, since investors in the former may become shareholders in the issuer (which represents a completely different risk to a straightforward debt investment).

The due diligence process will usually involve meetings between the lead manager and its solicitors, the relevant officers of the issuer (eg, the finance director, managing director, and other officers with particular knowledge of the business), and the issuer's auditors (both internal and external). The lead manager will usually conduct the meeting by asking detailed questions of the other parties in order to obtain sufficient information to be able to proceed with the issue and to prepare the prospectus (or listing particulars). An alternative approach to due diligence is for the lead manager to draft a list of detailed questions which is sent to the issuer. However, whilst this method is less time-consuming, it is also less flexible, and is more suited to frequent issuers, with high credit ratings, where there are likely to be few or no problems with the issuer and the information memorandum (or listing particulars) will be relatively straightforward.

The due diligence process provides the material for the prospectus (or listing particulars). The lead manager may be liable for any negligent misstatement or omission in these documents, and so he has a particular interest in checking that their contents are accurate and not misleading (see **20.6**). Obtaining the comfort letters in agreed form from the issuer's auditors (see **19.3.8**) is also part of the due diligence process following analysis of the issuer's accounts.

21.5 DOCUMENTATION

The principal documentation involved in a bond issue was discussed at **19.3.1**. The preparation and negotiation of these documents is the responsibility of the lead manager's solicitors. Preparation of the contractual documentation is expedited by the fact that most of the documents required for a bond issue comply with market accepted standards (eg, the agreement among managers will almost invariably use the ICMA standard form, and will not require any input by the solicitors). If the bond issue is to be listed, a draft of the prospectus or listing particulars must be sent to the appropriate listing authority. The UKLA usually requires a period of at least 10 working days in which to review a prospectus prior to its intended publication (Prospectus Rule 3.1.3). However, early application is encouraged, and most solicitors would want the draft particulars to reach the Authority at least three weeks before publication.

Preparation of some of the documents will continue through signing, and the process is only really complete on closing when the last documents of the issue are executed. The solicitors will prepare agendas for both signing and closing, which act as checklists for the process at each stage.

21.6 MARKETING

An important role of the lead manager is to help the issuer's directors in making presentations to potential investors (these are sometimes known as 'roadshows'). The roadshows are intended to familiarise potential investors with the issuer's business and portray the issue as a good investment. The roadshow may be held in a number of different countries in order to widen the audience of potential investors, although they are not usually necessary for well-known issuers for whose securities there is usually a regular demand. Solicitors are not generally involved in the roadshow process; however, the roadshow material should be scrutinised by the solicitors and the lead manager's compliance department to ensure it complies with ss 21 and 25 of the FSMA 2000 (which put restrictions on advertising).

Sections 21–25 of the FSMA 2000 make it an offence for any person other than an 'authorised person' (ie, authorised to carry on regulated activity under the FSMA 2000) to 'in the course of business, communicate an invitation or inducement to engage in investment activity' (or to cause the same) in the UK, unless its contents have been approved by an authorised person (or an exemption applies). The prohibition is widely drafted, albeit with various exemptions.

21.7 LAUNCH AND SYNDICATION

The launch date is when the bond issue is confirmed by formal public announcement. The date will be agreed between the issuer and the lead manager. Launch must await the completion of any due diligence and marketing processes and will, so far as possible, be effected when market conditions are most favourable (eg, avoiding launches of other competing issues).

On the launch date, the issue will be announced to the market (usually through online trading screens) and the lead manager will send the invitation 'telex' (now an 'electronic' document) to the financial institutions he has chosen to invite into the syndicate (the lead manager will already have spoken to the syndicate to gauge their interest, and so the invitation is merely a formal communication). The invitation shows the 'price' of the bonds (unless it is an equity linked deal, when pricing will not be made until the date of signing of the subscription agreement) as well as the fees and commissions the syndicate banks will receive. These are sometimes referred to as the issuer's 'all in cost' of funds, although it does not include legal fees, printing costs and agency fees.

The co-managers are usually required to respond to the invitation within 24 hours of receipt. Acceptance does not constitute a binding contract to subscribe: that is the purpose of the subscription agreement. It does, however, constitute a significant 'moral' obligation on the co-managers. Once all the co-managers have responded, the lead manager will know the level of interest in the issue, and can notify each co-manager of the number of bonds it is expected to take at issue by way of an 'allotment telex'.

Once the allotment telex has been sent, the draft subscription agreement is sent to each co-manager. The ICMA recommendations allow the co-managers at least two working days in which to review the agreement before it is to be signed.

21.8 LISTING

A listed bond is one which is formally quoted, listed or capable of being traded on a recognised stock exchange. Bond issues are not always listed, either through choice or an inability to comply with the stock exchange requirements. Most listed bonds will be listed on the stock exchanges in London or in Luxembourg.

21.8.1 Reasons for listing

Unlike most share issues, bond issues are not generally listed in order to use the exchange as a marketplace. Most trading (even of listed bonds) will take place away from the exchange (known as 'over-the-counter' trading) between banks and other financial institutions by telephone or online. The primary reason for listing a bond issue is to demonstrate that it has satisfied the requirements of the exchange. Since those requirements are generally intended to protect investors, attaining listed status makes securities more marketable. Some entities, such as pension funds and unit trust funds, are precluded (by legislation, regulation or their constitution) from investing in securities which are not listed. An issue must therefore be listed to attract their funds.

One specific advantage of obtaining a London listing of bonds is the 'quoted bond exemption' from UK withholding tax. This exemption allows a UK issuer to pay gross interest on both bearer and registered bonds. A listing on a number of other stock exchanges, including Luxembourg, will also enable the securities to qualify for the same exemption.

There are two main disadvantages associated with listing an issue: cost and timing. Listing authorities will charge a fee, whilst legal fees and lead managers' fees will be considerably higher for a listed issue because of the additional time involved in a listing application (particularly for a first-time issuer).

The timetable for issuing a listed bond will usually be longer than an unlisted one (particularly with respect to new issuers), because the UKLA will require time to review the documentation of an issue and the due diligence process will often be more in-depth.

21.8.2 Listing requirements

The requirements of the UKLA for admission to listing with respect to a bond issue are found in Listing Rule 2. The Stock Exchange reserves the right to impose any special condition it considers appropriate in the interests of protecting investors. Specific requirements of most types of bond issuer include the following:

21.8.2.1   Status

The issuer is duly incorporated (or validly established) and is operating in conformity with its constitution. If the issuer is a UK incorporated company, it must not be a private company.

21.8.2.2   Securities

The main conditions relating to the securities are:

(a)   the securities must conform with the law of the issuer's place of incorporation, be authorised under the issuer's constitution, and have any necessary statutory or other consents;

(b)   the securities must be freely transferable;

(c)   the securities must have an expected aggregate market value of at least £200,000 (unless securities of the same class are already listed). The Stock Exchange will allow a lower value if it is satisfied there will be an adequate market for the securities;

(d)   the entire class of a security must be listed;

(e)   convertible securities must convert into securities which are themselves listed on the London Stock Exchange or another 'regulated, regularly operating, recognised open market'.

The London Stock Exchange also has criteria for determining whether an applicant is suitable for membership.

21.8.3   Application procedure

The application procedure for listing bond securities on the London Stock Exchange is found in Listing Rule 3, supplemented by Listing Rule 17, and in Prospectus Rule 3. The main requirements of the procedure include the following:

21.8.3.1   '10 clear business day documents'

In general, issuers (through their sponsor) must submit two copies of specified documents to the UKLA at least 10 clear business days prior to their intended publication (see Prospectus Rule 3.1.3). For a bond issue, these documents comprise the requisite application form, the prospectus (which must usually be annotated to indicate compliance with the relevant paragraphs of the Prospectus Rules), two letters (the 'non-applicable' letter and the 'omission of information' letter) explaining why certain information does not appear in the prospectus and requesting the omission of information respectively, with contact details of individuals who can answer any UKLA queries. The 10-day time limit will not strictly apply to a bond issue, although a later submission might risk a delay to the listing. The UKLA will return copies of the documents with any comments it has.

21.8.3.2   Marked-up documents

Any 10-day documents which the UKLA amends (or which are altered after submission to the UKLA) must be re-submitted with the changes marked up.

21.8.3.3   '48-hour documents'

Listing Rule 3.4.4 requires the following documents, in final form, to be submitted at least two business days prior to the consideration of the listing application:

(a)   a complete application for admission of the securities; and either:

(i)   the approved prospectus or listing particulars; or

(ii)   a copy of a prospectus approved by another Member State (under the 'passporting' regime).

21.8.3.4   Listing charge

On the day of consideration of the listing application, the issuer must pay the appropriate listing fee (Listing Rule 3.2.2).

21.8.4   Continuing obligations

The responsibilities imposed on an issuer do not end once its securities are listed. There is a variety of 'continuing obligations' which the Listing Rules and Disclosure and Transparency Rules require an issuer to fulfil, primarily with regard to disclosing financial statements.

21.9   SIGNING

A signing meeting is usually held within two weeks of the issue being launched, although it may be longer if the UKLA is slow to approve the prospectus. The signing is usually a simple meeting of the parties and their advisers, although it will occasionally be held as a more formal ceremony.

The lead manager and its solicitors must be sure that certain aspects of the issue process have been completed before the signing. Fundamentally, they must ensure that:

(a)   the prospectus (or listing particulars) is in an agreed form (and agreed by the relevant listing authority);

(b)   the other contractual documents (ie, paying agency agreement, trust deed (or fiscal agency agreement), legal opinions and auditors' comfort and consent letters) are in final form;

(c)   the issuer (and any guarantor) has executed any resolutions necessary to authorise the issue, and has appointed an authorised signatory of the global note;

(d)   the common depository has been appointed.

At the signing meeting, the subscription (or underwriting) agreement is executed by the issuer and the syndicate members, and takes contractual effect. If the issue is to be listed, final copies of the prospectus will be signed by the issuer to be sent to the UKLA. There is also a substantial number of peripheral documents to be produced and/or executed at the signing meeting, and the lead manager's solicitors will produce a signing agenda, which is distributed before the meeting, to ensure that nothing is overlooked.

21.10   CLOSING

The closing is the final stage of the issue process, and usually takes place approximately one week after signing. It is the time when the issuer receives its funds and the bonds come into being, creating the issuer's debt obligation.

The lead manager's solicitors will produce an agenda to ensure that all the necessary matters are completed. Essentially, there are two sets of procedures which must take place at closing: documentary procedures and payment procedures.

21.10.1   Documentary procedures

The following matters are the responsibility of the lead manager and its solicitors, and must be completed before the closing meeting:

(a)   Admission to listing, if relevant, must be confirmed (subject to closing) by the relevant authorities.

(b)   The conditions precedent to the subscription agreement must be satisfied.

(c)   The auditors' closing comfort letter and the issuer's closing certificate must be in agreed form.

(d)   The legal opinions must be in agreed form.

(e)   All other documents associated with the issue must be executed or in an agreed form (those that have been executed in advance will be held 'in escrow').

It is vitally important that as many of these matters as possible are dealt with before the closing date to minimise the risk of any problems. This is primarily because the lead manager and 'would be' bondholders will have ensured that funds are already in place, awaiting instructions for transfer to the issuer on a successful completion. Any delay or, worse still, cancellation of the completion will be very expensive. The closing meeting is attended by the issuer (or its solicitor if it has already executed the necessary documents), the lead manager and its solicitors, the depository, and the fiscal agent (or trustee).

By the end of the completion meeting, the following documents should be executed (some may have been executed beforehand):

(a)   Trust deed (if appropriate).

(b)   Fiscal agency agreement or paying agency agreement.

(c)   Auditors' closing comfort letter.

(d)   Legal opinions.

(e)   Issuer's closing certificate.

(f)   Payment instructions from lead manager to the depository.

(g)   The temporary global note.

(h)   The permanent global note (if any).

(i)   Receipts between issuer and lead manager acknowledging payment and delivery.

The temporary global note is authenticated (ie, signed) by the fiscal agent (or paying agent) in order to give it legal effect, and is delivered to the depository for safe-keeping.

After closing, any documents still to be lodged with the UKLA (or relevant exchange) must be sent by the listing agent; the definitive bearer bonds (if relevant) must be security printed (this may take several weeks) and authenticated before the temporary global note is exchanged for the definitive bonds (alternatively, the temporary global note is exchanged for the permanent global note), in either case only after the relevant lock-up period.

21.10.2   Payment procedures

The payment procedures, also known as the 'closing mechanics', or 'payment against delivery procedures', involve the depositary and are adopted in most bond transactions. Co-ordination of the payment procedures is the responsibility of the lead manager.

21.10.2.1   Prior to closing

The lead manager will have notified the clearing system of the names and amounts of bonds to be allotted to the account of each syndicate member. Each syndicate member will also give payment instructions to the clearing system to the effect that its cash account is to be debited with the amount of money it must pay for the bonds, and the money credited to the lead manager's new issues account. The instructions are phrased so that the debit will be made only if the syndicate member is credited with the requisite number of bonds in its securities account (payment against delivery). The lead manager will also instruct the clearing system to debit its new issues account with the total amount of the issue to be paid to the account of the common depository, who will hold it until the temporary global note has been issued and delivered (ie, payment against delivery: see **21.10.3**).

21.10.2.2   At closing

The following matters occur 'simultaneously' at closing. The lead manager will authorise release of its payment instruction to the depository to transfer the money (already placed with the depository) representing the issue amount to the issuer. The depository will then transfer that money to the issuer's bank account once it receives the temporary global note.

The closing is now complete: the issuer has its funds and the depository holds the temporary global note on behalf of the clearing system. The clearing system will have credited the securities accounts of each syndicate member with an interest in the number of bonds for which they have subscribed, and each of their respective cash accounts will have been debited with the appropriate amounts.

21.10.3   Payment against delivery

Figure 21.2 below shows the flow of payments and bonds at closing for both Euroclear and Clearstream participants.

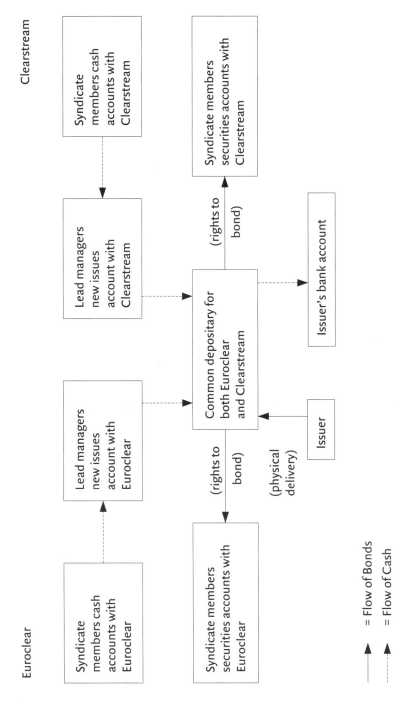

Figure 21.2 Closing procedures payment against delivery

Glossary

Acceleration	Declaring a loan due and payable before the scheduled repayment date, usually as a result of an event of default
Accordion facility	Also known as a 'trombone facility', it allows the borrower to approach some or all syndicate members after signing and request an extension of available commitment. It is uncommitted, but if the borrower persuades some banks to lend more, the other syndicate members cannot object to the increased commitment being added to the loan
Accrued interest	The interest which is being earned on a loan, bond or other security on a daily basis between two interest payment dates. Secondary dealings in securities such as bonds or notes will usually take place on an accrued interest basis so that they will be bought and sold at a price which includes the accrued interest, ie market price plus interest which has been earned on that loan, bond or note but not yet paid (sometimes known as the 'dirty price')
Advance	A utilisation of money under a loan facility (now more commonly known as a 'loan')
All in cost	The entire cost of the transaction quoted to the borrower or issuer by the lenders or lead manager, which includes fees payable to the lenders or managers. All in cost will not usually include legal costs
Alphabet facilities	A facility with different tranches of debt repayable at different times, and usually labelled 'A', 'B' and 'C' facilities
Amortisation	The repayment of a debt in stages
Ancillary facility	A bilateral facility, for example an overdraft or derivatives facility, between a borrower and one of its syndicate banks which is drawn as part of a syndicated revolving credit facility
Arbitrage	Making a profit through the small differences in price between markets, for example buying shares on the Tokyo exchange and selling them in Singapore. Usually low risk, but requires high volume to make money
Arranger	Usually, the bank or financial institution responsible for arranging a loan transaction (including the syndication)
Asset backed security	A security which has its interest and capital repayments provided by a generic group of assets (eg, mortgages) which produce income (aka securitisation)
Asset stripping	Acquiring a business with a view to breaking it up and selling the most lucrative parts rather than developing it (euphemistically: 'rationalisation')
Authentication	In securities issues, the physical signing by the fiscal agent or principal paying agent of a security (eg, bond or note) in order to give it legal effect
Authorised institution	Under the provisions of the Financial Services and Markets Act 2000, in the UK only 'authorised institutions', as defined in the Act, may accept deposits in the course of a deposit-taking business

Availability period	The time during which a borrower may draw down (or 'utilise') advances under a loan (also known as 'commitment period')
Back office	The various 'non-profit centre' operational departments of a bank or financial institution which deal with the 'behind the scenes' activities of the organisation (eg, the settlement and accounts departments). 'Front office' activities include trading and lending
Balloon repayment	A final repayment of principal on a loan transaction which is substantially larger than earlier repayment instalments
Bankers' acceptance	A bill of exchange, drawn on and accepted by a bank. By accepting the bill of exchange the bank is accepting full liability to pay the bill on maturity as the primary obligor
Base rate	A fluctuating interest rate, peculiar to individual banks and used by them as a reference point for lending rates to individuals
Basis point	One hundredth of one percentage point (eg, 45 basis points is 0.45%)
Basis rate	The rate used as a basis for calculation of interest under a commercial loan transaction (eg, Libor)
bbalibor	See Libor
Bells and whistles	Additional features of a debt transaction which are designed to attract investors
Bible	Complete set of conformed copy documents relating to a particular transaction
Bilateral facility	A loan facility between one bank and one borrower
Bill of exchange	A form of short-term IOU widely used to finance trade and provide credit
Bona fide	In good faith. A bona fide purchaser is one who believes he is entitled to buy, and the seller is entitled to sell
Book loss or gain	The difference between the original cost or book value of a security and its current market value (excluding accrued interest), ie an unrealised loss or gain
Book runner	The institution responsible for the syndication, documentation, distribution, payment and delivery of a new market issue of securities (or loan facility)
Brady bond	Paper issued in exchange for distressed commercial bank debt (particularly emerging market countries)
Bridge financing	Interim financing used before the intended long-term financing is put in place
Broker	A person or institution acting as an agent for buyers and/or sellers and charging a commission for his services, but who does not buy for his own account
Bullet repayment	Repayment of a debt obligation in a single instalment at the maturity date of the debt (ie, no amortisation)
Business day	A day on which banks are open for business in the relevant financial centre

Call option	In relation to a bond or note issue, a term which gives the issuer the right, but not the obligation, to redeem its securities before their specified maturity, normally at a specified price on a specified or determinable date. A premium may be payable on the exercise of the call option (cf 'put option')
Carve out	An exception to a representation or undertaking
Certificate of deposit	A negotiable bearer instrument evidencing a time deposit with a commercial bank, either interest-bearing or issued at a discount
Chinese wall	An artificial barrier restricting communication between different areas within an organisation, allowing them to act for parties who may have conflicting interests. The concept originated in securities houses, but is commonly used within large firms of solicitors (aka an 'ethical wall' or 'information barrier' – particularly in institutions with Chinese clients)
Clawback clause	A clause enabling one party to retrieve money already paid out. Often found in the agency provisions of syndicated facility agreements enabling an agent to recover money already paid out by it to a party, wrongly believing that the agent had received the corresponding payment from another party. This allows an agent to distribute money (eg, repayment instalments) to the bank syndicate without confirming receipt of the payment from the borrower, knowing that if he does not receive the monies from the borrower he may 'clawback' the monies paid out to the syndicate
Clean down	A requirement for the borrower to reduce its drawing under a revolving credit facility to zero (or a specified reduced amount) for a given period (eg, five days in every year) to demonstrate it is not being used for capital expenditure
Clean-up period	The period (commonly 90 days) after an acquisition during which the new owners are allowed to remedy any events of default without the banks taking action
Clearing system	An organisation through which purchase and sale transactions of securities are handled and cleared. The main systems in the euromarkets for bonds and notes are Euroclear and Clearstream
Club loan	A facility provided by a small number of banks taking a similar level of commitment
Collateral	The assets over which security is granted
Commercial paper	Very short-term debt securities (eg, between a week and a few months' maturity) issued under a programme typically by borrowers requiring working capital funding
Commitment	The specified amount of money agreed to be lent by a bank in a 'committed facility', or agreed to be invested by a manager in a bond or note issue
Commitment fee	An annual percentage fee payable to a bank on the undrawn portion of its 'commitment' under a 'committed facility'. The commitment fee is usually paid quarterly in arrear
Commitment period	See 'Availability period'
Committed facility	A financing or credit arrangement in which a bank is obliged to lend up to a certain agreed limit of money for a defined period of time, usually subject to a predetermined set of conditions

Conformed copy	A record copy of a final executed document in which all signatures and any other handwritten words (eg, dates or alterations) are printed in typed form. Conformed copies are used to make up the transaction 'bible'
Coupon	Refers to both the stated rate of interest on a bond or note, and also to one of a series of actual coupon certificates attached to a bond or note, evidencing interest payable at a specified date
Credit default swap (CDS)	A derivative used to hedge risk against default of an entity ('reference entity') or specific lending obligation (the 'reference obligation'). Essentially, the buyer pays a premium to the seller of the CDS to buy protection against loss on default. If the entity or obligation defaults, the seller will pay the buyer the par value of the defaulted obligation (usually a loan or bond): in return the buyer usually has to transfer the obligation in question to the CDS seller to recover what it can
Cross default	An event of default triggered by a default in the payment, or the potential acceleration of repayment, of other indebtedness of the same borrower or issuer
Data room	A place in which information about a target company up for sale can be viewed by potential purchasers. It may be a room at the vendor's solicitor, or may be a 'virtual' room online
Debt push down	Usually refers to moving debt around a group of companies (typically from parent companies down to operating companies) to maximise tax advantages. For example, an operating company making profits can use interest payments to reduce its corporation tax, whereas a holding company earning only dividends cannot
Deep discount securities	Non-interest bearing securities issued at a large discount to their face value
Dematerialised	Usually referring to securities which are not represented by physical certificates but are traded through an electronic exchange
Derivatives	Financial instruments that derive their value from underlying financial products and markets such as interest rates, exchange rates, share prices, etc (examples include options, futures, swaps)
Discount	The difference between the price of a security and its face value
Distressed debt	Debt which is, or which the lender believes will be, non-performing (ie, repaid late, partially, or not at all) and which is usually sold for substantially less than the value of principal outstanding ('below par')
Double dipping	A means of structuring finance leases to utilise the tax benefits on capital investments in more than one jurisdiction
Double taxation treaty	An agreement between two countries intended to limit the double taxation of income and gains, under the terms of which an investor in one country may be able to apply for an exemption or reduction in the taxes imposed on his income or gains by another country, or from his own country on the basis that such income or gains have already had tax levied on them. This type of treaty encourages trade and financial transactions between countries
Drag along	Usually refers to certain investors being forced to accept something if a percentage of other (usually higher ranking) investors voted in favour
Drawdown	See 'Utilisation'

Drawstop	An event under a loan facility which prevents a borrower from utilising the loan
Earn out	In an acquisition finance, where the purchase price for the acquisition varies in accordance with the performance of the business post acquisition
Eligible bill	A banker's acceptance which can be re-discounted at (ie, sold to) the Bank of England
Emerging market	A jurisdiction in which the debt and capital markets are new or developing areas (often 'developing' countries) (see also 'LDC')
Equity cure	In an acquisition financing, the ability of the private equity 'owners' to put cash into the borrower which is treated as reducing debt or increasing profit (or cashflow) to 'cure' what would otherwise be a breach of financial covenants
Equity kicker	A warrant or option to buy, or exchange, debt for equity and which is attached to certain debt instruments (generally found in leveraged management buy-outs)
Equity of redemption	A mortgagor's right to reclaim mortgaged assets on repayment of the secured debt with interest and costs
Escrow arrangement	Documents held 'in escrow' are executed documents given by one executing party to a third party (usually a solicitor) to hold to its order until a certain condition is satisfied, or event occurs. On the satisfaction of such condition or occurrence of event, the third party will usually be obliged to release the documents out of escrow to the other executing party
Exploding bridge	A facility in which the interest rate increases dramatically after a given period to act as an incentive to the borrower to refinance the facility
Face value	The nominal or par value of a security, rather than its market value at any particular time. It will be the amount due to the holder of the security on its maturity but exclusive of any interest or premium
Facility office	The branch or office of a bank through which the funds for a facility are provided. Also known as the 'lending office'
FCA	The Financial Conduct Authority is one of three new bodies (see also FPC and PRA) which will take certain regulatory functions from the Financial Services Authority by 2013. The FCA will have responsibility for conduct issues across the financial services industry.
Finance lease	A means of financing whereby one lessee acquires the use of an asset for most of its useful life (eg, an aircraft). Lease payments during the life of the lease are sufficient to enable the lessor to recover the cost of the asset, plus a return. The lessee takes the risks and rewards of ownership (so, eg, is responsible for insuring the asset), and may acquire the asset at the end of the lease
Finance vehicle	A subsidiary company, usually incorporated 'offshore', for use by its parent company for issuing debt securities and then 'on lending' the proceeds to the parent or other companies in the group. The finance vehicle (aka 'special purpose vehicle') will be used only for these purposes and is unlikely to have any assets of its own. The issue of securities by a finance vehicle will therefore have to be guaranteed (usually by the parent company)

Foreclosure	Forfeiture of a mortgagor's equity of redemption due to default in payment (of principal or interest)
FPC	The Financial Policy Committee is one of three new bodies (see also FCA and PRA) which will take certain regulatory functions from the Financial Services Authority by 2013. The FPC will be established in the Bank of England with responsibility for macro prudential regulation.
Front end fee	A fee calculated as a percentage of the principal value of a loan or issue of securities, which is payable once at commencement of the loan or at issue of the securities, as opposed to an annual percentage fee payable each year (also known as 'arrangement fee')
Front running	A practice, usually prohibited in the commitment letter, in which an arranger sells part of its commitment outside of the normal process during primary syndication, thereby achieving an advantage over other arrangers in the syndicate
FSA	Financial Services Authority
FSMA 2000	The Financial Services and Markets Act 2000
Fungibility	An object is said to be 'fungible' if it can be replaced by another object and still fulfil any obligation to which it is subject. Fungible objects are therefore described by weight, quantity or value, rather than specific description (the most common example is cash)
Fungible securities	Securities of the same issue, which are kept in the clearing system where the book-keeping is such that no specific securities are assigned to customer accounts by their serial numbers
Gilts	Securities issued by the British Government
Governing law	The jurisdiction to which the terms and conditions of transaction are subject
Grace period	The period of time given to a borrower or issuer in which it is allowed to remedy an event of default
Grey market	The 'market' in a new security issue, among financial institutions, which commences on the launch of a new issue (ie, before it is available to trade to the 'public') and ends when the securities are formally available at closing of the issue
Gross-up	A borrower/issuer may be required to gross-up payments it has to make to the lenders/investors, meaning it must make additional payments to compensate for withholding taxes, or similar deductions, which would otherwise reduce the amounts actually received by the lenders/investors
Headroom	Refers to the difference between a borrower's projected performance (eg, in its business plan) and the lower targets set for it to attain under its financial covenants
Hedge fund	A fund which is allowed to take relatively high-risk and 'innovative' positions with investors' money, agreeing to sell shares they do not yet own ('shorting' shares). The ethos behind hedge funds is to 'make good money in good markets but not lose money in down-turns'

Hedging	An activity employed by financial institutions or corporate treasurers to protect against loss due to market fluctuation in certain investments held by that organisation. Hedging is usually performed by counterbalancing a current sale or purchase of an investment by another future sale or purchase. The aim is to ensure that any loss on the current sale is offset by the profit on the future sale
High yield bonds	A bond (or note) with a low grade credit rating (ie, below investment grade), and which must therefore yield a higher rate of interest (or substantial discount) to attract investors
Hive down	Refers to the transfer of assets from a parent down to one or more of its subsidiaries ('hive up' is the opposite)
ICMA	The International Capital Markets Association, the regulatory body in the bond market, formed in July 2005 by the merger of the International Primary Markets Association (IPMA) and the International Securities Markets Association (ISMA)
Information memorandum	A document produced by the borrower and arranger of a syndicated facility to inform potential participants about the deal
Infrastructure finance	Providing finance for the acquisition of 'infrastructure' assets or businesses such as water, gas or electricity suppliers, ports, airports, telecommunications, windfarms, and transport franchises.
Interim facility	A short-form loan agreement, usually lasting only 30 days, which allows the bidder in an acquisition finance to demonstrate that it has immediate funds with which to purchase the target. The short-form facility is really just a negotiating tool to show serious intention to bid and to move quickly, and is often not utilised; the intention is to negotiate the usual 'long-form' loan documents to replace the short-form facility before it expires
IPO	'Initial Public Offering', ie the first ever issue of (usually equity) securities by a particular entity
Issuing house	The financial institution which organises and arranges the issue of new securities, also known as the 'lead manager'
Judgment currency indemnity	An indemnity sometimes included in credit facilities to protect the lenders against losses they may suffer if judgment is obtained against the borrower in a currency different to that in which the facility is denominated
LDC (Less Developed Country)	A common term for third world countries, primarily used to describe the debt of those countries, ie 'LDC debt' (see also 'Emerging market')
Lending office	See 'facility office'
Letter of credit	A written undertaking by a bank (the issuing bank) given at the request of, and in accordance with, the instructions of the applicant (the buyer) to the beneficiary (the seller), to effect a payment up to a stated amount of money, within a prescribed time limit, and usually against the production of stipulated documents
Libid (London Interbank Bid Rate)	The rate of interest quoted by banks operating in the London Interbank Market at which they are willing to borrow money (ie, bid for deposits in a particular currency)

Libor (London Interbank Offered Rate)	The rate of interest quoted by banks in the London Interbank Market at which they are willing to lend money, ie offer deposits in a particular currency. Note that 'bbalibor' is an average rate calculated for the BBA by asking a panel of banks to submit rates based on the question, 'At what rate could you borrow funds, were you to do so by asking for and then accepting interbank offers in a reasonable market size just prior to 11 am?'. The bbalibor rate is therefore closer to Libid than true Libor (see also **4.9.3**).
London Approach	Guidelines issued by the Bank of England encouraging support for troubled debtors rather than sale of distressed debt
London Code of Conduct	Published by the Bank of England: a guide to best practice in the wholesale money markets in London
London Stock Exchange	The London Stock Exchange plc (which trades as 'the London Stock Exchange') is the international stock exchange for the UK, but not the Republic of Ireland
Management buy-in (MBI)	The purchase of a business by 'external' managers. As with MBOs, most of the funding is from outside investors
Management buy-out (MBO)	The purchase of a business by its management (and sometimes employees). The managers invest a small amount of money, but most of the finance is provided by outside investors such as venture capitalists
Mandate	The authorisation from a borrower or issuer to his chosen arranger or lead manager to conduct the relevant transaction on the agreed terms. Usually given in the form of a letter signed by both parties
Margin	(a) in relation to floating interest rates, the rate of interest charged by the bank over and above the relevant cost of funding, such as Libor; (b) in relation to some financial markets (eg, the futures market), a deposit required to be paid by members of the relevant exchange for each transaction they carry out; (c) 'margin lending' is where the loan amount is of a lesser value than the amount of collateral given for the loan
Market flex	A term written into a commitment letter allowing the arranger unilaterally to change the terms of a facility if it cannot successfully syndicate
Matched funding	The process of matching a loan (asset) with a deposit (liability) of the same maturity
Maturity	The date upon which a debt is finally repayable
Mezzanine finance or debt	Usually high interest-bearing debt, where the lender receives little, if any, form of security for its loan and which ranks behind the 'senior debtors' so far as repayment is concerned. It is sometimes seen as halfway between debt and equity in terms of risk and reward
Monolines	Companies which provide a guarantee of debt securities issued by lower-rated issuers in return for an insurance premium. This 'monoline insurance' or 'wrap' can raise an issue rating from 'A' to 'AAA', so attracting more investors and reducing coupon for the issuer
New Global Note structure	A structure which requires global notes to be held by clearing systems (and not a common depository) to ensure they are eligible as collateral in the euro central banking system ('Eurosystem')

Non-recourse	A non-recourse loan is one with no comeback (or recourse) to a guarantor or parent company of the borrower. Non-recourse loans are usually used to finance a special project or purpose over which they are secured
Note	A widely used alternative label for 'bond' – see **17.5**
Off balance sheet liabilities	Obligations of a company which do not appear on its balance sheet. These can be of concern for lenders since they disguise the extent of the commitments entered into by a company
Opco/Propco finance	A finance technique in which an existing business puts ownership of its real property (ie, land and buildings) into one SPV (the 'Propco') and its operating assets into another (the 'Opco'). The Propco can raise finance for the business on very favourable terms because it only owns land, whilst the Opco leases the real property back from the Propco so that the business keeps trading
Option	The right, but not the obligation, to buy or sell an instrument at a specified price and up to a specified time in the future
Over-the-counter (OTC)	The purchase and sale of securities and other financial instruments which take place away from any stock exchange or other official financial exchange (eg, futures exchange). The eurobond secondary market is predominantly an over-the-counter market, irrespective of the fact that some of the securities traded will actually be listed on a stock exchange
Paper	Colloquially, securities such as bonds, notes, certificates of deposits and commercial paper
Par	The principal amount (the initial issue price) at which an issuer agrees to redeem its securities on their maturity (see also 'face value')
Parallel debt	A structure used in jurisdictions that do not recognise a security trustee. A parallel debt provision provides for a security agent to be owed an equivalent sum to that due under a loan facility (ie, two 'parallel' debts). This allows the security agent to hold security for the full amount of the loan. As the facility debt is repaid, the security agent debt is reduced 'in parallel' (and vice versa), so that the borrower only repays one debt.
Pari passu	Equally and without preference
Perpetual bonds or notes	Bonds or notes which have no scheduled maturity date and therefore are redeemable only under any call option that the issuer may have under their terms and conditions. Events of default in such issues will be very basic and will give rise to a winding-up procedure and not to redemption
PIK	Payment in kind, usually referring to a facility in which the borrower can roll-up interest and add it to principal to be paid when the loan matures (cf 'cash pay' where interest is paid as it falls due). May be found in mezzanine facilities for acquisition finance
Plain vanilla	A colloquial term used to describe securities or loan facilities with no additional features such as warrants, call options, multi-options, etc

PRA	The Prudential Regulation Authority is one three new bodies (see also FPC and FPC) which will take certain regulatory functions from the Financial Services Authority by 2013. The PRA will be established as a subsidiary of the Bank of England and be responsible for prudential regulation.
Private equity	A private equity house (also referred to as the 'sponsors', 'venture capital', 'equity' or the 'investors') is an organisation that creates funds by raising money from institutions, banks and high net worth individuals to invest in the acquisition of other companies or groups.
Private placement	An offer of securities made to a limited and prearranged number of investors
Professional Securities Market (PSM)	The PSM is a market created by the London Stock Exchange in July 2005 to enable companies to raise capital by issuing securities to professional or institutional investors. The key feature of the PSM is that it is 'unregulated' or, more precisely, 'exchange regulated' and so has a very flexible regulatory regime (eg, no requirement to report under IFRS, no restrictions on type or value of securities, etc).
Project finance	The financing of a specific project (eg, building a power station or toll road), the revenue from which will provide the lenders with repayment of their investment. The project also provides security for the lenders
Promissory note	An unconditional promise in writing, signed by the debtor, undertaking to pay a specific sum on demand, or at a fixed or determinable date in the future
Purple Book	Colloquial name for the old rules of the Financial Services Authority relating to listing on the London Stock Exchange. Now replaced by the Prospectus Rules, Listing Rules and Disclosure Rules
Put option	If contained within a bond or note issue, it will give the holder of the securities the right to call for an early redemption of the securities prior to their scheduled maturity (cf 'call option')
Redemption	The repurchase or repayment by an issuer (or borrower) of outstanding securities (or loans), in accordance with their terms, with the effect of extinguishing the outstanding debt
Repurchase agreements ('repos')	In capital markets, repos entail two simultaneous transactions: the purchase of securities (the 'collateral') by an investor from a bank or dealer; and the commitment by that bank or dealer to repurchase the securities at a specified higher price (or the same price with charges) on a specified future date (or on call). Repos are primarily used as a means of short-term funding and are governed by market standard terms and conditions
Rescheduling	In relation to debt obligations, the renegotiation and agreement of revised terms of a loan facility (usually involving the spreading of interest and capital repayments over a longer period) as a result of the borrower being unable to comply with the original terms
Reuters screen	A telecommunications system, subscribed to by banks and financial institutions, which provides regularly updated financial information relevant to banking and securities trading
Reverse flex	A clause in commitment documents for a loan that requires the arranger to push for lower pricing if the loan appears oversubscribed during syndication. The arranger is usually incentivised by taking a share of any cost saving

RIS	Regulatory Information Services: companies which provide information services to the capital markets and have been approved by the FSA Listing Rules as a vehicle for members to make announcements (see Listing Rules, Appendix 3 for a list of RISs)
Rollover	The renewal of a loan which has become repayable under a revolving credit loan facility
SEC (the Securities and Exchange Commission)	The US Federal Government agency charged with overseeing the US domestic securities market
Secondary market	The trading of securities which are already issued
Settlement	The process of clearing the paperwork involved in trading securities: ensuring the purchaser receives its securities and the seller its money. Purchases and sales must be reconciled between the different financial institutions involved in the trades. Settlement is dealt with by an institution's 'back office'
SPA	'Sale and purchase agreement' or 'share purchase agreement': the contract governing the acquisition of the target in an acquisition finance
Spread	Generally, the difference between two prices, but the term has other meanings in specific contexts
Standby letter of credit	A letter of credit issued by a bank as a form of guarantee. A beneficiary of arrangement will be able to make a drawing on the letter of credit merely by providing a certificate of non-payment of the underlying debt
Stapled financing	In an acquisition finance, where the bank advisers to the vendor offer a loan package to potential bidders for acquiring the target (the loan terms are 'stapled' to the back of the information memorandum relating to the target)
Stock lending	A transfer of securities from 'lender' to 'borrower' to meet a pre-existing contract of the borrower to sell securities. The 'loan' requires the borrower to replace the securities in due course, and cash collateral of 102–105% of the securities' value is usually taken
Structured finance	A financial structure specifically designed for a particular borrower
Subordination	A creditor is subordinated if its claim against the borrower ranks behind one or more other creditrs on insolvency. Subordination can be achieved by way of taking security, by contractual arrangements or by debt structuring (ie, lending at different levels of company within a group of companies) or a combination of all three
Swap	The exchange of one product for another, usually currencies, interest streams, or securities
T bill (Treasury bill)	A security issued by the US Government
Ticking fee	A fee to cover an arranger's commitment costs, and payable from when the arrangers underwrite a loan to when the loan documentation is signed
Toggle facility	Allows a borrower to chose whether to pay interest as it falls due, or roll it up and add it to the capital repayment ('payment in kind')

Tombstone	An announcement, usually placed in the financial press such as the *Financial Times*, made by either the borrower/issuer or the banks/lead manager, and announcing an issue of securities or provision of a loan facility. Tombstones are not intended as an advertisement to entice prospective purchasers, they simply contain a brief description of the issue or facility and a list of the participating banks or managers. The names of these banks or managers appear as a vertically presented list, hence the name 'tombstone'
UK Listing Authority (UKLA)	The colloquial name for the division of the Financial Services Authority responsible for admission of securities to listing
Undertaking (of a company)	All of a company's present and future assets
Utilisation	The borrowing of money under a loan facility (sometimes known as 'drawdown')
Withholding tax	A tax deducted at source on certain payments (usually interest or dividend payments)
Workout	Common term for the long-term rescue of a defaulting borrower by its bank(s) (and other creditors)
Zero coupon bond/ note	A non-interest bearing bond or note issued at a discount to its face value

Bibliography

Commercial lending

There are few, if any, books dedicated to the documentation of facility agreements; however, the following books address many of the legal issues that loan documentation raises:

Geoffrey Fuller, *Corporate Borrowing: Law and Practice* (4th edn, Jordans, 2009)

A good technical review of certain aspects of corporate borrowing.

Philip Wood, *Law and Practice of International Finance* (Sweet & Maxwell, 1995)

This is a series of 6 volumes, of which the most relevant are *Comparative Law of Securities and Guarantees, Comparative Financial Law* and *International Loan, Bonds and Securities Regulations*.

Security

Richard Calnan, *Taking Security: Law and Practice* (2nd edn, Jordans, 2011)

An exceptionally well written and thorough review of security issues: if you only read one book on security, make it this one.

Goode, *Commercial Law* (4th edn, Penguin, 2009)

Professor Goode's well-known book covers a number of aspects of taking security, as well as being an invaluable reference work for general commercial practice.

Goode, *Legal Problems of Credit and Security* (4th edn, Sweet & Maxwell, 2008)

A surprisingly readable collection of Professor Goode's lectures which covers a number of basic security issues in some depth.

Ellinger and Lomnicka, *Modern Banking Law* (5th edn, Oxford University Press, 2011)

Particularly useful review of secured lending.

Capital markets

Geoffrey Fuller, *The Law and Practice of International Capital Markets* (2nd edn, Butterworths, 2009)

A very useful text: *the* book for capital markets lawyers.

Dr Joanna Benjamin, *Interests in Securities: A Proprietary Law Analysis of the International Securities Markets* (Oxford University Press, 2000)

Stephen Valdez, *An Introduction to Global Financial Markets* (6th edn, Macmillan, 2010)

This is an excellent introduction to many different areas of banking and capital markets. Readable and informative.

General

Christopher Stoakes, *All you need to know about the City* (3rd edn, Longtail Publishing Limited)

A witty and readable demystification of the markets, players and products in the City of London. A very useful jargon-buster.

Michael Brett, *How to Read the Financial Papers* (5th edn, Century Business, 2003)

An unbeatable guide to jargon and concepts of the City in general and the financial world in particular. Aimed at laymen not lawyers, but contains very clear explanations and examples.

Michael Lewis, *Liar's Poker* (Coronet, 1999)

This is the story of the author's training and trading at the investment bank Salamon Brothers. The first half of this book is an hilarious account of investment banking; the second half is drier and more informative, but by this time you will be hooked. (Worth reading just to find out how to play 'liar's poker'.)

Index

364 day facilities 23
accepting houses 5
account officer 12–13
accounting principles
  representations 52
accounting regulations
  Companies Act 2006 71
  FRSs 72
  harmonisation 72
  IFRS 72
  legal effect 72
  small and medium-sized companies 71–2
  SSAPs 72
  summary accounts 73
  UK listing rules 72
Accounting Standards Board 72
Accounting Standards Committee 72
accounts
  company see company accounts
  groups see consolidated accounts
  regulations see accounting regulations
administration
  administrator appointment 188
  enforcement of security 160–2
administration expenses 100
administrative agent
  party to loan agreement 34
  syndicated facilities 24–5
administrative receivership
  enforcement of security 160–2
  receiver appointment 188
agents
  fiscal agent 224, 226, 231
  listing agent 226
  paying agent 226, 231
  principal paying agent 226
agent's fees 110
aircraft
  registration of security 173
amendments 111–12
amortisation 21
annual accounts 60
Area Credit Officer 13
arranger
  liability 25–6
  party to loan agreement 34
  syndicated facilities 24, 25–6
asset protection undertakings 83–6
  access to information and assistance 84
  acquisitions 85
  auditors 86
  cash collateralisation 84
  consents 83
  depositing money 84
  disposals 85
  dividends 85–6
  insurance 83

asset protection undertakings – continued
  lending 85
  licences 83
  liens 84
  negative pledge 84–5
  negative undertakings 84–6
  pari passu ranking 85
  positive undertakings 83–4
  securitisation 84
  shares 85–6
assets
  covenants protecting see asset protection undertakings
  current 61
  fixed 61
  giving rights over see security
  grouping 61–2
  intangible 79
  ordering 62–3
  restrictions on disposal 64
  unaudited revaluation 79
assignment
  equitable see equitable assignment
  legal see legal assignment
  priority of security between 174
  security 152
  statutory 152
Association of Corporate Treasurers 136
auditors
  eurobonds 227, 230
  negative undertakings 86
  qualification of accounts 69, 94
auditor's report 60
  eurobond issue 230
  qualifications 94
authority 37–9
  actual 37–8
  apparent 38
  ostensible 38

balance sheet 60
  assets
    current 61
    fixed 61
    grouping of 61–2
    restrictions on disposal 64
  bank's 62
  capital 63–4
  content 60–1
  depreciation 65
  IFRS requirement 65
  liabilities
    current 62
    long-term 62
    ordering of 62–3
  provisions 65
  reserves 63–4
  revaluation 64–5

balance sheet – *continued*
   sale of loan 122
   'snapshot' 65
   subsidiary undertakings 70
balloon repayment 21
Bank of England 6, 105
banks
   accepting houses 5
   balance sheet 62
   central banks 6
   commercial banks 4–5
   deregulation 5
   investment banks 5
   merchant banks 5
   ring-fencing 5
   syndicated facilities
      advantages to role 25
      tombstones 25, 30–1
   universal banks 5
Basel Committee 102–3, 104
basis points 47
bbalibor 43–4
bearer bonds 217–18
   anonymity 220
   claims of issuer 220
   clearing system
      Clearstream 221
      depository 222
      Euroclear 221
      investor 222
      participant 222
      safekeeping 222
   coupons 218
   priority 220
   promise to pay 218
   registered bonds compared 219–20
   talons 218
   terms and conditions 218
   title 220
   transfer 220
'bells and whistles' loans 19
bills of exchange 27, 209
'blue-pencil test' 111
'boiler plate' 102
bonds 4
   anonymity 220
   bearer bonds 217–18
      anonymity 220
      claims of issuer 220
      in clearing system 221–2
      priority 220
      registered compared 219–20
      title 220
      transfer 220
   claims and defences of issuer 220
   convertible 206
   definitive form 217–18
   description 203–4
   equity linked 206–7
   eurobonds *see* **eurobonds**
   exchangeable 207
   fixed rate 204
   floating rate notes 204–5

bonds – *continued*
    interest 204–5
    matched funding 204–5
    reverse 205
   form 215
    definitive form 217–18
    permanent global form 217
    temporary global form 216–17
   holder in due course 219
   issuer 212, 223
    claims and defences 220
   negotiability 219
    by mercantile custom 219
    by statute 219
    consequences 219
   permanent global bond 217
   priorities 220
   registered bonds 218
    anonymity 220
    bearer bonds compared 219–20
    claim of issuer 220
    priority 220
    transfer 220
   step-up or step-down 205
   temporary global bond 216–17
    meaning 216
    selling restrictions 216–17
    time constraints 216
    use 216–17
   title 220
   transfer 220
   transferability 218
   variable rate bonds 205
    cap 205
    collars 205
    floor 205
   with warrants 207
   zero coupon 205–6
book debts 185–6
borrower transfers 131
borrowers
   companies 2, 3–4
   governments 2
   local authorities 2
   municipalities 2
   partnerships 2
   sole traders 2
   supranational organisations 2
borrowing
   capital instruments 80
   deferred purchase agreements 80
   finance leases 80
   financial covenants 79–80
   guarantees *see* **guarantees**
   indemnities 80, 155–6
   instalment credit agreements 80
breach of condition 89
breach of intermediate term 89
breach of undertaking 91
breach of warranties 89
bullet repayment 21

call protection 118

cancellation
    fee 110
    of payment 102
cap 205
capacity
    to enter agreement
        position pre-CA 1989 36–7
        position post-CA 1989 37
        position post-CA 2006 37
        ultra vires transaction 36, 37
    to provide security 179
capital
    adequacy 102–5
    in balance sheet 63–4
    investment see capital markets
    realisation by sale of loan 121
    regulatory capital 102–5
    retained profit 64
    share capital 64
capital instruments 80
capital markets
    bills of exchange 209
    bonds see bonds
    certificates of deposit 208
    clearing system
        bearer bonds in 221–2
        bridge 211
        Clearstream 210–11, 221
        Common Code 211
        depository 222
        Euroclear 210–11, 221
        investor 222
        ISIN 211
        meaning 210
        operation of 211
        participant 222
        safekeeping 222
    commercial paper 207–8
    credit rating 212–14
        Moody 213
        Standard and Poor 213
    debt securities 200, 203
    domestic 200–1
    equity securities 203
    'Euro' 201
    eurobonds see eurobonds
    eurocurrencies 201
        use 201
    Euromarkets 201–2
    eurosecurities 201
    'foreign' securities 202
    illiquid 199
    International Capital Markets Association 211–12
    investment capital 199–200
    issuer 212, 223
        claims and defences 220
    loan facilities compared 200
    medium term notes 207
    primary market 210
    secondary market 210
    settlement see clearing system
    traders 210
    treasury bills 209

capital markets instruments 3–4
cash
    debentures 184–5
cash flow statements 60, 69
casino banking 5
central banks 6
certificates of deposit (CDs) 4, 208
charge
    fixed see fixed charges
    floating see floating charges
    meaning 152
choses in action 187
Clayton's case, rule in 157, 176–7
'clean-down' provision 20, 23
clear market 15
Clearing system
    bearer bonds 221–2
    bridge 211
    Clearstream 210–11, 221
    Common Code 211
    depository 222
    Euroclear 210–11, 221
    investor 222
    ISIN 211
    meaning 210
    operation of 211
    participant 222
    safekeeping 222
Clearstream 210–11, 221
cold-calling 12
collar 205
combination, banker's right of 160
comfort letters
    common intention 158
    eurobond issue 230
    jurisdictions 158
    legal effect 158
    quasi-security 158
    wording 158
commercial banks 4–5
commercial paper 4, 27, 207–8
commitment fee 110
commitment letter 14, 15, 16
    clear market 15
    market flex 15
    negotiation in good faith 16–17
commitment period 102
common depository 226–7
common law
    crystallisation of floating charge 147–8
    governing law 112–13
companies
    borrowers 2, 3–4
    capital markets instruments 3–4
    financing 2, 3–4
    gearing 3
    leverage 3, 77–8
    loan facilities 3
    retained profit 3
    share capital 3
    term loans 3, 20–2
company accounts
    assets

company accounts – *continued*
current 61
fixed 61
ordering 62–3
restrictions on disposal 64
auditor's report 60
balance sheet *see* **balance sheet**
capital 63–4
retained profit 64
share capital 64
cash flow statements 69
consolidated 69–70
cost of sales 67–8
depreciation 65
directors report 60, 68–9
dividends 68
extraordinary and exceptional items 68
financial statements 59–60
groups 69–70
liabilities
current 62
long-term 62
ordering 62–3
listed companies 72
manufacturing account 66
medium-sized companies 71–2
net profits 68
profit and loss account *see* **profit and loss account**
provisions 65
reserves 63–4
retained profits 68
revaluation 64–5
small companies 71–2
trading account 66
turnover 67
see also **accounting regulations**
concessions 79
conditions
remedies for breach 89
conditions precedent
bank's perspective 41
borrower's perspective 41
documentary 40–1
loan agreement 39–41
purpose 39
time limits 40
uncertainty 40
confidentiality letter 18
connected person
floating charge to 149
consent letter
eurobond issue 230
consolidated accounts
subsidiaries 69–70
contract
eurobond listing particulars 247
Rome Convention 113
set-off 159
contractual subordination
priority of security and 174
typical arrangement 174–5
use of 175

convertible securities
bonds 206
copyright 79
corporation tax 106
costs
fees *see* **fees**
increased 104–5
mandatory 105
security 162
see also **expenses**
counterparts 117–18
coupons
bearer bonds 218
eurobonds 234
replacement 235
covenants
defaults 91
financial
borrowing 80
capital expenditure 79–80
equity cure 81
examples 77–80
form 77
goodwill 79
incurrence 77
intangible assets 79
limits 77, 79–80
maintenance 77
meaning 76–7
minimum net worth 79
payments on account 79
ratios *see* **ratios**
research and development costs 79
tax provision 79
unaudited revaluation 79
see also **undertakings**
credit analysis 13
material adverse change 13, 15
credit clearance 13
credit rating
capital markets 212–14
Moody 213
Standard and Poor 213
credit risk 12
cross guarantees 140
cross-default clause 13

damages
misrepresentation remedy 57
debentures 35, 152
administrative provisions 188
administrative receiver appointment 188
administrator appointment 188
book debts 185–6
cash 184–5
charging clause 184–7
choses in action 187
collection of debts 188
crystallisation clause 188
execution by deed 189
further assurance clause 187
goodwill 185
land 184

debentures – *continued*
   negative pledge 187
   payment on demand 183–4
   plant and machinery 184
   power of attorney 188
   receiver appointment 188
   redemption of security 188
   shares 186–7
   stock in trade 187
   structure 183–8
   undertakings 187
      covenant to pay 183–4
debt securities 4, 203
   loan facilities compared 200
   see also **bonds**
debts
   distressed 130
   impaired 130
default
   action on 95–6
   breach of condition 89
   breach of covenant 91
   breach of intermediate term 89
   breach of undertaking 91
   breach of warranties 89
   cross-default 91–2
      into subsidiaries 92
   events of *see* **events of default**
   grace periods 96
   notification undertakings 83
   potential 96
   remedies 89
default interest 47
defaulting lender provisions 115–16
deferred purchase agreements 80
depository
   bonds 222
   eurobonds 226–7
depreciation
   balance sheet 65
directors' report 60, 68–9
disclosure duty 244
disclosure letter 54
distressed debt 130
dividends
   negative undertakings 85–6
   profit and loss account 68
double tax treaties 107
drafting
   aims 136
   ambiguity 136
   certainty 136
   clause construction 137
   creation of document 135–6
   de minimis 139
   definitions 141–2
   eiusdem generis rule 142
   'includes' 141
   keywords 140–2
   materiality 138–9
   'means' 141
   'might' 139
   'notwithstanding' 141

drafting – *continued*
   'parent companies' 140
   precedents 136–7
   qualifying an obligation 137–8
   reasonableness 139
   'subsidiary' 140–1
   techniques 137–9
   templates 136–7
   time computations 142
   user-friendly documents 136
   workability 136
   'would' 139
drop dead fee 110
due diligence
   account officer 12–13
   acquisition finance 14
   credit analysis 13
   credit clearance 13
   credit risk 12
   eurobond issue 251–2
   initial investigation 12
   margin 12
   ongoing information 14
   subsequent investigation 13–14
   term sheet *see* **term sheet**

EBITDA 119
***eiusdem generis* rule 142**
encumbrances 53
enforcement of security
   administration 160–2
   administrative receivership 160–2
   Enterprise Act 2002 161–2
environmental audit 54
environmental issues
   expert report 54
   remediation costs 53–4
   representations 53–4
equitable assignment
   advantages 127
   disadvantages 127–8
   form of notice 128
   legal compared 127
   non-disclosure 127
   partial assignment 127
   payments 127–8
   subject to equities 128
equitable lien 151
equitable mortgages 150
equitable right set-off 159
equity linked bonds
   convertible 206
   exchangeable 207
   with warrants 207
Euribor 44
eurobond listing particulars 228–9
   administrative bodies 243
   business overview 243
   civil liability
      contract 247
      FSMA 2000 245–6
      Hedley Byrne v Heller 246
      misrepresentation 247

eurobond listing particulars – *continued*
  contract liabilities 247
  criminal liability, FSMA 2000 247
  disclosure duty 244
    omissions 244–5
  financial information 243
  governing law 247–8
  incorporated information 244
  issuer 243
  jurisdictions 247–8
  liability for
    civil 245–7
    criminal 247
  Listing Rules 239–40, 253, 254
  management 243
  marketing 252
  material contracts 243
  negligent misstatement 246
  omissions 244–5
  persons responsible 242
  prospectus
    authority 241
    contents 241–4
    declaration of responsibility 242
    exemptions 240
    format 241
    general content 241
    listing particulars 242
    responsibility for information 242
    risk factors 243
    when required 240
  registration documents 243
    persons responsible 242
  repeated information 244
  risk factors 243
  securities, information about 244
  securities document 244
  shareholders 243
  supervisory bodies 243
  use of proceeds 244
eurobonds
  admission to Official List 239–40
  admission to trading 240
  allotment telex 228, 253
  auditors 227
  auditor's report 230
  closing
    documentary procedures 255–6
    payment procedures 256–7
  co-managers 224, 253
  comfort letters 230
  consent letter 230
  coupon 234
    replacement 235
  deed of covenant 232
  deed of guarantee 231–2
  default 235
  depository 226–7
  documentation of issue 227–32, 252
    agreement among managers 230
    allotment telex 228, 253
    auditor's report 230
    comfort letters 230

eurobonds – *continued*
    consent letter 230
    deed of guarantee 231–2
    fiscal agency agreement 231
    invitation telex 228, 252–3
    legal opinions 230
    list 227–8
    listing particulars 228–9
    mandate letter 228
    paying agency agreement 231
    prospectus 228–9
    subscription agreement 229
    trust deed 231
    underwriting agreement 229
  events of default 235
  fiscal agent 224
    advantages of use 226
    agreement 231
  further issues 238
  governing law 238
  invitation telex 228, 252–3
  issue
    authorised person 252
    closing 255–7
    documentation *see* documentation of issue
    due diligence 251–2
    flowchart 250
    further issues 238
    launch 252–3
    lead manager 255
    listing 253–5
    mandate 249, 251
    marketing 252
    payment 256–7
    signing meeting 255
    stages 249
    syndication 252–3
  issuer 223
  jurisdiction 238
  launch 252–3
  lead manager 223–4, 252–3
    responsibilities 255
  legal advisers 227
  legal opinions 230
  list of required documents 227–8
  listing
    10 clear business day documents 254
    48-hour documents 254
    application procedure 254–5
    charge 255
    continuing obligations 255
    disclosures 255
    Listing Rules 253, 254
    marked-up documents 254
    particulars *see* **eurobond listing particulars**
    reasons for 253
    requirements 253
    securities 254
    status 254
  listing agent 226
  listing particulars *see* **eurobond listing particulars**
  loan agreement compared 232
  London listing 239

eurobonds – *continued*
  mandate 249, 251
  mandate letter 228
  marketing 252
    authorised person 252
  meetings 235–6
  negative pledge 233
  notices 236
  parties to issue 223–7
  paying agent 226
    agreement 231
  payment 234, 256–7
    against delivery 257–8
    at closing 256–7
    prior to closing 256
  prescription period 235
  principal paying agent 226
  prospectus 228–9
  re-purchase 234
  redemption 234
  regulated market 240
  replacement of bonds and coupons
    235
  secured issues 224–5
  sponsor 224
  subordinated issues 225
  subscription agreement 229
  syndicate 224
  syndication 252–3
  taxation 235
  telexes
    allotment telex 228, 253
    invitation telex 228, 252–3
  terms and conditions 232–6
    coupon 234, 235
    events of default 235
    form, denomination and title 233
    governing law 238
    jurisdiction 238
    meetings 235–6
    negative pledge 233
    notices 236
    payment 234
    preamble 233
    prescription period 235
    redemption and purchase 234
    replacement of bonds and coupons 235
    status clause 233
    taxation 235
    where located 232–3
  trust deed 231
  trustee 224
    advantages of use 225–6
  underwriting agreement 229
  unregulated market 240
Euroclear 210–11, 221
Euromarkets
  'Euro' 201
  eurobonds *see* **eurobonds**
  eurocurrencies 201
    use of 201
  eurosecurities 201
  'foreign' securities 202

eurosecurities 201
  trading 210
events of default 89–98
  action on default 95–6
  bank's perspective 97
  borrower's perspective 97
  change of business 92
  change of control 92–3
  covenants 91
  cross-default 91–2
    into subsidiaries 92
  eurobonds 235
  general default 94
  grace period 96
  insolvency 93
  late payment 90
  litigation proceedings 93
  LMA definition 97
  material adverse change 94–5, 119
  potential 96
  proceedings 93–4
  qualification of accounts 94
  reasons for 89–90
  representations 90–1
  repudiation 94
  undertakings 91
  unlawful performance 94
  warranties 90–1
execution
  counterparts 117–18
  powers of attorney 117
  signatures 116–17
expenses
  administration 100
  requirement for 108–9
  see also **costs; fees**

facility fee 110
facility office 35
fees
  agent's 110
  cancellation 110
  commitment 110
  drop dead 110
  facility 109, 110
  fee letter 110
  front end 109
  justification 109
  types 109–10
  underwriting 109
  utilisation 110
finance
  need for 2
  raising *see* **raising finance**
finance leases 80
financial assistance
  guarantees as 157
  prohibition 180
  security as 180
Financial Conduct Authority (FCA) 6, 105
financial covenants
  borrowing *see* **borrowing**
  capital expenditure 79–80

financial covenants – *continued*
  equity cure 81
  examples 77–80
  form 77
  goodwill 79
  incurrence 77
  intangible assets 79
  limits 77, 79–80
  maintenance 77
  meaning 76–7
  minimum net worth 79
  payments on account 79
  ratios *see* **ratios**
  research and development costs 79
  tax provision 79
  unaudited revaluation 79
Financial Policy Committee (FPC) 6
Financial Reporting Council 72
Financial Reporting Standards 72
financial services
  FSMA 2000 131
Financial Services Authority (FSA) 6, 105
financial statements
  balance sheet *see* **balance sheet**
  cash flow statements 69
  profit and loss account *see* **profit and loss account**
fiscal agent 224, 226
  agreement 231
fixed charge cover ratio 78
fixed charges 146
  choice between floating and fixed 177
  mortgages *see* **mortgages**
  priority
    floating charges 173–4
    mortgage 173–4
fixed rate interest 45
floating charges 146–9
  administrator's costs 148
  avoidance of 149
  choice between floating and fixed 177
  crystallisation 147–8
    automatic 148
    certificate of non- 148
    common law 147–8
    post-crystallisation instrument 148
  disadvantages 177
  flexibility 177
  hardening periods 179
  later fixed charge 148
  meaning 146–7
  preferential creditors 148–9
  priority 148, 173–4
  recognition of 178
  to connected person 149
  to unconnected person 149
  weaknesses of 148–9
floating rate notes 204–5
  matched funding 204–5
  reverse 205
floor 205
force majeure 112, 229
fraudulent misrepresentations 56
front end fees 109

funding
  administration expenses 100
  broken 100
  capital adequacy 102–5
  capital markets *see* **capital markets**
  funding rate 102
  increased costs 104–5
  loans *see* **loan agreement**
  mandatory costs 105
  matched 29, 100
  prepayment fee 100
  rate 102
  regulatory capital 102–5
  see also **payment; prepayment**

gearing 3
gilts 209
Glass-Steagall Act 5
global transfer agreement 130
glossary 259–70
goodwill 79, 185
governing law
  comfort letters 158
  common law rules 112–13
  eurobond listing particulars 247
  eurobonds 238
  factors affecting choice 113
  guarantees 157
  jurisdiction where assets situated 113–14
  lex situs 180
  Rome Convention on contracts 113
  Rome II Regulation 113
  taking security 180
governments
  as borrowers 2
'grossing-up' 107–8
group accounts
  subsidiaries 69–70
guarantees 80
  continuing 157
  counter-indemnity 157
  cross guarantees 140
  eurobond issue 231–2
  evidence to bank 157
  evidenced in writing 157
  as financial assistance 157
  governing law 157
  indemnities and 155–6
  meaning 155
  power to enter into 157
  quasi-security 155–8
  reimbursement from borrower 156
  rights of guarantor 156–7
  secondary contract 156
  subrogation 157
  terminology 158
  undervalue transaction 157
  variation of contract and 156

hardening periods 178–9
  floating charges 179
  preferences 178
  undervalue transactions 178

hedging 47
Hedley Byrne v Heller 57, 246
Hibor 44
holding company 140–1

illegality 115
impaired debt 130
incurrence covenants 77
indemnities 80
  guarantees and 155–6
information undertakings 82–3
  financial 82
  insurance 83
  notification of default 83
  shareholder documents 82
Inland Revenue
  'hindsight test' 106
  withholding tax 105–8
innocent misrepresentations 56
insolvency
  events of default 93
  preferences 100–1, 178
  undervalue transactions 157, 178
  see also **administration; administrative
    receivership**
instalment credit agreements 80
insurance
  asset protection undertakings 83
  information undertaking 83
intangible assets 79
intellectual property
  registration 173
inter-bank provisions 114–15
interest
  apportionment 46
  associated costs 102
  bbalibor 43–4
  cap 205
  collar 205
  default interest 47
  Euribor 45
  fixed rate 44
  floating rate
    base rates 42–3
    Libor 43, 204
  funding rate 102
  hedging 47
  Libor 43, 44, 45, 46, 47, 118, 204, 205
  loan agreements 42–7
  mandatory cost rate 43, 47
  margin ratchets 46
  margins 46, 47
  overdraft facility 20
  periods 45–6
  ratchets 46
  rates 43–4
  reference banks 44–5
  revolving credit facilities 22
  screen rate 43–4
  'short' 106
  swap 47
  tick 47
  variable rate, Libor 205

interest cover
  ratios 78
intermediate (innominate) term
  breach 89
International Capital Markets Association 211–12
International Financial Reporting Standards 72
  balance sheets 65
  profit and loss account 68
International Securities Identification Number
  (ISIN) 211
invalidity, partial 111
investment banks 5
  ring-fencing 5
investment capital 199–200
issue of eurobonds
  authorised person 252
  closing 255–7
  documentation 227–32, 252
    agreement among managers 230
    allotment telex 228, 253
    auditor's report 230
    comfort letters 230
    consent letter 230
    deed of guarantee 231–2
    fiscal agency agreement 231
    invitation telex 228, 252–3
    legal opinions 230
    list 227–8
    listing particulars 228–9
    mandate letter 228
    paying agency agreement 231
    prospectus 228–9
    subscription agreement 229
    trust deed 231
    underwriting agreement 229
  due diligence 251–2
  flowchart 250
  issuer 223
  launch 252–3
  lead manager 255
  listing 253–5
  mandate 249, 251
  marketing 252
  payment 256–7
  signing meeting 255
  stages 249
  syndication 252–3
issuer
  eurobonds 223

jurisdiction 113–14
  agent for service of process 114
  Brussels Regulation 113
  choice of 114
  EU Regulation 113–14
  eurobonds 238
  lex situs 180
  Lugano Convention 113–14
  process agents in 114
  sale of assets 131
  taxation 107
  where assets situated 113
  see also **governing law**

'know your customer' 82

land
    debentures 184
    priority of security over 174
    registered 174, 176
    registration of security 173
    tacking 175–6
    unregistered 174, 175–6
late payment 90
law *see* governing law
Law Debenture Trust Corporation 224
lead manager
    eurobonds 223–4, 252–3
        responsibilities 255
legal advisers
    eurobonds 227
legal assignment
    absolute 125
    advantages 126
    borrower's payments 126
    disadvantages 126–7
    disclosure 125
    equitable compared 127
    meaning 125–6
    obligations not transferred 126
    rights not transferred 127
    rights transferred 126
    secured loan 126
    statutory 125
    transferable loan instruments 127
legal mortgages 150
legal opinions
    assumptions 193
    conclusion 196
    eurobond issue 230
    foreign counsel 195–6
    form 192–5
    opinion 193–4
    overseas jurisdictions 192
    persons providing 191
    preamble 192–3
    purpose 191
    qualifications 194–5
    secured lending 192
    use 191–2
lenders 4
    defaulting 115–16
lending
    negative undertakings 85
lending office 35
leverage 3, 77–8
    mandatory prepayment 101
leveraged acquisition facilities 26
lex situs 180
liabilities
    ordering 62–3
Libor (London Interbank Offered Rate) 43, 44, 45, 46, 47,
    118
    floating rate notes 204
    variable rate bonds 205
licences 79
lien 84

lien – *continued*
    common law 151
    equitable 151
    general 151
    particular 151
    statutory 151
liquidation
    set-off on 160
listed companies
    Listing Rules 72
    summary accounts 73
listing agent
    eurobonds 226
listing of eurobonds
    10 clear business day documents 254
    48-hour documents 254
    application procedure 254–5
    charge 255
    continuing obligations 255
    disclosures 255
    Listing Rules 253, 254
    marked-up documents 254
    reasons for 253
    requirements 253
    securities 254
    status 254
listing particulars, eurobonds 228–9
    administrative bodies 243
    business overview 243
    civil liability
        contract 247
        FSMA 2000 245–6
        Hedley Byrne v Heller 246
        misrepresentation 247
    contract liabilities 247
    criminal liability, FSMA 2000 247
    disclosure duty 244
        omissions 244–5
    financial information 243
    governing law 247–8
    incorporated information 244
    issuer, information about 242–3
    jurisdictions 247–8
    liability for
        civil 245–7
        criminal 247
    Listing Rules 239–40, 253, 254
    management 243
    material contracts 243
    negligent misstatement 246
    omissions 244–5
    persons responsible 242
    prospectus
        authority 241
        contents 241–4
        declaration of responsibility 242
        exemptions 240
        format 241
        general content 241
        listing particulars 242
        responsibility for information 242
        risk factors 243
        when required 240

listing particulars, eurobonds – *continued*
  registration documents 243
    persons responsible 242
  repeated information 244
  risk factors 243
  securities, information about 244
  securities document 244
  shareholders 243
  supervisory bodies 243
  use of proceeds 244
Listing Rules
  eurobonds 239–40, 254
litigation
  event of default 93
  representations 53
loan agreement
  amendment 111–12
  authority 37–9
    actual 37–8
    apparent 38
    ostensible 38
  availability 41–2
  bank's concerns 27–8
  borrower transfers 131
  borrower's concerns 28–9
  capacity
    position pre-CA 1989 36–7
    position post-CA 1989 37
    position post-CA 2006 37
    ultra vires transaction 36, 37
  conditions precedent
    bank's perspective 41
    borrower's perspective 41
    documentary 40–1
    purpose 39
    time limits 40
    uncertainty 40
  conditions subsequent 41
  contract 19
  contractual remedies 49
    see also **representations; warranties**
  control 36
  covenants *see* **covenants**
  date 34
  default *see* **default; events of default**
  definitions 34–5
  drafting *see* **drafting**
  eurobond compared 232
  execution 116–18
  facility clause 35
  facility office 35
  interest *see* **interest**
  interest periods 45–6
  interpretation 34–5
  lending office 35
  margins 46, 47
  multiple utilisation loan 42
    defaults 42
    representations 42
    utilisation notice 42
  parties 34
  privity of contract 34
  project finance 36

loan agreement – *continued*
  purpose clause 36–9
  ratchets 46
  representations in *see* **representations**
  repudiation 94
  schedules 116
  single utilisation loan 41–2
  time computations 142
  US and English law compared 118–19
  utilisation loans
    defaults 42
    multiple 42
    representations 42
    single 41–2
    utilisation notice 42
  utilisation notice 42
  warranties in *see* **warranties**
  working capital purposes 36
loan facilities
  364 day facilities 23
  ancillary facilities 23
  bankers' acceptance 27
  'bells and whistles' loans 19
  bilateral facility 23
  bills of exchange 27
  choice 27
  commercial paper 27
  committed 19
  companies 3
  debt securities compared 200
  facility office 35
  lending office 35
  medium-term notes 207
  overdraft 20
  'plain vanilla' loans 19
  revolving credit 22–3
  short-term lending 27
  'standby' facility 23, 27
  swing-line facility 27
  syndicated facilities 23–6
  term loans 3, 20–2
  'term-out options' 23
  uncommitted 19, 20
loan instruments
  sale of transferable 127
Loan Market Association 105, 130, 135–6
loan stock 4
loans
  selling *see* **sales**
local authorities
  borrowers 2
London CD 208
London Interbank Offered Rate *see* Libor (London
    Interbank Offer Rate)

machinery
  debentures over 184
maintenance covenants 77
management
  control by security interest 162
management accounts 70
mandate
  eurobonds 249, 251

mandate letter
  eurobonds 228
mandatory cost rate 43, 47
mandatory costs 105
manufacturing account 66
margin ratchets 46
margins 12, 43, 46, 47
  basis points 47
market disruption clause 44–5
market flex 15
material adverse change 13, 15
  event of default 94–5, 119
medium-sized companies
  accounting regulations 71–2
  auditing requirements 71–2
  delivering accounts 71
  true and fair view 72
medium-term notes 207
meetings
  eurobonds 235–6, 255
memorandum of satisfaction 172
merchant banks 5
mezzanine lenders 26, 101
Mibor 44
misrepresentations
  damages 57
  eurobond listing particulars 247
  fraudulent 56
  Hedley Byrne v *Heller* 57
  innocent 56
  Misrepresentation Act 1967 56
  negligent 56
  negligent misstatement 57, 246
  non-fraudulent 56
  remedies 56–7
  rescission 57
Moody's ratings 213
moratorium 160
mortgages
  equitable 150
  legal 150
  over land 149–50
  priority, fixed charges and 173–4
  statutory definition 153
multi-currency term loan 21–2
municipalities
  as borrowers 2

negative pledge 84–5, 159
  debentures 187
  eurobond transaction 233
negative undertakings
  acquisitions 85
  auditors 86
  cash collateralisation 84
  depositing money 84
  dividends 85–6
  lending 85
  liens 84
  negative pledge 84–5
  pari passu ranking 85
  securitisation 84
  shares 85–6

negligent misrepresentations 56
negligent misstatement 57, 246
negotiation
  in good faith 16–17
non-recourse transaction 129
notes 4
  floating rate notes 204–5
  medium-term notes 207
notice 115
novation
  advantages 124
  consent 124–5
  disadvantages 124–5
  disclosure 125
  easy syndication 124
  meaning 123–4
  moving obligations 124
  risk transfer 124
  secured loans 125

opinions *see* legal opinions
overdraft facility 160
  basic features 20
  'clean-down' provision 20
  interest 20
  maximum aggregate amount 20
  purpose 20
  standard terms 20
overseas companies
  registration of security 172–3
overseas jurisdictions
  foreign counsel 195–6
  legal opinions 192

parallel debt structures 181
'parent companies'
  dominant influence 140
  use of words 140–1
pari passu ranking 85
partial invalidity 111
participation
  funded *see* sub-participation
  risk 128, 129–30
parties to loan agreement
  administrative agent 34
  arranger 34
  borrower 34
  guarantor 34
  privity of contract 34
partnerships
  as borrowers 2
patents 79
paying agent 226
  agreement 231
payment
  cancellation 102
  commitment period 102
  early reduction 100–1
  eurobonds 234, 256–7
    against delivery 257–8
    at closing 256–7
    prior to closing 256
  prepayment 100–1

payment – *continued*
  repayment 99
performance
  unlawful 94
permanent global bond 217
personalty 176
'plain vanilla' loans 19
plant and machinery
  debentures 184
pledges
  constructively pledged 151
  delivery of asset 150–1
  meaning 150
  negative 84–5, 159, 187
    eurobonds 233
  practical difficulties 151
  rights of pledgee 150–1
positive undertakings
  access to information and assistance 84
  consents 83
  insurance 83
  licences 83
power of attorney 117
  debentures 188
preferences 100–1, 178
preferential creditors
  floating charge and 148–9
prepayment 100–1
  administration expenses 100
  broken funding 100
  mandatory 101
  order of application 100
  preference 100–1
  prepayment fee 100
  right to 108
prescription period
  eurobonds 235
primary market 210
  marketability 210
  traders 210
principal paying agent 226
priority
  assignment 174
  bearer bonds 220
  contractual subordination 174
  fixed charges 173–4
  floating charge 148, 173–4
  mortgages 173–4
  registered bonds 220
  security over land 174
privity of contract 34
profit and loss account 60, 65–6
  buying-in or manufacture 66
  cost of sales 67–8
  dividends 68
  extraordinary and exceptional items 68
  IFRS requirement 68
  net profit 68
  period 66
  retained profit 68
  structure 66–7
  trading (or manufacturing) account 66
  turnover 67

profits
  net 68
  retained 3, 68
project finance 36
prospectus
  eurobonds 228–9
provisions
  in balance sheet 65
Prudential Regulation Authority (PRA) 6, 105
purpose clause
  authority 37–9
    actual 37–8
    apparent 38
    ostensible 38
  bank's perspective 39
  borrower's perspective 39
  capacity
    position pre-CA 1989 36–7
    position post-CA 1989 37
    position post-CA 2006 37
    ultra vires transactions 36, 37
  control 36
  loan agreement 36–9
  resulting trust 39

qualifications
  auditors 69, 94
  legal opinions 194–5
quasi-security
  comfort letters 158
  guarantees 155–8
  negative pledge 159
  retention of title 159
  set-off 159–60
  third party support 155–8

raising finance
  banks *see* **banks**
  borrowers *see* **borrowers**
  lenders 4
  need for finance 2
ranking of debt 52
ratchets 46
ratios 77–8
  accounting policies 81
  defining terms 80
  fixed charge cover 78
  'frozen GAAP' provisions 81
  gearing 3
  information for testing 80–1
  interest cover 78
  leverage 3, 77–8
  using 80–1
realisation of capital
  sale of loan 121
receiver
  appointment by debenture holder 188
reference banks
  interest 44–5
  market disruption clause 44–5
  syndicated loans 44–5
refinancing 12
register of charges 172

registered bonds 218
  anonymity 220
  bearer bonds compared 219–20
  claim of issuer 220
  priority 220
  transfer 220
registration of security
  aircraft 173
  Bills of Sale acts 173
  Companies Act provisions 166–73
  compulsory registration 166
  consequences of non-registration 167, 172
  documents kept by company 172
  effect of 167
  form 168–71
  inaccurate 167
  intellectual property 173
  land 173
  late 167
  memorandum of satisfaction 172
  non-registration, consequences 167, 172
  overseas companies 172–3
  overseas registration 181
  procedure 166–7
  property already subject to charge 172
  purpose 165
  redacted information 167
  regime, CA 2006 166
  register of charges 172
  requirements for 166–7
  responsibility for registration 166
  security release 172
  ships 173
  time limit 167
regulatory capital
  increased costs clause 104–5
  origins 102–3
  risk weighting 103
  types 103–4
remedies
  breach of condition 89
  breach of warranty 89
  contractual 49
  damages 57
  default 89
  misrepresentations 56–7
  rescission 57
  waivers and 110–11
repayment 99
  amortisation 21
  balloon repayment 21
  bullet repayment 21
  term loans 21
  time computations 142
representations
  accounting principles 52
  admissibility in evidence 50–1
  application 57
  authority 50
  bank's perspective 55
  binding obligations 50
  borrower's perspective 55–6
  catch alls 54

representations – *continued*
  commercial 51–4
  contract law 56–7
  deduction of tax 51
  defaults 51, 90–1
  disclosure letter 54
  encumbrances 53
  enforcement 51
  environmental issues 53–4
  examples 49–54
  false 89
  governing law 51
  information 51–2
  legal 50–1
  litigation 53
  loan agreement 49–54
  misrepresentations *see* **misrepresentations**
  non-conflict 50
  power 50
  ranking 52
  repetition of 54–5
  stamp duty 51
  status 50
  in subscription agreement 229
  undertakings and 76
  validity 50–1
  winding-up proceedings 53
repudiation
  loan agreement 94
rescission
  misrepresentation remedy 57
research and development costs 79
reserves 63–4
retained profits 3, 68
retention of title 159
revaluation
  balance sheet 64–5
revolving credit facilities
  basic features 22
  'clean-down' provision 23
  purpose 22
  rollover 22
risk management 122
risk participation 128, 129–30
risk transfer
  sub-participation 129
rollover 22, 27
ruling off accounts 176–7

sales
  balance sheet 122
  bank's perspective 131
  borrower transfers 131
  borrower's perspective 131–2
  distressed debt 130
  equitable assignment
    advantages 127
    disadvantages 127–8
    form of notice 128
    legal compared 127
    non-disclosure 127
    partial assignment 127
    payments 127–8

sales – *continued*
    subject to equities 128
  global transfer agreement 130
  impaired debt 130
  jurisdictions 131
  legal assignment
    absolute 125
    advantages 126
    borrower's payments 126
    disadvantages 126–7
    disclosure 125
    equitable compared 127
    meaning 125–6
    obligations not transferred 126
    rights not transferred 127
    rights transferred 126
    secured loan 126
    statutory 125
    transferable loan instruments 127
  moving rights and obligations 122–3
  novation 123–5
    advantages 124
    consent 124–5
    disadvantages 124–5
    disclosure 125
    easy syndication 124
    moving obligations 124
    risk transfer 124
    secured loans 125
  prestige 122
  profit 122
  realisation of capital 121
  reasons for 121–2
  risk management 122
  risk participation 129–30
  securitisation 131
  sub-participation
    advantages 129
    consent 129
    credit risk 129
    disadvantages 129
    funded participation 128
    meaning 128–9
    non-disclosure 129
    risk transfer 129
    taxation 130
  syndication 122
  tax implications 130
  transfer of ownership *see* **transfer of ownership**
  types of asset 130
schedules 116
screen rate 43–4
secondary markets 210
securitisation 131
security
  applicable law 180
  asset control and stability 162
  assignment 152
  bank's perspective 162–3
  borrower's perspective 163
  capacity to provide 179
  categorising 145–6
  consensual 145

security – *continued*
  contractual subordination 174–5
    arrangement 174–5
    use of 175
  corporate benefit 179
  costs 162
  enforcement of
    administration 160–2
    administrative receivership 160–2
    Enterprise Act 2002 161–2
  EU Insolvency Regulation 180
  financial assistance 180
  fixed charges 177
  floating charges 177
  hardening periods 178–9
  lien 84, 151
  management control 162
  meaning 152
  memorandum of satisfaction 172
  mortgage *see* **mortgages**
  non-consensual 145
  notification requirements 181
  parallel debt structures 181
  pledge *see* **pledges**
  preferences 178
  prior 181
  priority
    assignments 174
    contractual subordination 174
    fixed charges and mortgages 173–4
    fixed and floating charges 173–4
    land 174
  quasi-
    comfort letters 158
    guarantees 155–8
    negative pledge 159
    retention of title 159
    set-off 159–60
  reasons for taking 160–2
  register of charges 172
  registration *see* **registration of security**
  release 172
  rights over assets 146–9
    fixed charges 146
    floating charges *see* **floating charges**
    rights not possession 146
  ruling off accounts 176–7
  statutory definitions 152
  tacking 175–6
  transfer of ownership 149–50
  UNCITRAL Model Law 181
  undervalue transaction 178
security trustee
  syndicated facilities 25
set-off 115
  availability 159–60
  banker's right of combination 160
  contractual 159
  equitable right 159
  liquidation 160
  meaning 159
share capital 3
share warrant 186

shareholder documents
  information undertakings 82
shares
  debentures 186–7
  dematerialised 186
  negative undertakings 85–6
ships
  registration of security 173
short-term lending 27
  bankers' acceptance 27
  bills of exchange 27
  commercial paper 27
  standby facility 27
  swing-line facility 27
signatures 116–17
small companies
  accounting regulations 71–2
  auditing requirements 71–2
  delivering accounts 71
  true and fair view 72
sole traders
  as borrowers 2
solicitors
  role of finance solicitor 6–7
special purpose vehicle 131
Standard and Poor's ratings 213
'standby' facility 23, 27
Statements of Standard Accounting Practice 72
stock in trade
  debentures 187
sub-participation
  advantages 129
  consent 129
  credit risk 129
  disadvantages 129
  funded participation 128
  meaning 128–9
  non-disclosure 129
  risk transfer 129
  taxation 130
subrogation
  guarantors and 157
subscription agreement
  eurobonds 229
  force majeure clause 229
  representations 229
  warranties 229
subsidiaries
  consolidated accounts 69–70
  cross guarantees 140
  cross-default into 92
  dominant influence 140
  own balance sheet 70
  use of word 140–1
supranational organisations
  as borrowers 2
swap 47
swing-line facility 27
syndicated facilities
  administrative agent 24–5, 34
  advantages to banks within 25
  arranger 24, 34
    liability of 25–6

syndicated facilities – *continued*
  bilateral 23
  leveraged acquisition facilities 26
  parallel debt structures 181
  sale of loan and 122
  security trustee 25
  structuring a syndicate 23–5
  tombstones 25, 30–1

tacking
  personalty 176
  registered land 176
  unregistered land 175–6
talons 218
tax credits 108
taxation
  corporation tax 106
  double tax treaties 107
  eurobonds 235
  'grossing-up' 107–8
  jurisdiction 107
  sale of assets 130
  sub-participation 130
  tax credits 108
  withholding tax *see* **withholding tax**
telexes
  allotment telex 228, 253
  invitation telex 228, 252–3
temporary global bond 216–17
  meaning 216
  selling restrictions 216–17
  time constraints 216
  use 216–17
term loan 3, 20–2
  amortisation 21
  availability period 21
  balloon repayment 21
  basic features 21
  bullet repayment 21
  commitment period 21
  committed facilities 21
  currency 21–2
  interest 22
  multi-currency 21–2
  purpose 20
  repayment schedule 21
  tranches 21
term sheet
  brevity 15
  conditions precedent 16
  content 15–16
  'inclusive' lists 15
  legal effect of 16
  meaning 14
  negotiation in good faith 16–17
  private equity 16
  reasons for 14–15
  sample 17–18
  'subject to contract' 17
  'unusual' provisions 16
'term-out options' 23
Tibor 44
tick 47

time limits
  conditions precedent 40
  registration of security 167
tombstones
  syndicated facilities 25, 30–1
traders 210
trading account 66
tranches 21
transaction at undervalue *see* **undervalue**
  transactions
transfer of ownership
  lien 151
  mortgages 149–50
  pledges 150–1
treasury bills 209
'true and fair view' 72
turnover 67

UNCITRAL Model Law 181
undertakings
  asset protection 83–6
    access to information and assistance 84
    acquisitions 85
    auditors 86
    cash collateralisation 84
    consents 83
    depositing money 84
    disposals 85
    dividends 85–6
    insurance 83
    lending 85
    licences 83
    liens 84
    negative pledge 84–5
    negative undertakings 84–6
    pari passu ranking 85
    positive undertakings 83–4
    securitisation 84
    shares 85–6
  bank's perspective 86–7
  borrower's perspective 87
  control using 75
  in debentures 187
  default 91
  form 75–6
  identity of borrower 86
  information 82–3
    financial 82
    insurance 83

undertakings – *continued*
    'know your customer' 82
    notification of default 83
    shareholder documents 82
  loan agreement 75
  loan type 86
  market conditions 86
  purpose 75–6
  representations and 76
  see also **covenants**
undervalue transactions
  guarantee as 157
  hardening periods 178
  security 178
underwriting
  agreement 229
  eurobonds 229
  fee 109
universal banks 5
unlawful performance
  event of default 94
utilisation fees 110

Volcker Rule 5

waivers 111–12
  remedies and 110–11
warranties
  contract law 56–7
  default 90–1
  in loan agreement 49
  remedies for breach 89
  subscription agreement 229
Wheatley review 44
winding-up proceedings
  representations 53
withholding tax
  banks and 106–7
  corporation tax 106
  double tax treaties 107
  'grossing-up' 107–8
  meaning 105–6
  sale of assets 130
  short interest 106
  tax credits 108
working capital facility 20
working capital purposes 36

zero coupon bonds 205–6